HIGHER and INTERMEDI

Administration

Ann Hackston
Margaret Darroch

Hodder Gibson

A MEMBER OF THE HODDER HEADLINE GROUP

Instructions for CD-ROM (in 'With Answers' edition only)

Insert the CD-ROM into the CD-ROM drive and select the required file(s) via the chapter headings and chapter sub-headings. If you experience difficulties using the CD-ROM please contact our Digital Customer Support Line on 0207 873 6448 or contact Hodder Gibson direct, as below.

The Publishers would like to thank the following for permission to reproduce copyright material:
Photo credits Page 48 © Ephraim Ben-Shimon/CORBIS; Page 59 Imagestate/Alamy

Every effort has been made to trace all copyright holders, but if any have been inadvertently overlooked the Publishers will be pleased to make the necessary arrangements at the first opportunity.

Although every effort has been made to ensure that website addresses are correct at time of going to press, Hodder Gibson cannot be held responsible for the content of any website mentioned in this book. It is sometimes possible to find a relocated web page by typing in the address of the home page for a website in the URL window of your browser.

Hodder Headline's policy is to use papers that are natural, renewable and recyclable products and made from wood grown in sustainable forests. The logging and manufacturing processes are expected to conform to the environmental regulations of the country of origin.

Orders: please contact Bookpoint Ltd, 130 Milton Park, Abingdon, Oxon OX14 4SB. Telephone: (44) 01235 827720. Fax: (44) 01235 400454. Lines are open from 9.00 – 5.00, Monday to Saturday, with a 24-hour message answering service. Visit our website at www.hoddereducation.co.uk. Hodder Gibson can be contacted direct on: Tel: 0141 848 1609; Fax: 0141 889 6315; email: hoddergibson@hodder.co.uk

© Ann Hackston and Margaret Darroch 2006
First published in 2006 by
Hodder Gibson, a member of the Hodder Headline Group
2a Christie Street
Paisley PA1 1NB

ISBN-10: 0-340-90561-1
ISBN-13: 978-0-340-90561-6

Impression number   10 9 8 7 6 5 4 3 2 1
Year   2011 2010 2009 2008 2007 2006

ISBN-10: 0-340-90560-3
ISBN-13: 978-0-340-90560-9

Impression number   10 9 8 7 6 5 4 3 2 1
Year   2011 2010 2009 2008 2007 2006

Cover photo © Randy Faris/CORBIS

Typeset in 10.5pt ITC Century Light by DC Graphic Design Limited, Swanley Village, Kent.

Printed and bound in Great Britain by Martin's the Printers, Berwick-upon-Tweed.

A catalogue record for this title is available from the British Library

C O N T E N T S

Introduction

The purpose of this book is to provide students, teachers and lecturers with the essential knowledge and skills needed to pass National Qualification Administration at level Intermediate 2 or Higher.

The first chapters of the book – Chapters 1–8 – deal with the knowledge needed for the Administrative Services units at both levels and the later chapters – Chapters 9–14 – deal with the IT aspects of the awards.

Throughout Chapters 1–9 there are activities for students to test their knowledge and understanding and to extend their skills.

- Tasks are designed to encourage further investigation.

- Check your Progress exercises are designed to test understanding and recall.

- Examples of the kind of questions which will be used in Internal Assessments are included in each of these chapters.

- Examples of the kind of questions which could be used in External Assessments are included in each of these chapters.

Having completed these tasks and questions, students should be well prepared to deal with both internal and external assessment requirements for Administrative Services and many of the theoretical aspects they need to know about IT.

In some of the topic areas identified in the Unit specifications, there may be overlap between chapters. The CD ROM which accompanies the 'With Answers' version of the book contains a breakdown of the learning outcomes for both levels covered by each chapter.

Chapters 10–14 deal with the IT and problem solving skills required for word processing, spreadsheets, databases, presentation software and using e-mail, e-diary and the Internet. The material in these chapters is laid out differently. Here the approach taken is essentially one of using graded exercise materials to enhance skills to the level required for the internal and external assessment. The tasks are split into In-tray exercises and each In-tray exercise contains a batch of documents. These documents are provided on the CD ROM which accompanies the With Answers edition of this book. Alternatively, the students can key in the documents themselves. In some cases these documents may be recalled for amendment as Day 2 exercises and again amended on Day 3. Each batch is clearly labelled whether it is appropriate for Intermediate 2 or Higher students. Work of this type is progressive and will encourage students to file their work in an appropriate way and will enable students to work toward the higher level skills needed for Higher.

The CD ROM which accompanies the 'With Answers' version of the book has the basic documents already keyed in and correction models at each stage. This will be particularly useful for the word processing and IT sections of the book. The 'With Answers' version also contains answers to all Tasks, Check Your Progress, Internal and External Assessment questions throughout the book.

SECTION ONE

Administrative Services

CHAPTER 1

Working Effectively

This chapter is all about working effectively in an organisation. Before you can contribute effectively to an organisation, you have to know what is expected of you in terms of your duties at work and you have to know how you are expected to behave in relation to people you work with and customers.

Intermediate 2 Level Outcomes:

This chapter includes from Intermediate 2 Administrative Services Outcome 1:

☆ **the roles, duties and qualities required of an administrative assistant – job descriptions and person specifications**

☆ **techniques to identify current skills and skills gaps – skillscan techniques**

☆ **effective communication – features, methods and barriers to good communication.**

It also includes from Intermediate 2 Administrative Services Outcome 3:

☆ **the uses of job descriptions and person specifications.**

Note: Customer service – the importance and benefits of good customer service is dealt with in Chapter 5.

Higher Level Outcomes:

It also includes from Higher Administrative Services Outcome 1:

☆ **the roles, duties and qualities needed of administrative staff at a senior level – job descriptions and person specifications**

☆ **personal development planning, action planning, setting your own targets and contributing to departmental targets, and monitoring and evaluating progress against these targets**

☆ **time management and task management techniques**

☆ **features and benefits of working as a team**

Note: Further information on planning and target setting at strategic, tactical and operational level can be found in Chapter 8.

What Are You Expected to do as an Administrative Assistant?

All organisations spend time on administration. In some organisations all employees are expected to do their own administration; in others, specialists are employed to carry out administrative tasks to support other people. All offices will have to:

- **handle information**
- **deal with people – both internal and external to the organisation**
- **follow procedures to ensure consistency.**

Handling information will include tasks like:

- **dealing with mail – both incoming and outgoing**
- **dealing with e-mails**
- **storing and retrieving information both manually in traditional filing systems and electronically using IT systems**
- **producing documents, usually using IT systems and copiers**
- **keeping records**
- **ensuring there is sufficient stationery and equipment to meet the office needs.**

Dealing with people will include tasks like:

- **making and taking phone calls and messages**
- **dealing with requests from other departments in the organisation**
- **dealing with customer enquiries and complaints**
- **reception duties.**

Following procedures will include tasks like:

- **keeping diaries up to date**
- **using flexitime/overtime procedures to log time at work**
- **recording any accidents accurately**
- **ordering goods and services using appropriate forms**
- **operating petty cash systems**
- **arranging meetings.**

 As a junior member of staff you are likely to have a supervisor who will monitor your work. You would be expected to:

- **operate as a member of a team**
- **follow existing procedures**
- **carry out routine word processing and IT tasks**
- **carry out routine administrative tasks such as filing, photocopying and dealing with mail.**

As you progress to a more senior post such as an administrator, you would expect your job role to change and your level of responsibility to change. You would be expected to carry out tasks like:

- **researching and analysing information**
- **responding to correspondence**
- **arranging events such as conferences and meetings**
- **making travel and accommodation arrangements**
- **making financial arrangements and monitoring payments.**

As a senior administrator or personal assistant you would be expected to take more of a managerial role which is likely to involve:

- **delegating jobs to others**
- **co-ordinating and monitoring the work of other people**
- **developing systems and procedures to ensure the smooth running of the organisation**
- **ensuring that work flow is smooth**
- **acting as 'stand-in' for a senior member of staff**
- **having an input into decision-making in the organisation.**

In addition to the duties outlined above most employers have a clear idea of the personal qualities they regard as important at each level in the organisation. Although you would be a real star if you had all the personal qualities below, you should remember that some jobs will give certain personal qualities a very high priority, e.g. a job where money is involved would rate honesty highly, while a job working in personnel would require discretion and the ability to deal with confidential information would be very important. The kind of words an employer might use to describe the ideal employee would be words like:

- **enthusiastic**
- **positive**
- **smart**
- **good with people**
- **able to work on your own**
- **good teamworker.**

When you are looking for a job you are likely to look in job centres, in local and national newspapers or you may be told of openings in local organisations by someone you know, perhaps through your school or careers officer. Organisations advertise jobs by outlining the main administrative tasks you would be expected to do.

Here is an example of an advertisement for a junior member of staff.

Job 1

Based in the General Office of a supermarket chain, the successful applicant should be familiar with word processing and spreadsheet applications and should have good communication skills, be enthusiastic and energetic. They will be expected to help with routine office work including mail, filing, photocopying and will be expected to provide support for buyers.

Here is an example of an advertisement for a more senior administrative role.

Job 2

Experienced administrative assistant/receptionist with Microsoft Word experience and a minimum of 2 years experience of office work. You will be required to deal with customers and staff a busy reception desk and should have a cheerful and friendly manner. You should be able to work quickly and accurately with large volumes of information with close attention to detail. You should have a good level of education and be able to work on your own. Full training will be given in database maintenance.

Here is an example of an advertisement for a personal assistant to someone in a senior management role.

Job 3

A personal assistant is required for a busy consultant in the Aberdeen area. The candidate must be fully conversant in Microsoft Word, Excel and Powerpoint and should be able to converse at a high level with clients. Good telephone manner and the ability to work well under pressure are essential. The successful candidate will be required to supervise clerical staff assigned to carry out short term contracts and may be required to work flexible hours for specific projects.

You will notice in each of these advertisements that there are two types of requirements:

1 the tasks you are required to do

2 the personal qualities that will be required of the applicant.

Task 1

Looking at the 3 jobs shown above and using the layout shown below, key in the tasks you would be required to do and the personal qualities required. You should either key in this form or your teacher/lecturer will give you an electronic version of the form Admin1task1

Junior Administrative job in supermarket office	
Duties	Personal Qualities

Experienced Administrative Assistant/Receptionist	
Duties	Personal Qualities

Personal Assistant	
Duties	Personal Qualities

If you write or phone for further details after reading a job advertisement, you are likely to receive a *Job Description* which clearly states the tasks you will be expected to do and will usually include hours of work and pay. You may also receive a *Person Specification* which will state the personal qualities expected of you.

Job Descriptions and Person Specifications

The job description and the person specification are important documents and together they will give you full details of the job and what qualities you would need to do the job well. Different organisations will use different layouts but the documents will contain similar information. Here are three examples of job descriptions and person specifications. Some organisations make a point of differentiating between *essential* and *desirable* skills and knowledge and *essential* and *desirable* personal qualities. You will look at this more closely in Chapter 4.

Job 4 Administrator in an insurance company

POST DETAILS			
POST NUMBER	001	**SITE**	Glasgow
JOB TITLE	Administrator		
DIVISION	Insurance Claims		
UNIT	Claims Management		
SECTION	Car Insurance Claims		
MANAGED BY	Carol Spartan		
SALARY BANDING	£13,044 – £14,740		
HOURS PER WEEK	35.0	**SHIFT**	No
FTE	1.00	**POST STATUS**	Permanent
ANNUAL LEAVE	20 – 25 Days		
NOTICE PERIOD	4 weeks	**OVERTIME**	Yes
PROBATIONARY PERIOD	3 months	**PLANTIME**	Yes
UNIT PLANS	01 Process and validate insurance claims 02 Manage and develop Unit staff 03 Provide an efficient and effective query service for claimants 04 Review and revise procedures for collecting information on claims 05 Clear claims and issue cheques or arrange repairs as required 06 Manage and develop Unit responsibilities 07 Maintain effective channels of communication with customers and the company 08 Investigate the possible use of new technologies and impact on business practices		

continued ➤

Job 4 continued

JOB DESCRIPTION	
Under supervision, act as a first contact for policy holders for enquiries related to claims:	
1	Assisting with the completion of claim forms
2	Assisting with the repair/replacement of vehicles involved in claims
3	Answering internal and external inquiries regarding insurance claims
4	Assisting with establishing procedures to support simplifying the claims function within the company
5	Contribute towards the organisation's continuous improvement initiatives and ensure personal compliance with documented processes

PERSON SPECIFICATION
Have experience of working in an administrative capacity in an office environment and/or be qualified to Standard Grade General Level, SVQ Level II or equivalent
Have the ability to prepare standard written communication and be able to communicate information clearly, including by telephone, using standard grammatical form, with a variety of internal and external customers
Be able to work with others and as part of a team
Be able to organise own work for given priorities, tasks and objectives; be able to identify, and propose solutions for routine problems
Be able to understand and carry out basic numerical calculations
Be customer focused
Be confident and competent in dealing with telephone enquiries
Preferably have experience with standard Word Processing and Spreadsheet packages

Job 5 Administrative Assistant in John Nicholls Department Store

Post Title	Administrative Assistant
Grade and Salary	GS1/2 £12,500–£14,200
Type of Post	Permanent
No. of Hrs per week	36
Function	To provide administrative support services to John Nicholls staff within the General Office which deals with enquiries from customers and visitors as well as dealing with correspondence and notes from staff and directors of the company.

continued ➤

ADMINISTRATIVE SERVICES

Job 5 continued

Duties and responsibilities
Present an efficient and caring image to staff, customers and visitors
To carry out word processing and reprographic duties as assigned
To ensure accurate and efficient maintenance of all filing and records systems
To undertake, as necessary, telephonist duties and reception duties
To support the administrative services of the organisation as required by the Office Supervisor
Any other duties as required within the remit of this post
Personal Qualities
Good communication skills including ability to deal with front office duties
Word processing qualification and experience of using Microsoft Word
Experience of working within a team
Preferably experience of using a switchboard
Ability to work to deadlines
Willing to develop skills in using IT

Job 6 Administrative Assistant in Audit Section in an accounting firm

Post Details	
POST TITLE	Quality Assurance Assistant
DIVISION	Audit
MANAGED BY	Supervisor Ellen Flanders
GRADE	5 £15,600 – £17,700 (target salary)
HOURS	35 + AGREED OVERTIME IF REQUIRED
SITE	Edinburgh
ANNUAL LEAVE	25 Days
NOTICE PERIOD	4 weeks
PROBATIONARY PERIOD	1 month
ADDITIONAL COMMENTS	All overtime will be paid at the rate of £8.50 per hour
OUTLINE OF DIVISION ACTIVITIES	Maintain the rigour of the organisation's audit and quality assurance procedures: Contribute to producing audit reports within agreed timescales Support auditors by providing historical audit reports and background information as requested Help improve the interpretation of standards

continued ➢

Job 6 continued

OUTLINE OF DIVISION ACTIVITIES (CONTINUED)	Work with others (internal and external) on quality assurance and auditing issues to enhance income generating opportunities and to assist convergence
	Contribute to reviewing processes to ensure continued efficiency and effectiveness
	Adopt an open attitude so that team is self-critical in approach, open to new ideas and readily co-operates with others.

The holder of this post will be responsible for the following

Plan visits of auditors

Make travel and accommodation arrangements for auditors

Provide auditors with all background information requested on the organisation being audited

Format and prepare audit reports to meet with the organisation's standard format

Provide advice and guidance on procedures

Monitor and log auditor expenses

Participate in auditor training events

Contribute towards the organisation's continuous improvement initiatives and ensure personal compliance with documented processes.

Person Specification

The successful applicant is likely to have the following attributes

Have at least two years' experience of varied administrative work in a similar environment

Be qualified to SVQ Level 3 or HNC level or equivalent

Have the ability to express themselves clearly, demonstrating confidence and self assurance

Be able to communicate well

Be able to lead, motivate and explain tasks and priorities to junior staff

Be able to use IT solutions for data management

Demonstrate competence with word processing and spreadsheet packages to produce reports or information for auditors

Be able to evaluate problems, interpret procedures and reach decisions to meet auditor enquiries

Be able to understand and use statistical information

Be able to use financial and management information data to produce reports for auditors

Be able to prioritise

Be self-motivated and demonstrate the ability to motivate others.

ADMINISTRATIVE SERVICES

Task 2

Use the Internet to find two advertisements for jobs in administration. From the information given complete the following pro-forma. This pro-forma may be given to you by your teacher as form Admin1task2. You could use websites such as www.s2jobs.com or www.scotlandsjobs.com or use a search engine to look for jobs in your local area.

Job Title	
Job Description	
Personal Qualities required	
Qualifications required	

Check your Progress

1   If you were applying for Job 4 write down how you could prove that you have the personal qualities required for the job.

2   Job 5 requires the job holder to work on the reception desk. Which personal qualities refer to this part of the job? Can you think of any other qualities which would be good for this type of work?

3   Look at Jobs 4, 5 and 6. What job is the most senior job? (You shouldn't judge solely on salary.) Why do you think this is the most senior job?

4   What qualities do all three jobs have in common?

Personal Targets

When employing staff all organisations will ensure that their policies and procedures aim to do the following:

- Recruit, develop and motivate people to help achieve the organisation's targets.

- Develop a structure which encourages co-operation and commitment to the organisation.

- Make the best use of the skills and abilities of their employees.

Most organisations will have formal procedures which have to be followed when recruiting new staff to ensure that recruitment is fair and that all potential candidates get the same opportunity to join the organisation. Once employees have been recruited they will usually be given the opportunity to participate in staff development to help them reach their full potential.

Regardless of where your job fits into the overall structure of an organisation you are likely to be involved in identifying development opportunities and setting targets for yourself as well as contributing towards the targets set by the organisation.

When you read a job description and a person specification together you should get a clear idea of the type of person and the experience required to carry out the role. However, these documents do not usually give you an indication of the standard required.

In many organisations there will be set standards for administration and these would normally be familiar to those making new appointments. These standards would be read and used along with job descriptions and they would also be used to compare what you do with the standard the organisation requires. Here are some examples of the kind of standards set by large organisations.

General Office Standards

- We will keep the reception area neat and organised to give a professional impression.
- We will tidy all desks at the end of each day.
- We will keep confidential work out of view and locked away at the end of each day.
- We will report any equipment faults or issues with other facilities as they occur.
- We will have an operational knowledge of all basic office equipment.
- We will open all e-mails each morning and access and read new e-mails regularly during the day.
- We will not use e-mail or the Internet excessively for private use.
- We are aware that sending rude or suggestive e-mails is regarded as a disciplinary issue.
- We will keep all records of addresses, e-mails and telephone numbers up-to-date.

Personal Effectiveness Standards

- We will be punctual at all times.
- We will look business-like at all times.
- We will have a positive, pleasant and helpful attitude to everyone.
- We will be prepared to cover all roles within our department.
- We will work together as a team and maintain good communication in the department.

Word Processing Standards

- We will achieve 100% accuracy in spelling.
- We will present all word processing in accordance with house style.
- We will meet turnaround times as agreed when a word processing request is received.
- We will keep a day file of all word processing.
- We will ensure that all files and folders are maintained in a logical and accessible way.
- We will maintain confidentiality at all times.

Telephone Standards

- We will all have a good working knowledge of the switchboard.

- We will staff the switchboard at all times during office opening hours except during fire alarms when Night Service will be used.

- We will answer all calls promptly within a maximum of 15 seconds.

- We will answer all calls in a polite and professional manner with the minimum greeting 'good morning/good afternoon' and the name of the organisation.

- We will ensure that if the required person is not available a message service will be offered to callers.

- We will pass on all messages to the relevant administrative support staff within 20 minutes of receipt.

- We will update the telephone extension list regularly and it will be readily available at the reception desk and on the company intranet.

You will see from the standards shown above that most overall work standards are written in very general terms. Within departments much more specific standards might be stated. For example, in word processing there is likely to be a folder with examples of accepted house styles for all commonly-used documents. If you are new to the organisation and do not know the layout of a report you can look up the folder.

Other organisations may encourage staff to undertake NVQs/SVQs to ensure they are operating at national standards. This will usually mean that the employee or trainee has to prove that they have certain essential skills common to all office jobs as well as certain optional skills which best reflect the job they currently do. Essential skills which are common to most administrative jobs will include things like knowledge of health and safety, teamworking skills, time management skills and IT skills. Optional skills will include things like dealing with invoices, following purchasing procedures, using shorthand skills, making travel arrangements and organising and recording meetings. For further information you should access the Council for Administration website (www.cfa.com) to see the standards currently required for Level II and Level III candidates.

Some organisations will test the level of potential employee skills either as part of the interview process or as part of the induction programme. This is often to ensure that new employees are correctly placed on the right salary scale. Other organisations ask employees to do a skillscan. A skillscan is an honest look at the skills you have in comparison with the skills required for the job.

Task 3

Job 1 has been analysed to identify the skills required for the job. This is shown below (Admin1task3). You should be honest in identifying the skills you have and those you need to develop.

Skill	No experience/ do not do this	Not very competent/ do this occasionally	Competent/ regularly do this	Very competent
Word processing skills				
Spreadsheet skills				
Telephone skills				
Face-to-face communications				
Written communications				
Listening skills				
Filing				
Dealing with incoming mail				
Dealing with outgoing mail				
Photocopying				

Every organisation does things differently and any new employee appointed will usually have an induction programme to introduce them to the organisation and ensure they know what is required of them. If an employee is not meeting the required standard, targets would be set to help them do so. These targets would be reviewed on a regular basis.

What are Targets or Objectives?

A target, or objective, is something which you are aiming to accomplish. A target or objective can belong to an individual, a team or a department.

Operational targets are the results you or your organisation want to achieve. They will normally be based on your contribution or your department's contribution to the organisation's overall business plan.

Developmental targets are what you agree to do or learn to improve your performance, knowledge or skills. These are usually developed with reference to the person specification and job description for a specific job role. Often an employee will use a skillscan of the type you completed in Task 3 to spot any gaps in their skills. The purpose of the skillscan is to identify the skills you have and any further training requirements you need.

Many organisations use personal development plans to help staff and management match their targets.

Personal Development Plans

A personal development plan (PDP) is usually a single A4 sheet which maps out how a person can develop skills and progress in his or her job.

Features

- It looks at the development of the individual employee.

- It is all about the aspirations of the employee.

- It looks at broad long-term development, usually for the next year.

- Development does not have to be related to work tasks.

- PDPs should be written in a structured way, recorded and reviewed. This usually means that you and your line manager:

  – agree long term targets

  – decide how to achieve them

  – break down the targets into short term goals

  – regularly review what you have done, usually at least twice a year.

- When PDPs are used in an organisation it is usual for all employees in the organisation to have one.

Setting Targets

Most organisations use a standard questionnaire to help set targets. Here are the kind of questions that might be asked.

- What do you want to get out of your job?

- How have you coped with the workload?

- What part of your job do you think you do well?

- What part of your job would you like to improve?

- What new/improved skills would improve your work performance?

- What resources would you need to improve your performance?

- What would help you feel more confident at work?

- What interests or abilities would you like to develop?

You will notice that all of the questions are very general and really apply to all employees from the managing director to the office junior. While it would be lovely if all of us could freely choose what skills we wanted to develop and what we wanted to do, obviously the requirements of the organisation have to be taken into account.

There will often be a formal system set up to ensure that the plans for the organisation as a whole are developed at different levels and the development plans of individuals have to fit into these overall organisational plans. Line managers should be familiar with the organisation's business plan and targets before they speak to staff. They should be aware of any new demands or job roles which will be asked of employees. It may be a complex task to

ADMINISTRATIVE SERVICES

match the needs of the business to those of the employee and often trade union negotiation is part of this process. Usually employees are provided with a copy of the company's targets or business plan to read before their career review or personal development planning meeting.

Agreeing Targets in Your Personal Development Plan

The line manager and the employee have to agree the targets. When you are drawing up a personal development plan you should remember the following:

- both you and your line manager have to buy-in to the process

- the resources of the organisation are limited so you may have to prioritise your targets

- you may need to compromise in your personal targets to suit the targets of the business

- the number of main targets are usually limited to three

- short-term targets should be SMART (specific, measurable, agreed, realistic and time-limited).

Some organisations use the term *performance management* alongside personal development planning but the performance management process is usually linked to judgements on previous performance and often to pay scales and increments. Performance management schemes usually concentrate on setting targets only for the workplace. The focus of a personal development plan should be positive for the employee and should concentrate on what will happen rather than focus on criticism of what did happen.

The Process of Personal Development Planning

Whether a personal development planning system or a performance management system is in place, all those being reviewed should prepare in advance for a review by:

- looking at progress made since the last review

- discussing progress by agreeing whether good progress has been made or no progress has been made

- discussing what contribution has been made to the overall goals of the organisation or department.

The reviewer or line manager should:

- ensure that the operational targets of the department are available

- ensure that all employees have a personal development planning session

- review all PDPs on a regular basis

- discuss, analyse and record performance with the person being reviewed.

Some organisations grade progress, others do not. If a grading is used it is likely to be very simple. This usually means each target will be judged as highly effective, effective or ineffective. If an ineffective grading is given, special attention would be given to that employee and a *performance improvement plan* may be introduced which would focus on the areas requiring improvement. The whole process is summarised on the following page.

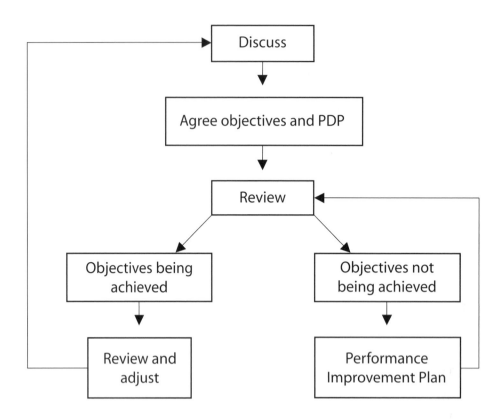

The process of personal development planning

Writing Clear Targets

It is very important that targets are SMART. This stands for

Specific – targets should detail precisely what you are going to do

Measurable – this could, for example, be a number or time

Agreed – with your line manager

Realistic – while your targets should stretch you, they must be realistic

Timebound – there should be a timescale attached to achieving the target.

If you write SMART targets you can more easily see if they have been met.

 Task 4

Try to write the following targets in a smart way

General target	SMART target
Learn to drive	
Save some money	

Development of the Targets

Development can take place:

- through formal training which is particularly useful where there are a number of people with the same targets and where new knowledge or skills are required

- in the employee's own workplace often by assigning a mentor or seconding the employee to a different department

- through self-directed development, i.e. organising and doing it for yourself.

There are basically two kinds of development:

- essential development which **has** to be undertaken to meet the targets

- desirable development which will enhance your performance or develop your potential but is not really a requirement of the current job.

Reviews

Some organisations have set review times, e.g. every three months, but it is quite common for organisations to allow reviewers to be flexible, particularly where a performance improvement plan is involved. High flyers may need to be reviewed more frequently than other employees.

Most PDPs have a feedback part of the form which gives the person being reviewed – sometimes called the reviewee – the opportunity to record what went well as well as what could be improved. All PDP meetings should give the reviewer the opportunity to recognise employees' achievements and progress. When development has been slow, the PDP can be used as a way of focusing on problem areas.

Monitoring and Controlling Achievement of Targets in Personal Development Plans

There is no point in setting targets in any plan unless there is also a system set up to monitor and control these targets, ensure that targets have been met and that any lessons have been learnt. It is important that any checks or monitoring activities are seen as constructive and designed to help you achieve your aims.

Here are some ways that targets or work can be monitored.

Buddy system. This is where an employee, particularly a new employee, is paired with a more experienced person, usually at the same level, who can be called upon for help and advice. This will usually be someone who is familiar with all the details of the job and the organisation.

Mentoring system. Here a more senior member of staff is assigned to an employee. This is not likely to be the employee's line manager. This senior member of staff can be relied upon to supply help and advice as well as knowledge of the organisation and how it works.

Line manager. This might involve the line manager doing periodic checks of work or discussions about progress of tasks to ensure that organisational policy is being adhered to and the required quality standards are being met.

Internal audits. Many organisations use some type of quality system to check that organisational standards and quality standards are being met. These internal audits are usually carried out by someone external to the department but internal to the organisation.

Task 5

You have just started this course in Administration. You will already be aware of the overall content of the course and will know what you are going to learn and the skills you are going to develop over the next few months. You can start the personal development planning process by trying to identify your needs and completing the first part of the PDP on the table below. Your teacher/lecturer will either provide you with Admin1task5 or you should key it in yourself.

Personal Development Plan	
Targets	Details
Personal Targets	

Action Plan		
Action	Resources needed	Target Date
Personal Targets		

Line Manager Comments	
Individual Targets	Personal Development Plan

continued ➤

Task 5 continued

Description of Performance
Very Effective, Effective, Underperforming, Unsatisfactory
Line Manager's Comments Review of Performance

Employee comments

Start off by answering the following questions and making notes.

1 What do you want to get out of this course?

2 How have you coped with the workload?

3 What part of the course do you think you do well?

4 What part of the course do you need to work at to improve?

5 What new/improved skills would improve your performance?

6 What resources would you need to improve?

7 What would help you feel more confident in this course?

8 What interests or abilities would you like to develop?

You should also think about your relationships

- with staff teaching the course

- with other students.

continued ➤

ADMINISTRATIVE SERVICES

ADMINISTRATIVE SERVICES

Task 5 continued

On the basis of your answers to the above questions (particularly questions 4, 5 and 6) you should complete the first part of the form detailing your course targets. You should then look at your personal targets and identify three personal targets on the basis of your answers to question 8. Remember to make your targets SMART.

Make sure you save your answers and targets calling the file by a new name.

Action Plans

An action plan can be part of your personal development plan or it can be a separate document. In the example we are using, the action plan is part of the personal development plan. This is where you identify how you are going to achieve the targets you have identified. It is important that this part is discussed with your manager – in your case your tutor, teacher or lecturer.

Task 6

You should now discuss your personal development plan with your tutor, teacher or lecturer. Look back at what kind of preparation you would be expected to do before having a review with your line manager if you were working in an organisation and prepare in the same way for your PDP review.

Check your Progress 1.2

1   Why do most personal development plans include targets for your personal life as well as your work life?

2   Why is it important to make targets SMART?

3   Why do you think highfliers might need more frequent reviews of PDPs?

The personal development planning process is all about you setting your own targets but as we have learnt these targets and objectives have to match with those of the organisation and the department.

The Organisation's Planning Process

On a wider scale we also need to look at the organisation's planning processes and ensure that your targets fit in with those of the organisation. For example decisions may have been made at a different level which will affect your personal development plan – an example would be the decision to change the software used in your organisation. This might have training implications for you and might mean you have to amend the training requirements you and your line manager identified in your personal development plan.

It is generally accepted that there are 3 levels – strategic, tactical and operational – in an organisation and some kind of planning activity will take place at each of these levels.

The strategic level is the highest level in the organisation. Decisions made at this level are made by those who run the organisation and focus on the overall direction of the organisation. Here are some features of a strategic plan. It will:

- cover all aspects of the organisation, e.g. the example mentioned earlier about software

- incorporate the overall goals of the organisation, e.g. areas which the organisation wants to expand or extend

- answer the question 'what if...?'

- be a long term plan (usually 5 years) which is monitored and amended annually

- determine the policy of the organisation and decide on priorities for the future

- need a lot of broad-based information usually from outside the organisation, e.g. competitor activity.

The next level down in an organisation will be the tactical level. Here are some of the features of a tactical plan. It will be:

- a shorter term than the strategic plan

- written and reviewed by middle managers

- centred around 'how to' and will concentrate on resource allocation and problem solving

- based on identified strengths and weaknesses in the organisation's current processes and operations

- focused on the organisation's structures and on trying to achieve the goals and targets identified at strategic level.

The operational plan will have the following features. It will be:

- a shorter term than the tactical plan

- undertaken by departmental managers or section supervisors

- reliant on co-operation with middle managers who write the tactical plan to ensure that their intentions are translated to this level

- centred on the problem of the individual department or section involved, e.g. The Finance Section's operational plan will only contain targets which are under the Finance Section's control unless a target is organisation-wide

- about monitoring the level of outputs like quality, cost effectiveness and profit and will aim to try and improve these.

You may remember when you started to look at personal development planning, it was suggested that you would be provided with information on operational/departmental plans before you spoke to your line manager. This is because you are likely to:

- be able to have an input into the operational plan and should be quite clear about your part in that plan. Many organisations have planning events to try to ensure that all employees:

    – have the opportunity to discuss proposals at operational level and

    – can feed back opinions to the tactical plan or strategic plan.

- be expected to have an overall knowledge of where the organisation is going – the strategic plan

- be expected to know how they intend to get there – the tactical plan.

Whatever the level at which plans are formulated or the purpose of the plans there will be certain similarities:

- Plans should have SMART targets.

- Priorities should be indicated for each target.

- The organisation's planning system should have a review process built in to ensure that the organisation is monitoring progress towards overtaking the targets.

- Reviews should take place on a regular basis.

- The planning process should log any alterations which are required due to changing priorities.

 # Working Effectively

All administrative roles will involve:

Planning – e.g. involvement in personal development planning and operational planning as well as planning your own work and the work of others.

Organising – e.g. organising your own work, managing your time and managing your own paperwork

Delegating – e.g. ensuring that work which can and should be done by others is allocated appropriately

Directing – e.g. ensuring that processes and procedures are managed

Controlling – e.g. ensuring that processes are tracked and controlled for monitoring purposes.

We are now going to look at some techniques to help in the above processes.

 # Time Management

Why is Time Management Important?

To work effectively you really have to manage your time. We all have our moments when we wonder what happened to the day and we seem to get nothing done but, in a business, time is money and every hour you spend at work costs your employer a lot of money. The cost to an organisation of an employee is not just the salary they are paid but the employer's National Insurance contribution, any pension contributions the employer makes as well as costs like the heating and lighting of the business premises, telephone costs, the cost of office furniture and computer equipment, and the provision of staff facilities, training, etc. Imagine then how expensive it is for an organisation to have a meeting of senior managers for two hours every week unless it has a definite purpose!

Much of the time we spend working is spent doing routine, unimportant tasks and research indicates that up to 80% of our time at work is spent on tasks of this type. Pareto's Law states that 20% of the time produces 80% of the results and 80% of the time produces 20% of the results.

For the individual, good time management skills usually mean that the employee feels more in control of their workload. This in turn means that the employee is likely to find working less stressful and will be required to spend less time in their place of work, leaving more space for quality time spent at home or in leisure activities. Good time management therefore results in benefits for both the employee and the employer.

Poor time management is usually shown by:

- getting less done than you expected

- an inability to meet deadlines set by your line manager

- spending much longer on some part of the job and then having insufficient time to do the rest of the job.

Poor time management can be the result of *time stealers* such as:

- time wasting – you doing things which are not a priority – sometimes called displacement activity

- not knowing what to do or how to start

- being unable to find the information you need to do the job

- putting off starting – this is known as procrastination

- re-doing one small part of the job over and over again until it is perfect

- having little incentive to do well – poor motivation, work overload

- interruptions by people – colleagues chatting and gossiping

- interruptions by telephone

- dealing with other people's work – often the result of absence

- dealing with a backlog of your own work

- meetings going on longer than expected

- flapping every time priorities are changed

- taking on too much work in the first place because you feel you have to say yes and help others

- failing to communicate clearly with either the person you are doing the job for or the person you are asking to carry out some tasks

- not prioritising work correctly resulting in some essential jobs not being done.

All of us are guilty of allowing our time to be stolen by some of the factors outlined above. The important thing when you are looking at how you manage your time is to identify what are **your** critical time wasters. For example, when revising for an exam you may find the first thing you do is make a drink and while you are making it, you turn on the television and you never actually get as far as studying because you get 'distracted' before you start.

ADMINISTRATIVE SERVICES

ADMINISTRATIVE SERVICES

 Task 7

When you start studying for an assessment or exam what time wasters result in poor time management for you? How can you stop these factors being a timewaster? Your teacher/lecturer will provide you with Admin1task7 or you should create a table with two columns: the one on the left headed 'Identified stops to good time management' and the one on the right 'How to avoid the stoppage'.

Most people recognise themselves as a morning person or an afternoon person or an evening person. This usually means that this is their best time for thinking, working quickly and studying. They feel that this is when they are at their best. You should know and recognise your *prime time*. If you have a choice about when to work on difficult things or when to hold an important meeting you should try and make sure it is in your prime time.

 Task 8

When is your best time? How do you know? Give examples of what has made you choose this time as your prime time.

 Task 9

You should now try to complete the following table. Your teacher/lecturer will provide you with Admin1task9 or you should key in the table yourself.

Time Stealer	How can you stop this stealing your time?
Interruptions by telephone	
Looking for lost papers	
Communicating problems	
Meetings going on longer than expected	
Re-doing one part of the job again and again	

Effects of Poor Time Management

From the employer's perspective poor time management skills result in:

- much of the time spent at work being wasted – some of it on displacement activities, i.e. spending time doing jobs that do not matter or could be done by someone at a lower level in the organisation

- staff becoming demoralised as work becomes very routine and seems to serve no purpose

- work not progressing as fast as management hoped

- targets not being achieved and the strategic and operational plans becoming meaningless

- new projects not being started as there is never any 'spare' time to progress new ideas.

There are lots of benefits to both individuals and the organisation of adopting good time management skills:

- It allows organisations to plan, delegate and organise employees more effectively.

- Everyone in the organisation can then be focused on their own tasks.

- Progress of projects can be traced and if there is a hold up it can be identified and extra resources allocated to it.

- Individual employees feel more in control of their work, i.e. they know what has to be done and they know when it has to be finished.

Managing your own time is important both in your personal life and in your workplace. Those who manage their time well have time to do everything. Those who are poor at managing their time achieve very little. Hence the saying if you want a job done, give it to a busy person.

Good Time and Task Management Techniques

Here are some techniques which might help you improve how you manage your time.

1. At the end of each day compile a *to do list* for the next day giving each job a priority and trying to note how long you expect to spend on the job. Try to stick to your list and tackle all the jobs with a high priority first. This means you are planning your day and will make you feel more in control. The timing element can also be used to your advantage. You should not be sitting waiting for something to happen, e.g. a long report to print or IT to get back to you; you should be able to identify a series of small jobs that can be done while you are waiting.

2. Try to prioritise your tasks. Most of them will fall into three main headings:
   - immediate action by you
   - some action by you but also some on-going work by you or others
   - information for reading, circulating, filing or disposing of.

   Develop your own code for marking tasks as one of the above categories and remember to set aside some time for both reading and prioritising. You can build this prioritising into your to do list.

3. At the end of each day try to clear your desk so that when you come in the next day you have a clear approach to your work and space to work in. This also allows other people access to any files you have been using. Again it will make you feel more in control as each day becomes a fresh start.

4. Make sure you do the most difficult tasks in your prime time when you are at your best.

5. Try to handle papers or tasks only once, i.e. read them, take any actions needed, and file them. This applies to e-mails too. If you deal with things promptly there is less chance of a backlog of work building up. It is important to finish a task, e.g. actually file the papers rather than just putting them in a filing tray which may build up yet another backlog.

6. Try to avoid being interrupted. If your interruptions are caused by people chatting to you at your desk you can try to make some physical barriers, e.g. make sure there is nowhere for people to sit near your desk, turn your chair side on so that you are not facing your colleagues, move to a quiet working space for a particular task. Some offices have quiet work times particularly first thing in the morning so that everyone gets a chance to do jobs which require concentrated effort.

7 You can improve your telephone call management technique by listing the calls you want to make and what you want to ask and have a set time for making your outgoing calls. Dealing with incoming calls is a bit more complicated. While some organisations might encourage you to you use their voice mail system and respond to all callers by the end of the working day, most organisations would prefer customers to get a response upon enquiry. Divert your phone if it is important that you are not interrupted.

8 Do not put off difficult tasks or those you don't know how to do. Seek help.

9 When you feel your concentration going and you know you are not working effectively, move on to doing something else.

10 While some time management systems will advise doing only one job at a time, others will advise working for a maximum of half an hour on one task and moving on to a different task. You should experiment and see which system suits you best.

11 If there is someone to whom you can delegate jobs, you should make sure you do delegate tasks to them. Be careful not to delegate only the tasks you don't like or really boring tasks – no-one wants to do things like stick on labels all day!

Task 10

From the list above identify three techniques you can use to help you manage your time more effectively. Use them consistently for three weeks.

Task 11

Evaluate your use of the three time management techniques you used. Did they work? Did you adapt them to suit your needs? Will you continue to use them? What did you gain from using them?

Check your Progress   **1.3**

1 Write some notes for a new member of staff in the office to help them manage their time.

2 Suggest a possible layout for a to do/priorities list.

3 Look at ways of prioritising or using a to do facility using your IT system or set up a template, e.g. as a word processing file and use this to help you prioritise your work.

Communication

Communicating with Others

In every survey asking employers what they want of employees, all rate good communication skills very highly. It is not only important that you can deal with customers or people outside your organisation but your ability to communicate well with people at all levels within the organisation is also important. Managers need to know what is happening to plan, co-ordinate and control operations and need to communicate information to ensure that targets and performance match. Good relationships between departments in an organisation depend on co-operation.

Communication can be vertical – downwards from your line manager to you or upwards to your line manager from you – or they can be horizontal or lateral between people at the same level in an organisation. Diagonal communication is usually between people at different levels and in different departments in an organisation where there is no clear line of authority, e.g. when a the sales manager needs the help of an IT technician.

Methods of Communication

There will be lots of different methods of communication used throughout every organisation. They can largely be categorised as:

- face-to-face communication
- oral communication
- written communication
- visual communication

Face-to-face communication

Face-to-face communication is good for exchanging views, generating new ideas, spreading information quickly through the organisation and encouraging co-operation. However, these advantages can be lost if those attending are unwilling to communicate or there is insufficient guidance or leadership to control proceedings. Here are some examples of face-to-face communication.

- Meetings which can be formal or informal. A formal meeting may have rules and conventions, such as restrictions on who attends. Some may think this acts as a barrier to communication but it is likely that most formal and semi-formal meetings will produce some kind of record of the decisions taken at the meeting (a minute of meeting or an action minute) and these are usually available to a wider audience than those who participated in the meeting. Many meetings will focus on joint problem solving by using people from different areas in an organisation to consult and decide on the best way forward. Brainstorming, where there is a free exchange of ideas, can also help generate new approaches. You will find out more about meetings later in your studies. Committees are often used as a way of delegating authority. These can be set up for a variety of purposes, e.g. to approve decisions such as budgets or audits or as a means of consulting between employers and employees.

- Interviews or one-to-one meetings are good ways of dealing with problems and queries while allowing confidentiality. You would expect any disciplinary hearings or grievance interviews to be face-to-face interviews although they may not be one-to-one. You would also expect an interview for any personal development planning or appraisal activities. Increasingly there is likely to be use of technology to improve face-to-face communication. Video-conferencing can be used to access face-to-face communications with those who are geographically dispersed. The two methods can be mixed so that you could have a video-conference link to a distant office so that a member of staff can join in a team meeting. The increased use of video links with computers will also increase face-to-face communication methods.

ADMINISTRATIVE SERVICES

Oral communication

Oral communication does not have the impact that face-to-face communication has but it does save travelling time and is less likely to take more time than anticipated. Here are some types of oral communication:

- telephones – static and mobile telephones, voice bank techniques and answering machines

- paging machines

- public address systems which work throughout an organisation to enable contact with one or all members of staff.

Written communication

Written communication has the advantage of permanence and traceability in an organisation. It is often helpful to retain a record of communication. Here are some examples of written communications:

- E-mail allows a brief informal written communication which can be printed in hard copy or saved electronically for future reference.

- Letters are still used, particularly for confidential internal information, e.g. appointments, redundancy, etc. They are mainly used for external communication and generally delivered by Post Office services with special arrangements for guaranteed, insured or urgent deliveries or overseas communications. They can also be sent by courier if urgency of delivery is a priority, e.g. a lawyer may choose to use this method.

- The memorandum is used as part of the internal mail system of an organisation and is usually placed in an internal re-usable envelope.

- Reports or papers. These could be formal reports or papers prepared to allow a number of people to review complex facts or arguments and make a decision. This kind of document can be published internally or it can be a source of information to external people who have an interest in the organisation – stakeholders, such as shareholders, or the general public. This kind of publication has the advantage of allowing people to study the information in their own time. The information will usually be presented in a formal, impersonal style allowing the reader to form their own opinion without being sidetracked by emotional reactions or conflicts which often occur at meetings. Annual reports are issued by many organisations not just for shareholders but also for employees. The employee version will often focus on the information employees want to know like welfare benefits, industrial relations and manpower planning.

- Forms. A lot of information flows into, around and out of organisations on forms. A well-designed form can be completed quickly, can usually be e-mailed and will contain all essential information.

- Notice boards are often used as a cheap way of transmitting a lot of information to a large number of people. They must be maintained on a regular basis or information will quickly go out of date. Many organisations use an internal newsletter, magazine or bulletin board as well as a physically located notice board. While much of the information here is likely to be informal like social events, retirements or staff benefits, it is also likely to have health and safety and insurance information included.

- An organisational handbook is often used to draw together relevant information about the business which affects each employee. It is likely to be given to the employee at induction and can be added to at any time. It is likely to contain information on:

    – the organisation structure

    – the organisation's history and background

    – products, services and customers

    – rules and regulations – e.g. claiming expenses, parking permits

    – conditions of employment – e.g. pay structure, hours, holidays

    – standards and procedures about health and safety

    – the organisation's procedures for dealing with grievances, discipline, salary review

    – facilities available for employees.

Visual communications

Charts, pictures, films, graphs, photographs and slides can all be used to communicate information. Most people can remember a picture better than the written word. Think about the letter K from Kellogs Corn Flakes or the colour of the wrapping paper from a bar of Cadbury's Dairy Milk. These are recognisable visual images which communicate a product to you.

 Task 12

Think of an example of when you would use face-to-face communication in preference to oral communication. Why would you consider face-to-face necessary?

 Task 13

Many organisations now use a telephone interview as part of their selection procedure. They use it prior to interviewing candidates. Why do you think this is popular?

Barriers to Effective Communication

To work effectively good communication is essential. Difficulties often occur because of faults or barriers in the communication process. Sometimes these barriers to communication are referred to as noise. Noise is caused by incomplete information, too much information or a lack of clarity in the information. Some examples of barriers or faults in communication are given below.

- Some information may be missed out. We all tend to summarise information as we pass it on, particularly if we do not fully understand all the content. This can often be as a result of technical jargon which is only fully understood by specialists.

- There are occasions when we all suffer from information overload, e.g. after being on holiday you probably come back to a pile of letters. Some may be junk mail while others may be really important but can easily be missed simply because you are swamped by communications.

- Information gets distorted. It may be changed as it is retold and passed from one person to another or it may be misinterpreted when passed downwards in the organisation.

- When a message is given orally, sometimes the verbal communication conflicts with the body language of the person giving the message. The tone of voice, roll of the eyes or the way the information is given, e.g. as an afterthought, may give the impression that the information is not really important and this can lead to confusion.

- Differences in background, age and personality can often lead to confusion. We all have different sets of vocabulary we use on different occasions. For example, you are likely to speak very differently to your friends compared with the way you speak to your grandparents. You will speak differently to your teacher or lecturer and your younger brother or sister. This will not only be in terms of the slang words and phrases used but your verbal communication is likely to be at a different speed too. If you know someone is very sensitive and 'takes everything the wrong way' you tend to be very careful with what you say to them.

- People do not always hear what is said. This might be because they are nervous, e.g. at an interview or talking to a doctor, or it might be because it is bad news and they are 'filtering' it.

What is important is to recognise that even in the best of organisations there will be some barriers to good communication and as a result, organisations have to ensure that lines of communication work effectively.

Informal Communication

We have concentrated so far on formal communication methods. Every organisation also has a well developed informal communications system usually known as the *grapevine*. People like to gossip and indeed gossip is now viewed as essential for good mental health. Informal communication takes place over a cup of tea at work, on the way to or from work, in the corridors, at lunch, etc. The problem with informal communication of this type is that it may contain inaccurate rumours as well as some truth. Here are some features of the grapevine.

- It acts fast – often we learn information through our informal contacts first and then the information is communicated officially.

- It works selectively – some information will not pass through the organisation in this way. There is no guarantee who will hear information through the grapevine just as there is no guarantee that information will always go through the grapevine.

- It usually operates only in the workplace and once you are outside the workplace it ceases to work, e.g. if you are off sick or on holiday.

- It only works when there is a formal communication system. It does not fill gaps left by formal systems.

- It is useful and works at all levels in the organisation.

Effective Communication

Here are some ways you can ensure the communication is effective

- Make sure you understand what the message is yourself before you try to pass it on.

- Ensure it is technically correct – the spelling, grammar and vocabulary is acceptable and that technical terms, if used, are used correctly. Where possible use plain English.

- Make sure you are using the correct 'tone'. People can be very sensitive about the way they are spoken to or the way you write something to them.

- Ensure the language is appropriate for the person who is receiving the communication. Will the recipient understand what is being communicated? (Remember: you do not speak to a three year old the same way you speak to your friends.) At the same time remember not to patronise people by talking down to them.

- Make sure you indicate if a response is required – this is often useful to ensure understanding.

- Communicate the information in the most appropriate way, e.g. e-mail, phone call, letter, using any recognised house-styles, e.g. layout of letters or standard paragraphs in e-mails.

- Try to ensure you are using more than one way of communicating essential information, e.g. you might agree a date for a meeting at the end of one meeting and then send out the minutes with the date of the next meeting on them, or you might send an e-mail to all staff and also put a notice on the notice board.

- Ensure you get your timing right. When you send a memo or e-mail can be crucial. Try not to send out information first thing on a Monday when there may be lots of other items needing attention.

- Listen to any comments or problems, they may indicate a gap in your skills.

- Limit the use of jargon.

- Be concise – too much information is lost.

- Try to limit the length of the communication chain – passing it on leads to distortion.

What happens if communications are poor?

- Poor communications waste time as you will usually have to make individual explanations, correct things which are wrong or chase up responses. If people find particular e-mails or memos or letters difficult to deal with they go to the bottom of the pile.

- You will interrupt people at their busiest times and they will not deal effectively with your communication.

- You will not get prompt action to last minute requests.

- You may have to follow-up your initial communication to seek clarification. Reminding people tactfully is another skill.

Task 14

Discuss the following situations in groups and identify why communication was not effective and what could have been done to improve communication.

1   You have a doctor's appointment and asked your boss for time off just as she was going into a meeting. The next day she accuses you of not telling her you were leaving early.

2   You receive a call from a former employee asking for your boss's home address. She gets angry when you refuse to give it to her.

3   You have completed an application form for a job and realise that the closing date is tomorrow. You take a chance and post the application form first class.

4   A member of staff frequently repeats comments made by your boss about other people's work so that his opinion becomes common knowledge in the office.

ADMINISTRATIVE SERVICES

Task 15

Many of us use the wrong words in the wrong place. See if you can get these right.

1 principal/principle

Fill in the blanks.

The main _____ of the new system is to ensure that all time is logged effectively and the _____ intends to check data to ensure its accuracy.

The _____ purpose of carrying out this check is to ensure that everyone records data in accordance with the _____ laid down in the staff handbook.

2 formally/formerly

Write down what each of these words mean.

3 to/too/two

Fill in the blanks.

There are _____ many people wanting ____ undertake this course so we are going ___ have ___ divide them into ____ groups. If your name is in group one you will require _____ report ____ the Board Room at ____ o'clock on Friday ____ start the course.

4 there/their/they're

_____ were so many volunteers wanting to do that course that they were asked to put _____ names down on a waiting list. _____ going to be informed as soon as _____ is another course available.

Team Working

Part of your job is likely to include working with other people in a team. As part of your job you may be in several different teams. Teams are likely to have a common purpose, a common leader and a common identity. The team is likely to work towards accomplishing an agreed goal. There are benefits to both the organisation and to individuals of effective team working.

What makes a team effective?

- It is very important that all members of the team have a clear idea of what they are there to achieve and believe in these shared goals and objectives. An external threat is likely to bring a group even closer, e.g. the threat of redundancy. An outstanding success will have the same effect.

- Shared knowledge among members of the team means there will be better coverage of any absences, members will be able to support each other because they know what is happening and this in turn will lead to customers receiving better service.

- An effective team may impose its own rules and checks on team members who do not conform to the agreed objectives, e.g. general disapproval of those who do not pull their weight.

- There should be clear and transparent procedures and processes that are known to all members of the team. These should include procedures for reviewing the achievements of both the team and the individuals within the team. Better quality of service results when all involved know the processes and procedures they are supposed to follow.

- It is very important to choose people who have different skills and personality traits to contribute to the team dynamics. At the same time an effective team will be able to work with and communicate with all parts of the organisation.

- The balance of different skills and personalities in the team should encourage members of the team to express their opinions and feelings openly and honestly and decisions should be reached by agreement. It is important that the strengths of the individuals in the team are used for the benefit of the team. The strengths and weaknesses of individuals can often be balanced within a team.

- A leader with an appropriate leadership style that suits the way the team works will help maintain the team.

- The longer the team is together the more effective it is likely to be because they have a shared history.

- Small teams or teams where members are carrying out similar job roles are likely to be the most cohesive as they have less complex relationships.

- When a group meets regularly and frequently, it is also likely to be more cohesive.

Effective team working has benefits for both team members and the organisation. Here are some of the benefits to team members.

- The individual team members benefit in terms of the support they receive from other team members.

- A good team will resolve any conflict within the team itself. As a result there are likely to be fewer underlying tensions for the individual to deal with.

- Individuals learn well with the support of a team environment where there are likely to be both experienced and less experienced staff and therefore a ready supply of mentors.

- Members of a good team tend to be happier at their work.

As far as the organisation is concerned effective team working is likely to lead to higher productivity. Where people work well together there are likely to be lower levels of:

- staff turnover
- absenteeism
- accidents
- complaints
- errors in work.

Working with others

One of the personal qualities many employers say is important is the ability to work with others. It is only through working well with others that effective teams can be formed and, as we have seen, good teamwork can bring a lot of benefits to both individuals and organisations. If you are going to work as part of a team you should try to remember the following guidelines.

- Every member of the team should be open and honest in their dealings with others in the group.

- All members of the team should have a clear idea of their objectives and roles.

- Use any mistakes – your mistakes or mistakes of the team – to help improve what you or the team do.

- Use competition and conflict within the team to reach agreement. Try not to get to the stage where sides are identified and formed.

- Use relationships to build support and trust: no one should feel isolated or threatened by their actions, e.g. just because you disagree with someone this should not mean you are alienated by the rest of the team – a good team will talk openly about your point of view and as a group decide on the best course of action.

- Ensure that activities such as meetings are productive and stimulating. Meetings without a purpose can be frustrating and time-wasting.

- Ensure that there are opportunities for everyone to contribute to any team decisions so that everyone has an equal interest in the success of the decision. This may be difficult when there are a number of part-time or job-sharers involved in a team.

- The team should try to recognise, acknowledge and compliment personal development which contributes to the team effort.

What do you have to do to be an effective team member?

There are certain characteristics which you can recognise in successful and effective team members. Here are some of them. Team members:

- have the ability to co-operate and share in decision making

- have a willingness to listen to and accept other people's ideas and suggestions

- are willing to modify their own ideas and develop proposals and decisions jointly

- are ready to undertake tasks which contribute to only a part of the greater project under the direction of a group leader

- are happy to see praise and recognition go to the group rather than the individual

- are willing to come up with ideas which could be 'shot down'

- are prepared to do a fair share of the group's tasks and not just coast along as part of the group without really contributing

- support other group members and the group's work

- are willing to accept responsibility as a group member for the actions of the group.

What causes conflict within a team?

All businesses benefit from good strong teams but teams go through different stages. We cannot always choose who we have to work with and while a team may be very carefully chosen to have different personality types in it, people move on and sometimes teams no longer work well together. There can be many reasons why there can be conflict within a team.

- Interpersonal differences like personality clashes, differences of opinion, lack of understanding of interests. There can be jealousy between members and differing beliefs and values can lead to problems.

- Unclear job responsibilities can cause confusion and it is always in the interest of the team to clarify roles and responsibilities.

- Ineffective communication among team members may result in a lack of understanding of how your job fits into the overall 'big' picture.

- Heavy workloads for some team members or unfairly split workloads may lead to underlying tensions. While a team should take advantage of the individuals' skills and expertise, some individuals may feel they have more to do than others.

- Following this, those who see themselves as contributing a lot to the team may feel they do not receive the recognition they deserve.

- Some team members may feel they lack challenge.

- Different objectives and priorities among team members may mean that some members feel they are not advancing as quickly as they expect and that their full potential is not being developed.

When there is conflict within a team it can lead to disruption in the work of the team. When the focus switches from the team to conflict between the team members the aims and purpose of the team can be ignored, so it is very important to try to retain harmony in a team. When you are working with a team you have to acknowledge that people have different roles; some will be leaders, some will be followers, some will be outspoken and some will be quiet. To get the best out of a team, you need to have an effective leader.

What is leadership?

Leadership can be defined as the ability to get the best out of your team in any given situation. A good team leader brings big benefits to both the team and the organisation. The leader of a team has to concentrate on:

- getting the job done

- keeping the team operating as a team

- keeping the team effective and on track to meet its targets

- supporting the individuals in the team

- balancing the needs of the task, the team and the individuals within the team.

Leadership skills can be identified as CARE skills.

Cognitive skills – the ability to think clearly and the ability to analyse problems. This person makes decisions based on reasoning not impulse.

Action skills – knowing how to delegate, motivate and communicate and using these skills to gain co-operation from members of the team.

Relationship skills – knowing how to act like a leader and develop the social skills needed to build trust and effective working relationships between members of the team. A good leader:

- is interested in other people

- is a good listener

- does not blame others for what goes wrong

- is sensitive to the needs and expectations of others.

Expert skills – having the necessary technical skills and knowledge required for the job. This person is able to lead by example because of background skills and knowledge.

A good leader requires different skills for each situation and a leader of one group may not work well as a leader in another situation.

The benefits of good leadership

- The team works to common objectives and targets which are agreed and supported by all members of the team. Everyone knows what the team has to do and also their individual roles in any activity. The specific tasks within the overall job are allocated to those best able to do them and this is accepted and understood by all members of the team.

- The team is able to understand its targets and how these fit in with the overall organisational objectives.

- The team is not just a group of individuals but acts as one body with team members supporting each other as and when required.

- The team is prepared to put in extra effort above and beyond what is usually expected of them.

- The team is motivated to do the job as effectively as possible but also aims for excellence, not just 'going through the motions'.

Where poor leadership is in evidence, the team and the organisation will be affected in the following ways:

- The group will be unclear on what they have to do and as a result resources may be wasted and the job may not be done properly.

- The group is unlikely to be motivated. They will take longer than anticipated to meet their targets and may never reach them.

- As morale is likely to be poor, there is likely to be high staff turnover as team members will not want to stay in an environment which does not reward or sustain them.

- Individuals working separately are less effective than a team working properly together.

- A team with poor leadership is likely to do the minimum required – just sufficient to complete the job. They are unlikely to be able to work under pressure or sustain a standard of work for any length of time.

Internal Assessment

Here are some examples of the kind of questions you might be asked as part of your internal assessment.

1 Describe the purpose of a skillscan. (4)

2 Outline three personal qualities required of an administrative assistant. (3)

3 Describe three barriers to effective communications. (3)

1 Outline two personal qualities you might see in a person specification for a senior administrator that you would not find in a more junior post. (4)

2 Describe three consequences to an organisation of poor time management. (6)

3 Outline two reasons why organisations monitor targets. (4)

4 Describe two benefits to an organisation of a new member of staff joining an effective team. Describe two benefits to the individual. (4)

External Assessment

Here are some examples of the kind of questions you might be asked as part of your external assessment at Higher. An estimate of the marks assigned to each question is indicated and it would be anticipated that each question would form part of a larger question.

1 Compare the use of a person specification with a job description. (6)

2 Compare and contrast the roles of an administrative assistant and a senior administrator. (8)

3 Why is effective team working so important to organisations? (8)

4 Discuss the role of the review process in personal development planning. (6)

ADMINISTRATIVE SERVICES

CHAPTER 2

The Work Environment

This chapter is about the factors affecting you and your role in the work environment. It looks at working practices, contracts of employment, health and safety issues and health and safety legislation.

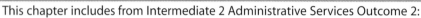

Intermediate 2 Level Outcomes:

This chapter includes from Intermediate 2 Administrative Services Outcome 2:

- ☆ **working practices including full-time, part-time, flexi-time, job-share and home-working, and the benefits to the employee and the organisation**
- ☆ **types of contracts of employment (permanent and fixed-term) and the benefits to employee and the organisation**
- ☆ **health, safety and security issues**
- ☆ **current legislation affecting health and safety, including display screen equipment regulations.**

Higher Level Outcomes:

It also includes from Higher Administrative Services Outcome 2:

- ☆ **the impact of changing working practices including outsourcing and career breaks**
- ☆ **the effect of the work environment on employee morale and wellbeing**
- ☆ **the various laws that affect the work environment, including HSAWA 1974,**
- ☆ **methods employed to communicate organisational and legal requirements**
- ☆ **consequences of breaches of organisational and legislative procedures.**

Note: Legislation affecting security of information and computer misuse is dealt with in Chapter 9.

Flexible Working Practices

Employers have introduced flexible working practices for a variety of reasons. These include: global competition, changes in technology, retention of valued staff, skills shortages and the effects of demographic changes.

In addition the needs of customers are changing. People's lives are much busier today and, as a result, they are demanding high quality services outside traditional hours – hence the increase in 24-hour banking and insurance call centres and 24-hour mail order catalogue services, such as NEXT and Freemans. Retailers, under strong competitive pressures, have had to extend opening hours following both a demand for longer weekday openings and the Sunday Trading Act 1994, which allows 6 hours trading on Sundays. Employees also want and/or need working hours that fit in with their domestic and other work commitments.

One of the most important aims and objectives of the Human Resources Department is to make the best use of its most valuable (and probably most expensive) resource – its staff. Interest in flexible working arrangements allows them to investigate better ways to recruit and retain valued staff, meet changing customer requirements, cut costs and boost productivity.

Flexible working practices cover the many different variations of work, workers and the workplace. The range of practices may include any of the following:

Flexibility of work. In order to attain or retain staff, employers may offer a wide range of *flexible working arrangements* including part-time, job-share and flexi-time. Employees may be able to choose their work location, i.e. home-working.

Flexibility of workers. Employers can use contingency staff on temporary, part-time or fixed term contracts to cover holidays and busy periods, encourage a more flexible workforce and reduce the organisation's labour costs.

Flexibility of the workplace. In order to save space (and therefore money) hot-desking may be introduced. This is an arrangement whereby workers do not have their own desks but are allocated work space according to their needs – workers may keep their personal belongings in lockers when not in the office.

Organisations who embrace these and other flexible arrangements are described by buzzwords such as 'family friendly organisations'.

Flexibility of Workers

One way of encouraging flexibility of workers is through adoption of the flexible firm model – shown below. This shows a method of identifying and using core and peripheral jobs. Permanent 'core' employees are supplemented by temporary and part-time staff as and when required.

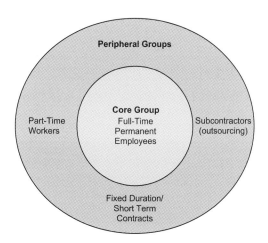

The flexible firm model

The core group tends to be characterised by employees with full time, permanent status. These jobs are central to the longer term future of the organisation. Employees in this group are more likely to:

- be highly flexible and adaptable

- benefit from adequate training and development

- enjoy good career and promotion prospects

- enjoy a higher degree of job security than employees in peripheral groups.

Employees will have to work the hours which are set out in their contract of employment – typically 9a.m. to 5p.m. over 5 days per week over 48 weeks per year. Research indicates that workers in the UK work longer hours than their European counterparts – 4 million employees in the UK regularly work over a 48 hour week. Visit the Department of Trade and Industry website (www.dti.uk) to find out more.

The term peripheral is generally used to cover, in particular part-time and fixed, limited-duration contract working.

Part-time Work

Part-time work involves working fewer hours a week, month or year than a standard full-time contract required by the organisation. Part-time refers to the number of hours worked whereas temporary (as opposed to permanent) refers to security of employment. Therefore an employee can be a permanent part-timer or a temporary part-timer.

The rights of part-time workers have recently changed with the introduction of the Part-time Workers (Prevention of Less Favourable Treatment) Regulations 2000. Part-time workers cannot be treated less favourably than their full-time colleagues. Visit www.dti.gov.uk to find out more about the rights of part-time workers.

How does it work?

Example 1

Mary Smith is Head of the Human Resources Department and has been employed by John Nicholls for 10 years. Mary manages 18 people, mainly administrative and support staff. She has been working a four day week for over a year and takes Tuesdays, Saturdays and Sundays off. She feels she works more effectively than when she worked on a full time basis – previously she was juggling looking after elderly parents and her family with a full-time job. She feels she is now enjoying a better work–life balance. She reports that her stress levels have reduced considerably .

Both employer and employee have to consider the potential advantages and disadvantages to this form of working arrangement.

Advantages to the employer

- Flexibility and cover. The organisation may only wish work to be carried out at certain times, e.g. peak times (in the case of call centres this may be in the evenings).

- Recruitment and retention of staff. The organisation may be able to recruit and retain staff who can combine caring for family members and carrying out their job. It is generally more cost effective to retain existing staff than recruit and train new staff.

- Productivity. Research indicates that productivity and motivation of part-time staff is good. Workers are more likely to stay fresh, energetic and creative in the hours that they work. Absenteeism is also likely to be low.

Disadvantages to the employer

- It may be difficult to organise training events to fit in with part-time hours of work.

- More effort may be required to support and manage part-time staff, for example, to ensure effective use of accommodation and resources.

Advantages to the employee

- Access to work. It enables part-time workers to combine work with family commitments thus enjoying the 'best of both worlds' – this is sometimes called the life–work balance.

- It may allow the part-time worker to keep abreast of developments in their field which is particularly important for those anticipating return to full-time employment. Some workers also report an increase in self-esteem and confidence due to the mental stimulation work provides.

- Lower stress levels than when trying to 'juggle' full time employment and family commitments.

Disadvantages to the employee

- Low pay. Although employees should benefit from the same basic rate of pay as full-time colleagues their gross pay will be lower because they are working shorter hours.

- Training. Many part-time workers have fewer opportunities to go on training courses and may therefore have fewer opportunities for promotion.

- Status of part-time workers. Many part-time workers feel they are not regarded as highly as their full-time colleagues.

Fixed term Contract (non-permanent)

A fixed term contract is issued with a fixed start date and fixed end date and may be issued to cover special situations such as:

- maternity leave of staff
- busy periods, Christmas and holiday periods
- sickness or other long-term absence
- project work which is of a fixed time-scale, e.g. 1 or 2 years.

Although the contract has a maximum duration it can be extended. However, there is no promise of renewal of a contract.

Advantages to the employer

- They allow the employer to use staff to cover busy periods and cover absence.

- Workers may be more committed because they hope to gain a permanent position within the organisation.

- Employer does not have to renew the contract.

- It allows the employer to 'try out' employees.

Disadvantages to the employer

- More administration is involved when contracts are to be renewed.

- Employees may not be as motivated as permanent staff.

Advantages to the employee

- They may suit workers who do not want to be tied down for long periods of time.

- Workers may enjoy a higher rate of pay to compensate for lack of permanency.

Disadvantages to the employee

- Many workers report a lack of feeling of belonging to the organisation because of the fixed duration of the working arrangement.

- There is less job security.

Note: Under the Fixed-term Employees (Prevention of Less Favourable Treatment) Regulations 2002 employees have the right to the same terms of condition of employment as permanent employees. Visit www.acas.org.uk to find out more.

Outsourcing

The subcontracting ('outsourcing' or 'contracting out') of certain activities, particularly non-core activities, is where the organisation engages a supplier to perform a non-core activity, e.g. cleaning, catering or payroll, instead of employing more staff. The perceived benefits to the organisation are:

- The ability of the organisation to agree short term contracts with the subcontractor to ensure performance and low cost are maintained.

- The ability to cancel contracts without the associated obligation of providing for staff should the service provided not meet suitable standards.

- Savings in recruitment and training.

However, there may also be disadvantages to the organisation such as lack of control over the subcontracted staff (perhaps they show lack of commitment and motivation) and the services they provide. The only way an organisation can show dissatisfaction is by not outsourcing for a second time.

Check your Progress [2.1]

1 How could the introduction of flexible working arrangements enable an organisation to satisfy customer needs more effectively?

2 What is meant by the term flexible working arrangements?

3 Discuss whether or not John Nicholls would benefit from employing staff on a fixed term contract basis and why?

4 What is meant by the term outsourcing?

5 John Nicholls wishes to improve its customer relations by setting up an after-sales service call-centre. The Human Resources Department has decided to outsource this work. Discuss the potential benefits and problems they may have of outsourcing this work.

Job-Sharing

In many ways job-sharing has developed because of some of the problems associated with part-time working. Job-sharing is a working arrangement where two people voluntarily share the duties and responsibilities of one full-time position, with salary, holidays and other benefits shared on a pro rata basis according to the number of hours worked.

How does it work?

Example 2

Megan Smith and Sarah Scott share a job as supervisors in the Clothing Department. The supervisory role is split equally between them. They alternate less frequent tasks such as chairing team meetings and carrying out staff appraisals etc. as Megan works all day Monday and Tuesday and Wednesday mornings while Sarah works Wednesday afternoons, all day Thursday and all day Friday. They have a lunch-time overlap on Wednesdays to discuss confidential or staff matters.

There are potential advantages and disadvantages to job sharing.

Advantages to the employer

- Two people bring two sets of skills and experience to a job.

- Improvements in productivity because people working reduced hours tend to be fresh, energetic and creative in the hours they are working.

- Continuity – if one person is off sick or on holiday at least part of the job is still being done.

- Absenteeism may fall because of the increase in employee morale and well-being due to reduced hours.

Disadvantages to the employer

- There are extra costs involved in providing extra staff accommodation and resources such as lockers, desks, laptops. There may also be extra training costs.

- Communication and hand-over difficulties between sharers could cause a problem.

- There are more staff to manage.

Advantages to the employee

- Job-sharing allows the employee to keep up-to-date in their professional and skilled work without a full-time commitment.

- It eases the return to work for those who have not worked full-time for some time, e.g. after long-term sick leave or maternity leave.

- It enables carers of children and the elderly to 'balance' time at home and work.

Disadvantages to the employee

- Job-sharing may not provide enough money to live on.

- Sharers frequently say they put in extra (unpaid) work.

Flexible Working Hours

Flexible working hours or flexi-time schemes allow employees to choose, within set limits, the times they start and finish work. The organisation sets a core time where employees must be present, other than authorised absence, e.g. core time might be 10a.m.–11.30a.m. and 2p.m.–3.30p.m. Employees will also be expected to work an agreed number of hours within an accounting period (usually a month). They usually permit an employee to carry over any excess or deficit in hours beyond an accounting period, with the option of taking 'flexi-leave'.

How does it work?

Example 3

Donald Henderson works full time in the Lighting Department and Ann Henderson works part-time in Customer Services Department. They have a son, Stephen, aged four, who goes to nursery four days a week. Ann takes Stephen to nursery and starts work later in the morning. Donald finishes work early in the afternoon and collects Stephen from nursery.

Both employer and employee should consider the potential advantages and disadvantages of flexible working hours.

Advantages to the employer

- A computerised time system helps build a clear picture of attendance, absenteeism and overtime.

- It can reduce or eliminate punctuality problems and the need to discipline staff for being late. People who are always late can make up their time later in the day or take a shorter lunch.

- It reduces absence rates. Staff can organise personal appointments like dental appointments in flexi-time.

- Helps attract and retain staff.

- It can also help organisations who have extended their opening hours, i.e. branches of banks which are now open between 8a.m. and 6p.m.

Disadvantages to the employer

- Extra costs include: the purchase and maintenance of recording equipment.

- Increased heating, lighting and security costs due to longer opening hours.

- A heavier burden is placed on managers as they have to organise the level of staff cover needed at any particular time.

- Making decisions on when people can take a 'flexi day' and ensuring there is enough staff and supervisory staff available to cover this.

Advantages to the employee

- It gives greater freedom to people to organise their working lives and suit personal needs.

- Travelling can be easier, cheaper and less stressful if outside peak times.

- Organisations show their trust by allowing staff to take responsibility for their work and staff are not disciplined for not being in at the start of the day. This can create an improved working environment.

- If people stay late to finish a task they can take the time off later in the accounting period.

Disadvantages to the employee

- If staff already have a degree of flexibility which is allowed informally, they may feel that a formal scheme may place more restrictions on them.

- The length of core time and the flexible time period are key issues here.

- Some employees may lose overtime payments.

- There may be variations between departments in the way the rules are interpreted and this may cause resentment.

Check your progress 2.2

1 John Nicholls is planning to introduce a pilot flexi-time scheme next month. Outline the possible benefits and costs to the employer of the introduction of such a scheme.

2 Discuss whether or not you would like to work flexi-time and why?

3 Under what circumstances would job-sharing be an attractive proposition to you?

Home-working/Tele-working

These are arrangements where an employee spends all or some of his or her working week working from home. They may be working using home as a base, or working partly in an office and partly at home. 'Based at home' can mean that a worker spends most of the working week there. Home-working and tele-working arrangements have developed due to advances in communications technology (see chapter 9 for details on advances in ICT) and have enabled many organisations to have smaller offices.

How does it work?

Example 4

The Purchasing Team at John Nicholls spend a lot of their time at various suppliers' locations and as a result split their time between home and office. They have networked computers with electronic mail to keep in touch with suppliers and stores within the organisation. John Nicholls pays for their mobile phones and they have a dedicated business line in their homes as well as wireless laptops.

John Morton works as a public relations consultant for John Nicholls. John works for many different organisations dealing with information for the media as and when needed. The output is easily measured (pay rates are per hour) and the work is delivered by electronic means (fax, e-mail or telephone). Technology has made it increasingly easy for people like John to deliver both text, voice and images from remote locations such as his home in Arran.

Working from home

Again there are advantages and disadvantages to both employer and worker.

Advantages to the employer

- Employers may retain staff because they can balance work with looking after children and/or elderly parents.

- Freeing up office space and other associated savings offsets equipment costs for home workers.

- Higher productivity because of improved concentration and fewer interruptions at home.

- Increased motivation and commitment because there is no travel involved.

Disadvantages to the employer

- Home-working is not suitable for all jobs, i.e. some jobs involve extensive face-to-face contact with customers.

- It is not suitable for all employees. Employees must be able to work on own and be quite self disciplined.

- The costs of equipment and training.

- A different style of management is required for managing remote workers.

Advantages to the employee

- A better work–life balance.

- The ability to access different types of work without changing location.

- It can reduce (or eliminate) travel time and also reduce stress.

- The employee can choose their own work schedule, e.g. work at night.

- Childcare and/or elderly care costs can be reduced.

Disadvantages to the employee

- Self discipline is required. The employee needs to set their own goals.

- Employees may feel isolated with little or no social contact. Evidence suggests that a compromise of this arrangement is best, i.e. the ability to work some of the time in the office and some of the time at home.

- Employees may not have the space at home.

To find out more about tele-working visit www.tca.org.uk

Hot-desking

Hot-desking is an arrangement whereby workers do not have their own desks but are allocated work space according to their needs – workers will keep their personal belongings in lockers when not in the office. Hot-desking relies on the assumption that a predictable proportion of people are going to be away from their desks at any given time, i.e. sales people and other home-workers/tele-workers. Many organisations insist employees depersonalise their desks so that they can be used by anyone. This means no photos or personal belongings in individuals' workspaces. In some organisations workspaces may be allocated on a first come first served basis, e.g. Call Centres, but in others workspaces can be booked in advance.

The growth in hot-desking is due to the increased cost of providing permanent office space for all employees, the increased dependence on information technology and the increase in home-working/teleworking.

How does it work?

Example 5

Maintenance, System Support and Security staff provide 24 hour cover at John Nicholls. The amount of space allocated for the staff reflects the number of people likely to be present at one time rather than the total number of people in the team. John Nicholls have requested staff in the above teams to depersonalise their desks so that any member of the team can use any free desk/computer to complete necessary paperwork and carry out computer related tasks. Staff will logon with their ID and password. Lockers are allocated to all 'hot-deskers' to keep personal belongings safe.

Example 6

Other 'hot-deskers' at John Nicholls are the Purchasing team (they are also known as home-workers/teleworkers). Again, the amount of space allocated for the Purchasing team reflects the number of people likely to be present at one time rather than the total number of people in the team. John Nicholls insist on depersonalisation of the shared space.

There are potential advantages and disadvantages to the employer.

Advantages to the employer

- Corporate office costs will be lower.

- Staff can be in control of where they work.

- Staff can work in a wide range of locations.

- The movement of people between desks can prevent cliques forming.

Disadvantages to the employer

- Morale and productivity may be adversely affected if staff are continually working with strangers.

- Depersonalisation, due to the elimination of private space, can result in a higher turnover of staff. The company will have to bear the additional costs of recruitment and training of new staff. Organisations should seek advice on how to combat these feelings and may need to ensure strong team spirit is encouraged in other ways, e.g. team meetings.

Career Break

A career break is an extended period of leave from work. The intention is that the employee will return to work at the end of the agreed period either at the same level or to the same job, retaining all or most of the service related benefits. During the break the employer and employee keep in touch by a variety of means.

Career breaks offer employees the flexibility of combining family and other commitments with work. Career break schemes were first introduced by high street banks and the Civil Service. They allow organisations to keep valuable staff who might otherwise leave, thus reducing the costs of staff turnover and ensuring a return on investment in skills and training made in the past.

It is essential that retraining opportunities are made available for staff after a career break otherwise skills will become outdated in their absence. Keeping in touch with the employees during their absence is vital so that employees do not become totally isolated from the workplace. It should be noted that for most employees taking a career break will affect their continuity of employment. If, however, they continue to work flexibly (e.g. on a job-share basis) their service will be continuous.

Impact of Flexible Working Practices on the Organisation

- The provision of flexible working arrangements means that employers can recruit and retain valued staff and meet changing customer requirements more easily.

- Costs can be cut by using peripheral workers, e.g. fixed term contracts to cover busy periods and boost productivity.

- The quality of work is often greater if employees are able to choose a working arrangement which allows them to balance work with commitments at home. It usually results in increased productivity and improved morale (workers are more energetic).

- The reduction of stress means less time is taken off work.

- The introduction of hot-desking means that savings in office space can be made or office space can be used for other purposes.

Impact of Flexible Working Practices on the Individual

- Individuals can access work and training when they otherwise may not have been able to, e.g. when they have to look after young children/sick relatives.

- The individual can balance work with other commitments.

- Stress levels are reduced, while energy, motivation and commitment are increased.

Check your progress

1   In what way do you think the increasing use of information technology and electronic communications at John Nicholls could change work arrangements?

2   Discuss the possible benefits and drawbacks for both the employee and employer of tele-working/home-working and career breaks.

3   Describe the impact of flexible working practices on both the organisation and the employee.

Contract of Employment

The employment contract is central to the activities undertaken by the Human Resources Department. After recruiting and selecting suitable staff the Human Resources Department will draw up a contract of employment. This may be updated due to promotion, changes to salary, etc. At the end of employment, the Human Resources Department will be involved with termination of the contract due to retirement, redundancy or dismissal, etc.

The relationship between an employer and an employee is laid out in a contract of employment. Under the Employment Rights Act 1996, an organisation is required by law to issue an employee with a written statement of the main terms and conditions of employment within eight weeks of commencing employment. Any changes to the written statement must be given to the employee within four weeks of the changes taking effect.

The statement must include the following items:

- name and address of employer
- name and address of employee

- job title and grade

- date of commencement of continuous employment (for those workers on a fixed-term contract a clause will be included which specifies the date at which the contract terminates)

- duties attached to the job

- hours of work (i.e. full-time, part-time, job-share)

- location (home address will need to be given here for home-workers/tele-workers)

- working times and breaks

- pay details

- holiday entitlement

- sickness and absenteeism

- pension inclusion/exclusion

- disciplinary rules and procedures

- grievances procedures

- notice requirements.

The Human Resources Department may have to issue varying contracts of employment including permanent (of no fixed duration), fixed term (a contract of employment which is of a fixed duration), job share, home-working agreements, etc.

Considerations such as place of work, duration and insurance will have to be considered for non-standard contracts of employment.

Below is an example of a written statement of particulars of employment for the restaurant and catering assistant at John Nicholls.

JOHN NICHOLLS

STATEMENT OF PARTICULARS OF EMPLOYMENT

This statement dated 7th March 2004 sets out the main terms and conditions of your employment with John Nicholls, 47 Great Emperor Street, Glasgow, GF1 7JN (hereinafter referred to as the 'employer' or the 'Company') and meets the requirements of Section 1 of the Employment Rights Act 1996.

Employee:

Brian Smith (hereinafter referred to as the 'employee').

Collective Agreements:

There are no collective agreements regulating and pertaining to the terms of your employment.

Changes to Terms of Employment:

Any changes or amendments to the terms of your contract of employment, agreed between the parties, will be communicated to you in writing within one month of them taking effect.

continued ➤

JOHN NICHOLLS continued

Employee Handbook:

The Employee Handbook is available from your centre manager for you to consult.

Commencement of Employment:

Your employment with the employer commenced on 20th February 2004.

Continuous Employment:

Previous employment with your last employer is not recognised as part of your continuous period of employment with John Nicholls.

Job Title:

The title of the job which you are employed to do is: Restaurant and Catering Assistant.

The Company reserves the right to change your duties on a temporary or permanent basis from time to time, as determined by the needs of the business. Significant permanent changes to your duties will not be made without consultation with you.

Reporting arrangements:

You will report directly to your line manager, Margaret Dougal.

Duties and Responsibilities:

This level of post is subject to the following duties and responsibilities:

- To work closely with the manager in all matters concerning the management, development and operation of the restaurant.

- To prepare and serve food.

- To operate the cash register.

- To wait on tables.

- To participate in the implementation of policies.

- To provide advice and support to other members of staff.

- To ensure the smooth running, cleanliness and safety of all areas of the operation.

- To provide advice and support when required to other members of staff for discipline referrals.

- To dress neatly and in-line with company uniform; any extreme hairstyles, visible tattoos and/or piercings must be pre-approved by management.

Other duties:

- Support the company's other training and commercial activities when required.

- Complete any other tasks as requested by the Chief Executive, Ann Horton.

continued ➤

ADMINISTRATIVE SERVICES

JOHN NICHOLLS continued

Probationary Period:

Your employment is subject to an initial probationary period of three months during which your performance will be monitored. This probationary period may be extended by the Company at its discretion. At the end of the probationary period, your performance will be evaluated and the Company will confirm in writing to you its decision regarding your continued employment.

Your employment may be terminated on one week's notice given by the Company at any time during or at the end of your probationary period (including any extensions to the probationary period).

Place of Work:

Your usual place of work is 47 Great Emperor Street, Glasgow F1 7JN but you may be required to work at other outlets (if applicable) temporarily from time to time as the Company may reasonably require.

Payment of Wages:

Your salary is £6.50 per hour, payable weekly in arrears by cash. Your hourly rate of pay will be reviewed in the month of September of every working year and any changes required by law will be implemented by 1st October of the same working year.

Performance:

Your performance will be reviewed and as such an appraisal procedure will be conducted twice yearly from the date of commencement of your employment with the employer.

Hours of Work:

Due to the nature of the business, the employer cannot guarantee the employee set or fixed hours for any period of time. Hours will be agreed with each employee on a mutual basis and before the commencement of any work undertaken.

Your normal hours of work are 25-48 hours per week with normal working hours to be from 8.30a.m. until 10p.m., although you will be expected to undertake such hours as necessary to carry out your duties to the Company's satisfaction

Shift patterns will be organised by way of a rota system and your hours of work will be communicated to you two weeks in advance.

Overtime:

In addition to your normal hours of work, you are required to work any necessary additional hours in order to carry out your duties to the Company's satisfaction. Payment for these hours will be at your normal rate, unless otherwise agreed in advance. You will not be required to work more than 48 hours in any working week.

continued ➤

JOHN NICHOLLS continued

Annual Holidays:

The Company's holiday year runs from 1 April to 31 March.

Holiday entitlement is accrued from your 1st day of work. Holiday accrual entitlement is calculated on the basis of 1/52 of the annual entitlement for each complete week worked for hourly paid staff. You are entitled to 20 days (inclusive of 8 days public) paid annual holiday entitlement each year. Part-time employees will accrue annual holiday entitlement on a *pro-rata basis*. Entitlement is accrued at the rate of 3.04 hours (.38 days) for each week actually worked.

When you will be able to take your leave entitlement will be subject to the exigencies of the service. Holiday dates must be agreed mutually with management and the employee must provide the employer with at least 14 days notice of his/her intention to use holiday entitlement where possible.

Public Holidays:

Employees are entitled to 8 days' public holidays each year which will be confirmed at the start of each year by the Company but will usually include, subject to regional and national changes:

Christmas Day

January 1

(Employees will only be entitled to these public holidays which fall on their normal working days.)

Employees who are absent from work, other than on authorised annual leave, on a public holiday, or on the working day immediately preceding or following a public holiday, will not be entitled to payment in respect of that day.

Further details of the rules in respect of annual and public holidays entitlement are set out in the Employee Handbook.

Absence and Sick Pay:

If you are absent from work for any reason and your absence has not previously been authorised by the Company, you must inform the Company by 8.30a.m. on your first day of absence.

If you are absent from work due to sickness or injury and comply with the requirements of the Company's absence procedure, you will be paid Statutory Sick Pay in accordance with the provisions of the legislation.

Further details of the rules in respect of absence reporting and the rules governing the payment of sick pay are contained in the Employee Handbook.

Pension:

The Company does not operate an occupational or contributory Group Personal Pension scheme. However, you can access a 'Stakeholder' pension, details of which can be found in the Company's handbook.

continued ➤

ADMINISTRATIVE SERVICES

JOHN NICHOLLS continued

Notice:

After being employed by the Company for a minimum of one month you are required to give one week's notice of any intention on your part to terminate your employment with the employer.

You are entitled to receive the following notice of termination of employment from the Company:

If you have completed more than one month but less than two years' continuous service with the employer:

One week.

If you have completed more than two years' continuous service:

One additional week for each complete year of service up to a maximum of 12 weeks after the completion of 12 years' service.

The Company reserves the right to make payment in lieu of notice. This payment will be equivalent to your normal salary and will not include any other contractual benefits.

Disciplinary Rules and Procedure:

The Disciplinary Rules applicable to you are set out in the Employee Handbook. You are strongly advised to read them.

Appeal Procedure:

If you are dissatisfied with any disciplinary decision taken in respect of you, you have the right to appeal. Further details of the Appeal Procedure are set out in the Employee Handbook.

Grievance Procedure:

The Grievance Procedure applicable to you is set out in the Employee Handbook. You are strongly advised to familiarise yourself with it.

Appeal Procedure:

If you are dissatisfied with any decision taken in respect of a grievance lodged by you, you have the right of appeal. Further details of the Appeal Procedure are set out in the Employee Handbook.

Other Employment:

You must devote the whole of your time, attention and abilities during your hours of work for the Company to your duties for the Company. You may not under any circumstances, whether directly or indirectly, undertake any duties of whatever kind during your hours of work for the Company.

Personal Property:

The Company does not accept responsibility for loss or damage to employee's personal property howsoever caused.

continued ➤

JOHN NICHOLLS continued

Confidentiality:

(a) The employee shall not make use of, divulge or communicate to any person (save in the proper performance of his/her duties) confidential information of or relating to the Company which he/she may have received or obtained as a result of or in any connection with his/her employment by the Company. This restriction shall continue to apply after the termination of his/her employment without limit in point of time but shall cease to apply to information required to be disclosed by law.

(b) All notes and memoranda of confidential information concerning the business of the Company which shall be acquired, received or made by the employee during the course of his/her employment shall be the property of the Company and shall be surrendered by the employee to someone duly authorised in that behalf at the termination of his/her employment or at the request of the Company at any time during the course of his/her employment.

Data Protection:

The employee consents to the Company holding and processing both electronically and in hard copy form any personal and sensitive data relating to the employee for the purposes of employee-related administration, processing the employee's file and management of its business, for compliance with applicable procedures, laws and regulations and for providing data to external suppliers who administer the employee's benefits solely for the purpose of providing the employee with those benefits.

Redundancy Payment:

The employer does not operate a contractual scheme for the payment of redundancy pay on the event of an employee's employment being terminated by reason of redundancy. Any employee with more than 2 years' continuous service with the employer or an associated employer is entitled to a statutory redundancy payment only.

Acknowledgement:

I acknowledge receipt of this statement, and confirm that I have read it. I also confirm that I have read the Employee Handbook. Where the terms of this statement and the Employee Handbook conflict, the terms contained in this Statement shall prevail

Employee's signature_____   Date_____

Director's signature_____   Date_____

Check your Progress

1 Outline at least six of the main features of a contract of employment.

2 What do you understand by the terms **permanent** and **fixed term** contracts?

Office Environment

Like any member of staff, you will benefit from working in a pleasant working environment. Far-sighted companies are realising that the creation of a pleasant working environment, taking into account the needs of its employees and health and safety requirements, is likely to increase productivity, improve efficiency, and boost the morale and well being of its employees. In turn a good environment will encourage staff to stay. Environment includes heating, lighting, ventilation, noise, décor, furniture and ergonomics.

Ergonomics is the study of the relationship between man and his working environment. Furniture can be designed so that you expend the minimum amount of energy and physical strain to do any task. Movement should be natural, rhythmical and symmetrical, so work tools and equipment should be within easy reach, and you should work sitting down where possible in an adjustable, supportive chair. Desks should be at a convenient height.

In a big organisation it is the role of the facilities manager to deal with the work environment. This will include dealing with:

- premises
- health and safety (including heating, lighting and method of air conditioning, etc.)
- space planning
- layout
- equipment
- décor
- maintenance
- acoustics.

It may also include aspects of security.

For information

Have you heard of sick building syndrome (SBS)? This is a term given to those office buildings where staff complain of generally feeling unwell – this can lead to time off work due to sickness. Symptoms include headache, sore throat, dry cough. Poor air conditioning and poor lighting are given as possible reasons for SBS. Visit www.unison.org.uk/safety to find out more.

The Health and Safety at Work (HSAWA) Act 1974 has done much to make personnel responsible for designing office space more aware of factors they must take into consideration to avoid accidents, the spread of colds and flu, etc. Information on HSAWA is detailed later in this chapter.

Check your Progress

2.5

1   What is meant by the term ergonomics?

2   What impact do you think a well-designed office layout will have on both the employee and the employer?

Cellular Office Design

Cellular office, or traditional design, is the name given to the concept of separate rooms of varying sizes for individual workers, or group of workers. In this type of layout the various departments of the company are divided into several rooms of different sizes to suit their functions.

Advantages of cellular office design

● Ensures the privacy of the group or individual, e.g. can hold confidential discussions.

● Noise level is kept to a minimum.

● Security of information is easier – doors can be simply closed or locked.

● It is easier to control levels of heating and lighting.

Disadvantages of cellular office design

● When staff work on their own they may feel isolated – social contact may be limited.

● Office space is lost due to the creation of internal walls and doors.

● It does not have same flexibility of layout, for example to allow for future expansion.

● It is more difficult to ensure correct workflow as the movement of staff and documents around the office may be restricted.

● It is more difficult to share resources as the same equipment may be needed in each of the rooms, e.g. laser printers.

● It is more expensive to heat and light individual offices.

An open plan office

Open Plan Layout

Open plan layout or landscaped office design is based on the concept of large areas of floor space with no dividing walls. Large areas of floor space are broken up into functional areas with acoustic screens, filing cabinets and plants providing any division of space required.

How does it work?

Example 7

John Nicholls has recently introduced an open plan style office. Facility managers have taken into account the size, type and quality of space required – the need for some staff to share space ('hot-desking') – and the necessity to share facilities. Café areas have been provided which can be used for informal meetings. The provision of enclosed meeting rooms allows for privacy and confidentiality and provision of quiet zones for uninterrupted report-writing. Acoustic panels are used to help reduce the level of noise.

Advantages of open plan design

- Easier supervision of staff – everybody is working in an open area which can be seen by one supervisor.

- Economy in floor space, lighting and heating – no space is lost to internal walls and doors.

- Flexibility of layout – any expansion or change of work or procedures (and consequent increase of staff and equipment) can be accommodated.

- Minimises movement of staff and documents. Delays in the flow of work caused by moving papers and people from room to room are eliminated.

- Communication between staff is easier. You can see if a member of staff is at his or her desk by simply looking around.

- Morale of staff is enhanced by the pleasant, spacious appearance of the office.

- A more sociable atmosphere is created because artificial barriers between people working at different levels in the organisation are removed.

Disadvantages of open plan office

- More noise. One person's phone call or meeting may disturb everyone.

- Encourages chit-chat amongst staff so staff can be more easily distracted.

- Lack of privacy can be a problem, especially if disciplinary or personal issues are involved.

- Staff may have difficulty reaching agreement about appropriate levels of lighting, heating and ventilation.

- Managers can be distracted by routine matters.

- More chance of infections being spread throughout the office.

ADMINISTRATIVE SERVICES

The following checklist identifies some of the factors you will have to consider when designing an open plan layout.

John Nicholls – Factors to consider when designing open plan office

Have all legal aspects such as:

- space planning
- adequate toilets
- adequate heating
- lighting and
- method of air conditioning been satisfied?

Has consideration been given to efficient flow of work such as:

- ensuring workers and equipment are grouped together to assist communication?

Has consideration been given to aesthetics such as:

- the use of pleasing and co-ordinated colours for décor, fabrics and surfaces etc.?

Have noise problems been minimised such as:

- the use of acoustic screens and barriers (can ensure up to 46% sound reduction)?

Has privacy and confidentiality been ensured such as:

- the creation of meeting rooms or quiet areas?

Has flexibility of layout been ensured such as:

- allowing for future expansion of office (for instance, increase in number of staff and equipment), e.g. flexibility in wiring?

Check your Progress   2.6

1   Discuss the advantages and disadvantages of an open plan office layout for both the employer and employee.

2   How can management overcome the disadvantages of the open plan office?

3   What can you do to ensure the efficient flow of work when designing the layout of your office?

Health and Safety Legislation

In order to create a safe and healthy working environment for both staff and visitors to your organisation everyone must adhere to health and safety legislation. As an employee you have a key role to play in ensuring that the people in your own work area are not only aware but actually co-operate with any new requirements and procedures. The main Act of Parliament regarding health and safety in the office is the Health and Safety at Work Act 1974 (HSAWA). This act imposes duties on **both** employer and employee and imposes financial penalties (and even closure) on those who do not follow its requirements. It is therefore important that you are alert to health, safety and security hazards.

Health and Safety Policy Document

Individual responsibilities and arrangements will be specified in an organisation's Health and Safety Policy document – in accordance with the Health and Safety Information for Employees Regulations 1989, your organisation has a legal requirement to provide a written statement on health and safety. The Health and Safety Policy document states an organisation's commitment to health and safety and sets out a framework to enable an organisation to provide and maintain safe and healthy working conditions.

Note: Health and safety legislation is constantly changing and you should refer to appropriate websites for updates. A useful website is that of the Health and Safety Executive (www.hse.gov.uk).

Task 1

Look up the Health and Safety Executive website and find out the name of the six UK regulations covering health and safety in the workplace. Discuss the key duties of the employer and employee under each regulation.

Task 2

An employee was walking along a corridor when she tripped over one of a number of bags which had been left on the floor. There had been numerous complaints of bags being left in the corridor prior to the accident. However, no action had been taken. The employee sustained an injury to her back and a serious sprain. She was on sick leave for a considerable time and then had to retire on medical grounds.

What breaches could your employer be liable for?

Information and Communications from Employers

In a big organisation, the human resources department will usually arrange in-house information and training sessions on health and safety for all new members of staff – this will be delivered as soon as possible upon commencement of employment. (This is in line with the Health and Safety Information for Employees Regulations 1989.) This information will usually be part of a new employee's induction programme.

To help record that all aspects of health and safety have been covered the organisation will produce an **Induction Checklist** for new staff to your office which will include:

- the organisation's Health and Safety Policy document – usually in a Health and Safety folder

- an overview of employer and employee responsibilities

- arrangements for general health and safety communications

- first aid and accident reporting procedures

- fire and other emergency procedures

- location of evacuation routes and assembly points

- an overview of Health and Safety (Display Screen Equipment) Regulations 1992

- an overview of Control of Substances Hazardous to Health Regulations 1994

- health and safety inspections

- an overview of Data Protection Acts (1998), Computer Misuse Act (1990) and Copyright, Designs and Patents Act (1988)

- likely consequences of failure to comply with company policy.

While induction is the most likely way of communicating health and safety information, here are some other ways of telling staff about health and safety:

- **Intranet** Many organisations create a health and safety folder which has the Health and Safety Policy document and procedures and other related information such as workplace checklists and accident report forms.

- **Notice boards** These can be used to provide general information. Remember this information must be updated regularly and notice boards should be kept tidy by removing out-of-date information.

- **E-mail, memo or newsletter** Changes to procedures can be communicated in this way. It is important to date the bottom of the document to allow for identification of the most up-to-date version. This also ensures each member of staff receives their own copy.

- **Training sessions** These can be used to keep staff informed and to disseminate information, e.g. on risk assessment when staff move to different jobs.

- **Posters** This is an excellent way to communicate prohibitions, i.e. 'you must not do'. They are usually a red circle on a white background with a diagonal bar across. Examples include no smoking and no entry. Posters are also designed to give warnings to people – i.e. alert staff to a hazard. This type of poster will have a yellow background with a triangular border and a symbol and/or lettering in black. Examples include warning of an uneven floor or slippery surface. Posters are also used to inform people of what they must do, for example, keep fire doors shut or wear hearing protection. Posters can also be used to communicate safe conditions. They will have white lettering and/or symbols, for example, fire exit and drinking water. Many organisations display a health and safety poster informing staff of health and safety provision in the workplace (in accordance with the Health and Safety Information for Employees Regulations 1989).

- **Videos and role playing** exemplify and encourage good practice, for example, working at the VDU, lifting heavy objects. Fire drills are used on a regular basis to familiarise staff with procedures.

- **Safety meetings** Employees can be kept up to date with any changes and new regulations, codes of practice or guidelines. Most large organisations have Health and Safety Committees which include both union and management members to ensure all staff have a channel of communication about health and safety issues.

There is no 'best' method of communicating information to employees – much will depend on the organisation and your job role. Health and safety legislation is constantly changing and being updated and it is important to give all members of staff **up-to-date** information relating to new developments and practices. Identification and promotion of good practice should also be encouraged.

Enforcement of Health and Safety Legislation

Health and Safety Executive (HSE) inspectors and local authorities share responsibility for the enforcement of health and safety legislation. The powers of the enforcement officers include:

- entering and inspecting premises at any reasonable time (even unannounced)

- taking photographs, samples of water, measurements, etc

- interviewing and asking people questions if they think this is essential

- issuing improvement notices

- issuing prohibition notices

- prosecuting people and organisations.

There are penalties for failing to comply with health and safety legislation. If health and safety issues are identified inspectors and local authorities will try to negotiate an improvement by serving an improvement notice but may need to:

- close premises

- issue fines

- prosecute, which may result in imprisonment.

Employee Responsibility

It is not just the organisation which is held liable because employees also have a responsibility to work in a safe and proper manner, co-operate with their employer in order to comply with all statutory duties and requirements affecting safety, and not to interfere with or misuse anything in the interest of health and safety. Failure to comply with these requirements can lead to disciplinary action and even prosecution.

> ### Task 3
>
> **1** Who enforces health and safety legislation?
>
> **2** What are the powers of the enforcement authority?
>
> **3** What are the consequences to the employer of failing to comply with health and safety legislation?
>
> **4** What are the consequences to the employee of failing to comply with health and safety legislation?

Common Security and Confidentiality Measures

Organisations will have a range of security measures in place regarding control over entrances and exits, visitors, buildings, protection for staff and equipment and security of information – measures will vary depending on the size of the organisation and the nature of the work.

Access to buildings

Where sensitive information is being stored, many organisations will employ security guards and may use closed circuit TV (CCTV) to monitor visitors. Here are some other measures to prevent unauthorised access:

- Minimise the number of entrances and exits.

- Issue identification passes to staff.

- User identification, for example, electronic keypad or card reader, required to gain access to rooms where confidential information is stored.

- Only issue keys to nominated personnel.

- Check all rooms at end of each day to ensure windows and doors are locked.

- Use security guards to prevent unauthorised access which could lead to theft and vandalism.

Security of visitors

- Visitors should report to reception which should be manned at all times.

- Reception should be informed of expected visitors.

- Visitors should be asked to sign in and out and issued with an identification pass.

- Visitors should never be left unsupervised.

- Visitors should return pass and sign out at end of visit.

Security of equipment

Here are some of the security measures organisations can take to ensure security of equipment:

- Tag or security mark all computers and valuable pieces of equipment.
- Make sure equipment is stored in a safe place.
- Lock away small items of equipment when not in use.
- Carry out a regular audit of equipment.

Security of staff

Here are some security measures organisations can take to ensure staff are safe:

- Install security cameras and CCTV.
- Ensure visitors are monitored.
- Install toughened glass screens and panic buttons where staff are in contact with members of public.
- Provide personal alarms.

Security of information

Under the Data Protection Act, every organisation has an obligation to protect manual and computerised records. Here are some of the security measures organisations can take to ensure security of information:

- Ensure that only authorised users can get into the computer system – this is usually done by giving access to users through passwords. These passwords usually have to be changed on a regular basis, for example, once a month. Remember that these passwords should not be given to anyone else or be written down. Logging into the system allows the system administrator to check who is doing what because what you have accessed can be traced.
- Make sure VDUs are located away from areas the public can access.
- Use screen savers so that information can be hidden from passers by or when employees are not at their desks.
- Back-up procedures must be established to prevent accidental loss or damage.
- Store all disks in a secure location.
- Put procedures in place regarding storage, distribution and disposal of printed documents.
- Remove access from employees who leave the organisation – they may take financially sensitive customers or financial information with them.
- Levels of access. Often the level of access you can gain is triggered by one of the passwords. For example, if you were the financial director of an organisation, you would have access to most information but you would be unlikely to have access to personnel records.
- Electronic safeguards such as:
  - A virus and content scanner is usually installed to ensure that data coming into the organisation is checked for known viruses. This may mean a slight delay in receiving data from those outside the organisation while it is checked. This software needs to be regularly updated.

– A firewall is the term given to a software barrier which will protect your system from 'intrusion'. The firewall and anti-virus software should be updated on a regular basis so that it is ready to reject any new viruses. These updating downloads are usually called patches.

– Intrusion detection systems act like burglar alarms and can identify potential intruders trying to get into the system. This is a sophisticated system and should be considered if the organisation runs a website or has a high profile which might attract attacks.

Confidential documents

These should be monitored by ensuring distribution is restricted only to those who should have access to the documents and by sending them in sealed envelopes. Confidential documents should always be shredded when no longer in use.

Task 4

Organisations will have a range of security measures in place regarding control over information, visitors, staff and equipment. Discuss the measures an organisation will take to ensure security over each of the above.

Internal Assessment

Here are some examples of the kind of questions you might be asked as part of your internal assessment:

1a Outline five main features of a contract of employment. (5)
  b Outline one advantage and one disadvantage to the employer and the employee of a fixed term contract. (4)

2a What is meant by hot-desking? (2)
  b Give one advantage of hot-desking to the employer and one disadvantage to the employee. (2)

3 Outline methods used by organisations to prevent unauthorised access to premises. (4)

4 Outline the legislation an organisation must adhere to when working with VDUs. (6)

External Assessment

Here are some examples of the kind of questions you might be asked as part of your external assessment. An estimate of the marks assigned to each question is indicated and it would be anticipated that each question would form part of a larger question.

1 Describe the benefits to the organisation of providing staff-friendly working practices. (4)

2 Compare and contrast cellular and open plan offices. (8)

3 Discuss four ways of keeping employees up to date with health and safety legislation. (8)

4 Describe three features of current legislation concerning activity at the workstation. (3)

CHAPTER 3

Meetings

This chapter is about planning, conducting and supporting meetings. In some organisations, particularly those in the public sector, meetings form a big part of their activities.

Meetings are a necessary part of organisational life. Face-to-face discussion allows for clear communication and should help bond a team and encourage team approaches to problem solving. While many people regard meetings as a waste of time, this opinion is often based on attending meetings which are held even though they may not be necessary. Remember it is expensive to hold meetings so the more elaborate and lengthy the meeting, the more costly it is.

Face-to-face communication in the form of a meeting is usually needed where:

- **a large amount of information has to be given to an identified group of people**
- **the timing of giving that information is significant**
- **there is an element of persuasion involved in not only delivering information but persuading people to buy into the information**
- **ideas have to be exchanged**
- **problems have to be solved collectively.**

Meetings can be described as formal, semi-formal and informal meetings. A formal meeting is usually held for a specific purpose and will usually be held on a regular basis, for example, meetings of the Board of Directors of a company might be held monthly. Formal meetings will also be procedural and will usually have a set of 'rules' which govern how they are conducted. These meetings will usually have a documented record of what was discussed and an administrator would be responsible for organising and recording the decisions and outcomes of the meeting. An informal meeting does not usually have to follow the organisation's procedures. It can be very informal – a meeting over a coffee break would constitute an informal meeting. Usually a line manager or a team leader will lead the meeting and there is unlikely to be a formal chairperson. Notes are not always taken.

In between these two types of meeting are the most common meetings which take place in business. You should think of them as semi-formal meetings. Examples of this type of meeting might be everyone in one department meeting once a week for an update. Although no formal minute is held, the department manager may well file their notes on what was discussed. This type of meeting is usually held for the purpose of:

- keeping all staff informed

- tracking progress towards targets

- collectively identifying any action needed

- bonding teams together.

This chapter refers to the processes and procedures involved in formal meetings. Here are some kinds of formal meetings which occur in business.

Annual General Meeting (AGM)

All public limited companies have to hold an annual meeting for their shareholders. The rules which govern the conduct of this Annual General Meeting (AGM) are written into the Companies Acts. The main purposes of the AGM are:

- to elect the directors and office holders

- to discuss the performance of the company. This will usually mean:
    - accepting the directors' report
    - accepting the auditors' report
    - agreeing the dividend to be paid to shareholders
    - looking at the accounts and balance sheet of the organisation

- to look at the strategic plans of the organisation for the following year.

Other organisations such as clubs and associations also have AGMs, held for the same purposes and to give members a chance to find out the direction the organisation is going in and air their opinions. You may have attended an AGM if you belong to a club or organisation.

Extraordinary General Meeting (EGM)

This is a meeting which is open to all shareholders or, in the case of a club, members. It is normally held to discuss a particular issue which is of crucial interest to the organisation and one which the directors or office bearers feel cannot wait until the AGM, for example, a potential take-over bid or a crisis over money.

Both an Annual General Meeting and an Extraordinary General Meeting have to be organised to meet with the requirements of the Companies Acts if they are being called by a limited company. This would mean they had to ensure sufficient notice of the meeting was given to all those eligible to attend so that they could make arrangements to come to the meeting.

ADMINISTRATIVE SERVICES

Board Meeting

In between Annual General Meetings, the business of a limited company is carried out by directors. These directors hold board meetings at which company policy is discussed and decisions are made. In turn they may appoint committees to look at specific areas of work and report back to the directors. These committees are also likely to hold formal meetings.

There are many types of committee, for example:

- Advisory Committee which is set up to look at particular issues and make recommendations to the Board of Directors.

- Joint Committee which is formed to help improve communications between different interest groups, such as trade union and management.

- Standing Committee has a specific remit which it deals with on a regular basis; for example, health and safety

- Executive Committee which is set up with particular powers to make decisions in one particular area; for example, this might be in the area of pay negotiations. Any decisions made would be binding on the organisation.

- Ad Hoc Committee is formed for a particular purpose and once that purpose is achieved the committee will disband. For instance, a 25th Anniversary committee would organise events to celebrate the 25th Anniversary and at the end of the celebrations there would be no need to continue to have a committee.

- Sub-committee. If one of the above committees wanted some members to look at a particular aspect of business and report back to the board or some other committee, it would form a sub-committee; for example, to deal with a staff dinner dance as part of the 25th Anniversary celebrations. All of the sub-committee business would be about the staff dinner dance.

All formal meetings have to meet the rules that the organisation has laid down for them. These will be usually be listed in the company's Articles of Association or the club's Constitution or local authority's Standing Orders. This means that formal meetings have to:

- be constituted correctly – the chairperson must be present or an appropriate substitute person nominated

- be attended by the minimum number of people required. This minimum number is called a quorum

- have properly elected office bearers. Full details will be found in the Articles of Association, Constitution or Standing Orders. The main office bearers are:

  - Chairperson who is responsible for leading the meeting (Full details of his/her role follow)

  - Secretary who provides the administrative support required

  - Treasurer who is responsible for providing financial information to the meeting

- be properly convened. The relevant notice must be given prior to calling the meeting and must be given to all those who are entitled to attend. The timescale and membership will be written in the Articles of Association, Constitution or Standing Orders.

Documentation for Meetings

Certain documents are commonly used when dealing with meetings. The layout of these documents and how they are used will vary from organisation to organisation. The examples given here are typical of what you might find in business.

Notice of Meeting

This is a simple notice which tells those eligible to attend the type of meeting, where the meeting is to be held, the date and the time. It is often combined with an agenda so that a single sheet is sent to those invited to attend. The original notice for a formal meeting will usually be signed by the secretary and copied. The Notice of Meeting must be sent to all eligible to attend and in the case of a formal meeting a set period of notice has to be given prior to the meeting. A formal meeting which includes people external to the organisation will have the organisation's full name and address at the top of the notice.

Agenda

An agenda is a list of the items which will be discussed, listed in the order of discussion. An example of a notice and agenda is shown below.

John Nicholls

NOTICE OF MEETING

A meeting of the Pay and Salary Negotiating Committee will be held in the Board Room at 1230 hours on Wednesday 24 November 20...

AGENDA

1   Apologies for absence

2   Minutes of previous meeting

3   Matters arising from minutes

4   Long Service Bonus Scheme

5   Review of Pension provision

6   Any other business

7   Date of next meeting

Margaret O'Hara

Secretary

Today's date

Some of the items on the agenda are what are called 'standard items'; that is, they occur on virtually all agendas. The standard items are:

Apologies for absence. This allows the Secretary to make a note of those unable to attend. This might be important at a later stage and may need to be referred to if members query who was present when something has been discussed.

Minutes of the previous meeting. These will normally be sent to members prior to the meeting but they can be read out loud at the meeting. This item gives those attending the meeting the opportunity to discuss the accuracy of the minutes and make any amendments before they are signed by the chairperson.

Matters arising from minutes. Often actions will be pending or decisions may have had to be postponed at the last meeting until members have a greater knowledge of situations. This item gives those attending the meeting the opportunity to find out about the up-to-date position or report back to the others at the meeting.

Any other business. This allows people to raise matters of general relevance but which do not warrant a great deal of discussion. If an important issue is raised here it should be dealt with by the chairperson and incorporated as a major item in the next agenda.

Date of next meeting. This ensures that general agreement is reached about an appropriate date for the next meeting.

These standard items usually take up the position shown in the example agenda – items 1–3 and the last 2 items. If you were to look at the agendas of particular types of meetings you would be able to identify other 'standard items' peculiar to those types. For example, you would expect to find a report by the sales manager in a monthly sales meeting, or a report by the club treasurer at a golf club business meeting.

When preparing an agenda you should remember the following.

- Avoid too many items for discussion at any one meeting. 'Manageable' is the key word. There should be sufficient items to make the meeting worthwhile but not so many that discussions will be rushed.

- Each agenda item must be clear to members so that they know what is to be discussed.

- The order of the items should be logical.

Chairperson's Agenda

This document is not always used. It is basically an agenda with space for the chairperson to make their own notes. It is usually only prepared for formal meetings but can be used to help a less experienced chairperson. Below is an example of the same agenda as on page 72, prepared for the Pay and Salary Committee, but this time it has been prepared for the chairperson.

John Nicholls

CHAIRPERSON'S AGENDA

Pay and Salary Negotiating Committee – 24 November 20..

	AGENDA ITEM	NOTES
1	Apologies for absence – Mary not coming	*Lewis not there either*
2	Minutes of previous meeting – should be OK; check date of AGM	*OK*
3	Matters arising from minutes – report on new rate of pay for 18 year olds	

continued ➤

John Nicholls continued

AGENDA ITEM	NOTES
4 Long service bonus scheme – remember new time scales – from 5 years Pass out bonus chart showing amounts Discuss amounts and length of service	
5 Review of Pension provision – being reviewed by Directors Form sub-committee?	*Sub-committee* *Committee concerned about changes*
6 Any other business	
7 Date of next meeting – January?	*January 25 am*

The information inserted on the left hand side would have been available when the agenda was keyed in. The information hand-written on the right would be written in by the chairperson just before or at the meeting.

Minutes of Meeting

This is the official record of the meeting. Most participants will take their own notes but part of the duties of the secretary will be to take an official record of the meeting, usually called the Minutes. Minutes can have different layouts. Three types of minute are shown on the following pages. The first type is a traditional record of the proceedings recording the decisions taken. The second is a full action minute which is a more brief note of the decisions taken with an extra column identifying the action which has to be taken and who will take it. The third example is a short action minute. The problem with the shortened action minute is that it does not give details of what was discussed at the meeting but only records any on-going or subsequent actions identified. This means it is not suitable for all meetings. This is why many organisations prefer the compromise of a full action minute like the second example given.

Some features of minutes are worth noting:

- Language used is formal.

- The minute is written in the past tense.

- The minute is written in the third person.

- Arguments are not given, only resolutions, conclusions or decisions.

- Resolutions must be worded exactly as given at the meeting.

- Actions must be noted.

- Once the group has agreed that the minute is an accurate record, it should be signed by the person who chaired the meeting.

- Items discussed are often numbered to match the agenda items although not all organisations number items. Examples of both are included.

- Copies of the minutes are sent to all who attended.
- Those attending are listed at the top of the minutes with the chairperson's name first and the secretary's name last and the others attending in alphabetical order.

Example 1 Minutes

John Nicholls

MINUTES OF MEETING

Minutes of the Pay and Salary Negotiating Committee held in the Board Room at 1230 hours on Wednesday 24 November 20…

PRESENT

Jean Brass (Chairperson)
Linda Delmonte
Parveen Khan
John McGregor
William O'Leary
Jim Woods
Margaret O'Hara (Secretary)

1   APOLOGIES FOR ABSENCE

Apologies were received from Mary Brown and Lewis Macphie

2   MINUTES OF PREVIOUS MEETING

The Minutes of the previous meeting were taken as read, agreed and signed by the Chairperson.

3   MATTERS ARISING FROM THE MINUTES

The Chairperson reported that a new rate of pay had been proposed for 18 year olds following the company training scheme. The proposal was that the rate of pay be £9.50 per hour. This amount is £3.00 per hour greater than the statutory minimum. It was agreed that this proposal should be accepted. The Chairperson agreed to inform the Finance Director and agreed to remind him that it is the Committee's belief that salaries should reflect work done rather than age.

4   LONG SERVICE BONUS SCHEME

The Chairperson tabled a paper showing the amount of proposed long service bonuses and their relationship to length of service. Following discussion on the proposed scales, the Committee agreed the long service bonuses were a significant improvement on previous figures and voted to accept the new proposals.

5   REVIEW OF PENSION PROVISION

The company pension scheme is currently being reviewed by the Directors. As this is a complex area, it was agreed that a sub-committee consisting of Linda Delmonte, Parveen Khan and John McGregor should be formed to discuss the proposals in

continued ➤

Example 1 Minutes continued

detail and report back to this Committee at the next meeting. It was agreed that this sub-committee should seek advice from both the Company Secretary and the relevant trade unions about the figures given. It was agreed that the Committee's concern about any changes to the pension provision should be formally noted.

6 ANY OTHER BUSINESS

John McGregor reported that the Christmas bonus would be paid in the January salary payments. For those who were paid weekly this would be in the second week in January.

7 DATE OF THE NEXT MEETING

It was agreed that the next meeting would be held on January 20 at 1430 hours.

Jean Brass

Date of signing

Example 2 An Action Minute

JOHN NICHOLLS

MINUTES OF MEETING	ACTION
Minutes of the Pay and Salary Negotiating Committee held in the Board Room at 1230 hours on Wednesday 24 November 20…	
PRESENT	
Jean Brass (Chairperson)	
Linda Delmonte	
Parveen Khan	
John McGregor	
William O'Leary	
Jim Woods	
Margaret O'Hara (Secretary)	
APOLOGIES FOR ABSENCE	
Apologies were received from Mary Brown and Lewis Macphie	
MINUTES OF THE PREVIOUS MEETING	
The Minutes of the previous meeting were taken as read, agreed and signed by the Chairperson.	

continued ➤

Example 2 An Action Minute continued

MINUTES OF MEETING	ACTION
MATTERS ARISING FROM THE MINUTES	
The Chairperson reported that a new rate of pay had been proposed for 18 year olds following the company training scheme. The proposal was that the rate of pay be £9.50 per hour. This amount is £3.00 per hour greater than the statutory minimum. It was agreed that this proposal should be accepted. The Chairperson agreed to inform the Finance Director and agreed to remind him that it is the Committee's belief that salaries should reflect work done rather than age.	*JB inform Finance Director of acceptance of training scheme rate of pay.* *JB inform Finance Director of Committee view on pay linked to age.*
LONG SERVICE BONUS SCHEME	
The Chairperson tabled a paper showing the amount of proposed long service bonuses and their relationship to length of service. Following discussion on the proposed scales, the committee agreed the long service bonuses were a significant improvement on previous figures and voted to accept the new proposals.	*JB inform Finance Director Long Service Bonus Scheme accepted.*
REVIEW OF PENSION PROVISION	
The company pension scheme is currently being reviewed by the Directors. As this is a complex area, it was agreed that a sub-committee consisting of Linda Delmonte, Parveen Khan and John McGregor should be formed to discuss the proposals in detail and report back to this committee at the next meeting. It was agreed that this sub-committee should seek advice from both the company secretary and the relevant trade unions about the figures given. It was agreed that the committee's concern about any changes to the pension provision should be formally noted.	*LD, PK, JMcG to meet before January to research and discuss proposed pension changes.*
ANY OTHER BUSINESS	
John McGregor reported that the Christmas bonus would be paid in the January salary payments. For those who were paid weekly this would be in the second week in January.	
DATE OF THE NEXT MEETING	
It was agreed that the next meeting would be held on January 20 at 1430.	
Signed *Jean Brass* Chairperson Date 28 November 20..	

Some action minutes are even more brief than the example shown above, with only the initials shown in the right hand column. Here is a further example of a brief action minute based on the same meeting.

Example 3 An Action Minute

ACTION MINUTES

DATE OF MEETING:		24 November 20..
PRESENT:		Jean Brass (Chairperson), Linda Delmonte, Parveen Kahn, John McGregor, William O'Leary, Jim Woods, Margaret O'Hara (Secretary)
ACTION	**BY WHOM**	**TARGET DATE**
Inform Finance Director of acceptance of training scheme rate of pay and Committee view on pay linked to age.	JB	By 1 December
Inform Finance Director Long Service Bonus Scheme accepted.	JB	By 1 December
Sub committee to meet before January to research and discuss proposed pension changes.	LD, PK, JMcG	Before next meeting

Supplementary Papers

Most meetings will require the consideration of reports and papers submitted by the chairperson or other members. These are usually sent out prior to the meeting along with the notice and agenda and the minutes from the previous meeting. If papers are not ready at the time the notice and agenda are being sent, they can be tabled at the meeting. When acting as a secretary, you should bear the following guidelines in mind.

- Try not to send too many papers to be read prior to the meeting. Too much information will put people off reading it altogether and they may forget to bring the papers to the meeting.

- Where possible try to include an executive summary of each lengthy document.

- Large documents which require extensive reading and understanding should not be tabled at a meeting in anticipation of a discussion.

- Be careful about distributing confidential information. It may fall into the wrong hands.

- It is often a good idea to number supplementary papers and indicate which supplementary paper will be referred to at each agenda item by adding the supplementary paper number to the agenda item.

Attendance List

This is often used where expenses can be claimed by participants. You would prepare a list of those you were expecting to attend and they would sign in. You also have a double check available when preparing your minutes.

Organising Documents

Regular meetings often refer back to decisions made in the past. It is therefore important that you are able to locate notices, agendas, minutes and supplementary papers quickly and easily.

The administrator or secretary should systematically file all of the papers for each meeting. The meetings should be in date order with the most recent papers at the front of the folder or file. Electronically held documents should be filed in the same way, systematically creating a folder for each meeting and putting all relevant documents into that folder.

There should always be spare documents available at the meeting in case participants do not bring their own copies.

In some organisations meetings are numbered and each item is given a sequential number. For example, if you were recording meeting number 25, the first item on the agenda would be 25.1. Each paragraph in the minutes would usually be numbered under this system so if item 25.3 had three paragraphs in it they would be 25.3.1, 25.3.2, and 25.3.3.

Organising Venues

Most meetings will be held as internal meetings usually in the organisation's own rooms. As secretary you will need to know the size and capacity required for the meeting, the layout of furniture required for the meeting and the availability of suitable accommodation. Most organisations will require you to pre-book accommodation and you will usually have to identify any resources required in the room, such as data projector or flipcharts, preferably at the time of booking. You will also need to know the catering facilities needed.

In addition, where you are booking accommodation which is external to the organisation, you will usually have to know any budget restrictions or any organisational preferences for particular hotels or conference facilities. Car parking may also be a consideration where external facilities are being used. To check that you are getting best value you will probably be asked to make enquiries and gather estimates from several different venues so that you can do a genuine comparison between costs, quality and catering.

Task 1

Prepare an Agenda and a Chairperson's Agenda for the next meeting of the Social Committee at John Nicholls which is next Friday at 2p.m. The Boardroom has already been booked. Apart from the standard items on the agenda you should include the following items: Children's Christmas Party, Staff Christmas Party and the Charity Fun Run. You have received apologies from Jim Martin. Save and print a copy of your completed notice and agenda.

Task 2

Prepare the next Agenda and Chairperson's Agenda for the Pay and Salary Negotiating Committee at John Nicholls. Use the minutes of the last meeting to work out what will come up at the next meeting. Save and print a copy.

Check your Progress

3.1

1   What is the purpose of an agenda and how does it differ from a chairperson's agenda?

2   What are the main differences between a formal meeting and an informal meeting? Give an example of each type of meeting.

3   Why does the chairperson sign the minutes? How would you suggest filing the minutes?

The Role of the Secretary

The administrative support required for meetings is usually provided by the secretary. The secretary will have administrative duties to carry out before the meeting, on the day of the meeting, during the meeting and after the meeting.

Before the Meeting

- You must ensure that the accommodation is booked in advance and that it meets the requirements of the meeting. You may be asked to indicate the layout of the room; for example, will you all sit round one table or will it be theatre style where everyone faces the front to listen to the chairperson? You might also have to book 'break-out' rooms so that private discussions away from the main body of the meeting can be held. This might be needed, for example, for pay negotiations between unions and management.

- Order any refreshments required, including water, during the meeting. Any special dietary requirements should also be ordered in advance.

- You should clarify any special equipment required such as data projector, notebook, OHP, DVD, etc. and ensure it is booked well in advance of the meeting.

- Prepare and circulate the relevant documents – notice, agenda, minutes of previous meeting and any supplementary papers, remembering to have a few spare copies for the day of the meeting. If this is not a regular meeting or a regular meeting venue, you should include directions in your documents. If available, book any car parking required or ensure that car parking arrangements are included in information sent to participants in advance.

- If participants do not know each other it is often a good idea to prepare nameplates or badges and/or a seating plan.

- Make a note of any apologies received and try to ensure that the results of any actions assigned to these members are available to the meeting.

- Inform the press if the meeting is open to the public and likely to be reported.

On the Day of the Meeting

- Check the room is satisfactory and meets your requirements such as seating layout as requested, heating and lighting.

- Check resources are as ordered and that they are working.

ADMINISTRATIVE SERVICES

- Inform reception of the meeting and the room and if the organisation has a secure entry arrangement, ensure that reception has a list of the names of those expected at the meeting.

- Ensure signs are available to direct visitors to the appropriate room.

- Ensure a Meeting in Progress sign is available.

- Arrive at the meeting room early to welcome visitors and place nameplates.

- Ensure that there are pens, paper and water available in the room and that you have spare copies of the documents circulated prior to the meeting.

- Have an attendance list in the room for signing.

- Ensure you have a copy of the Minutes of the last meeting available for the chairperson to sign.

- Inform the switchboard that you are unavailable for calls or delegate a colleague to accept your calls.

At the Meeting

- Try to make sure you are sitting beside the chairperson so that you can pass relevant papers and clarify any uncertainties.

- Read the Minutes if required. (This is usually only needed if they have not been circulated in advance.)

- Inform the meeting of any apologies received.

- Ensure the chairperson signs the Minutes of the last meeting.

- Take notes at the meeting including any actions which have to be followed up after the meeting. While these will be the basis of the minutes of meeting later on, you should not try to take notes in the way you are going to key them in. Just make sure you have a note of all decisions and actions.

- Make sure everyone signs the attendance list.

- Distribute expense claims if required.

After the Meeting

- Clear and tidy the room, remove direction signs and the Meeting in Progress sign, if used.

- Let any colleagues who have provided cover know that the meeting is finished.

- Read over your notes and key up the Minutes as soon as possible after the meeting.

- Once you have keyed up the Minutes you should check with the chairperson that they are an accurate account of the meeting before you duplicate or e-mail them to the other people who attended the meeting.

- You should always try to follow up any actions you have to do immediately after the meeting, otherwise you may get sidetracked by other things and forget to do them. Your actions are likely to include things like writing letters or researching information.

- Prepare a list of actions the chairperson has to do before the next meeting.

- Write the date of the next meeting into your diary. If this is an internal meeting and you are using an electronic diary system you should prepare this as an invitation and send it to all those entitled to attend.

- If you had any files or individual papers at the meeting, ensure they are returned to the correct cabinets and files.

- Start the Agenda for the next meeting.

- Put a note in your diary as a memory jogger, to remind you when you have to prepare the next Notice and Agenda.

Consequences of Inadequate Preparation for Meetings

It is really important that, as secretary, you make effective arrangements for any meetings, because your reputation, as well as the image of your department or organisation, will suffer if arrangements are not as they should be. It is important to have a routine when you are dealing with regular meetings and this might mean writing reminders in your diary of tasks to be completed prior to a meeting. For example, you may remind yourself three weeks before a meeting to send out the notices and agenda. Here are some of the consequences of being poorly prepared.

- Your reputation or that of the chairperson might suffer.

- In the worst case, you may have to postpone a meeting because you are not prepared properly, for example, if you had not given the members of a formal committee sufficient notice of the meeting, you would have to change the date as it would not be in accordance with the rules of the committee.

- A poor agenda may result in the meeting over-running.

- If the members of a committee feel they have been messed about, for example, if the accommodation or catering is inadequate or of a poor quality, they may feel reluctant to attend another meeting.

- Non-receipt of papers in advance of a meeting may result in insufficient or ill-informed discussion.

- If you have not followed procedures you may invalidate any decisions made. For example, if the fact that there were insufficient people attending the meeting to make a quorum was ignored, the meeting and any decisions taken at it would be invalid.

The Role of the Chairperson

The chairperson is probably the most important person at any meeting. A good chairperson will direct the course of the meeting and ensure that objectives are met. It is important that the chairperson of any committee has the respect of the other members. The chairperson will often be voted in by the other committee members indicating their acknowledgement of his or her experience and competence. Additionally, the chairperson is expected to show tact and fairness in their dealing with issues and members. The chairperson should be impartial and objective when decisions have to be made.

As well as these personal qualities the chairperson also has the following responsibilities.

- Making sure the meeting is set up and run according to the Standing Orders of the committee and that a copy of these Standing Orders are available in the meeting room, in case they are needed for reference.

- Ensuring that the minimum number of people to form a quorum are present.

- Starting the meeting on time.

- Signing the minutes of the previous meeting as an accurate record of what happened, once this has been agreed at the meeting.

- Taking each item to be discussed in the order it appears on the agenda or getting the agreement of the meeting to change the order, in exceptional circumstances.

- Sometimes difficult or complex ideas or topics have to be discussed and it is part of the role of the chairperson to:

  - introduce the ideas or topics

  - explain the issues and ensure everyone understands them

  - know when to keep quiet

  - try not to over-influence the other committee members.

- Keeping a sense of balance is important and the chairperson has to make sure that everyone has a chance to speak and air their views. The other side of this is the chairperson's duty to make sure that no one member monopolises the meeting. The chairperson will often have to steer the meeting back to the original point.

- Sometimes discussions can go on for a long time. The chairperson has to judge when there has been sufficient discussion and draw the discussions to an end prior to taking a decision. Ideally the chairperson will sum up the discussions which have taken place.

- A good chairperson will try to make sure that the wording of any motions is clear to everyone before a vote is taken.

- Putting matters to the vote when required, announcing the result of voting and summarising decisions so that everyone knows what decisions have been taken. This allows decisions to be recorded properly and accurately.

- Ensuring that after the committee has voted or taken a decision, the secretary has a note of the decision and the wording of any motions.

- In a formal committee the chairperson will often have certain powers, for example, he may have the casting vote if there is deadlock.

- Closing or adjourning a meeting.

- Between meetings the chairperson will act on behalf of the committee, along with the secretary, to deal with any matters which cannot wait until the next meeting.

- Taking follow-up actions as agreed by the committee.

The Role of the Committee Member

While the role of both the chairperson and the secretary are very important, there are certain personal qualities and attributes which all the committee members should have.

Prepared. Although committee members may not be as experienced at the chairperson, they should come to the meeting having done their homework. They should have read the minutes of the last meeting, read the agenda and read over any supplementary papers distributed prior to the meeting.

Interested. Not all discussions will interest all members equally but they should all try to concentrate on the arguments and discussions.

Committed. When decisions are made they often involve actions for those attending the meeting. Those who are prepared to serve on committees have to be prepared to put in some work between meetings as well as attend meetings. This is particularly true of those attending meetings as the representative of others.

Listening skills. Most of the time spent at a meeting will be spent listening. No meeting should be dominated by one person.

Articulate. Committee members have to be prepared to present their arguments in an articulate way or they will not 'win' the argument. They also need to know when to stop talking or this could also lose them the argument.

Task 3

Give an example of when you would choose to hold an informal meeting rather than a formal meeting and explain why you would choose to keep the meeting informal.

Task 4

If you were taking over the role of a secretary for a series of formal meetings, where would you expect to find the 'rules'. What kind of things would you expect to find in the 'rules'?

Commonly Used Terms at Meetings

Here are some terms which are used in meetings and what they mean.

Abstain	Refrain from voting. If a member eligible to vote decides not to vote he or she is said to abstain from voting.
Address the chair	Sometimes called to speak through the chair. Before speaking each person must say 'Mr Chairman' or 'Madame Chairperson' and then start speaking. This ensures that only one person speaks at a time.
Adjournment	The meeting is discontinued until a later date. Usually a new date will be agreed but if it is not the adjournment is described as sine die – without another date being decided.

ADMINISTRATIVE SERVICES

Amendment	A change or alteration to a proposed motion, for example, adding words, changing words or deleting words. Usually done prior to a vote being taken. Any amendments must be proposed and seconded in the same way as the original motion.
Ballot	A written vote which is usually taken to preserve secrecy.
Casting vote	A second or additional vote held by the chairperson and used when there is deadlock and a decision has to be made.
Ex Officio	Literally means 'by virtue of office'. Certain members of a committee may be included 'ex officio', for example, the company accountant may always be on the Finance Committee.
In camera	The meeting is not open to the public – a private meeting.
Lie on the table	Those at the meeting agree that nothing should be done about a particular issue at the moment. No action should be taken.
Majority	The greater number who have voted either for or against a motion.
Motion	A proposal which is put before the meeting. It may be described as a motion being moved by a member of the committee. The motion has to be proposed and seconded in formal meetings. Motions will usually be discussed at the meeting and the proposer will usually be allowed the **right of reply** – to comment after all discussion has taken place. The motion is then voted on. After voting at a formal meeting the chairman would announce:
	The motion is carried – it is agreed.
	The motion is lost – it has been rejected.
	The motion is carried unanimously – everyone is favour of the motion.
No confidence	A vote usually taken 'against' the chair to indicate that the other members are not happy with the decisions taken. The Chair would usually have to stand down.
Point of order	A question or query raised about whether the correct procedures are being followed. Often requires reference to the Standing Orders.
Postpone	Put off, delay or defer a meeting or a decision.
Proposer	The person who moves or proposes a motion.
Proxy vote	If one member is unable to attend a meeting, arrangements can sometimes be made to appoint a proxy – a substitute person to vote in their place.
Quorum	The minimum number of people who have to be present for the meeting to be valid. When a quorum is formed, the meeting can be described as quorate. If insufficient numbers are present it is inquorate.
Resolution	Once a decision has been made at a formal meeting, it becomes a resolution.
Rider	An addition to a resolution after it has been passed. This will usually add to, rather than alter, a resolution.

Seconder	The person who puts their name to supporting the proposer of the motion.
Standing orders	The rules under which the committee operates. This will include information on the notice to be given before meetings, the quorum and election of office bearers.
Unanimous	All members have voted in favour of the motion. It would be described in the following way: The motion was carried unanimously.
Verbatim	A word for word record of what was said at the meeting.
Vote	A vote for a motion can take the form of a show of hands, where those eligible to vote say yes or no by raising their hands; a ballot, where voting is done secretly; or go into division, where those eligible to vote go to an allocated place, for example, one side of a room.

Check your progress 3.2

1   Read over the following passages and make sure you understand them. Make a note of any part you do not understand and look back at the text. Try to note what would be recorded in the minutes.

   a   Before the meeting began the Secretary put the Meeting in Progress sign up on the door, checked that a quorum was present and indicated to the chairperson that the meeting could begin.

   The Chairperson welcomed all present to the meeting and asked the secretary to read out any apologies from Alan Forrest and Ann Beattie. The Chairperson asked if the minutes could be taken as read and it was agreed that the minutes were an accurate record of the meeting. The Minutes were duly signed and dated by the Chairperson.

   b   John Smith proposed the following motion 'That the presentation takes place in the Royal Scot Hotel on 27 January'. This motion was seconded by Wendy O'Hara. Discussion followed and the motion was unanimously carried. The following amendment was proposed by Jim Forrest 'That the presentation takes place in the Royal Scot Hotel on 27 January and that all members of the Marketing Department, past and present, be invited'. This amendment was seconded by Sahiba Khan. The amendment was lost.

   c   Due to the severe snow storm the Chairperson proposed that the meeting be adjourned. This was seconded by the Secretary. The meeting was adjourned sine die.

2   Why is it important to be properly prepared for a meeting? If you were going to be on holiday at the time of a regular committee meeting for which you are secretary, what kind of things would you write down for someone to check on the day of the meeting?

continued ➤

ADMINISTRATIVE SERVICES

Check your progress *continued*

3.2

3 The following are the key words used when a motion is proposed at a formal meeting. Complete a description of the process, in your own words.

The motion

The proposer

The seconder

An amendment was proposed and seconded

Following discussions, the proposer used the right to reply

A vote was taken and passed

The resolution

A rider

4 Explain in your own words the meaning of the following terms:

Casting vote

Action Minutes

Verbatim

Quorum

Abstain.

Use of Technology and Networks in the Organisation and Conduct of Meetings

Increasing use of IT in business has had a huge effect on how people work, communicate and meet. The possibility of using remote meetings as an important way of communicating within business is now a reality. Here are some of the ways technology can be used in meetings.

E-diaries

Traditionally, regular meetings were held on a set day and time each month but with the advent of shared e-diaries it may no longer be necessary to do this.

- Using e-diaries for internal meetings means that appropriate dates and times can be set to suit all.

- This facility allows the secretary to invite people to a meeting and once they have accepted the invitation, it will be automatically logged in their e-diaries.

- Both acceptance and non-acceptance of an invitation will be notified back to the secretary issuing the invitation and providing him or her with a list of those expected.

- E-diaries also make any changes to the meeting venue, date or time, easy to alter and communicate to other members.

- An e-diary allows the secretary to flag up key dates (for having materials ready for distribution, items to be included in the agenda, etc.).

E-mail

- Where previously all papers had to be printed and circulated, often they are now circulated electronically and the recipient may choose whether or not to print copies of the documents or merely to read them.

- Documents can be recalled on screen at meetings.

- Proposed amendments can be edited and sent back with alterations indicated in different colours.

- Where a distribution is made electronically, it is advisable for the secretary to ensure that receipt and opening of all documents is logged on their e-mail system.

- Documents can be filed electronically and may be retained in this way. The official set of minutes is still likely to be held in hard copy for ease of access at meetings but could be kept electronically as well, usually with some kind of password control so that the content cannot be altered. Where some signature is required, usually it is acceptable for an e-mail from, for example, the chairperson to accompany the minutes saying that this is an accurate statement of the meeting.

Video Conferencing

Increasing use of video conferencing is being made by all organisations, many of whom have specific video conferencing facilities set up within their offices. Essentially a video conferencing system is a set of television monitors with cameras which can be linked. Video conferencing is particularly useful for geographically distant members of the same organisation to talk to each other. Many small business centres and colleges also have facilities which can be hired by individuals or other organisations. Individuals usually use web-cams – individual PC cameras. The technology involved in these two systems is likely to merge over the next few years.

Advantages of using video-conferencing

- There are monetary savings because staff are not required to travel and the associated accommodation and subsistence costs do not have to be met.

- Time is saved as a result of staff being able to remain in their usual working environment.

- If certain individuals are unable to attend or technical difficulties are encountered, the meeting can be recorded.

- It allows face-to-face communication to take place more frequently with remote locations.

- It allows people who may not have had the opportunity to attend to follow proceedings.

Disadvantages of using video-conferencing

- Technical issues may arise and it is advisable to have technical support standing by which may add to the costs.

- Hiring of video conferencing facilities is expensive.

- The chairperson has to develop new skills as there may be a time delay on transmissions and the chairperson will have to ensure that each group is clear about when they can and cannot be heard. It becomes very important to address the chair.

- It is often difficult to ascertain if everyone has heard all the arguments.

At a video conference it becomes very important to:

- ensure that everything is working before the meeting begins
- summarise regularly
- ensure that all participants can be viewed as well as heard, preferably by having a technician present to work the camera or by having only a small group of participants involved
- address the chair so that only one person is speaking at a time.

Audio conferencing

Audio conferencing is to some extent the poor relation of video conferencing as only the voice input is heard. Think back to the section on communication where it was identified that the best communication takes place when more than one method of communication is used. Often it is preferable to be able to see those involved rather than only hear them. For short in-house meetings a three or four way conversation is easily manageable through most organisations' telephone systems.

Advantages of audio conferencing

- It can be an effective way of saving time.
- It allows a cheap way of transferring brief information.
- Any additional equipment is easily attainable and usually already incorporated in high quality telephone extensions.
- It is effective for internal meetings.

Disadvantages of audio conferencing

- Face to face contact always leads to better communications.
- Participants often multi-task when talking on the phone, for example, dealing with e-mails at the same time.
- In many open plan offices conversations would be overheard so it should not be used where confidential information is being discussed.

Internet and Network Meetings

Instant messaging and the use of web cams and chat rooms/discussion groups has resulted in communication, both visual and written, to be made almost instantaneously. Additionally, e-groups or e-forums which are closed communication groups, allow pre and post meeting discussions to take place. In this type of group you can use your e-mail address and are automatically sent any information others put on the e-group. One of the problems about using e-groups is that they tend to be unmonitored and as a result all information may not always be accurate.

Mobile Phones and Video Phones

Increasingly the use of mobile phone technology also has an input to this area. Video phones are now increasingly common – you can see them being used on the television news to transmit messages from difficult areas like war zones and you can buy mobile phones to use

with this facility yourself. This enables anyone to be linked to another phone or a meeting, albeit it is likely to be for a short time only. The field of vision is likely to be small so this technology is not usually used for group to meet with group but rather for one to meet with many.

Most people now own a mobile phone and many organisations are now seeking to limit the use of personal phones during working hours. A certain amount of telephone etiquette is now building up. This will often include restricting the receipt of calls at your desk or requesting that mobile phones be switched off before meetings start. While the use of a mobile phone will mean that the owner can be contacted at any time, the use of a phone during a meeting would be distracting for others attending the meeting and would be regarded as bad manners.

If an emergency call or special call is expected during a meeting, special arrangements will have to be made, for example, the recipient could inform those attending at the start that a call is expected and leave the phone on silent but on the table and ask to be excused to take the call. What should not happen is that calls are automatically answered, disrupting business and distracting others. There may be situations when it is important to the meeting that news is current and in this case receiving a call might be deemed to be important and necessary to the meeting.

Internal Assessment

Here are some examples of the kind of questions you might be asked as part of your internal assessment at Higher.

1 Explain the use of one of the following documents:

Chairperson's agenda

Attendance register

Action minutes. (3)

2 Explain the difference between:

Annual General Meeting

Extraordinary General Meeting. (2)

3 Explain two of the following terms:

   a seconder

   b adjournment

   c abstain

   d quorum. (2)

4 Describe how one of the following might be used to help organise or conduct a meeting:

   a e-mail

   b e-diary

   c video-conference. (2)

External Assessment

Here are some examples of the kind of questions you might be asked as part of your external assessment. An estimate of the marks assigned to each question is indicated and it would be anticipated that each question would form part of a larger question.

1 Outline the role of the Secretary on the day of the meeting and explain the possible consequences of not carrying out this role effectively. (8)

2 Compare and contrast the use of e-mail and e-groups to aid communication with committee members. (8)

3 Differentiate between the costs and advantages involved in holding a traditional meeting and a video conference if your organisation does not have its own video-conferencing facilities. (8)

4 Outline the process which would usually be followed at the start of a business meeting up until the specific agenda items for the meeting are being discussed. (8)

5 Compare and contrast the use of traditional minutes and action minutes. (4)

C H A P T E R 4

●● Recruitment and Selection

This chapter is about the recruitment and selection process. It also covers staff development processes and procedures relating to staff welfare.

Higher Level Outcomes:

 This chapter includes from Higher Administrative Services Outcome 3:

☆ **job descriptions/person specifications**

☆ **internal and external advertising**

☆ **applications**

☆ **tests/interviews**

☆ **employment checks**

☆ **staff appraisal process including CPD and staff training**

☆ **procedures relating to staff welfare including counselling, grievance and disciplinary procedures, absence management and staff-friendly issues.**

Note: Further information and exemplars of job descriptions and person specifications can be found in Chapter 1.

Recruitment and Selection

Recruitment and selection is one of the main activities of the Human Resources (HR) Department in any organisation. The process must be effective as it is a costly activity for the organisation in terms of both time and money. The recruitment process begins when the need for a position is identified. Selection is concerned with choosing the best person for the job – usually you will have to choose from a number of people. If a Human Resources Department had a mission statement it might be something like:

To have appropriately skilled and highly motivated and professional staff who demonstrate superior performance in an environment of continuous change.

Does a Vacancy Exist?

With the ever increasing costs of recruiting and selecting staff the first step is to establish whether or not a vacancy actually exists. Many questions will need to be asked such as:

● Would it be more cost-effective to outsource the job?

● Will the job be same in 12 months time?

● Can the job be shared amongst existing staff?

ADMINISTRATIVE SERVICES

ADMINISTRATIVE SERVICES

Job analysis

Jobs are looked at very carefully before they are advertised and often a job analysis will be carried out to help establish the need for the job. The job analysis determines the main features of the job, in particular the duties, the end results which are expected and relationships with other jobs in the organisation. Once the need for a vacancy is determined, approval is agreed with the appropriate line manager prior to starting the recruitment process. The steps involved in the recruitment process are shown below.

RECRUITMENT & SELECTION PROCESS – INTERNAL/EXTERNAL CANDIDATES

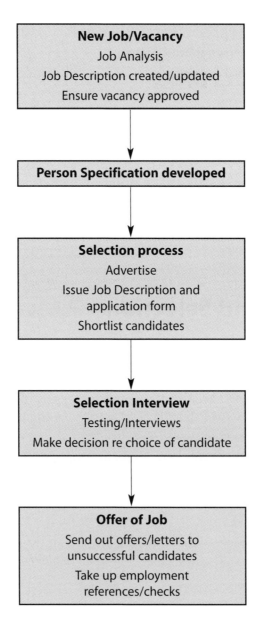

After the confirmation of offer has been received, Induction is arranged and a Contract of Employment is drawn up

Job Description

The next step is to draw up (or update) a job description. As you have learnt from Chapter 1 the job description clearly defines the duties and responsibilities associated with the job. It may include any constraints, for example, working at a different location. It determines what tasks have to be done in the job and may be reviewed and updated to meet the changing needs of the organisation.

Person Specification

After determining what tasks have to be carried out, a person specification will need to be drawn up which states the personal qualities and attributes needed to do the job. This is a summary of the most important knowledge, skills and characteristics required in order to be able to do the job to the required standard. For further person specifications see Chapter 1. When using a person specification for recruitment purposes, features are often labelled under the headings 'Desirable' or 'Essential'.

JOB SPECIFICATION   John Nicholls

Job Title: Information Desk Assistant   **Grade: 1**

Location: Glasgow   **Responsible to: Customer Services Manager**

	Essential	Desirable
Qualifications		4 O'Levels/Standard Grades or SVQ Level 2 in appropriate discipline
Work Experience	Relevant work experience in the Business Environment	
Skills	• Excellent oral/written communication • Numerate	• Keyboard skills • Telephone skills
Special Attributes	• Ability to work as part of a team • Ability to work under pressure • Ability to listen • Communicate sensitively • Confident • Unflappable	• Take ownership for own work • Care about standards
Specific Training	None	None
Other Requirements	None	None

A person specification is a useful tool to help ensure every candidate is treated equally and fairly in the interview process, i.e. measured against the same criteria. Usually the person specification and job description are used together to determine full details of what has to be done in the job and the qualities needed to do the job well.

Task 1

What are the differences between a job description and a person specification?

Task 2

Make up a job description and person specification from the information given below using a layout of your choice.

A human resources assistant is required for the HR Branch, Edinburgh. Responsible to the Human Resource Manager, the post holder will work as an integral part of a small pro-active HR team, providing an efficient secretarial and administrative service. The post holder should have at least 2 years' experience in an office environment and possess an SVQ Level II or equivalent.

Good communication skills are essential. Excellent keyboard and IT skills are also necessary along with the ability to prioritise your own workload within a busy environment. Good organisational skills and the ability to work under pressure are also essential. Ability to take shorthand is desirable. The job involves receiving and assisting visitors, carrying out word processing and reprographic duties. The new HR assistant will also have to undertake any telephone duties when necessary and will also be expected to maintain the manual and computerised filing system. The job will also involve assisting with the organisation of interview rooms/events.

Internal and External Advertising

Once the job description and person specification have been drawn up, the next step in the recruitment process is to advertise the job – a decision has to be made whether to carry this out internally (within the organisation) or externally (outwith the organisation). It is crucial that the Human Resources Department get this right – they have to attract potential candidates with the necessary skills, knowledge and attributes to fill the job. This process must also be cost effective. Often organisational policy is to advertise all posts internally before going outside the organisation. The posts would be advertised internally via the corporate intranet, on notice boards and in weekly newsletters. If the posts advertised do not receive responses from suitable candidates, the vacancy will then be advertised externally through newspapers, magazines, professional journals, job centres, schools, colleges, agencies and the Internet.

Advantages of internal recruitment

- It is less expensive to advertise internally than externally.

- It is less expensive to interview and select internal candidates – expenses do not need to be paid.

- It requires less expensive induction and training processes.

- The recruitment process may be quicker because of the above and because less notice needs to be given.

- Existing employees will have the opportunity to enhance their career.

- Further job opportunities may be created as a result of recruiting internally.

- The organisation can make use of its pool of existing workers.

- Candidates are known to the organisation so there is less chance of selecting the wrong person.

- The motivation of the existing workforce may be enhanced due to a good internal promotion policy.

Disadvantages of internal recruitment

- There will be a smaller pool of workers to choose from.

- The company will need to advertise another job (quite often lower-end jobs) if the new job is filled by an internal candidate.

- There is less opportunity to bring new skills, ideas and experience into the organisation.

- There can be a lack of stability in work teams due to team members regularly moving to other positions.

- There can be a lack of ownership of tasks due to employee expectations of moving on to another job

Some organisations will choose to advertise externally rather than recruiting from within the organisation. The method of recruitment may depend on the nature of the job which needs to be filled. There are various methods of recruiting staff from outside the organisation:

- Local newspapers are usually used to advertise unskilled and semi-skilled jobs.

- National newspapers are usually used to advertise professional and managerial positions.

- Technical/professional journals are used to advertise professional and managerial positions.

- Job centres are usually used to advertise unskilled and semi-skilled jobs and temporary jobs.

- Agencies are usually used to advertise temporary positions such as administrators, secretaries, bank staff, IT staff, nurses and some specialist staff such as software engineers.

- The Internet is now used to advertise a wide range of occupations including graduates. E-recruitment now plays an important role in the recruitment and selection processes. The use of e-mail and the Internet is fast becoming an integral part of recruitment and selection strategy. Visit www.hr.com and www.erecruitment.com to find out more.

Advantages of external recruitment

- The organisation attracts a wider pool of workers from home and abroad. European job seekers often use the Internet to search for jobs in other EU countries.

- There is more chance of recruiting a 'good-fit' because the organisation is recruiting from a wider pool.

- New workers can bring new skills and innovation to the organisation.

Disadvantages of external recruitment

- It is more expensive than recruiting from within the organisation:
  - costs of advertising in local/national newspapers and technical/professional journals
  - more costs involved in interviewing and selecting candidates and
  - more costs involved in induction and training processes.
- Existing employees will not have the opportunity to enhance their careers.
- The recruitment process may be slower.
- Candidates are not known to the organisation so there is more chance of selecting the wrong person.

Assuming you have attracted appropriately qualified and skilled people from internal/external advertising, you can then move to the next stage of the recruitment and selection process – the selection of staff.

Staff Selection

The staff selection process first of all involves sifting through the application forms and CVs to make up a shortlist and then invite appropriate candidates for interview.

**John Nicholls
Department Store**

Application Form

Application for appointment of:
Job reference Number:

PERSONAL DETAILS

Surname	Tel: (home)
Other name(s)	Tel: (business)
Title (e.g. Mr Mrs Miss Ms)	
Address	
	Do you hold a full current driving licence?
Town	
Postcode	
Previous surname (if any)	Do you own a car?

CAREER HISTORY

Present Appointment position	Employer and address
Date of appointment	
Renumeration and Grade (if applicable)	Employees supervised:
Description of Duties (add further sheets if necessary)	
Reason for leaving	

PREVIOUS APPOINTMENTS AND EMPLOYERS

Employer's name and nature of business	Appointment held	Dates From	To	Grade/Salary on leaving	Reason for leaving

EDUCATION

Secondary School / College / University	Dates From	To	Qualifications gained	Grades	Date

OUTSIDE INTEREST (hobbies etc.)

What are your main interests and leisure activities outside work?

MEMBERSHIP OF PROFESSIONAL BODIES (state whether by examination)

Body	Membership Status	Since

NON-QUALICATION COURSES ATTENDED (Course, Organising Body and Dates)

An application form

The application form

There are several advantages of a well-designed application form:

- Information about all the candidates is in a standardised format.

- It enables candidates to give full information about themselves outlining their knowledge, skills and experience which are specifically required for the job advertised.

- The HR Department can match each completed application form with the person specification and job description to ascertain the candidate's suitability for the job. This will allow the organisation to draw up a shortlist of suitable candidates for the job.

Check your Progress 4.1

1   Outline five methods of advertising externally for staff.

2   Outline three ways of advertising internally for staff.

3   Outline the advantages and disadvantages of advertising internally for staff.

The selection interview

The selection interview, together with other documentary evidence such as qualifications, application forms and references, is the most influential factor used in deciding on the right candidate for the job. The interview gives the employer the opportunity to assess whether or not the candidate will be able to perform well in the job. It also gives the employer the opportunity to assess the candidate's motivation for the job. The interview is a two-way process so it also gives the potential candidate lots of opportunities. The candidate has the chance to build upon what they have written in the application form and to learn more about the job and the organisation. It gives the candidate the opportunity to ask questions and decide if they want to take up any job offer given.

Successful interviews will only occur when the interviewer is properly prepared. The interviewer should bear in mind the following points before the interview.

- Book an appropriate interview room

- Match the person specification against the application form to decide on areas to investigate at the interview.

- Read all other relevant documentary evidence – CV, references, etc.

- Decide on suitable questions to ask the candidate to ensure that the interviewer obtains the information they want to get from the candidate.

- Confer with colleagues who may also be present at the interview to:
  - ensure you are both taking the same approach
  - identify who will ask what questions and
  - identify areas for further discussion.

- Decide whether or not there is a need to carry out any testing, for example, a word processing test.

Other skills have to be developed to conduct effective selection interviews. These include:

- listening and observing skills
- questioning skills
- the ability to build and maintain rapport with the candidate
- the ability to summarise and make relevant notes about the candidate
- the ability to control the interview.

Staff conducting interviews must also be aware that all interviews must be conducted within the law – all candidates must be treated fairly and equally.

In reality, however, many interviews are not carried out in a systematic way because the interviewers do not possess the appropriate knowledge and skills to interview effectively. For example, staff may not have received any training and/or do not have the prerequisite experience of conducting interviews.

Another problem associated with the selection interview is that some candidates are known to exaggerate their skills, experience and ability. Other candidates may possess excellent interview techniques which allow them to perform well at the interview. These candidates may not necessarily perform as well in the job.

Check your Progress 4.2

1 What factors must the interviewer consider prior to conducting an interview?

2 List the main qualities required by the interviewer in order to conduct a successful interview.

Tests

To help them decide who to employ, employers often use selection tests to provide useful additional information about the candidate. These can be used to supplement the information about the candidate from the application form and interview. Tests can be used to identify the candidate's personality profile, reasoning skills and aptitudes.

Two of the main types of tests are skills tests and psychometric tests.

Skills tests are used to ascertain existing skill levels and to find out if the candidate has the ability to do the job (for example, typing and shorthand skills, communication skills, numerical ability).

Quite often organisations will use psychometric assessments to obtain a profile of the candidate covering both personality and intellectual ability. These tests have been developed by psychologists. Organisations may buy these standard tests and should ensure that they are applied under the recommended conditions and marked by trained markers. Psychometric tests include personality tests and aptitude tests.

A personality test is used to explore a candidate's personality traits. It can help identify strengths and weaknesses and ascertain whether or not the candidate is a team player, a risk taker, cautious, aggressive, etc. Universities are to introduce personality tests to identify bright students from poorer backgrounds. They feel too many academics rely on the interview favouring confident teenagers coached in the 'right answers'. Visit www.education.guardian.co.uk to find out more.

Aptitude tests are designed to measure an individual's level of verbal, numerical and diagrammatic reasoning.

Task 3

Visit www.aptitudeonline.com to try out an aptitude test.

Medical tests are used by some professions (such as the police and fire service) to ensure candidates are physically able to carry out the activities required in the post.

A problem associated with testing is that the tests can make people feel quite nervous and as a result candidates may not perform well. However, some bought-in tests are used by many organisations to ensure reliability and validity of results. Only properly qualified staff should analyse the scripts of personality tests to avoid misleading results and avoid unfair discrimination claims.

Reference/employment checks

Once a decision has been made regarding the candidate, references and employment checks can be requested. These should simply confirm that the information given by the candidate in the application form is accurate. Interviewers know that candidates are nervous at an interview and a good interviewer will try to get a more rounded picture of how candidates perform in their normal day-to-day activities. Rigorous employment checks are prerequisite to any offer of a job in the police force, hospitals and schools or any job which involves working with children or other vulnerable groups.

Staff Development and Training

After finding the right candidate for the job the next challenge for the organisation is to keep them! This leads us on to another very important activity of the Human Resource Department – assisting with supporting and developing its most valuable resource, its staff.

What is the difference between development and training in the organisation?

- Training is the learning activity to gain specific knowledge and skills in order to carry out the job.

- Development is concerned with future needs rather than current ones. It focuses more on career growth than immediate performance.

If the organisation is to achieve its goals, the Human Resources Department has to make sure that there is sufficient staff with the necessary expertise at every level of the organisation to get the job done now and in the future. This involves making sure that the staff are given every opportunity to prepare for future roles and responsibilities.

Staff Appraisal

A staff appraisal process is one way to review current performance and help identify and evaluate the training and development needs of staff and thus improve work performance. This is done by appraising current strengths and weaknesses of staff and assessing their career development potential. Most staff appraisal policies apply to non-manual workers.

Here are some benefits of staff appraisal:

- It allows creation of a personal development plan.

- It identifies future training and development needs.

- Staff are allocated duties most suited to them where they can contribute best to the overall efficiency of the organisation.

- It provides a basis for annual salary reviews in particular where pay is related to individual merit.

- It assists with succession planning.

- It can improve communication channels within the organisation through regular open communication.

- It improves motivation of the individuals in the organisation.

- It encourages self-assessment.

Both the employee and employer have to plan for the review. (See Chapter 1 regarding planning for a personal development interview.) Usually the process starts with the completion of an appraisal form. Then an appraisal interview is conducted by the relevant line manager. This usually happens once a year. The appraisal process should be viewed as an opportunity for honest and open self-assessment. Any training and development requests from members of staff usually relate to the job role. Goals set at the appraisal meeting will reviewed at the next appraisal meeting.

Performance is often graded, for example, 1–5. In this case 5 would be the highest (highly effective) and the gradings would drop down through 4 (effective), 3 (satisfactory), 2 (ineffective), 1 (very ineffective). Staff who receive higher grades may be considered for promotion or pay increases but often this is not guaranteed.

Remember, every organisation may use and carry out staff appraisal differently. As you can see from the diagram below, at John Nicholls, the department store we are studying, appraisal is linked to pay. This may not be the case in all organisations.

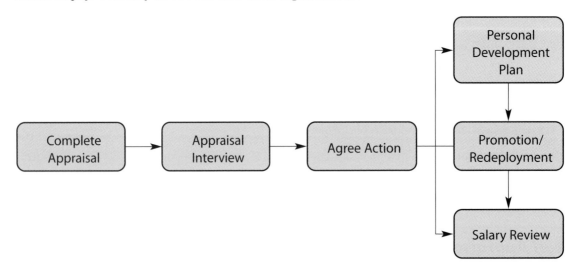

The appraisal process at John Nicholls

STAFF APPRAISAL

Name:

Department:

Date of Review:

Reviewed by:

The following should indicate dates for achievement/action and what to do, where appropriate

1 Performance over the past year:

2 Personal goals, targets and objectives for the year ahead:

3 Specific areas of personal improvement and development plans agreed:

4 Relevant training recommended for the next year:

5 Realistic ambitions and career objectives agreed:

Signed .... Job holder. Date:

Signed .... Line manager. Date

Copies to be kept by both parties (during following year) and on personal file.

A staff appraisal form

ADMINISTRATIVE SERVICES

Not everything goes well at appraisal interviews. Here are some problems associated with the appraisal interviews (The appraiser is the person carrying out and recording the appraisal interview. The appraisee is the person being appraised.):

- The appraiser may not possess the necessary interview skills.

- The appraiser may rely on their own perceptions, own likes/dislikes about some of their subordinates to reflect any assessment made about the candidate.

- Where pay is linked to appraisal, employees/appraisees may try to hide any difficulties in the job in order to obtain a pay increase.

- There can be loss of morale where staff expectations regarding promotion are not met.

Check your Progress — 4.3

1   What is the difference between training and development?

2   What is the purpose of staff appraisal?

3   Outline the steps involved in the staff appraisal process at John Nicholls.

4   Outline some of the problems associated with the appraisal interview.

Continuing Professional Development (CPD)

Research indicates that if businesses are to grow and prosper in today's rapidly changing technological environment, the use of continuing professional development as a tool must be fostered to ensure businesses address likely skills shortages.

Continuing professional development – often shortened to CPD – implies both the commitment of the individual and the commitment of the organisation. In order to implement a CPD system, the member of staff must make a commitment to develop and move on in some way and that commitment should be endorsed and actively supported by the organisation.

One of the goals of the Scottish Executive's Minister for Enterprise and Lifelong Learning is to foster lifelong learning which will benefit both society and the economy. In order for businesses to thrive, the acquisition of knowledge, skills and experience cannot stop after full-time schooling but must continue throughout life. Visit www.scotland.gov.uk to find out more.

There are obvious advantages to the organisation of committing to CPD, including:

- improved performance of the organisation

- satisfied customers

- motivated employees.

Advantages to the individual of undertaking CPD include:

- Improved employee performance because they are equipped with new skills and experience.

- Job security. Employees who are multi-skilled and versatile can adjust to changes in the work environment more easily.

- The reduction of stress. Employees can cope with any changes to their job more easily.

- Increased motivation and job satisfaction.

- Access to further promotion due to development of skills and experience.

- It may lead to an increase in salary.

Training

Training will start with induction training and should then be continuous throughout employment to ensure that the employee is equipped with the necessary up-to-date skills, knowledge and experience needed. Many organisations in the UK are committed to ensuring that they have a well-trained workforce to allow them to grow and prosper. Many of these organisations have been recognised as Investors in People. Investors in People is a national quality standard launched in 1990 to encourage UK businesses to invest in staff training and development. In order to achieve Investor in People status, organisations are measured against rigorous quality standards. This quality system ensures that a systematic approach to staff development and training is adopted throughout the organisation and involves analysis of training and development needs of staff, planning the training activities, carrying out training and development, and finally evaluating the activity. Visit www.investorsinpeople.co.uk to find out more.

In-house and external training

In all organisations much of the training will be done in-house, but there may be occasions when it is appropriate to send employees on specific external courses.

Training at the workplace may be:

- on-the-job – done in the course of the employees carrying out their normal work, for example, job rotation or work shadowing

- off-the-job – removing people from their own work environment, for example, to a computer suite for IT training perhaps using the company's own training facilities.

Many organisations employ their own full-time training staff and seek assistance from specialists when required. External training may take place at a college, university or private training centre and may also involve a secondment opportunity.

There are obvious advantages and disadvantages of in-house training.

Advantages of in-house training

- Employees may feel more comfortable in familiar surroundings.

- It is more cost-effective than external training.

- It can be more easily tailored to meet individuals' and organisations' needs, for example, induction training.

- It can be arranged as and when necessary.

Disadvantages of in-house training

- Employees can be easily distracted and interrupted if they are in their own workplace.

- In-house trainers may lack credibility.

- Staff may have to wait until a training course is timetabled, i.e. a course will only run when there is a sufficient number of employees identified.

ADMINISTRATIVE SERVICES

Advantages of external training

- It is more likely to lead to a formal qualification, i.e. at college or university.

- It may take the form of a secondment which can widen employees' experience.

- Employees are not as easily distracted by interruptions in a different environment.

- Employees can cascade new knowledge and skills to other staff on return to the workplace.

- Employees have the opportunity to widen their perspective, the ability to network with others, exchange views and ideas, which can enhance motivation and encourage new ideas.

Disadvantages of external training

- It is more expensive than in-house training.

- The employee may not pass any exams or assessments which form part of the course.

- The organisation has little control over the length and content of training course and it may not address all needs of the individual and the organisation.

- Monitoring of attendance may be required for some employees, for example, skillseekers.

Check your Progress 4.4

1 What is meant by the term CPD?

2 Why do you think it is important for the organisation to encourage its staff to commit to CPD?

3 What is meant by in-house training and external training? Give examples of training courses which are more suited to each type of training.

Staff Welfare

Another important activity of the Human Resources Department is to meet its obligations in relation to welfare of its employees. Traditionally, the employer emphasis was on meeting health and safety requirements but enlightened employers are now taking a much wider approach to the well-being of their employees. They are aware of the business benefits of developing policies over and above statutory requirements. Here are some of the benefits:

- improved sickness and absenteeism levels

- earlier resolution of grievance problems

- increased output

- increased motivation and retention

- happier staff.

Welfare policies are also known as 'staff-friendly policies'. The welfare role will vary greatly between organisations but here are some examples of welfare services which may be provided:

- Services (counselling) for the individual including organisational procedures to deal with absence and illness, bereavement, domestic and personal problems. Procedures will also

be in place to deal with employment issues including grievance and disciplinary procedures, stress, financial and legal problems.

- Group services including promotion of good health and lifestyle, sports and social services, medical provision, work–life balance initiatives, crèche facilities, etc.

Counselling at work

Organisations may use their own trained counsellors or they may employ the services of an external counselling body. Expert advice can be given to cover job issues such as grievance and disciplinary procedures, harassment, stress in the workplace, absence and illness (short and long term) etc. In some cases career development advice may come under this area, for example, when hours have to be shortened to accommodate changing personal circumstances.

Unbiased advice may also be available to cover personal problems such as bereavement, breakdown of relationships and stress, in order to help resolve issues quickly. Various organisations may provide support to the employee, for example, by giving time off to look after sick relatives.

Individuals are encouraged to take responsibility for their own problem situations whether they be work related or personal. However, the counselling role may sometimes be inappropriate. For instance, where it becomes apparent that an employee may not be able to change, such as continued alcohol abuse, other procedures may then be necessary to resolve the situation.

Grievance and disciplinary procedures

The HR Department gives advice and helps administer and monitor the grievance and disciplinary procedures of the organisation. It will assist with the maintenance of effective employee relations which is also essential to ensure success of the organisation.

Details of grievance and disciplinary procedures are normally included in the contract of employment which is usually issued when someone starts a new job. Many organisations also include these procedures in their organisational procedures manuals.

These procedures are necessary to make sure that every employee is treated in the same way in similar circumstances. They also ensure that complaints are dealt with fairly, reasonably and quickly and that they are compliant with current legislation.

Disciplinary Procedures

All employees are expected to maintain an appropriate standard of behaviour in the workplace, such as:

- good timekeeping
- good attendance
- honesty
- maintenance of confidentiality of information at all times.

Disciplinary procedures will be instigated by management where an employee does not meet these or other standards set for their job. The Advisory Conciliation and Arbitration Service (ACAS) provides independent and impartial advice on discipline and grievance issues to both the employer and employees. Visit www.acas.org.uk to see a model of good practice for disciplinary and grievances practices and procedures and to find more about their role.

ADMINISTRATIVE SERVICES

Disciplinary procedures will involve several stages:

- verbal warning
- written warning
- final written warning
- suspension (with/without pay)
- dismissal.

In cases of gross misconduct, for example, theft or malicious damage to property, employees may not be given prior warning and may go directly to suspension or dismissal.

During any disciplinary action, an employee will be given the opportunity to present his or her case and a fellow employee, or where appropriate a trade union member, can usually be present at any hearing. Employees subject to disciplinary action will usually have the right to appeal.

Grievance Procedures

Grievances are raised by employees to management when employees feel they are genuinely aggrieved, for example, because of racial and sexual harassment or other issues relating to the work environment, such as being demoted. Again grievance procedures will involve several stages.

- Employee raises grievance with immediate supervisor.
- If the matter is not resolved the employee has the right to take the issue to the next level of management. The employee can take a representative.
- If the matter is still not resolved the employee has the right to meet with senior management and can, again, take a representative with them.
- If the employee is still not satisfied they have the right to appeal to the Managing Director.

Time limits for each stage are set to ensure a speedy solution to overcome problems. An employee can take their case to ACAS when issues are not resolved within the organisation. Cases may go to an industrial tribunal before they are settled. Evidence suggests that where an organisation has excellent channels of communication there will be few, if any, grievances.

Check your Progress 4.5

1   What is the difference between a grievance procedure and a disciplinary procedure?

2   Outline the stages involved in disciplinary and grievance procedures.

Procedures for dealing with absence and illness

The Human Resources Department will assist will the effective management of absence and illness. Sick leave costs British companies around £11 billion every year, that is around 166 million lost working days! Effective control and absence management is essential because every occurrence of staff absence or illness is money lost. It is, however, essential to combine a caring and supportive attitude towards the health and well-being of staff with firm action against those who may abuse the system. Maintaining contact with the employee when they are not at work is important to help ascertain when, or if, the employee will be able to come back to work and to allow future plans to be made.

Problems associated with staff absence and illness include:

- disruption to the flow of work

- dissatisfaction amongst other workers

- additional workload of staff who are at work.

Procedures for managing short term and longer term staff illness and absences will vary from organisation to organisation but will be included in the organisation's procedures manual. Usually the HR Department will work closely with line managers and the Occupational Health Unit or counsellors, if relevant. In cases of persistent absences a welfare counselling service may be used, for example, where an employee has been sick on three separate occasions.

Task 4

Visit the Tesco website to find out how they are dealing with problems with staff absences and illnesses.

Cases of longer term illness, usually taken to be absences extending beyond 28 days, will not go unnoticed but the HR Department must provide support and treat matters with sensitivity. Return to work must be encouraged, perhaps with the introduction of health and welfare services. A welfare counsellor or mentor may be introduced to discuss mutual concerns and where appropriate agree:

- a modified workload for an agreed period

- phased return to work

- temporarily reduced hours.

In all cases the return to work must be planned with appropriate review dates. Support from an HR manager, line managers and counsellors is essential to ensure that employees receive full entitlement to benefits and are treated reasonably, fairly and in accordance with Employment Law.

Staff welfare – other services

With a shrinking population it is even more important that organisations hold on to the staff they have. As a result many organisations now offer an increasing range of staff welfare services. Many organisations are now realising the business benefits of making a commitment to improving and maintaining the health and fitness of their workforce. A national award is given to businesses in Scotland – Health at Work Campaign (SHAW) – who show a commitment to improving the health of their workers.

Task 5

Visit Scottish Health at Work Campaign (SHAW) at www.shaw.uk.com and www.shawlanarkshire.org to find out how businesses in Lanarkshire are reaping the benefits of improved business performance due to less time off work because of sickness and/or stress.

Many organisations have in-house health and fitness/sports studios or provide staff with access to local facilities. This service may include:

- health and fitness evaluation
- the designing of healthy lifestyle programmes
- provision of fitness classes
- access to sports such as tennis, badminton and five-a-side football
- physiotherapy, massage and other related services.

Some organisations provide health care by employing their own nurses, doctors and dentists or by 'buying in' this service for part of the week.

Work–life balance initiatives

Flexible work patterns

You have already looked at the increasing move towards more flexible working and more flexible contracts in Chapter 2. Organisations have found that staff are less likely to be absent where flexible work patterns are available which fit in with family responsibilities and other commitments. Staff are usually invited to apply for changes to their working arrangements and consideration will be given to the individual and needs of the organisation. This is because some working arrangements may not suit the needs of a particular department.

Leave Arrangements

Some organisations provide leave arrangements over and above those normally expected. Normal leave includes annual leave, maternity leave, parental leave, paternity leave and adoption leave. The additional leave may include:

Carer's leave – an entitlement to take time off to deal with certain unexpected or sudden emergencies involving a dependent.

Special discretionary leave – this covers requests from members of staff for short periods of paid and/or unpaid leave in circumstances not covered by other policy provisions.

Childcare – many organisations now provide nursery facilities and Kids Clubs which run during school holidays. These facilities may be in partnership with local authorities.

Career development opportunities – many organisations offer a range of development opportunities in conjunction with the organisation's training and development policy, such as secondments and sabbaticals.

Other services may include provision of free hairdressing, subsidised canteen and free car parking. Social and recreational events and activities may be promoted such as an annual outing or Christmas party or sporting competitions.

Check your Progress　　　　　　　　　　　　　　　**4.6**

1　Why is it important for the HR Department to monitor closely all cases of sickness and absence in the organisation?

2　Outline some of the support strategies an organisation can put in place to assist a worker back to work after a prolonged period of absence.

3　Discuss four 'staff-friendly' services provided by organisations in the UK today.

Internal Assessment

Here are some examples of the kind of questions you might be asked as part of your internal assessment.

1　Discuss internal and external recruitment. (6)

2　Discuss two different types of test used during the selection interview. (4)

3　Outline three advantages to the organisation and three advantages to the individual of committing to continuous and professional development. (6)

4　Outline two benefits to an organisation that develops 'staff friendly' policies over and above statutory requirements. (2)

External Assessment

Here are some examples of the kind of questions you might be asked as part of your external assessement. An estimate of the marks assigned to each question is indicated and it would be anticipated that each question would form part of a larger question.

1　Discuss the purpose of a job description and a person specification for the post of human resources assistant. (4)

2　Employers use the selection interview as a source of information to make a decision on recruitment of staff. Outline two advantages and two disadvantages of the selection interview for both the candidate and the employer. (4)

3　Discuss in-house and external staff training. (6)

CHAPTER 5

Customer Service

This chapter is about dealing with customers. Customers can be both internal and external and you will have to know how you are expected to behave in relation to people you work with – internal customers – as well as people who buy your products and services – external customers.

Intermediate 2 Level Outcomes: ⫸

This chapter includes from Intermediate 2 Administrative Services Outcome 1:

☆ **the importance to the organisation of good customer service:**
- **mission statements**
- **benefits of good customer service**
- **the impact of poor customer service.**

Higher Level Outcomes: ⫸

It also includes from Higher Administrative Services Outcome 5:

☆ **the importance of customer service policies to the organisation including:**
- **customer care strategy**
- **service level agreements**
- **complaints procedures**
- **methods of evaluating policy such as satisfaction surveys, focus groups and market research.**

Customer Care Strategy

To try to ensure customer care is high on the list of priorities many big organisations will have a customer care strategy which gives a written outline of their policy and plans for dealing with customers. This customer care strategy is written to try to ensure that customers get:

- what they want
- to the standard and specification they want
- with predictable reliability or quality
- at a price which suits their needs.

In order to ensure that customer needs are satisfied, the organisation should try to ensure that customers are dealt with in a consistent and transparent way. A customer care strategy will include the organisation's policy and plans for:

● ensuring the quality of the organisation's customer care

● measuring and testing that customer needs are satisfied

● ensuring that service level agreements are in place

● dealing with any customer complaints.

Mission Statements

Most organisations have an overall mission statement which gives a short statement of the main intentions of the organisation. Mission statements can tell you a lot about a business. A mission statement is a cross between a slogan and a summary of the organisation's aims. It can be used in many different ways but a good mission statement should be able to tell people about your organisation and ideals, in seconds. It should tell the world what your organisation stands for. It is ideal if everyone in the organisation can have some input into writing the mission statement. It is also important that everyone who works for the organisation knows and believes in its mission statement.

Most mission statements are very short – three sentences at the most.

Task 1

Find out the mission statement of Marks and Spencers, your local FE college and one other organisation with which you are familiar. Do you think these statements give you an idea of the organisation's values?

Ensuring the Quality of Customer Care

Most organisations agree that looking after customers is important. Generally speaking, if the organisation doesn't look after its customers, it will go out of business because it will get no repeat business. However this is not always the case. Here are some examples where the standard of service you give your customers will not affect the organisation – in the short term.

● The organisation may compete on price not customer care. Think of very cheap shops – you do not expect fancy surroundings or very good after sales service. You shop there because of prices and as long as the organisation offers cheap prices you will continue to shop there despite other factors – assuming price is really important to you. Recent surveys now indicate that customers do not always put price above other factors in determining customer choice – loyalty, convenience, image, etc. may all play a part.

● You may not have to compete with anyone else because you are the only supplier of certain goods or services. Local authorities and many public sector organisations come under this heading but so do local shops and services, for example, the only pub in a village or the only dentist for 50 miles. Your customers still have a choice – they may choose to do without the goods or services.

- You may supply goods or services in a sector where no-one else bothers about customer care. Listen to comments about builders or plumbers. All you need here is one organisation in the sector to start improving customer service and all of the others will have to follow suit if they wish to remain competitive.

- You may have a unique product or service which no-one else has thought about supplying, for example, a new invention or a new service. The number of customers you attract, however, is likely to be a short term phenomenon because in the longer term other organisations will enter the market.

In judging how well a product or service meets their needs, the customer considers factors like:

- Reliability of the service or product – does it work every time?

- Consistency over a period of time – how did this product or service compare with the last one purchased?

- The speed and flexibility of delivery – can the customer get the product or service when they want it?

- Courtesy and attitude of staff in the supplying organisation – this covers all staff from those dealing with telephone calls to those supplying the goods or the service.

- Information given about the service or product – was it accurate, informative, appropriate? How did the organisation's staff react to requests for help?

- The reputation of the organisation.

What we usually think of when we talk about customers is people who buy our goods or services but remember these are external customers. You also deal with internal customers – people internal to your organisation – the people you work with and for. It is equally important to ensure that your internal customers also get satisfaction.

Task 2

In groups of four you should think of an example of good service and an example of bad service which you or your family have experienced and then try to identify what made it good or bad. You should find one person to speak about each of the experiences in the class so that you can get together and identify several features of good service and several features of bad service.

An example of good service	What made it good
An example of bad service	What made it bad

Most people find they can think of lots of examples of bad service and few of good service.

The three foundations of good customer service and meeting customer expectations are:

- Keeping customers well informed of progress and changes, sometimes called setting and re-setting expectations.

- Under-promise and over-deliver. If you make promises ensure they can be kept by allowing yourself some flexibility. For example, if you promise to do something by Friday and you cannot keep that promise your customer will be annoyed but if you manage to do the job by Wednesday, your customer will be pleased.

- Go the extra mile by delivering consistently high quality service.

Why is Customer Service Important?

It is important to treat all customers well but treating them well has benefits for the organisation as well as the customer.

- Good internal customer relations mean employees work better together as a team. The whole organisation's reputation is enhanced. Outsiders see people and the organisation as one.

- All organisations can benefit from good publicity from happy employees and happy customers – and the opposite. Think back to the example of good customer service and bad customer service you discussed in Task 2. You may not be able to remember the good story but you are likely to remember the example of bad customer service and which organisation gave bad service. Remember, people talk! As an employee you should try to make sure the talk is positive.

- Good external customer relations are likely to mean regular repeat orders. Customers who are happy with the services they receive become loyal customers. Think about where your family does its weekly shopping. It is likely to be in the same place each week if you are satisfied customers.

- In turn, increased customer loyalty results in bigger turnover and increased market share.

- Good publicity enhances the organisation's reputation and will have many hidden results. For example, having a reputation as a good employer will mean that when the organisation advertises for new staff it should attract high quality candidates.

The Impact of Poor Customer Service

Customer care is important at all levels in an organisation. Many people will form an opinion of an organisation from the way they are spoken to by the telephonist or caretaker.

- Bad publicity results from poor customer service as people always tell others about their experiences.

- A poor reputation is difficult for an organisation to turn around and a poor reputation has implications for recruitment, falling market share and the impact of any advertising the organisation undertakes.

- Customers who are dissatisfied do not come back. Many people do not complain about poor service, they simply do not return resulting in falling income. Think of how you react to a disappointing meal in a restaurant.

- In extreme cases the organisation may be subject to legal action. This will involve legal costs for the company and may involve compensation payments.

- Increased resources have to be spent on sorting out problems with customers.

Task 3

Consider what steps will be taken to ensure consistent good service is experienced by all customers. Look at the websites of the following organisations – John Lewis, Scottish Power and Dixons and see what they have written about customer satisfaction and customer service. You could also check with your school or local college to see if they have a student charter.

Surveying Customer Satisfaction

Often organisations survey customers or ask for feedback to ensure that high standards of customer service are being met. This allows organisations to work on improving their customer service. Within all organisations, jobs are interconnected with employees depending on each other for support and service. This is sometimes called the service chain. While organisations tend to survey external customers, they do not tend to survey internal customers to the same extent.

After a customer has used an organisation's services or products the selling organisation may wish to know what the customer thought about the service or the goods they received. The organisation can check satisfaction using different methods such as:

- a written survey such as a pre-printed form or questionnaire which is posted out to the customer with a reply-paid envelope

- telephoning the customer and asking a series of pre-set questions

- e-mailing a customer with a questionnaire/written survey for on-line completion

- holding a meeting of customers (usually called a focus group). While some questions may be pre-determined, discussions may stray from the questions asked

- face-to-face interviews which can be done at the point of sale or later on but are usually on a one-to-one basis

- membership groups of customers who are prepared to identify with the product or service and feed back information regularly

- 'mystery shoppers', where the treatment of potential customers is experienced by people employed for the purpose

- suggestion schemes which are often used for both internal and external customers

- freephone or video booth opportunities.

Written surveys

The most common types of surveys used are written surveys.

Advantages of written surveys

- A written survey gives the customer the opportunity to comment and makes them feel valued.

- A questionnaire can be issued immediately after the customer has had dealings with the organisation and the experience is still fresh in the customer's mind.

- Written surveys are completed by individuals in isolation, uninfluenced by other peoples' experience as customers.

- A permanent record is created which can be compared with previous surveys over a period of time.

- Results can be analysed and statistics extracted by computer.

Disadvantages of written surveys

- The number of responses received from written surveys is usually very low and may not be representative of the whole customer base.

- The people who respond may only be those who are either very satisfied or very dissatisfied and the results may not, therefore, be very accurate.

- Written surveys are costly in terms of time. The survey has to be prepared, printed and sent out, and it may take some time for responses to be returned. The responses then need to be summarised and analysed. Software packages are available to help with this task.

- The wording of questions is crucial. Questions should be pre-tested to ensure they are unambiguous, clear and understandable. Those being surveyed are unlikely to seek clarification of any questions which they do not understand but are more likely not to complete the questionnaire.

- Many surveys are based on box ticking so that the customer can indicate the level of satisfaction with the service received. This type of question tends to be inflexible.

Telephone surveys

Telephone surveys are becoming increasingly used with a huge rise in the use of call centres which undertake these surveys. Most telephone surveys are outsourced.

Advantages of telephone surveys

- They are a useful public relations exercise making all those contacted feel valued.

- They generate instant data which can be used for fine tuning customer service strategies.

- This kind of survey is cheap compared with other methods, particularly when it can be outsourced to a specialist call centre.

- Responses can usually be entered directly into a software package.

- Any ambiguous questions can be explained.

Disadvantages of telephone surveys

- Customers may resent being interrupted at work or at home at the time of the call.

- Customers may think there is a hidden agenda like trying to sell some other product.

- Questions often have to be very simple when only given verbally. Complex questions cannot be used.

- If the organisation has outsourced the survey to a third party they may not be able to explain the question to the customer if the customer does not understand what is being asked. Those asking the questions may not be interested in any additional comments made by customers or may miss important points.

- They may only reach certain groups of customer.

Focus groups

Focus groups bring together groups of customers for the purpose of feeding back information on products or services.

Advantages of focus groups

- A pre-determined number of customers can be invited to a focus group so you can guarantee the number of responses.

- The organisation gets instant feedback from a focus group. They do not have to wait until information is returned and analysed.

- Those invited to a focus group will feel valued and are likely to give more positive responses than they might on a written survey.

- The dynamics of the group may lead to an infectious positive feedback.

- Customers may give more considered responses because everyone is given the opportunity to speak.

- Any questions which the customers do not understand can be clarified or re-worded so that they can be clearly understood.

- Additional questions can be asked to probe any issues which arise.

Disadvantages of focus groups

- There may be a time delay between the customer buying the product or service and the meeting of the focus group.

- All customers cannot be invited to the focus group so the organisation is sampling responses right from the start.

- The interaction of the individuals in the group may lead to an infectious negative experience and feedback.

- They tend to be irregularly held events.

- Focus groups can be expensive to run as expenses will have to be paid and appropriate accommodation booked for meetings.

Face-to-face interviews

Face-to-face interviews may be deemed appropriate in some cases, especially where information is confidential, for example, if research is being done into financial services. Here interviews are usually on a one-to-one basis.

Advantages of face-to-face interviews

- These are usually one-to-one allowing for interaction between interviewer and interviewee.
- They allow for more subtle questioning.
- They can be useful for expanding basic statistical information.
- They are often used as a way of identifying major issues for a more comprehensive survey.

Disadvantages of face-to-face interviews

- They can be longer and more time-consuming.
- They are less structured and therefore often more difficult to summarise what has been reported.
- They are expensive.
- Few people are reached by this type of interview as it is labour intensive.

Membership groups

Membership groups usually grow out of some kind of brand loyalty, for example, a particular product which is seen as having a cult following. To some extent members have already shown a brand loyalty by joining the group.

Advantages of membership groups

- They are often formed for 'defensive' reasons: these groups often act as watchdogs or good ambassadors for a product (for example, Reliant Robin clubs, Harley-Davidson owners).
- They create real brand loyalty.
- Their activities often create a more desirable product for the public in general and their existence may even increase demand.
- They allow the organisation to keep tabs on what these customers do, for example, with supermarket loyalty cards.

Disadvantages of membership groups

- The feedback often is biased in favour of the product.
- Membership of the group may mean that the members are treated differently from other customers.

Mystery shopper

A mystery shopper is where customer service is sampled by someone acting as a 'real' shopper who logs and evaluates the service received.

Advantages of the mystery shopper

- This gives a really clear *sample* of what a potential customer might experience.
- It is good for giving a starting point for other types of survey.

Disadvantages of the mystery shopper

- It does not allow for variations in the standard of service throughout the organisation.
- It is likely only to assess front line customer service.
- There may be hostility from the company's employees.

ADMINISTRATIVE SERVICES

Suggestion schemes, video booths and freephone lines

Other kinds of surveys and feedback arrangements include suggestion schemes, video booths and freephone lines dedicated to customers.

Advantages of suggestion schemes

- These are good for internal use, particularly if there is a reward attached, for example, a voucher for each suggestion adopted.

- They work well with regular customers, for example, in the hospitality industry, to ensure the organisation is providing what is required.

Disadvantages of suggestion schemes

- Many customers ignore the opportunity to complete feedback slips and as a result feedback may focus on very good or very poor customer service.

Advantages of freephone lines or video booth

- They allow customers to react to service immediately as they are often in-house.

- They allow customers reporting poor service to remain anonymous.

Disadvantages of freephone lines or video booth

- If used on their own they can be very reactive rather than pro-active, in that those who respond are likely to be reacting to very good or very poor customer service.

Customer Service Level Agreements

A Customer Service Level Agreement (SLA) sets expectations between the customer and the provider. It addresses five key aspects:

- What the supplier is providing.

- How the supplier will deliver on those promises.

- Who will measure the delivery and how.

- What happens if the provider fails to deliver as promised.

- How the Service Level Agreement will be reviewed.

It is a means of opening up communication between customer and supplier. A service level agreement ensures responsibilities are documented and this in turn allows customers to know what to expect. A service level agreement will usually have two elements to it – service and management.

The service element will document items like:

- the services provided and those not provided, for example, carriage of goods might be extra

- the conditions of service, for example, what the customer has to do in terms of timing of order

- the standard of service, for example, turnaround times for the service or supply of goods

- the responsibilities of both parties

- any costs involved in providing extra services

- what happens if this agreement is broken.

The management elements will include items like:

- how effectiveness will be measured and tracked
- how any complaints should be reported and addressed
- how any disagreements will be settled
- how the agreement will be reviewed and revised.

Before an agreement is drawn up the parties concerned should:

- know exactly what they are looking for in terms of giving service and what service they are prepared to accept. This means that the organisation providing the service should not make rash promises which are unlikely to be kept. All promises should be realistic – remember under-promise and over-deliver

- know what the other party is prepared to accept in terms of an agreement. Both parties should ideally have an idea of the kind of agreement they expect to enter into

- have a clear understanding of the process of working together. Good negotiations and flagging up potential difficulties are the keystone of good customer relationships.

The agreement should be developed, discussed and negotiated and this may take several weeks or months in big contracts. Once a draft has been decided it should be circulated to all concerned prior to being signed. This gives everyone a chance to make alterations or raise issues. If this phase is carried out correctly, buy-in from all those concerned can be expected.

It would be normal, prior to the final document being signed, to ensure that processes (for tracking, reporting progress, etc.) are developed in a way that satisfies both parties. There will also usually be a point of contact established to ensure that it is working, reviewed regularly and that all staff meet the service level agreed.

Here is an example of an internal service level agreement for printing services in John Nicholls department store.

John Nicholls Print Rooms: Statement of Service

This sets out the level of service that you can expect from John Nicholls' Print Rooms. All that we ask is that you tell us precisely what your requirements are. It is important that you tell us the correct page count, the number of copies you need, and which unit or section you are in – and that you do this on our Print Room Request forms. You can also add special instructions, if they are required – the Print Room staff can help you with this. Remember printed copies can be sent to us in hard copy or by e-mail. All requests received will generate an e-mail receipt which will indicate when the order can be uplifted.

You can find the request form on the John Nicholls Intranet, under Print Room.

Quality Consciousness

We will make proof copies of all jobs and will check them conscientiously. We will also sample copies throughout the run to make sure that the quality is consistently high. You can check a proof of your job before we start your print run. There is a special box to request this service on our Print Room Request form.

continued ➤

Confidentiality

If you request it, we can store confidential documents in our safe throughout the print run. We will also return any confidential waste to you. We'll make whatever special arrangements you request so that your document is controlled as much as is necessary. For example, we can run the job at specific times with a member of your staff on hand to supervise.

Booking Production Time

You can reserve production time in advance. This will help to guarantee production when our deadlines are tight. For example, if you need 5,000 copies of a 100 page document you can arrange with us that we will provide you with 200 a day until your order is complete.

Turnaround Times Provided

We will schedule your job as soon as we are told about it. This means that we can give you an estimated time of completion within one hour of receiving your order. We guarantee that all requests for copying will be carried out within 48 hours of receipt.

Production of Orders

Moderately-sized print jobs can be produced next day – provided that we receive your order by 12 noon. For example, if you need 20 copies of a 15 page document for a meeting on Wednesday afternoon – get it to us before noon on Tuesday and it will be ready.

Here are our contact names and our locations

Karen Thoms	Glasgow	Ext 2437
Cecilia McManus	Hightown	Ext 3357
Paul Brydon	Edinburgh	Ext 4487

Here is an example of an extract of an external Service Level Agreement John Nicholls Department Store has with an On-Line catalogue provider called IS.

The On-line Catalogue as used by John Nicholls should be available to all Internet customers. IS guarantees that:

The On-line Catalogue will be available 24 hours a day, 7 days a week excepting revision times which will not exceed 2 hours in any one day up to a maximum of 5 days. Any more than this will constitute a violation.

The IS Customer Care Team will respond to service incidents that affect users within 1 hour, and update the website with a status message within 15 minutes. IS will resolve any problem within 2 working days. Missing any of these deadlines would constitute a violation.

This SLA may change to reflect the improvement and/or changes to technology. It will be reviewed every 6 months and updated as necessary. When updates are deemed necessary, the customer will be asked to review and approve any changes.

Penalties

1>5 violations	Penalty of £500 reduction in fees
5>10 violations	Penalty of £2000 reduction in fees and a corrective action plan.

Why are Service Level Agreements Important?

SLAs allow organisations to set boundaries and expectations for both the supplier and the customer. They allow key performance indicators to be established. The supplying organisation can clearly see where they have not met standards and where they have failed. The customer can also see where service has fallen short of expectations and might reasonably expect some compensation.

> ### Check your Progress 5.1
>
> 1   You are a member of the Healthy Eating Committee in your school/college. You want to gauge customer opinion of the food provided in your centre. You want feedback quickly so that it can be actioned quickly. What type of customer survey would you recommend carrying out and why?
>
> 2   Why do organisations want to have service level agreements with their suppliers?

Complaints Procedures

In all organisations things do go wrong sometimes. Complaints can be an opportunity for the organisation to show commitment to their customers and demonstrate that complaints are handled effectively. When things do go wrong your customers should know how to contact you and complain. Most organisations have an established complaints procedure which enables them to log complaints and ensure they are dealt with in a way which informs future customer service. Software packages are available to help with this process.

Organisations will operate a system where:

- Any complaints received, regardless of how they are made – verbal, e-mail, phone, in person or written – are logged and given a reference number.

- Those who handle complaints are given careful training and are skilled in apologising, listening, establishing the facts, agreeing with the customer what to do and then, crucially, doing it.

- A specific customer liaison department or special mailbox or even the chief executive's name is used. It is often effective to have the same person deal with the complaint from start to finish, giving the customer a person to refer to.

- All complaints received are acknowledged immediately, usually in writing, along with details outlining the process of investigation which will take place with key times, for example, 'We will investigate your complaint and will contact you again within five working days'.

- All complaints are given a high priority. Clear timelines should be established to ensure prompt investigation and any deviation from the given timelines should be communicated to the customer.

- The result of the investigation is communicated to the customer and, if appropriate, compensation of some kind may be offered.

- The process of investigation is tracked internally.

- All complaints are reviewed on a regular basis by a senior member of staff to identify any patterns or issues which the organisation should address.

- The complaints procedure is transparent and available to all customers and known to all staff.

Here is an example of John Nicholls' customer complaints and feedback procedure.

Customer Complaints and Feedback Procedure

We are committed to ensuring that all our customers receive the best possible service from John Nicholls. However, we realise that sometimes our customers may experience problems. We also recognise that complaints are a valuable form of feedback on our goods, services and delivery. We use this feedback to identify the root causes of any complaints and to ensure that as a result of this feedback, improvements are made to our processes for the benefit of our customers.

We promise you

- We will listen to you.

- We will make every effort to understand the reasons for your complaint.

- We care that we have failed to meet your expectations.

- We will try to resolve your problems at your first point of contact.

- We will offer fair solutions quickly.

- We welcome positive feedback from all our customers about our goods, services and staff.

Making a complaint

You can make a complaint to any of our staff who will do their best to resolve any issues there and then. If your complaint cannot be resolved immediately or if the matter is very serious, you should ensure the complaint is formal. Formal complaints and feedback should be made in writing, by fax or by e-mail to any member of our staff.

Your complaint will be entered into our formal complaints process and will be acknowledged within 2 working days.

You can expect to receive a considered response within 10 working days. If we cannot resolve the issue within 10 working days, we will keep you informed of the delay and will give you a date by which you can expect a full response.

If you are unhappy with the response we make you should contact the Managing Director, directly. He will review your complaint and our response and a reply will be sent to you within 5 working days.

Task 4

Look up the customer service section for Sainsbury's (www.j-sainsbury.co.uk), Debenhams (www.debenhams.co.uk) and one other shop of your choice and identify their procedures. How clear are they?

Task 5

See if your school or college has a complaints procedure. Would you know what to do if you had a complaint?

Quality Management Systems

The responsibility for the approach taken to managing quality rests with management. Over recent years there has been a much greater emphasis on the whole concept of quality and how an organisation measures up against others in the same field – think about league tables of exam results and hospital waiting lists. Quality management includes monitoring standards to ensure that products and services conform to the standard customers want, so customers have a big influence on setting the quality demanded.

Quality standards will influence appearance, safety, availability, after-sales support, customer service and value for money. The attainment of any quality standard has to have commitment and participation of all members of staff – this is often known as buy-in.

Many organisations follow particular quality standards for their industry, e.g. Chartermark, ISO 9000, Scottish Quality Management System, British Standards BS5750 and European Foundation for Quality Management (EFQM). In some industries it is common practice only to deal with organisations who hold a particular quality standard. Most of these standards involve organisations providing evidence of continual monitoring and quality improvement activities as well as quality manuals which set out policy, procedures and quality standards which are followed by all in the organisation. The accent is on quality assurance and quality improvement rather than quality control – that is to say that organisations are looking to ensure that the quality of what they do is maintained at a high level and that improvement of standards is constantly being sought as opposed to correcting what has gone wrong.

Total Quality Management

Total quality management (TQM) aims to improve the quality of products and services through on-going review and feedback and then subsequent refinement. The main principle of this system is that it aims to improve quality through pleasing the customer – the customer's needs are valued above all else. This customer can be internal as well as external. The next person in a production chain or service chain is as important to the organisation as the final customer. Although TQM can be costly to initiate, it should save money in the longer run because much less time has to be spent dealing with complaints or faulty goods.

The adoption of a total quality management approach means that:

- Everyone in the organisation has to understand the importance of TQM.

- Management have to show commitment by providing resources needed to set up and run the system.

- All staff have to be consulted and involved in setting standards and trained in the systems adopted.

- A team approach has to be encouraged as well as an open atmosphere which encourages people to identify improvements.

- A quality plan has be to be written and agreed and should include not only procedures and standards but also arrangements about checking that quality standards have been met.

- There will be a constant striving for quality improvement.

Total quality management has four main elements which have to be managed:

1   Quality has to be defined at each stage of the process.

2   Commitment of all staff is very important.

3   A system where quality can be measured.

4   A method of ensuring quality.

1 Defining quality

The main principle is that the customer defines quality, so much time and effort will go into customer research to find the quality they want, the service they want, the standard of safety, the cost, etc. of the product. Research will be done using some of the methods outlined earlier in this chapter. Remember, though, that there is a customer at each stage in this system so quality has to be defined throughout the production or service process.

2 Commitment

The organisation will usually show its commitment to quality in various ways:

- In its mission statement – most organisations have a qualitative statement.

- In customer service agreements clearly outlining the rights and obligations of supplier and customer.

- In a quality manual or operational handbook which outlines all procedures in the organisation.

- In standard operating procedures which indicate how consistency will be achieved.

- In a quality auditing system which monitors that consistency has been achieved.

- By training staff and involving them in ensuring quality.

3 Measuring quality

Here are some things the organisation will have to do to support total quality management. They will need:

- to ensure that there is appropriate documentation to set out requirements clearly, to record progress and the quality achieved

- to ensure record keeping is accurate and consistent

- systems which review, monitor and feed back information

- comprehensive job descriptions for all posts in the organisation

- some kind of appraisal or performance management system which includes targets

- to provide clear instructions, information and standards which are understandable to all.

4 Ensuring quality

Methods of ensuring quality standards have been met have to be developed. This can be helped by using the following techniques.

- Benchmarking against other standards. This could involve comparisons with another provider in the same area or with the industry's averages or industry's best. Sometimes it is difficult to get reliable figures for comparison, for example, with NHS figures and in education.

- A quality circle is a group which meets regularly to try to make improvements and solve problems. Ideally a quality circle will include people from different levels in the organisation, in particular those who form part of the service chain where areas interact.

The quality cycle can be summarised in the diagram below.

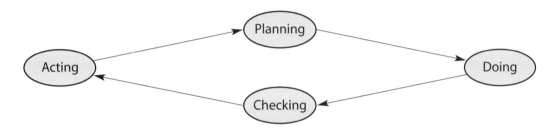

The planning phase is where the problem is defined and information is collected to determine the scope of the problem. In the doing phase, a solution is developed and implemented and a way of measuring effectiveness is decided on. In the checking phase the results are confirmed using before and after comparisons. In the acting phase results are documented and processes are changed.

Internal Assessment

Here are some examples of the kind of questions you might be asked as part of your internal assessment at Intermediate 2.

1   Outline two benefits to the customer of a customer service policy. (2)

2   Outline two benefits to the organisation of a customer service policy. (2)

3   What is a mission statement and why is it important? (4)

Here are some examples of the kind of questions you might be asked as part of your internal assessment at Higher.

1   Describe two possible effects of bad customer service for the organisation. (4)

2   Explain the benefits of providing effective customer care for the organisation. (4)

3   Outline the purpose of a service level agreement and describe two benefits of having service level agreements. (4)

4   What is a focus group and when would it be used? (3)

ADMINISTRATIVE SERVICES

External Assessment

Here are some examples of the kind of questions you might be asked as part of your external assessment. An estimate of the marks assigned to each question is indicated and it would be anticipated that each question would form part of a larger question.

1   Describe the consequences of poor customer service to the organisation. (2)

2   What is a mission statement and why do organisations choose to have one? (4)

1   Compare and contrast two different methods of gauging customer opinion. (8)

2   Outline the importance of a customer service policy. (6)

CHAPTER 6

Functional Departments

This chapter is about the functional departments in an organisation and the kind of activities carried out in each department. It also looks at some documents which are used by organisations.

Intermediate 2 Level Outcomes: ▯▯▯➡

It includes from Intermediate 2 Administrative Services Outcome 3:

☆ **the role of the Sales, Purchasing, Finance and Human Resources departments**

☆ **the kind of activities carried out in each of the above departments**

☆ **the use of business documents.**

Note: Application forms, job descriptions and person specifications are covered in Chapters 1 and 4. Contracts of employment, holiday rotas, staff rotas and training request forms are covered in Chapter 4.

Functional Grouping

All organisations are different. Not only do they have different priorities but they have different structures and it is therefore difficult to define a 'typical' business organisation. However, most businesses do have to carry out certain activities, for example, dealing with the accounts, marketing and selling their goods and services to customers, purchasing goods or raw materials, and dealing with staff and staffing issues. Often these activities and the people who do them are grouped together within an organisation and when this happens the groupings are called functional sections or functional departments.

Advantages of functional grouping

Each section or department is likely to have a manager or section head who will be closely involved in the overall performance of the organisation as a whole. There are certain advantages to organisations of grouping together staff who work on similar areas.

Functional grouping can:

- **lead to more efficient use of resources**
- **ensure staff in each functional area all follow the same 'code of practice' or sets of procedures**
- **allow employees to develop real skills in certain areas, for example, dealing with VAT and Customs and Excise**
- **provide a clear promotional structure for staff**
- **improve communication and support for staff in a specialist area**
- **allow good team working practices to develop**
- **develop better co-ordination within the department.**

Disadvantages of functional grouping

On the other hand having specialists working together in groups may result in:

- **processes becoming very routine and boring**
- **poorer communication between departments**
- **a slowing down of communication between different parts of the organisation as people often see other departments as having nothing to do with them and buck passing can become common**
- **decisions taking a long time to be reached.**

The following functions are likely to be carried out in most organisations: Sales (which will usually include marketing), Purchasing, Finance and Human Resources.

Sales Department

The main function or role of this department is to create orders for the goods and services of the organisation. Many organisations employ large sales forces, for example, sales staff in a retail department store like John Nicholls or sales representatives geographically distributed across the country, Europe or even the world. If the organisation sells mainly to individuals, as opposed to other organisations, it is likely to have a bigger sales force.

Here are some of the major activities the sales department will have to carry out for the organisation.

- It will control and organise the selling and distribution of the organisation's products and services.

- It will handle communications with customers.

- It will have systems established to deal with enquiries, orders received, distribution arrangements and any problems encountered.

- It may have an input into discussing the creditworthiness of customers.

- It will draw up a sales plan with appropriate targets which have to be met by different sections of the organisation. In a department store this would mean sales targets for the toy department, ladies clothing department, electrical department, etc. In the case of an international operation, there might be individual sales targets for each country where the organisation is represented, for example, Poland, France, India.

- It will provide summaries of previous sales figures and comparisons of current results with targets, highlighting where targets were not met and where results were better than anticipated.

- It will provide information on the level of profit made from the current sales levels.

- It will deal with guarantees, warranties and other after-sales service (unless a specialist department is involved or these are outsourced to another organisation).

- It will link closely with and may even include the warehousing or distribution section of the business to ensure that goods are available and can be distributed to customers by agreed dates. This is greatly helped by computer technology – sales staff can now check stock in warehouses on a terminal and can tell customers when new deliveries are due. Stock sold can be re-ordered immediately or even automatically.

Many sales departments include a marketing section or specialist marketing staff. Marketing is responsible for ensuring that customers' needs are understood and taken into account at all times. This part of the department would be expected to:

- carry out market research to find out what customers want

- ensure that products which are being designed and developed or bought in for re-sale will satisfy the needs of customers

- ensure that the products available are at the right price and available in the right quantities

- ensure that prices which are competitive in the market will still give an appropriate return to the organisation and will still be priced right for customers

- conduct promotional activities to encourage sales

- make sure that the products are available where customers want them

- ensure customer satisfaction by doing surveys and dealing with any complaints.

The sales department may also include a warehouse and distribution section which is responsible for running a cost effective way of making sure goods reach customers at the right time and in the right condition. This would include:

- keeping a check on both inward and outward movements of stock

- ensuring goods are kept in the correct storage conditions, for example, at the correct temperature

- ensuring goods are rotated and that older goods do not end up being wasted because of the way they have been stored or because they are past their sell-by date because of the way that goods have (or in this case have not) been rotated

- watching stock levels are neither too big or too small

- ensuring that all paperwork is in order before goods are received or sent out to customers

- maintaining a secure system of stock control to minimise theft.

You will look at some of the business documents used in this department, such as quotations, delivery notes, invoices and credit notes, later in this chapter. The sales department will also keep records on its customers, their credit rating and their sales history.

The Purchasing Department

In some organisations the purchasing function is concentrated in one department. This is particularly the case when goods are being produced by the organisation as opposed to bought in and resold by the organisation. The main activities of the purchasing department will be:

- ensuring that sufficient stocks of raw materials, goods and components have been purchased to enable production lines to run efficiently without hold-ups

- predicting demand for all raw materials or goods the organisation is likely to demand. This is particularly important when the goods or raw materials come from overseas or have a long delivery time

- obtaining all goods and services at the best possible price and also on good credit terms from regular suppliers

- ensuring that all goods are delivered on time

- ensuring that the goods delivered are of the right quality

- linking closely with any store or warehousing facilities in the organisation to make sure that there is sufficient space to store the goods purchased. Internal requests for goods (requisitions) will either go direct to the purchasing department or to the stores/warehousing section of the business. An example of an internal requisition form is shown below. You will see that it is like a simplified order form – it performs the function of an internal order form.

REQUISITION FORM	
REQUISITION SLIP	
From (Name of the department requiring the goods)	
Quantity	Description
Special Requirements (for example, the date when the goods are required)	
Date	Authorised by (Signed by an authorised person)

In addition to requisition forms the purchasing department will use enquiries, orders and stock control records. You will see some of these documents later in the chapter.

Finance

The finance department is concerned with three main activities.

- Financial accounting, i.e. managing the capital and the cash funds of the organisation. This function is concerned with raising money from banks and investors and making sure that the interest is paid on loans or dividends paid to shareholders.

- Management accounting. This aspect is concerned with providing the managers of the organisation with sufficient financial information to help them make decisions. This will include predictions and forecasts as well as analysis of past activities. This section will negotiate budgets within the organisation, usually with managers, and highlight alternative courses of action.

- Financial reporting, i.e. collecting and presenting facts and figures used in financial and management accounting. The information will be gathered in a systematic way to show the profit of the organisation and the assets held – producing ultimately the profit and loss account and the balance sheet.

The main purposes of any financial reporting system are to:

- provide managers with information to ensure they have financial knowledge of the areas under their control

- help managers formulate budgets and plans based on estimates of spending and income

- allocate expenses in accordance with the plans laid down by senior managers

- use standard procedures which can be audited by an external body

- ensure that there are procedures for checking differences between budgets and actual spending so that spending can be controlled

- ensure that all financial information is recorded accurately

- store records in a secure way which is accessible to authorised personnel

- have appropriate records available for inspection by the organisation's auditors, the Inland Revenue (for tax purposes) and Customs and Excise (for VAT purposes)

- gather information for the end of year accounts.

Part of the duties of this department may also focus on assessing and controlling the level of credit given to customers by establishing a credit limit based on their ability to pay and their past history with the organisation. The finance department deals with the organisation's financial records, expense claims, cheques and bills received, as well as the records required for tax purposes & VAT. It will also be involved with receiving payment from customers and for issuing invoices and statements along with the sales department.

Human Resources Department

The human resources (HR) department, sometimes called the personnel department, plays an important role in any organisation, acting as an adviser (for example, in terms of Health and Safety), an enabler and a facilitator (such as bringing together those who are in dispute over pay). You have already looked at some of the activities carried out by the Human Resources Department. Additionally, the HR department is responsible for:

- Manpower planning which includes determining what overall staff requirements the organisation has in the long term as well as short term planning such as co-ordinating holiday rotas and staff rotas. Some of this departmental planning may be carried out at departmental level but is likely to be done using a system devised by HR.

- Co-ordinating and arranging all of the training requirements of the organisation and will also co-ordinate any career review or appraisal arrangements. Training requirements will be identified through the career review or personal development planning process as well as through the organisation's overall strategic and operational plans.

- The administration of salaries, although this may be jointly undertaken with the finance department, especially when expenses are involved.

- All issues involving employees including industrial relations, pay negotiations and any issues where staff feel they have a grievance.

- Keeping accurate and up-to-date records on employees. This would include any training undertaken which would be logged in the employee's Continuing Professional Development record. Much of the information held by the HR department is regarded as confidential.

Many of the above functions will be carried out jointly with the relevant department, for example, if the sales department wanted to recruit more sales people both departments would be involved; or if a member of the finance department felt he was being bullied and took out a grievance against his manager the two departments would also work together.

There are many types of ducuments used in the HR department. Some of these have already been looked at in Chapter 2 and Chapter 4 – application forms, job descriptions, person specificstions, contracts of employment, personal development planning forms. Additionally you would expect to see holiday rotas, staff rotas, annual leave sheets, career review or appraisal forms, forms for requesting training, training evaluation forms, self certified sickness forms and forms for recording continuing professional development. In some organisations, such as where staff are working with the young or vulnerable, you might also find Disclosure information on employees.

Example of a Holiday rota for June and July for John Nicholls

Department	Manager	Week Beg 01/06/..	Week Beg 08/06/..	Week Beg 15/06/..	Week Beg 22/06/..	Week Beg 29/06/..	Week Beg 06/07/..	Week Beg 13/07/..	Week Beg 20/07/..	Week Beg 27/07/..
Furniture	Kamal Ahmed		▓							
Cosmetics	Rena Carter				▓		▓			
Bathrooms	Susan Shields			▓		▓				
Cosmetics – JN only	Loraine Duval							▓	▓	
Ladies Clothing	Naiem Reda					▓				
Children's clothing	Anne Wilson									
Gents Clothing	Alistair McKay						▓			
Electrical	Jeff Quigley									
Household	Ellen Divers		▓							
China	Ruby Dalziel			▓						
Glassware	Gordon Stratford			▓						
Soft furnishings	Gary Davidson				▓	▓				
Accessories	Sandra Melbourne									▓
Gifts	Sonia Ben Arefi									
Toys	Gail Shields					▓		▓	▓	
Sports	Orla Coyle						▓			

Check your Progress

6.1

1   Why would a furniture manufacturer have a separate sales department?
    Outline the likely role of the sales department in that organisation.

2   What are the benefits to an organisation of having a centralised functional
    department for purchasing?

Documents used in Buying and Selling Goods

Although there are an increasing number of ways of selling goods, such as telephone ordering
and buying on the Internet, many organisations still organise their buying and selling on paper-
based systems. This is particularly the case where goods are imported and exported. The
following is a summary of the use of the common documents used in a business transaction.

A transaction is shown below using the documents we will look at.

Buyer		Seller
Enquiry	→→→	
	←←←	Reply with catalogue, price list, quotation or estimate
Order	→→→	
	←←←	Advice Note if special arrangements for delivery have to be made
	←←←	Goods and Delivery Note
	←←←	Invoice
Faulty or wrong goods	→→→	
	←←←	Credit Note
	←←←	Statement
Cheque	→→→	

Transaction of buying and selling goods

An Enquiry

Enquiries about products can be made by telephone, in person or in writing. A written enquiry
is sent from the potential buyer to the seller. An enquiry from one business to another would
normally take the form of a letter printed on headed paper or a specially printed enquiry form.
It would detail what information the enquirer wanted to know. This could be a request for a
catalogue, a request for prices, details of products or services and information on delivery
charges and delivery dates. It could also be a request for an estimate where catalogues do not
exist, such as an estimate for building work or repair to a car. The potential buyer might send
out several enquiries to different potential suppliers. Let's look at a transaction where
John Nicholls Department Store is looking to buy 100 leather handbags from a supplier called
Mojo Bags. Here is an example of an enquiry sent by John Nicholls to Mojo Bags.

John Nicholls

47 Great Emperor Street
GLASGOW
GF1 7JN
Telephone 0141 5688000
E-mail purchasing@JNstores.co.uk

Enquiry

SM/KL

5 June 20..

The Sales Department
Mojo Bags
46 Great Rushford Street
NORWICH
NN6 7RS

Dear Sirs

We are interested in purchasing the following products which we saw at the recent Handbag International Trade Show in Milan.

100 Fortuny leather bags

Could you please let us know

- the colours available
- the price per bag
- the time it would take for an order of this size to be delivered
- if delivery is included in the price and
- any trade discount we would receive on this order.

I look forward to hearing from you.

Yours faithfully

Sandra Melbourne
Manager

Quotation, Price List and Catalogue

A quotation is sent by the seller to the buyer in response to an enquiry and is often accompanied by details of the products. For example, the supplier might send back a catalogue with a price list. A price list will give a detailed list of all products with their prices whereas a catalogue is usually illustrated and usually only includes pictures of some of the range of products available. Often a catalogue will have the price list printed separately rather than printed prices appearing beside the goods illustrated in the catalogue. This allows the

organisation to update their price list without the expense of changing the printed catalogue which is usually a glossy, more expensive document. An estimate is usually sent where it is a big job or several different kinds of workers are involved, for example, building work. An estimate indicates approximate prices. Firm prices are shown in a quotation.

Quotations will often be timebound, and will include a statement like 'this price stands for 28 days from the date of this quotation'. Terms are usually stated in a quotation. By terms we mean any discounts available to other traders – trade discount or any discounts available for settling the bill promptly such as a cash discount. The supplier may offer discounts for big orders or to regular customers or to new customers they wish to attract. Any delivery charges will be detailed and the likely delivery time will be indicated. A quotation can be a form or a letter. Here is an example of a quotation sent from Mojo Bags to John Nicholls.

Mojo Bags

46 Great Rushford Street
NORWICH
NN6 7RS
Telephone 01298 587609
E-mail mojoworks.co.uk

TT/HG

9 June 20..

Ms S Melbourne
John Nicholls
47 Great Emperor Street
GLASGOW
GF1 7JN

Dear Ms Melbourne

Thank you for your enquiry about Fortuny Bags. We had a huge number of orders for Fortuny bags as a result of the Milan show and consequently orders will take a minimum of 4 weeks from receipt until despatch. There is no charge for delivery and we use Fastrak Services who guarantee UK deliveries within 48 hours.

The bags are available in Navy, Black, Red and Tan. I enclose a copy of our catalogue with sample leathers attached.

The trade price per bag is £50 + VAT and in cases where orders exceed £500 a 10% discount will be given to new and existing trade customers.

If there is anything else you need to know please do not hesitate to get in touch.

Yours sincerely

Ishmail Ravi

Ishmail Ravi

Enc

Order

Once the potential customer has decided where they are going to place the order they will complete an order form and send it to the seller. Often there will be an order form in a supplier's catalogue. If you, as an individual customer, were to order from a mail order catalogue you would normally complete a pre-printed order form produced by the seller but in business it is usual practice for the buyer to order on the buyer's own stationery.

All orders are numbered sequentially – this is important to prevent fraud and help in the auditing process. Usually only certain people in an organisation are allowed to order goods and often an authorised signature is asked for, i.e. someone who is authorised to order goods by their job remit or the level of their post. There are likely to be limits on the value of goods which can be ordered at any one time or by any one person. In large organisations, orders often have to be placed through the purchasing department and the purchasing department may also make decisions about where orders are to be placed. This is usually so that the organisation can buy in bulk. A good example of this would be when stationery, like photocopying paper, is ordered. It would be more economical for the organisation to send in one big order than for each department to order their own supplies. A big order would cost less and would require only one delivery.

An order will contain a description of the product, a catalogue or reference number, the quantity ordered and the address where the goods are to be delivered. Notice it does not *have* to contain the price although many order forms do have prices on them.

Here is an example of the order which would be sent by John Nicholls to Mojo Bags for the goods they want.

Order No | AD 49867/108 | **John Nicholls**
47 Great Emperor Street
GLASGOW
GF1 7JN
Telephone 0141 5688000
E-mail purchasing@JNstores.co.uk

14 June 20..

Mr I Ravi
Mojo Bags
46 Great Rushford Street
NORWICH
NN6 7RS

Please supply the following

Item	Catalogue No	Quantity
Fortuny Bags Black	365/11	40
Fortuny Bags Navy	365/12	25
Fortuny Bags Red	365/13	25
Fortuny Bags Tan	365/14	10

DELIVER TO: The above address

AUTHORISED BY: *Sandra Melbourne*

Advice Note

An advice note is often sent by the seller to the buyer to inform them that the goods are ready for despatch. It is often a copy of the delivery note (see below). It is very important to have an advice note if special arrangements have to be made prior to the delivery, for example, if it is a very bulky item which requires special lifting equipment or it is a huge order which will take up a lot of space. Many organisations, particularly those dealing with routine repeat orders which require no special arrangements for delivery to be made, no longer use advice notes.

Delivery Note

A delivery note is sent at the same time as the goods from the seller to the buyer. It is usually prepared at the same time as the advice note and often the invoice (see below) and will have exactly the same details. It is the responsibility of the person receiving the goods to ensure that the goods delivered correspond with those detailed on the delivery note. Any differences (sometimes called discrepancies) must be detailed on the note and should be confirmed by the person delivering the goods.

The delivery note will have the number of items ordered as well as their reference numbers but will not have prices. It is often a copy of the invoice with the prices blanked out. The purpose of the delivery note is to enable the buying organisation to check what has been delivered and allows the buying organisation to put the items received into their stock control systems. A copy of the delivery note will be kept by the delivery person as proof of delivery. It is important that the buying organisation does not sign for something which is not there because they will be charged for what they have signed for. Delivery notes should be checked against the order which was sent for the goods. Here is an example of a delivery note from Mojo Bags.

DELIVERY NOTE

Mojo Bags
46 Great Rushford Street
NORWICH
NN6 7RS
Telephone 01298 587609
E-mail mojoworks.co.uk

Vat no 675/75876/32

14 July 20..

Goods delivered to:

John Nicholls
47 Great Emperor Street
GLASGOW
GF1 7JN

Order Number: AD49867/108

Item	Catalogue No	Quantity	Unit Price	VAT	Total price
Fortuny Bags Black	365/11	40			
Fortuny Bags Navy	365/12	25			
Fortuny Bags Red	365/13	25			
Fortuny Bags Tan	365/14	10			
Total					

Goods received by Name (printed) Jim Ward

Signature   *Jim Ward*

Date 14 July 20..

Invoice

An invoice is a bill sent from the seller to the buyer for the goods which have been supplied. If the buyer only buys occasionally the seller will expect the buyer to pay the invoice when they receive it or within a month. If, however, the buyer is a regular customer the seller may send the buyer a monthly bill called a statement (see below).

All invoices should be carefully checked against the delivery note and order reference to ensure that every item ordered has been received and the calculations on the invoice should also be checked before payment is authorised. Here is an example of the invoice that Mojo Bags would send to John Nicholls.

Mojo Bags

46 Great Rushford Street
NORWICH
NN6 7RS
Telephone 01298 587609
E-mail mojoworks.co.uk

INVOICE

Vat no 675/75876/32

20 July 20..

Goods delivered to:

John Nicholls
47 Great Emperor Street
GLASGOW
GF1 7JN

Order Number: AD49867/108
Invoice Number: 9008

Item	Catalogue No	Quantity	Unit Price	Total price
Fortuny Bags Black	365/11	40	£50	£2000.00
Fortuny Bags Navy	365/12	25	£50	£1250.00
Fortuny Bags Red	365/13	25	£50	£1250.00
Fortuny Bags Tan	365/14	10	£50	£500.00
Total		100		£5000.00
Trade Discount 10%				£500.00
Subtotal				£4500.00
VAT				£787.50
Amount Due				£5287.50

Payment should be made in 30 days from date of Invoice

Cheque

Most organisations settle their bills by means of a cheque, although many now use computerised systems to pay regular suppliers. A cheque is an order to the banker to pay the named person or organisation the amount stated in words and figures.

Often there are two vertical parallel lines printed through the middle of a cheque – this is known as a crossing. Crossed cheques can only be paid into a bank account, they cannot be exchanged for cash. This is a security measure to try to reduce fraud. If the cheque is passed on to a third person it would have to be endorsed, i.e. signed on the back by the person to whom it was made payable. The bank will usually ask for proof of identity from the third person. Most cheque books have a counterfoil or a front sheet to help organisations keep a note of when they wrote the cheque, who received it and the amount.

Here is the cheque which would be sent by John Nicholls to Mojo Bags to settle the invoice on the previous page. You should note that if John Nicholls traded regularly with Mojo Bags they would not settle their account when the invoice came in; they would wait until they received their monthly statement.

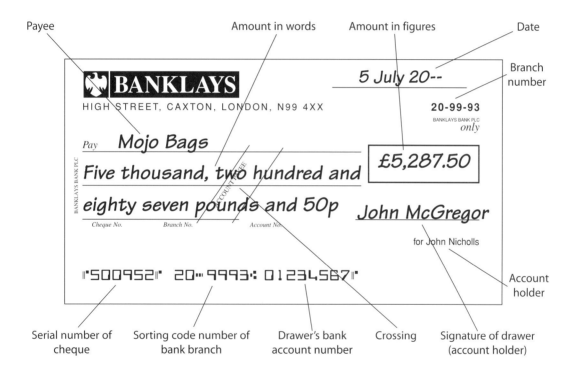

The cheque will have printed on it the name of the Bank and the address of the branch where the account is held. This is known as the DRAWEE.

Space for the date to be written.

A code number at the at the top right – this is the sort code number unique to this branch of the bank.

Space to write in the name of the person or organisation who will receive the money. This is known as the PAYEE.

Space to write the amount being paid, in words for pounds and figures for pence, for example, five thousand and twenty four pounds – 62 pence.

Space to write in the amount being paid in figures.

Space for the signature of the person who is writing the cheque. This is know as the DRAWER.

The name of the organisation or person who is the account holder.

At the foot of the cheque there are three sets of numbers in the following order:

The cheque number

The branch code number – sort code number which also appears at the top right hand side

The account number.

Credit Note

Sometimes things go wrong with goods or with the buying and selling process. If goods are faulty or damaged they have to be returned to the supplier. Goods will also be returned if they are not the goods ordered or if they are not of the quality expected or if you have been overcharged. When this happens the goods would be returned from the buyer to the seller. The seller would then send the buyer a credit note.

A credit note ensures that the amount billed in the invoice is effectively reduced. The amount of the adjustment would be indicated in the next statement sent from the seller to the buyer. Let's assume that one of the bags ordered by John Nicholls was sent back to Mojo Bags. A credit note would be issued by Mojo Bags.

Mojo Bags

46 Great Rushford Street
NORWICH
NN6 7RS
Telephone 01298 587609
E-mail mojoworks.co.uk

CREDIT NOTE

Vat no 675/75876/32

30 June 20..

Goods delivered to:

John Nicholls
47 Great Emperor Street
GLASGOW
GF1 7JN

Order Number: AD49867/108
Invoice Number: 9008
Credit Note Number: 425

Item	Catalogue No	Quantity	Unit Price	Total price
Fortuny Bags Black	365/11	1	£50	£50.00
Total		1		£50.00
Trade Discount 10%				£5.00
Subtotal				£45.00
VAT				£7.88
Amount of Credit Note				£52.88

Statement of Account

When a buyer and seller trade on a regular basis a statement or statement of account will be sent to the buyer from the seller, at the end of each month. This statement is a picture of the buyer's account in the seller's accounting system and should detail every invoice sent as well as any credit notes issued and any payments received. The buyer's account will be shown as follows:

- any outstanding balance owed by the buyer to the seller

- added any goods purchased that month along with the relevant invoice number

- less any payments received by cheque from the buyer

- less any credit notes issued by the seller to the buyer.

Here is an example of a statement sent by Mojo Bags. We have assumed they trade regularly with John Nicholls for this document. Not all of the transactions shown on this statement have been detailed in full.

Mojo Bags

46 Great Rushford Street
NORWICH
NN6 7RS
Telephone 01298 587609
E-mail mojoworks.co.uk

Statement

Vat no 675/75876/32

30 July 20..

John Nicholls
47 Great Emperor Street
GLASGOW
GF1 7JN

Order Number: AD49867/108
Invoice Number: 9008
Credit Note Number: 425

	Debit	Credit	Balance
1 June Balance			£190.00
14 June Invoice	£5287.50		£5477.50
30 June Credit Note		£52.88	£5424.62
5 July Cheque	£5287.50		£137.12

Check your Progress 6.2

1 What should you check before paying an invoice and why?

2 Under what circumstances would an organisation **not** pay the amount requested on an invoice?

Internal Assessment

Here are some examples of the kind of questions you might be asked as part of your internal assessment for Intermediate 2.

1 Describe the activities undertaken by the HR department. (3)

2 Outline the use and purpose of a delivery note. (2)

3 What is a job description and why is it useful to both the employee and the employer? (2)

External Assessment

Here are some examples of the kind of questions you might be asked as part of your external assessment. An estimate of the marks assigned to each question is indicated and it would be anticipated that each question would form part of a larger question.

1 Describe two documents you might have to deal with if you were the administrative assistant in the sales department. (2)

2 Outline the main activities of the finance department. (2)

3 Why are only certain people in an organisation allowed to issue purchase orders? (2)

CHAPTER 7

Travel

This chapter is about procedures for arranging and paying for business travel and accommodation.

Intermediate 2 Level Outcomes: ⫸

The chapter includes from Intermediate 2 Administrative Services Outcome 5:

- ☆ **information required before arranging business travel and accommodation**
- ☆ **factors affecting choice of method of travel and accommodation**
- ☆ **documentation relating to travel and accommodation**
- ☆ **methods of payment.**

As an administrator you may well be involved in arranging and monitoring business travel and accommodation both within the UK and/or overseas. If this is part of your remit you will have to adhere to organisational policy and procedures regarding booking and paying for travel and accommodation. The organisational policy and procedures will determine the amount which is to be spent to prevent costs escalating. This will affect the method and class of travel, type of hotel, size of hire car, etc. These procedures will vary between organisations – if you work for a small organisation your line manager may have complete authority over all travel and accommodation arrangements. However, organisations that are involved in a lot of travel may well have a centralised service which means that specialist staff will arrange all the travel and accommodation requests and deal with payment in line with organisational policy.

Careful planning is essential to ensure that time is not wasted, travel and accommodation costs are kept to a minimum and any preferences and constraints are taken into account.

Here are some of the details you must obtain right at the start of the planning process:

- name of the traveller(s)
- purpose of the trip
- destination
- date of departure
- date of return
- any individual preferences for travel/accommodation
- special requirements
- budget of the trip if applicable.

Some organisations may require staff to complete a standard form prior to a business trip to ensure that the administrator receives all the necessary information to prevent any misunderstandings. Here is an example of a travel and accommodation request form. Note that this form has to be signed and dated – this may be useful for audit purposes. Some organisations may simply ask for the same information in any written form, such as memo, e-mail or fax. It is obviously better to have this information in writing to avoid any mistakes or misunderstandings.

Travel/accommodation request form

TRAVEL/ACCOMMODATION REQUEST FORM

Name of traveller(s)	
Department	
Purpose of trip	

TRAVEL/ACCOMMODATION DETAILS

Place of Visit	
Departure Date and Time	
Return Date and Time	
Accommodation (grade/single/double) Smoking/Non Smoking* (delete as required)	
Method of Travel	

OTHER REQUIREMENTS

Itinerary Required	☐
Passport/Visa	☐
Medical requirements	☐
Insurance requirements	☐
Currency/money arrangements	☐
Dietary requirements	
Driving requirements	
Customs arrangements	
Any other requirements	
Signed:	Date:

Booking Travel and Accommodation

After obtaining clear details of travel and accommodation you may have to research a wide range of information to allow you to organise travel and/or accommodation. Useful sources include paper-based information, computer-based information and travel agents/travel organisations.

Paper-based sources

- Timetables – rail, ferry and airline timetables.

- Maps – town maps, route maps.

- Guides such as the AA and RAC handbooks and *Hotels and Restaurants in Great Britain* which give useful information on accommodation in Great Britain. Berlitz and Michelin guides give local information on the country to be visited including information on time differences, cultural information and places of interest.

- Leaflets on *Health Advice for Travellers*, published by the Department of Health.

It is also useful to keep a list of favourite hotels in the UK and abroad, a list of consulates of frequently visited countries, a list of local car hire firms, etc.

Computer-based Sources

- CD-ROMs – specific information on towns such as AA and RAC guides

- Internet – it is increasingly easier to access up-to-date travel and accommodation information on the Internet. This can also save you time and money – you can book direct and can often benefit from special discounts. You can bookmark sites that you use regularly which will save you time searching for a particular site.

  Here is a list of some useful sites:

  www.ryanair.com
  www.airline-network.co.uk
  www.directferries.co.uk
  www.eurostar.com
  www.streetmap.co.uk
  www.mapsonus.com

Travel Agent

You can use the services of a travel agent which can save you time and money. Many travel agents provide a complete business travel service to help organisations manage travel and provide more choices to the traveller. Travel agents can access an on-line reservation system such as *Galileo* which has access to over 470 airline suppliers, 23,000 car rental locations and 57,000 hotel properties, etc. One of the main benefits of this system is access to the most up-to-date information and access to the best possible prices – visit www.galileo.co.uk to find out more.

Many organisations use a preferred travel agent but research the information they wish prior to booking through the travel agent.

Travel Organisations

It may be sometimes necessary to contact travel organisations direct as this could save time and money. For example, if you book through a travel organisation such as Expedia you can save money in the booking process because there are fewer agency and administrative costs involved than going through a 'traditional' travel agent. Examples of travel organisations include:

Air

Aer Lingus
Air Canada
EasyJet
KLM UK

Bus

First Group
National Express
Scottish Citylink

Rail

Rail Europe
Scotrail

Sea

Caledonian MacBrayne (for Scottish islands)

You can contact travel organisations for information relating to the country you wish to visit: passport offices and consulates for information on passports
department of Health for information on health
AA, RAC for information on travel insurance.

Factors Affecting Choice of Method of Travel and Accommodation

Before you choose a method of travel and accommodation, consideration must be given to:

- Organisational policy and procedures. An organisation may have rules about what hotels and airlines can be used because they want to benefit from loyalty schemes or frequent traveller programmes. These schemes allow the traveller the opportunity to collect points which can lead to upgrades and free nights at their hotels or free flights and upgrades and, in the case of organisations, may allow the organisation bigger discounts. The organisation may also have rules about class of travel, mileage allowance, subsistence allowance, and the distance to be travelled before overnight accommodation can be allowed. Guidelines may be given on health and safety issues such as insurance, arrangements for vaccinations/inoculations, length of trips and driving times.

- Purpose of the trip. This may well affect choice of method of travel, for example, if the traveller needs to take display materials the administrator will have to investigate ways of packaging and make arrangements with the airline, rail service or a car hire service for transportation.

- Time available. It may well be an urgent business trip so may be limited to choice of method of travel. Consideration must also be given to the time the traveller will be away from work (this will cost the organisation money).

- Preferences of the traveller – they may prefer certain airlines and hotels.

- Constraints, such as medical arrangements, visa requirements, bank, holiday and religious festivals, driving regulations.

- The budget available. Employees on a different grading may be allocated a different budget.

Methods of Travel

The four methods of travel are air, road, rail and sea.

Air travel

Advantages include:

- savings in time – in many cases this is the fastest method of travel

- secure car parking facilities (you can also have your car valeted while you are away on business)

- good in-flight facilities – some airlines have installed payphones, laptop computers and faxes

- improved airport facilities, i.e. restaurants, shops, meeting rooms, executive lounges

- improved network of airlines across Great Britain which are nearer city centres which means that travel time can be reduced.

Disadvantages include:

- higher cost

- travel to and from airports

- restrictions on luggage you can take

- delays due to inclement weather

- long check-in times are often required

- travel time can be increased if departure is delayed

- jet lag due to time differences on long flights.

Road Travel

Road travel can mean using your own car, using a hired car or hiring a taxi.

Private car/car hire

Advantages include:

- traveller can suit themselves – they're not tied to flight/rail times

- traveller can choose route – they can use quickest and best roads

- relatively cheap.

ADMINISTRATIVE SERVICES

Disadvantages include:

- can be tiring if a long journey

- there can be delays if roads are busy

- can get lost if unfamiliar with the roads – traveller will need necessary maps and other related documentation

- can break down – you should make sure the traveller carries relevant documentation (in case of accident/breakdown)

- additional cost of toll roads – you should ensure the traveller is aware of these and has necessary change

- different driving regulations in other countries – the traveller will need advice on this.

Travel by taxi

Advantages include:

- convenience

- traveller does not have to worry about parking

- can be quick

- traveller does not have to worry about reaching their destination if unfamiliar with the area.

Disadvantages include:

- can be expensive, especially for long journeys

- sometimes difficult to book or call taxis, i.e. at peak times

- if roads busy there can be delays.

Travel by train

Advantages include:

- comfortable method of travel – the traveller can undertake work while at their seat

- less tiring than flying

- quite fast (improved rail links means faster trains)

- seat reservations can be made in advance of travel

- good on-board facilities – most trains include an on-board catering service (some first class services have telephone, television, photocopier and fax machines installed).

Disadvantages include:

- travel time can be increased if the train is delayed

- seat is not guaranteed if you do not reserve in advance.

Channel Tunnel

Advantages include:

- fast – Eurotunnel offers the fastest route to France crossing from Folkstone to Calais in under 35 minutes. The Eurostar train also goes from the heart of London to the heart of Paris.

- traveller can take their own car

- loading and unloading is quick and easy

- frequent shuttle service, for example, shuttle service from Dover to France runs four times per hour

- efficient customs arrangements in place which means time is not wasted

- relatively cheap

- little chance of getting seasick!

Disadvantages include:

- operating difficulties can cause delays and even cancellations

- travelling to France through the Channel tunnel is the least exciting of cross channel options.

Travel by sea

Advantages include:

- traveller can take their car on most services

- relatively fast

- secure quayside parking

- excellent on-board facilities – cafes, bars, restaurants, cinemas, gym and sauna – on some ferries services the traveller can pay a supplement to access meeting areas with access to a desk, telephones and fax facilities

- comfortable – can book sleeping cabin accommodation.

Disadvantages include:

- not as fast as air travel

- delays and cancellations due to inclement weather

- travel sickness if seas are rough

- ferry ports may not be near city centres.

Once a decision has been made regarding method of travel, many organisations require the completion of a travel request form. This will be passed on to the person processing the travel arrangements such as your Travel Department or travel agent. Here is an example of a travel booking form:

ADMINISTRATIVE SERVICES

Travel booking form

Form TB1		John Nicholls
Ref:	**TRAVEL BOOKING FORM**	47 Great Emperor Street
		Glasgow
		GF1 7JN
		Tel: 0141 548 8000
		Email: administration@jnstores.co.uk

To: _____

       _____

       _____

OUTWARD JOURNEY 1

| Date: | Dept Time:
Arriv Time: | Mode of Transport: |
| From: | | To: |

OUTWARD JOURNEY 2

| Date: | Dept Time:
Arriv Time: | Mode of Transport: |
| From: | | To: |

RETURN JOURNEY 1

| Date: | Dept Time:
Arriv Time: | Mode of Transport: |
| From: | | To: |

RETURN JOURNEY 2

| Date: | Dept Time:
Arriv Time: | Mode of Transport: |
| From: | | To: |

Reason for travel:

| Cost Centre: | Account Code: |

Signed: _____

Date signed: _____

Authorised by: _____

Date authorised: _____

Check your Progress
7.1

1 Describe the advantages and disadvantages of the following methods of travel:

Air

Rail

Sea

Road.

2 What factors would you need to consider before deciding on the most appropriate method of travel?

3 Outline the main areas which may be covered in the organisation's travel and accommodation policy and procedures.

4 Outline the type of information and services available from the following sources which will help plan for the next business trip.

Travel agent

Internet

Travel organisation.

Booking Accommodation

It is essential that the administrator checks the location of the hotel to ensure that time is not wasted getting to and from appointments. If a long journey is involved, it is essential that the accommodation has adequate facilities to allow the traveller time to exercise, relax and refresh. Here are details of some of the facilities offered by hotels which will assist the traveller:

- restaurant on site
- 24-hour room service
- connection for laptop
- air conditioning
- satellite television
- direct dial phone
- mini bar
- hairdryer
- trouser press
- automatic wake-up call
- money exchange
- valet parking

- valet/laundry
- multi-lingual staff
- fitness centre, sauna
- beauty parlour
- business centre
- city transportation.

Before booking accommodation the administrator should check the following:

- departure/return dates
- cost is within the agreed price limit of the organisation, i.e. within budget. Also a good idea to check that the cost includes the price of breakfast
- preferences of the traveller, for example, smoking/non-smoking, type of hotel, facilities required, i.e. gym and meeting room, special requirements
- location of the hotel
- facilities
- check-in and check-out times – you may have to let the hotel know if traveller is arriving late to avoid re-letting the room
- car parking facilities, where appropriate
- method of payment. Three common methods include:
  - request for hotel to invoice you for the amount
  - through your travel agent
  - credit card.

Many organisations will require the completion of an accommodation booking form. Here is an example of an accommodation booking form. Once completed, this will then be sent to the person arranging the accommodation such as the administrator, the Travel Department or travel organisation.

Accommodation booking form

Form ACB1	John Nicholls
Ref:	47 Great Emperor Street
	Glasgow
	GF1 7JN
ACCOMMODATION BOOKING FORM	Tel: 0141 548 8000
	Email: administration@jnstores.co.uk

To: _____

_____

ACCOMMODATION 1

Date:

No of Nights:

Town/city:

Name of Hotel	1st choice:
	2nd choice:
	3rd choice:

Additional comments:

ACCOMMODATION 2

Date:

No of Nights:

Town/city:

Name of Hotel	1st choice:
	2nd choice:
	3rd choice:

Additional comments:

Reason for Stay:

Cost Centre: Account Code:

Signed: _____

Date signed: _____

Authorised by: _____

Date authorised: _____

ADMINISTRATIVE SERVICES

Unless a travel agent is used for booking accommodation, the administrator will have to contact the hotel to make the reservations and confirm the booking. This will usually be done in writing. The most common method of payment is credit card where the business traveller will settle his account by credit card at the end of the trip. The credit card could be a company credit card or the traveller's own card. If a traveller uses their own card the amount spent would be claimed back later.

Here is an example of a letter which would be sent to the hotel confirming a booking which may have been made by telephone or perhaps e-mail. It is a good idea to give a copy of the confirmation letter to the traveller which they can add to their travel documentation.

Example letter confirming hotel booking

John Nicholls
47 Great Emperor Street
GLASGOW
GF1 7JN
Telephone 0141 5688000
E-mail administration@JNstores.co.uk

Ref: AB/MD/1025

Today's Date

Reservations
The Inn at Woburn
George Street
WOBURN
Milton Keynes
MK17 9PX

Dear Sir/Madam

RESERVATION NUMBER 26773

Further to our conversation earlier today, I confirm my reservation of a standard double room for two nights from 2 June 2005 for Mr Anthony McMurray. Please note that Mr McMurray will not be arriving at the hotel until at least 2200 hours on Friday 2 June.

I confirm that your room rate of £125 includes a full English breakfast and VAT. Please note that Mr McMurray will settle the account by credit card.

If you have any further queries, please do not hesitate to contact me.

Yours faithfully

Amy Brogan
Administrative Assistant

Jet Lag, International Time Zones and DVT (Deep Vein Thrombosis)

When organising travel the administrator will have to consider the health and safety requirements of the traveller – for instance, it is important not to make the schedule too tight and to make sure that the traveller has enough time to relax between appointments. Before a flight is selected the administrator will have to consider jet lag. Jet lag causes the traveller to feel fatigue, discomfort and disorientation due to crossing different time zones. It may be that you should allow the traveller a day of rest before their first appointment. Visit www.timeanddate.com which is a comprehensive guide to the different time zones around the world.

The traveller can be given advice on how to reduce jet lag, for instance drinking plenty of fluids to avoid dehydration, avoiding alcohol, doing gentle exercises to reduce discomfort and swelling of the feet. Go to www.nojetlag.com to find out more about combating jet lag.

Deep vein thrombosis (DVT) – clotting of the blood in any of the deep veins – is an added potential problem for 'at risk' travellers who are immobile for extended periods of time. The problem is most often linked with air travel, but the risk is also reported amongst those travelling by train and automobile. Exercise and avoiding dehydration are said to reduce the risks of DVT. Upgrades can ensure that the traveller has more leg room to do light leg exercise. Visit www.travelhealth.co.uk for further information.

Itinerary

The itinerary is the main document the administrator will prepare when arranging travel and accommodation. This is a summary of all the travel arrangements, accommodation and events. It is obviously important that all arrangements are recorded accurately to avoid missing flights and appointments, etc.

An itinerary will have the following information:

- Heading with the name of traveller, date and purpose of the trip.

- Precise times of travel. Always use the 24 hour clock for this.

- Exact travel details – method of travel will be detailed, such as air, rail. The details should also include check-in times, name of airport, departure times and flight numbers. Travel by ferry should include details of seat reservations and sleeping berths.

- Accommodation details – hotel name, address and telephone number.

- Details of business meetings including location and times and information on clients.

- Other documentation (if appropriate) might include:

  - documents which are necessary for a meeting

  - passport – all UK nationals traveling outwith the UK will need one

  - visa – needed for entrance to certain countries

  - insurance – personal and vehicle cover (usually covered in the organisation's insurance policy)

  - tickets for trip

  - letters and faxes of confirmation of hotel booking and car hire

  - emergency numbers for credit card insurance cover

  - vaccination certificates.

Here is an example of an Itinerary:

Example of an itinerary

Itinerary for Anthony McMurray
Trip from Glasgow to Bruges – Thursday 1 June to Monday 4 June 20..

Thursday 1 June

1000 hours   Collect hire car from Avis Rent-A-Car, 70 Lancefield Street, Glasgow, G3 8JD Tel 0141 221 2827. Leave your own car with Avis to collect on your return.

Drive to Woburn

1800 hours   Arrive at the Inn at Woburn
George Street
Woburn
Milton Keynes
Tel 01525 290441

One night bed and breakfast

Friday 2 June

0800 hours   Depart Inn at Woburn for Ferry Port at Ramsgate

1100 hours   Check in at Ferry Terminal (check in 1 hour before departure)

1200 hours   Depart Ramsgate for Zeebrugge

1600 hours   Arrive Zeebrugge
(3 hour crossing but remember Europe is 1 hour ahead of us)

Drive to Novotel Brugge Centrum
65B Katelijnestraat
800 Brugge
Belgium
Tel 3250337533

2 nights bed and breakfast

1700 hours   Meeting at hotel with Anton Leffe, Head of Fashion Designs, Brel Sport & Leisure. Meeting will last all afternoon.

Mr Leffe has arranged evening meal with clients from the Henin Tennis Group.

Saturday 3 June

0900 hours   Drive to Brussels
Attend launch of Summer Leisure Wear, Henin Tennis Group
Conference Centre
Novotel Grand Place
120 Rue de Marche Aux
Brussells 1000
Tel 3225143333

continued ➤

1400 hours	Presentation on new range of summer wear – presentation has been e-mailed in advance of meeting (Agenda, Attendance List, Floppy Disk and handouts in your Travel File)
	Launch event will last all day.
1700 hours	Drive to Bruges
1830 hours	Arrive Novotel Bruges Centrum for evening meal

Sunday 4 June

0900 hours	Depart hotel for Zeebrugge Ferry Port (Check in 1 hour before departure)
1030 hours	Depart Zeebrugge for Ramsgate
1230 hours	Arrive Ramsgate (UK 1 hour behind Europe)
1330 hours	Drive to Stratford Upon Avon
1730 hours	Arrive Thistle Hotel
	Waterside
	Stratford Upon Avon
	Tel 0870 333 9146
	One night bed and breakfast
2000 hours	Evening meal at the hotel with Frank McGregor, Head of Marketing (UK), Brel Sport & Leisure Group

Monday 5 June

0900 hours	Depart Stratford Upon Avon
	Drive to Glasgow
1600 hours	Arrive Avis Rent-A-Car. Leave hired car and pick up your own car

Check your Progress 7.2

1   Draw up a checklist of factors an administrator must consider before booking accommodation.

2   Describe eight hotel facilities required by the traveller on long trips.

3   Why should you be aware of international time zones when arranging travel?

4   What advice can you give to your boss, who will travelling from Glasgow to Miami, to help minimise jet lag?

5   Outline the information you will need to include in an itinerary.

6   What additional documentation might your boss need during a business trip to Japan?

Methods of Payment

Currency

It is useful to have some local currency for routine expenses such as cup of coffee, train ticket or money to tip a porter. However, you should try to keep cash to minimum to avoid loss or theft.

To find out the currency of a particular country and exchange rate go to:

www.x-rates.com
www.xe.com

These sites offer foreign exchange rate conversions.

Credit cards/debit cards

Credit and debit cards are used and accepted worldwide as payment for goods and services. Most hotels now require credit/debit card details before allocating rooms to ensure payment. A major advantage is the ability to obtain instant cash from ATMs and banks no matter where you are in the world, without the burden or worry of carrying large amounts of cash or travellers' cheques for the trip.

Losing a card is a disadvantage as the ability to replace it is hampered due to the lack of a permanent address and the timescale involved in banks providing replacements. Furthermore, banks add extra charges onto customers for using their cards for payment or obtaining cash whilst abroad. Although these tend to be small amounts they do add up during a trip. The main credit cards are Visa and Mastercard. Those who travel a lot on business will often be issued with a company credit card.

Travellers' cheques

These are still a relatively common method of payment abroad. These can be issued by banks, building societies and some travel agents. The advantage of using travellers' cheques is that travellers do not have to carry large amounts of cash and if travellers' cheques are lost or stolen they can be refunded. Although travellers' cheques are accepted in some countries as a method of payment, in other countries the traveller may need to cash them in at a bank or hotel where a surcharge may be added and proof of identification required.

Cheques

Personal cheques can also be used to settle bills throughout the United Kingdom. (Please see Chapter 6 for more information regarding cheques.) Cheques are not accepted abroad. The advantage of using a cheque is the ability to pay a bill which will not be taken out of a bank account for several days. Furthermore, they also save the need to carry large amounts of cash. Disadvantages include the need to produce a valid cheque guarantee card which may also limit the amount an organisation accepts. Unfortunately more and more retailers and petrol stations are refusing to accept cheques and insist on payment by card or cash only.

Checking and Verying Expenditure

On return from the business trip the traveller will be required to complete an expenses claim form in order to claim back any out-of-pocket money. This will have to checked and verified to ensure that:

- no errors have been made and the amount is correct
- expenses claimed are within the budget allocated
- receipts are included.

Invoices received from hotels, travel agents and travel organisaitons will also have to be checked and verified to ensure that there are no errors. Common discrepancies can arise where an organisation has been charged for additional nights' accommodation or where they have been charged for parking but should not have been.

Here is an example of an expenses claim form:

Form CL1
Ref:

John Nicholls

EXPENSES CLAIM FORM

Name:

Visit Date:

Departure Date and Time:

Department:

Return Date and Time:

Travel:

Air/Rail/Bus Fares/Car Parking fees

Total = £

(all receipts must be included)

Accommodation

Total = £

Private Car: …. Miles @ 30 pence

Total = £

Subsistence

Total = £

Total Expenses

= £

Signature of Employee: _____

Date: _____

For John Nicholls Use only

Travel Payment	£
Accommodation payment	£
Subsistence	£
Date entered on system	
Date authorised	

Check your Progress 〔7.3〕

1 What are the advantages to the business traveller of using Visa as a method of payment abroad?

2 What is the purpose of the expenses claim form? Why do you think travellers will be asked to include receipts?

Internal Assessment

Here are some examples of the kind of questions you might be asked as part of your internal assessment.

1 The human resources manager is going on a business trip to Canada next month. Outline the information required by an administrator before arranging his business travel and accommodation. (4)

2 **a)** Indenify the main document required for a business trip to Canada. (1)

b) Outline the purpose of the document. (1)

c) Suggest four pieces of information the document should include. (4)

External Assessment

Here are some examples of the kind of question you might be asked as part of your external assessment. An estimate of the marks assigned to each question is indicated and it would be anticipated that each question would form part of a larger question.

1 The finance manager will be attending the launch of a new sports line in Paris later next week. Outline the benefits of travelling by Eurostar (train) from London to Paris as opposed to air travel. (8)

2 Discuss three main factors you will need to consider before arranging travel and accommodation for the trip to Paris next week. (6)

3 Outline one advantage and one disadvantage of paying for goods and services while abroad using each of the following:

a) credit card (2)

b) travellers' cheques (2)

c) currency. (2)

CHAPTER 8

Information and decision making

This chapter is about decision making. For an organisation to run effectively, employees at all levels have to have good, accurate information on which to base their decisions. This chapter covers the different levels of decision making which take place in an organisation and the kind of information required to make good decisions.

Higher Level Outcomes: →

This chapter includes from Higher Information Technology for Management Outcome 1:

☆ **the nature of information**

☆ **sources of information**

☆ **features of good information**

☆ **types of decisions and types of information required to support decisions.**

Note: Chapter 1 also includes information on strategic, tactical and operational levels and how they contribute to planning processes.

Organisations have to ensure that there are:

● **adequate facilities for staff to access the information they require to do their jobs**

● **sufficient storage and retrieval systems to ensure that the information can be easily accessed by those who need it**

● **appropriate ways to communicate the information both within the organisation and to and from external bodies.**

Good information and communication technology systems (ICT) can help make all of these facilities available to organisations of all sizes.

What is Information?

Every organisation processes raw data into information. Processing means the data is collected, checked, organised, analysed, stored and distributed within the organisation. This information is then used for:

● monitoring and controlling performance. This usually takes the form of comparing past performance with current performance

● measuring performance. Making comparisons within an organisation between different parts of the business or comparing the organisation's performance with others in the sector

- anticipating future trends and opportunities

- decision making.

Information is the knowledge and background all businesses need to function well. Information is only of value if it is:

- relevant to the purpose and the person who wants it

- complete and unfiltered

- accurate

- clear and easy to understand

- consistent in both layout and quality – this in turn will give people confidence when using it

- communicated to the right person

- adequate in terms of volume – not too much and not too little

- delivered at the right time.

There are two main types of information.

1   Quantitative information is mainly statistically based. This kind of information can be measured. An example of this type of information would be the Christmas sales figures for the retail sector or for each department in John Nicholls.

2   Qualitative information is more concerned with opinions. In this book the chapter on customer service (Chapter 5) is likely to contain mainly qualitative information, for example, what did customers think of particular products.

Both types of information are essential to organisations and are used to inform managers in the decisions they take.

Where do Decision-makers get their Information From?

Information comes from many different sources:

- paper-based sources such as books or internal reports

- electronic sources such as CD ROMs, the Internet

- oral sources such as television, presentations.

Additionally, here are some terms associated with information sources.

Primary Sources

This is where the organisation gathers information solely for its own purposes. The organisation can gather this information from external sources as we saw when we looked at customer service and considered tools like focus groups and questionnaires. The purpose of this type of information gathering is usually very specific and focused, for example, customer satisfaction, trial of a new product, political opinion poll. Alternatively, an organisation can gather information from internal sources – their own data.

Here are some features of primary data.

- It is expensive to gather and to analyse if it is external information but if it is internal information for internal use, the information may already be there.

- It may be difficult to source as you may be trying to find out information which other organisations regard as commercially sensitive.

- It is usually gathered for a particular purpose and so it is very focused on what the organisation wants to know.

- The organisation has control over what it investigates.

- The information gathered is confidential to the organisation unless it decides to sell it on to another organisation.

- The information can be gathered in the organisation's preferred timescales and updated regularly as long as the organisation is prepared to bear the costs.

- The accuracy of the information can be checked because the organisation has access to the original information gathered.

Secondary Sources

Here information has been gathered by someone else for their own purposes but bits of the information gathered are relevant to another organisation. In the case of John Nicholls it might use information which is gathered on shopping habits and money spent in Edinburgh and Glasgow city centres. Reference books, CD ROMs, the Internet, government research and statistics, and commercial market research carried out for other people would all come under this heading.

Here are some of the features of secondary information.

- The organisation using secondary information does not always know the main purpose of collecting the information and there may have been a motive behind collecting it in a particular way, for example, would you trust a survey done by tobacco companies about the harmful effects of smoking?

- If this external information is available to your organisation, it will be available to other organisations too and may have been available to them before you knew of its existence. The timing of your access to this type of secondary information may indicate how important it is to your organisation.

- The organisation may have to filter through the secondary information available to find the bits which are relevant to their needs. This can be time-consuming and expensive.

- The organisation will not have any say on how the information is laid out or presented.

Internal Sources

This kind of information is available only within an organisation and is often crucial in helping the managers manage the organisation properly. Most of the information managers deal with on a day to day basis will be internal information – much of it will be of no interest to anyone outside the business, for example, sickness records and holiday rotas, but some of it might be of interest to competitors, such as the level of sales in each department.

The organisation has to set up systematic ways of gathering this type of information, probably by using bought-in or specially written software packages. This usually means that there are hidden costs of installing appropriate hardware and software as well as staff training costs.

On the plus side, though, as the producer of internal information you can check its accuracy and you can choose how and when to gather the information. This kind of information is very useful at certain levels of the organisation, for example, how much stock has been sold, how does that compare with this time last year, when will it have to be re-ordered, etc. Most staff can see the benefit of having this kind of information which means they buy-in to providing it accurately and on time.

External Sources

This refers to any kind of information gathered from outside the organisation, such as a local paper outlining planning permission for a new department store which is going to be built, or an independently produced market research survey comparing on-line buying with city centre buying habits. All information costs money to collect and the organisation may need to pay for externally collected information. It is, however, useful to have information of this type which looks at the wider picture. Senior managers need to know what is going on in the whole sector, not just inside their organisation.

Task 1

Using the above classifications describe the following pieces of information using the words primary, secondary, internal and external. Remember you can use more than one word.

a Market research done by Mintel – a market research organisation.

b Local government report on the effect of improved public transport.

c Sales report from the Furniture Department of John Nicholls.

d Customer survey on ladies clothing.

Regardless of how the information has been sourced, all organisations will have to decide if the information they have is in usable form. You can receive information in lots of different ways.

Written information

This is usually in the form of, for example, reports, articles, minutes, memos, letters, print-outs from Internet searches. Most people like dealing with written information because:

- it can be re-read and kept until required
- it can be filed as a permanent record
- the information can be compared with other sources.

Remember written information does not have to be in hard copy; it can be saved and read on screen.

Oral information

This covers face-to-face communication, telephone, video conferencing, presentations, meetings, etc. (all the forms of communication you looked at in Chapter 1). Giving information orally has certain advantages over other ways of getting information because:

- it allows for better discussion

- it ensures understanding as probing questions can be asked

- it is often a quick way of spreading key points

- it becomes more personalised as you know who has the information.

However, if important information is being exchanged a written record is often kept of the exchange.

Numerical information

This is a very precise and accurate way of giving information but to many people is not easy to understand. The advantages of using this type of information are:

- it allows comparisons to be made, using ratios and percentages

- it allows forecasts to be made, based on past experience

- it can form the basis of graphical information (see below).

Graphical information

This will include pictures as well as charts and graphs. The advantages of this type of information are that:

- many people remember an image better than words

- major points (such as a dramatic rise or fall in sales) can be easily seen

- pictures or graphs lend themselves to making comparisons immediately apparent.

Features of Good Information

Good information is essential for all organisations. Organisations have to decide what is good information and what is not good information for making decisions. The quality of their decision-making will depend on the information they use. Poor information quality leads to poor decision-making. The quality of information can be judged under the following headings.

Timing Operational decisions particularly depend on having up-to-date information available at the time it is needed. Much internal information will therefore be geared towards regular management meetings. Where information is required on a regular basis, it should be scheduled into work plans and to do lists.

Relevance One of the problems of using secondary data is the relevance of the data gathered. Information required by an organisation has to pertain to the decisions to be made. If you are overwhelmed with too much information you tend not to read any of it. Good organisations ensure that relevant information is available and that full data can also be accessed if required. Often personal assistants filter information or prioritise it on a need to know basis rather than nice to know basis so that the person they are working for only sees the relevant parts they need for decision making.

Accuracy The accuracy of information depends on the way it was gathered and the way it was handled as data. Errors can be made at the gathering stage, at the input of data stage and at the analysis stage. For example, the response to a question might be wrongly entered on a form or wrongly keyed in or mistakes could be made in analysing the result. Accuracy of information depends on tight systems being used and spot checks being carried out to determine if there is a margin of error.

Objectiveness The information should be gathered from an objective point of view rather than being gathered to prove a particular point. Think back to the cigarette company collecting data on damage caused by cigarette smoking. What do they want to find? Is this likely to be objective?

Available and Accessible The information has to be readily accessible to anyone in the organisation who might need it. This does not mean it is not kept securely (a password could be used) but if information is available in an organisation it should be available to anyone in the organisation who needs it. People who guard information and stop others getting it are bad news for the organisation as a whole.

Cost Effective Organisations will have to determine whether the cost of buying the information from secondary sources or setting up systems to gather primary data are worth the expense involved. Cost should be considered in terms of time as well as money.

Complete There needs to be a check that all of the information has been received otherwise the analysis will not show the entire picture. There is no point in having only some of the information. For example, if you are looking for sales figures for the month and two departments' figures are missing, you cannot find a complete figure. Additionally, there has to be sufficient detail to enable decisions to be made. There needs to be a balance between the information being complete and being concise enough to work with.

Traceability This is different from accuracy because it includes the ability to verify the completeness of the data as well as the accuracy of it. In accounting the term audit trail is used to identify the step by step process of finding out the original source of data.

Organisations which function well will have a well-developed information system where people, procedures and equipment are used to process data and provide reliable information for the organisation. The kind of information each level in the organisation will need for making decisions is summarised below. Decisions will be made at different levels in the organisation – strategic, tactical and operational. This can be shown diagrammatically.

Levels of decision making in an organisation

Types of Decisions

Decisions taken will reflect the types of problems to be solved and the level in the organisation at which decisions have to be taken.

A structured problem is one that is routine and repetitive. These are the kinds of problems which can be decided by a set of guidelines and standards. An unstructured problem, on the other hand, is one for which there is no definite way of finding a solution. This kind of problem requires the problem solver to use judgement, experience, intuition and common sense as well as any past precedent as a guide.

Operational Decisions – Short Term

Operational managers will usually take decisions which deal with the day to day operations of the organisation. There are always a certain number of decisions which have to be made for an organisation to continue to perform (such as who will work overtime, when to order new stock). The decisions made at this level will be aimed at controlling operations. The operational manager's decisions are likely to:

- be structured decisions

- be taken according to the organisation's guidelines

- be repetitive in that they occur regularly (such as how much stock to buy)

- have an impact on the organisation which is short-term

- have an immediate effect

- be quick to take because managers understand the relationship between the variables (for example, does this customer get more credit – what are the risks to the organisation?)

- have a nearly guaranteed outcome (if I do A then B will happen)

- be short term decisions

- be concerned with 'making it happen'.

The kind of information required by the operational manager to make effective decisions is likely to be:

- primary information

- detailed information

- information which is internal to the organisation

- routinely produced information which is likely to come out at a regular time in a particular organisational format and which is understood by the people who produce and use it

- quantitative in that it will be based on figures and will have targets, levels, ratios, etc. which can be analysed or benchmarked against 'success'

- accurate – the relevance of the information depends on the level of accuracy

- historical information which deals with returns on what has already happened

- documented. Guidance is likely to be available within the organisation to help make decisions more consistent. There might be handbooks/software/flowcharts to help people make decisions.

Tactical Decisions – Medium Term

Tactical managers will usually take decisions which involve allocating and controlling the organisation's resources. They are the middle level managers who are responsible for implementing policy decided at strategic level.

Tactical managers usually take decisions which are:

- medium term and likely to impact on the organisation in a matter of weeks or months rather than immediately

- what could be called semi-structured decisions, i.e. all the possibilities will not be known. However, many of the decisions at this level may also be structured and relatively routine decisions

- likely to have some guidelines within the organisation but often the tactical manager will have to use their intuition to help make the decision

- likely to have a more unpredictable outcome than decisions taken at operational level

- likely to involve comparing current performance with past performance and likely future performance

- likely to deal with the question 'how to'.

The kind of information required by tactical managers to make decisions at this level is likely to be:

- mainly primary information but also some secondary information

- usually information which is internal to the organisation

- mainly quantitative, often with an accounting bias like budget, cash flow statements, information on staffing levels. However, there will also be some qualitative information

- less dependent on things which have happened in the past than operational decisions

- systematically gathered information which allows comparisons to be made

- less dependent on the detail and numerical accuracy than the operational manager requires but with more emphasis on the wider picture and the effects any decisions will have on the whole organisation.

Strategic Decisions – Long Term

Strategic managers are those who are responsible for the strategic decisions involved in running the organisation. They will be involved in planning objectives, setting goals, assessing if they have been met and changing plans if required. Managers at this level will decide how the organisation will work towards reaching those goals. They will plan the long term objectives of the organisation.

Strategic managers usually take decisions which are:

- long term. It is likely to take several months or even years for the true effect of decisions to become apparent

- broad in outlook and consider not just the organisation in isolation but all external factors

- used to provide the basic outline and guidelines of how the organisation will run in the future

- repetitive in that they are revisited on a regular basis (such as, what will we produce?) However, they are not so repetitive that they will have catalogued guidelines to help make the decision as the context for making the decision will constantly be changing

- unstructured and complex. Everything that has to be considered will not be known (for example, what will our competitors do?)

- 'what if' decisions.

The kind of information needed to make strategic decisions is likely to be:

- Information which is external to the organisation – information about competitors, the market generally, the economy, suppliers, consumers and the overall industry outlook.

- Imprecise information. Since much of the information needed is not under the control of the organisation, it will often have to depend on what it can gather from secondary sources.

- Information with a high level of uncertainty of the outcome of any decisions taken. Decisions at this level are risky – some work; some do not.

- Information which has a long term impact on the organisation.

- Information on the profitability of the organisation as a whole and different segments within the organisation, as well as comparative information with other organisations.

- Information on the availability of new capital and the cost of borrowing money.

- Information on staffing levels, both current and future levels.

Internal Assessment

Here are some examples of the kind of questions you might be asked as part of your internal assessment.

1 Explain what is meant by quantitative information and give two examples of information which would be used by both operational and tactical managers. (3)

2 Explain why strategic managers use mainly externally sourced information. Give two examples to illustrate your answer. (3)

3 Compare and contrast primary and secondary information using examples. (4)

External Assessment

Here are some examples of the kind of questions you might be asked as part of your external assessment. An estimate of the marks assigned to each question is indicated and it would be anticipated that each question would form part of a larger question.

1 What is meant by good information? Describe four features of good information with examples. (8)

2 The three levels of management – strategic, tactical and operational – need different levels of detail, source information from different places and deal with different questions. Explain what is meant by this. (8)

3 John Nicholls, a department store, gathers information from focus groups of customers and pays for market research to be carried out on the buying habits of consumers in the Edinburgh area. Compare and contrast these methods of gathering data and identify possible uses for the information gathered. (8)

SECTION TWO

Information Technology

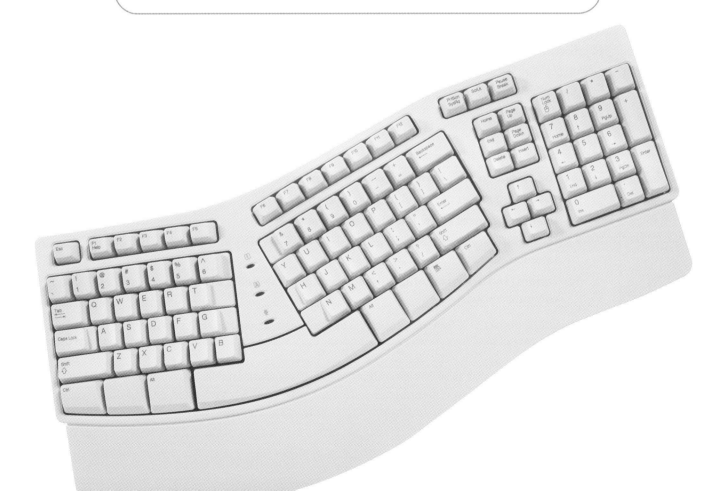

ICT: Its Uses and Impact

This chapter looks at information technology and electronic means of communicating as well as the impact on current working practices.

Intermediate 2 Level Outcomes:

This chapter covers Intermediate 2 Administrative Services Outcome 4.

Describe the uses of the Internet and office technologies:

- ☆ **the Internet, its uses, advantages and disadvantages**
- ☆ **features of electronic file management**
- ☆ **uses and features of other electronic means of communication**
- ☆ **benefits of e-commerce to the customer and the organisation**
- ☆ **the main purpose of current legislation in relation to data protection, copyright and computer misuse.**

Note: Some electronic means of communication – electronic diaries, e-mail, voicemail and fax have also been covered in Chapter 1 Working Effectively, Chapter 3 Meetings and Chapter 11 E-diary the Internet. Video and audio conferencing and web cams and Internet meetings have been covered in Chapter 3.

Higher Level Outcomes:

It also contains the content for Higher Information Technology for Management Outcome 2.

Describe the impact of ICT on workflow, working practices and management and security of information:

- ☆ **the impact of ICT on workflow**
- ☆ **the advantages of data management systems to organisations**
- ☆ **the consequences of poor data management systems**
- ☆ **the importance of electronic file management**
- ☆ **the importance of organisational procedures for security and confidentiality of information**
- ☆ **current legislation concerning security and confidentiality of information and computer misuse.**

Note: The impact of ICT on working practices has already been covered in Chapter 2.

More and more business is now being conducted using electronic means. Increasingly people all over the world are able to communicate with each other quickly and cheaply by using electronic means. Here are some of the ways they communicate using the Internet.

An On-line Service provider

This is a business which provides its subscribers with the facilities to communicate with each other using e-mail, on-line conferences and discussions and access to an unlimited number of third party information providers. Subscribers can get access to up-to-date information on, for instance, share prices, news stories, newspapers etc. Examples of on-line service providers are America Online and Compuserve. The Internet itself is a service but it is not centrally controlled and does not function for profit. Similar, but much smaller in scale, are bulletin board services which usually concentrate on a single theme and are usually non-profit making.

E-mail

This is a system where documents prepared or filed on a computer can be transmitted to another computer using a 'mailbox' system. The mailbox stores the message until it is accessed by the user. The person receiving the message can read, print, reply, store, distribute or delete messages received. The e-mail system will also give users the ability to save copies of messages sent.

Increasing use of networked systems – where computers are linked together – has resulted in e-mail being the most common form of communication within and between organisations. Here are some of the advantages of using e-mail:

- It is extremely quick. Even with virus checking it will be quicker than postal delivery.

- It is cheap. The major cost involved is installing the network or linking to an existing network.

- It can deal with text, photographs, drawings, spreadsheets, indeed virtually any kind of data. Beware of the size of file you are sending though. Unless you know the person receiving the e-mail is on broadband, you may tie up their machine for some time. Also some organisations limit the size of the files receivable by employees and may also reject files which contain photographs.

- Once a file is stored electronically it can be sent – it does not need to be keyed in a second time or scanned in.

- Messages can go to a number of people at one time. You would normally do this by keying in all the addresses in the first address line. In the second address line e-mail systems usually have a place for cc, standing for carbon copy, meaning that you are sending this *for information* to someone else. The third address line is bcc which means a blind carbon copy. Addresses entered here cannot be seen by the original recipient of the e-mail.

- E-mails are confidential. You can only access your e-mail with a password. Your e-mail can only be accessed if your password is known.

- E-mail addresses can be accessed anywhere – a very useful facility for people who travel a lot, for example, sales representatives who can access their e-mails using laptops and telephone connections or wireless technology.

- Personal digital assistants (PDAs) are now available with limited computer facilities on a basic Windows environment as well as e-mail. Some PDAs are also available with phones built in. These allow you to deal with your e-mails, use the Internet, text message and phone by using what could be described as a mini-computer. You need to resynchronise the PDA regularly with your PC.

I N F O R M A T I O N   T E C H N O L O G Y

- You can trace if an e-mail has been opened.

- You can create automatic messages, for example, 'thank you' when you open a message. This lets the sender know you have received the message.

- You can create a message to let people know you are out of the office or on holiday.

Task 1

Using your e-mail:

- Look at your address book and make sure you have at least four single addresses and at least one group.

- Set up a group in your address book with three or four friends in your class. Let them know you are now doing Task 1 and ask for an acknowledgement. Include your teacher/lecturer in the group.

- Set up a folder in your e-mail for all e-mails received for this chapter. Save the acknowledgements received into this file.

- Set up a folder for each of the in-tray exercises you will soon be undertaking in Chapter 10. Check to see how many there are. When you complete these in-tray exercises your teacher/lecturer will let you know which ones should be sent by e-mail and which should be printed.

- Set up an automatic message to indicate you will not access your e-mails during the next school or college holiday.

- Make sure you know how to print an e-mail.

E-mail Etiquette

Just as there are acceptable ways of writing business correspondence, so there are acceptable ways of dealing with e-mails. This is known as e-mail etiquette. Here are some of the important rules:

- Be brief and to the point.

- Always read over an e-mail before you send it to make sure it makes sense.

- Remember to check your spelling and punctuation.

- Answer promptly or you defeat the point in using e-mail.

- Make sure you answer any questions asked.

- Only attach necessary files.

- If you are using the reply facility, check who is receiving a copy of your e-mail – it may be going to more than just the person you think!

- Do not write in capitals – this is perceived as SHOUTING.

- Most organisations will have an automatic disclaimer that says they are not tied to any agreements made in an e-mail on behalf of their organisation.

- Do not forward chain letters, jokes, racist, sexist or gossipy comments. Remember e-mail is still written business correspondence.

- Avoid using urgent and important unless the e-mail really is urgent and/or important.

- Use cc sparingly.

Many organisations will have an Internet and e-mail policy which will stipulate quite clearly what is and what is not permissible practice within the organisation. This may well be linked to their anti-virus system which might prohibit photographs being sent or received at work, prohibit the use of music files or limit personal use of the Internet to break times, etc.

 Task 2

Look up the website www.emailreplies.com and look at the advice given on writing e-mails and the sample e-mail policy.

Discussion groups

This is one of the facilities provided by a service provider and it is a virtual room; that is, a room; which does not exist in reality but exists virtually, where a private discussion can take place. It is really a channel for communication – the word 'room' being used to communicate the idea of a private meeting.

 Task 3

Visit the Google website (www.google.com) to see how you would go about joining a group, tracking your favourite topics and creating your own group.

Here are some of the facilities a discussion group can have.

- It can be open to anyone or it can be restricted to members.

- It can be put into categories so that other browsers can find it easily.

- You can screen off old messages and read some samples from the last few subscribers.

- You can choose to read only messages by their title.

- You can respond easily.

- You can hide your e-mail address so that it is not available to all.

- You can remove your old posted messages – useful in case you change your mind about what you have said.

Discussion groups allow people in different locations to follow the thinking and arguments of others using the Internet as the means of communication.

INFORMATION TECHNOLOGY

At the stage of setting up a group you can decide if the group is open to the public or only open to members and you will be asked to classify it so that people can find it. You will be asked to give the group an e-mail address and describe who it is aimed at. This is to ensure that people interested in participating in discussion can find your group quite easily.

Instant Messaging

This is a type of communication service that enables you to create what is really a private chat room or a private discussion group with another individual user. Once connected you can exchange messages and comments in real time and share files with others. It enables you to communicate over the Internet like a telephone conversation, only it is text-based. This communication is in real time – it occurs immediately. Usually when someone is on your private chat list and you are on-line, you are notified when they come on-line. This system was originally devised and developed for home users but many organisations now use this facility in their office systems.

Here are some arguments for and against using this system in business.

- It allows answers to be sent quickly without the delay customary in e-mails and voice mail.

- It is inexpensive.

- IT managers argue that it can breach security systems because it can bypass the systems.

- In can act as a distraction rather than a productive tool.

A Mailing List

A mailing list is a list of e-mail addresses identified by a single name such as mysteryshoppers@jnicholls.com. When an e-mail message is sent to the mailing list name, the message is automatically forwarded to all the addresses on the mailing list. In addition there are now mailing list servers that manage centralised mailing lists for groups of users. You would buy into using these facilities by paying the providing company and this would enable you to search the lists available for current mailing lists of interest to you (for example, for running a mailshot when you wanted to launch a new product into a new market). The companies which sell the mailing lists ensure that they are kept up to date. This would help you target the right people.

Sending a message to a mailing list is known as broadcasting a message; that is, sending the same message simultaneously to a chosen group of users.

The Internet as a Source of Information for Business

The Internet is gradually taking over as the primary source of reference information. There are, indeed, lots of advantages of using the Internet for business information.

Advantages

- It saves time as you do not have to leave your desk to find the information – think how long you might have to wait for information on train times either at a station or on the phone.

- It operates 24 hours a day, 7 days a week, so you do not need to wait until information sources are open to find out information. The information can be sourced when you need it as you do not have to wait for other people to come back to you with the relevant information.

- There is a lot of information to choose from, as you will find when you do a search using a search engine.

- Increasingly it can be accessed anywhere – not necessarily in the office – by using personal digital assistants and through mobile phone and wireless technology.

- Finding information is quick.

- Finding information on the Internet is relatively inexpensive.

- You can print the information if you need to.

- You can save information to file.

- It allows access to information which formerly would have only been available in hard copy.

- Even if a charge is made for some of the information it can be paid for by credit card and is still obtainable immediately.

- Search engines allow you to ask questions and the information is usually shown in the sites most commonly accessed.

There are however some disadvantages.

Disadvantages

- You do not always know the accuracy of the source of the information.

- As no-one is in charge of the Internet, there is no policing of the information on it. Some information may be old or inaccurate but has not been removed.

- Information may not always be well organised and therefore it may take you some time to find the correct information.

- Some websites are not stable and you may find you cannot get into the information you want easily. Sometimes you get into a loop and keep going back to the same spot; other times it crashes or does not let you into the page you want. Before you give up on any site though, do make sure you read the screen carefully. There can often be instructions there which you may have missed.

- It is easy to get distracted when looking for one thing because you tend to wander into other topics.

- You can waste a lot of time finding the right information.

- You can suffer from equipment or software problems or, if you are not working with broadband, some sites may take some time to access or download information.

- A poorly designed website may lose, rather than win, customers. It must be stable with good, quick links and professional-looking graphics. Most organisations have their websites professionally designed and maintained.

INFORMATION TECHNOLOGY

1 You have been asked to set up a mailing list for the members of the Finance Committee. Why will this help you in your job?

2 Why are many fan clubs set up as discussion groups?

Networks

A computer network is formed when computers are connected together or connected to the same peripherals such as printers and scanners. As they grow, most businesses require more than one computer and as soon as more than one computer is needed in an organisation, it becomes cost effective to install a network and link the computers.

Most businesses using more than one computer will set up a LAN – a local area network. This will allow staff to share information, software and peripherals. There are two common types of LAN: peer-to-peer and client/server.

Peer-to-peer Networks

In peer-to-peer networks the connection is simple – two or more computers are connected allowing them to share files and programs. This is a cheap, straightforward way of creating a simple network but it can be slow. If there is a breakdown in one of the connected machines in a peer-to-peer system, the others will not be able to function.

Client/server Systems

In client/server systems one computer acts as a server where the files and programs are kept and the other computers act as clients and are connected to the server. Servers are powerful computers which are dedicated to:

- managing the file servers or disk drives in use. Any user on the network can store files on the server

- managing the printers

- managing the network traffic; that is, the information which goes round the network.

Often the server performs no other tasks besides the server tasks.

Clients are computers or workstations used by individuals to run applications. The individual workstations rely on the main server for resources such as files, processing power and output devices. This is sometimes called two-tier architecture. If there is a breakdown in one of the client computers the other client computers will not be affected. They will only be affected by a breakdown in the server.

The advent of wireless technology has meant that much of the cabling that used to be needed for a network is no longer required.

There are certain advantages to using networks.

- They improve communications between employees and between the organisation and customers.

- They allow information to be shared which makes the business more efficient and more profitable.

- The cost of hardware can be lower because printers, scanners, storage facilities and Internet access can be shared by several computers.

- Staff can deal with lots of customers at the same time as they can access customer and product information from a central source.

- Standard information, such as training materials and directories, can easily be made available to everyone in the organisation.

- As network administration can be centralised, fewer IT administrators are needed.

- Data can be backed-up centrally.

Task 4

Consider the following situation.

If John Nicholls didn't have a network each PC terminal would need its own printer attached and the only way data could be transferred between PCs would be by saving it to disk and passing on the disk. Some people might back up their data, some might not. Everybody is likely to have a copy of everything – probably in hard copy – but it is difficult to know if you have the most up-to-date version.

What would change if John Nicholls had a network?

Local Area Networks – LANs operate well when everyone in the organisation is based in the one place. As business grows, however, organisations often have to think about different types of network. Here are some other kinds of networks which are variations on LANs.

Campus-area network (CAN) – computers within a limited geographical area such as a campus of a college or university.

Metropolitan-area network (MAN) – a data network designed for a town or a city – often used by local education authorities for schools in their areas.

Home-area network (HAN) – a network contained within a user's home that connects a person's digital devices.

While most networks still remain connected by wiring, it is becoming increasingly common to connect computers and peripherals without wiring – wireless networking. Here are some advantages of wireless networking.

- Laptop users can use their laptops anywhere in their office building without having to keep logging in and out if they change location. This means time, and therefore money, is saved.

- Better access to information leads to greater accuracy of information being used (for instance, up to date figures on bed availability in hospitals or stock availablility in storerooms will help work flow).

- No wiring is needed, therefore there is greater flexibility available in accommodation used. Computer wiring will not dictate the layout of rooms which in turn means a better return on investment in accommodation.

- It allows for easy hot-desking. (See Chapter 2.)

- Employees are likely to be happy because it is easy to use and flexible.

VPN

When you need staff to connect to your centralised system from home or while travelling, a virtual private network (VPN) allows this by creating a secure link between their computer and the main system. This protects the information for those who log on, send or receive.

WAN

WAN stands for wide area network and here terminals are spread over large geographical areas. If your business starts operating in more than one location a WAN allows you to connect two or more LANs. The Internet is an example of a WAN.

Intranet

An intranet stores information on a central system at a private Internet address. Employees can access the information they want from wherever they connect to the Internet. This is useful for employees whose job involves travelling or working from home – it allows them to access information about jobs, forms and what is happening at their base office. Use of an intranet allows the organisation to quality control the information and also to keep it up to date without having to keep reprinting hard copies of documents. Take the example of a form for claiming expenses being updated – it is done once, put on the intranet and can then be downloaded for all to use. It also discourages individuals from keeping a stock of forms in filing cabinets. Some examples of data which might be stored on an organisation's intranet would include phone directories, policies, procedures, forms, social events, newsletters or bulletin boards, training opportunities and the organisation's events diary.

Extranet

Some organisations also open up their intranets to partners such as suppliers and customers. The Scottish Qualifications Authority (SQA) is an example of this. The SQA has a website which is available to the public, with different parts of the website targeted at different people and also a secure part of the website which includes information like examination papers and student records. Access to the secure part of the website is restricted to password holders. Other examining bodies will have similar arrangements.

All of the above types of networks improve communications for business. When you are using networks it becomes even more important to ensure that electronic files are managed properly.

Good Practice in Electronic File Management

In many networks it is possible to access other people's data files. It is therefore really important that all the people accessing data files follow the same kind of procedures. In some systems others may be able to access your files for read-only but in systems where the data is all shared, they may be able to alter data too. If the data must be kept secure you may have to password protect it.

- When you are saving data it is best to save documents on to a central location – usually your network area – because it makes back-ups easier.

- Gathering data into like kinds allows you to set up folders and sub-folders. You might decide to have a folder for each committee you provide secretarial services for and within that folder you would have a sub-folder for each meeting. Within that sub-folder you would have the agenda, minutes, attendance list and any supplementary papers you had at the meeting. This will make it easier for you to locate this information later and for others to locate it in your absence. Generally speaking you should not have more than three levels of folder.

- Think of your network space as a filing cabinet. Within the filing cabinet you will have a number of drawers – your folders – and within the drawers, a number of files – sub-folders – and within these files, documents – electronic files.

- File documents regularly and check that you have filed them in the right place – just as you would in a paper-based system.

- Check the default in the programs you are using. You should be aware how a document will be saved and where it will be saved if you do not give it a specific name, in each program you use.

- You should be aware of the file extensions used in each of the programs you use regularly.

- If you are unable to locate a file you recently used, use the history button to check the files most recently used.

Consequences of Poor File Management

When everyone depends on using the same set of files, data management and file management become very important. Everyone should try to adhere to the same high standards of file management as there can be consequences for the organisation if they do not.

- If you do not follow the same standards and ways that everyone else files information, no-one will be able to find the files you are responsible for – including you.

- If people in the organisation cannot find the information you file, it will slow up business and lead to a break in the workflow, great annoyance and a lot of time wasted.

- If file name conventions and practices are not followed by all, it will lead to confusion. Confidential information may be left in files which can be accessed by all, if the same practices are not adopted by everyone.

- If housekeeping tasks of tidying and deleting files are not followed regularly, more time will be wasted and systems will slow down.

- Ensuring that only current versions are usable is important when files are shared and any historical data which is kept should be locked in read-only files to ensure that only authorised users access the correct current version.

- Poor data management will cost the organisation money as time is wasted.

- Poor data management is also likely to cost the organisation customers (for example, if your files have not been updated or information of previous business cannot be found because it has been misfiled).

- There may be legal implications if data is mishandled.

Connecting computers can have drawbacks. When all computers are linked, one person's problems may become everyone's problems. For example one person may import a virus which goes on to affect the whole system.

(Backing up and security aspects of good file management are detailed below.)

Database Management

It is vitally important that a systematic approach to storing information is taken throughout the organisation. A good database management system will allow each part of the organisation to share information and enable access to a common database. This means that:

- Data is not stored several times over in different places.

- The one set of data can be kept up to date.

- Lots of information is available to everyone rather than lots of people having only a little information.

- Security can be determined by granting access to read-only information to all but updating only to a few named people.

- Less time is spent updating information or finding files.

A good example of this type of system would be the SQA (Scottish Qualifications Authority) which has records on everyone who has sat a Standard Grade, National Qualification, Higher National Certificate or Higher National Diploma. Results can be read by staff in schools and colleges with special passwords but can only be changed by specialist staff within SQA. Similar systems are operated by other examining bodies.

Good data management will depend on a number of factors which are detailed below.

Hardware and Software Choices

Successful organisations will usually have an organisational policy about what kind of hardware and software is used in the organisation. In the case of hardware there will often be a rolling programme of replacement of hardware and decisions about speed and capability of systems will be made by experts. Often large organisations choose one supplier for all their computer hardware needs as this can cut costs.

Software

The software chosen by an organisation will depend on the main purpose of the organisation. Many organisations use off the shelf software like Microsoft programs and they may even tailor parts of it to suit their own needs. Here are the common types of software in use.

- Utility programmes which will help routine computer tasks like filing, searching for files and organising files.

- Communications software to help the flow and transfer of data.

- Applications software such as word processing, spreadsheet, database and presentations software – usually an integrated package which allows data to be transferred easily from one package to another.

- Customised or tailored software – either software which has been specially written or which has been specially adapted for the organisation.

Storing information

Decisions will be made about how information is to be stored. Here are some of the ways electronic data can be stored:

- On network disk storage areas which can be accessed by designated staff.

- On floppy disks which can be protected by making them read-only.

- On CD ROMs which can hold a vast amount of information and can be easily stored.

- On pen drives which are portable and easy to use.

- On worm disks. These are 'write only read many' disks which allow you to write data on to the disk once only. The data is permanent and can be read many times but cannot be altered. This type of storage is often used by the media and for photographs as it is best suited to archiving materials.

- On magnetic tape (sometimes called streaming tape) which is often used to back-up data. As data is stored sequentially it is a less flexible way of storing data but it is a cheap method.

Inputting information

Although keyboards are still the most common method for inputting data, there are other ways of inputting data into electronic format.

- Voice data entry allows input to go via a microphone and the data is then displayed on a screen for editing and subsequent entry.

- Scanners and optical character recognition (OCR) systems allow you to store text and symbols in a format computers can read. The information can then be edited and manipulated like any computer file.

- Touch screens are display screens with a touch sensitive panel which allows you to point to objects on the screen. This is a good interface for a limited amount of input or for those unfamiliar with computers.

- Hand held devices, such as personal information managers, or other hand held computers, such as those used in supermarkets to check prices and stock levels.

Security precautions

Special security precautions should be taken where data is used and shared. Keeping data secure doesn't just fall to those who manage computer systems, however. Here are some physical and technical safeguards all organisations should take to secure data:

- Protecting premises with alarm systems and security guards.

- Keeping computers away from areas which the public can access.

- Restricting access to the building to those who need access for business purposes and ensuring that all visitors are signed in.

- Ensuring that power supply to computers is stable.

- Using encryption for sensitive data.

- Ensure that those with portable facilities – those who travel as part of their work – are subject to the same security measures:

  - keep portable facilities safe and secure

  - use passwords

  - protect portable facilities when they are being transported and

  - ensure data is backed up on a regular basis.

- Those who work at home should consider:

  - who else uses the computer. Members of the family? Does this put business data at risk?

  - if the computer is physically secure

  - whether the computer is running other data which might corrupt business data

  - if data has to be backed up. If so, how will this be done?

  - how the business will ensure that sensitive data is deleted from the computer if an employee leaves.

Task 5

Look up the Internet and see what the following words mean:

encryption
hacking
firewall
virus

The second stage of keeping data secure is usually what people call data security. Data security is very important because:

- lost data will take time and trouble and expense to replace

- business information and contact details may be of interest to your competitors

- VAT and accounting information must be kept in its entirety

- employee information, such as payroll and personnel details, are private

- new product developments might be confidential

- losing customer data would affect sales and turnover.

Data protection

Here are some of the security measures which will help to ensure security of data on networks.

- Ensuring that only authorised users can get into the system – this is usually done by giving access to users through passwords. These passwords usually have to be changed on a regular basis, for example, once a month.

- Logging into the system allows the system administrator to check who is doing what. What you have accessed can be traced.

- It is important to remove access from employees who leave the organisation – they may take financial or sensitive customer information with them.

- Levels of access. Often the level of access you can gain is triggered by one of the passwords. For example, if you were the financial director of an organisation, you would have access to most information but you would be unlikely to have access to personnel records.

- Electronic safeguards.

  - A virus and content scanner is usually installed to ensure that data coming into the organisation is checked for known viruses. This may mean a slight delay in receiving data from those outside the organisation while it is checked. This software needs to be regularly updated.

  - A firewall is the term given to a software barrier which will protect your system from 'intrusion'. The firewall and anti-virus software should be updated on a regular basis so that it is ready to reject any new viruses. These updating downloads are usually called patches.

  - Some organisations use filtering or scanning software which searches e-mails for specific words or phrases, usually obscene or discriminatory words, and does not allow them to be delivered.

  - Other software monitors the websites employees are accessing or filters the type of website they are able to access in order to prevent misuse.

  - Intrusion detection systems act like burglar alarms and can identify potential intruders trying to get into the system. This is a sophisticated system and should be considered if the organisation runs a website or has a high profile which might attract attacks.

- Adoption of an e-mail and Internet policy for all staff. Usually staff are reminded of this policy as soon as they log on to the Internet.

- Staff should be discouraged from opening e-mails when they are unsure of the sender.

Disaster Recovery and Back-ups

Apart from the precautions mentioned above, all organisations have to have a plan to recover from accidental loss of data as a result of things like theft, fire, flood or deliberate sabotage (like an act of terrorism or a virus). Most organisations will have a disaster recovery plan which details how buildings would be evacuated, how data would be backed up and held in another building or in a fire/bomb-proof area. Most large organisations try to ensure that their plans are set so that they could recover sufficient data to be operating again within 24 hours of any disaster.

Back-ups allow organisations and individuals to continue business even if data has been lost. Some of the data may never be recovered but most organisations make arrangements to back-up data every 24 hours so that only 24 hours of data would ever be lost. Best practice for backing-up data would include:

- giving the responsibility for backing-up to one person only with a designated second person to cover for absence

- using a different disk to back-up each day of the week and have a schedule for rotating the disks

- holding the back-ups on a different site, such as swapping disks with another organisation or keeping back-ups in a bank.

Task 6

Outline how you back-up data on your current system.

E-commerce

Using the Internet as much as we do for communication, it is inevitable that this use affects the way we do business. E-commerce is the term given to the process of trading electronically. This is usually done on the Internet, using web pages to sell your goods.

Advantages to the organisation

- The organisation will effectively have a shop which is open 24 hours a day, 7 days a week.

- There will be no overheads for staff or rent, with no upkeep other than keeping the web pages up to date.

- A good website can provide information on your product directly to those who want to buy it, when they want to buy it. Your organisation can even receive orders when no-one is there.

- You have a worldwide market place.

- Presentation, placement, display, selling and paying for goods is all done on screen as an automated process.

- The web pages are usually set up as a database with templates determining the layout and spaces for price, product, description etc.

- A good navigation system to guide potential buyers through the on-line catalogue is needed. Once they have found the right type of product, they drill down to find the product that suits their needs exactly.

- There will often be a shopping basket in which to deposit bought products using drag and drop techniques.

- Market research and customer profiling becomes very straightforward as you can trace exactly what a customer bought and where their interests lie.

Advantages to the individual

As a customer you can use e-commerce to:

- buy when you are most relaxed
- buy when you want – 24/7
- have access to a worldwide base of suppliers
- buy with no pressure from sales people
- buy without having to travel
- have your goods delivered to you.

The Impact of ICT on Workflow

ICT has had a revolutionary effect on the work done by organisations and the way that work flows through an organisation. Work flowing through an organisation is usually seen in terms of:

Input → Process → Output

Here are some of the effects that ICT has had on the input, processing and output of data.

Input

- Information is gathered from a wider area.
- Information is keyed in only once and can then be used by many people.
- Information is gathered more quickly from within and outwith the organisation.
- There is less time involved in transferring information from one part of the organisation to another.
- External enquiries can often be dealt with by the first person contacted, rather than having to wait for a named administrator, which leads to better customer service. Think of call centres and how they can deal with banking, credit card and insurance information.

Processing

- Greater use of ICT has meant that information can by shared by all in an organisation leading to greater accuracy.
- Sharing information means better quality information and better decision making at all levels.
- Processing data using commonly used software has resulted in work being done more quickly and often more accurately. Think about how long it might have taken you to produce a report for your manager if she was away on business. You might have had to key in the report and post it to her, wait for a reply and then amend. This can usually done very quickly using e-mail, particularly if your manager has a PDA. Or think about how you would use a database to search for selected information.

- Less staff need to be employed on routine tasks. For example, in the past photocopies had to be taken, sent and retained in different parts of the organisation but now manual filing is less used and electronic files can be accessed by all. This drop in routine activities allows staff to move on to other more interesting tasks.

- More use of ICT has allowed more flexible working practices which in turn means that best use can be made of staff time. Staff being able to access office files at home has led to increased home-working as well as hot-desking and enables staff to use time in the office for meetings and face-to-face communication while using their home time for activities which require thinking and solitary work. (See Chapter 2 for further information on flexible working.)

- Greater use of ICT has meant that one worker does not have to wait until someone else is finished with a document and has returned it to a central location, as most systems allow more than one person to access the same document at the same time.

Output

- Finished documents and communications can be sent out at any time to people who may not be able to receive communication by post, for instance, if they are travelling.

- Data and documents can be updated regularly and quickly and can be accessed by authorised users wherever they are based.

- Output can be set up to be in a standard format making it easier to read and understand.

- Presentation software can ensure that company presentations are presented in a systematic and standardised way.

- Output can still be monitored by supervisors before being distributed.

Current Legislation

As an effective member of staff in any organisation you must be aware of current legislation in the workplace. You should be familiar with the main principles of any law and how you and the organisation are affected by current legislation. These principles will often be communicated to you by posters, for example, on health and safety or copyright, or may be part of your induction programme or part of ongoing staff development. No-one expects you to be able to interpret the law in detail but you should be aware of the main purposes of the legislation on copyright, data protection and computer misuse.

Copyright

Copyright gives the creators of certain kinds of material rights about how these materials can be used. The Copyright Designs and Patents Act 1988:

- covers copying, adapting, distributing, communicating to the public electronically including broadcasting, renting or lending copies to the public and performing in public

- is to ensure that exclusive ownership is maintained and no unauthorised copying of materials takes place

- covers materials as soon as they are recorded, in writing or any other way, such as books, films, music and computer programs.

If you wish to copy other people's work you need to get permission from the owner and this often involves paying a fee. Many organisations pay a blanket fee to specialist agencies to allow them to copy extracts from materials without individual permission having to be sought for each piece of material copied. For example, for printed works the agency is the Copyright Licensing Agency but a similar agency exists for performing rights and video performance. These agencies collect money on behalf of the authors, composers and performers involved.

Photocopying

In an office environment you are most likely to be dealing with written material. If an organisation has paid a blanket fee to an agency of the type mentioned above, a notice will usually be displayed, for example, beside the photocopier, with details of the licence agreement. In addition you can copy materials if:

- you are copying them for your own private study
- your are copying them for the purpose of review
- you are copying them for research which is non-profit making
- you include an acknowledgement of the author and the title of the publication in your final script
- you are reporting current events
- you are using them for judicial purposes
- you are using them for educational use.

However, if you are making multiple copies or copying a large proportion of the materials, you may still need permission.

Copyright is often indicated with the copyright symbol © and the name of the owner of the copyright. On other materials you may find the term 'all rights reserved' or 'no part of this publication may be reproduced or transmitted in any form or by any means without permission'. You may have noticed this kind of warning at the start of DVDs. You should not copy this type of material without permission.

Software

The second area where business organisations have to be careful is in their use of software. Each organisation must ensure that:

- the organisation has sufficient licences for the software in use
- employees do not copy software
- the content of CD ROMs is not printed and copied
- CDs and software are not copied
- information from the Internet is not copied without permission.

Note that although material on a website is protected by copyright in the same way as material in other media, as websites are accessible all over the world you may not be able to enforce this law outside the UK.

Data Protection Acts 1984 and 1998

The purpose of these Acts is to balance the rights of individuals and the lawful rights of others for using their personal information. Those who process information – the data controllers – have certain obligations, while those whose data is recorded – the data subjects – have certain rights. If your organisation is involved in processing personal information, it has to notify the Information Commissioner's Office, pay a fee and register. It will then have to comply with the following principles of good information handling. The data must be:

- fairly and lawfully processed – see below for a full definition of fairly processed

- processed for limited purposes

- adequate, relevant and not excessive

- accurate and up to date

- not retained any longer than is necessary

- processed in accordance with the individual's rights

- secure

- not be transferred to countries outside the EU unless the country has adequate protection for the individual.

To clarify what is meant by fairly processed, a minimum of one of the following conditions must be met for personal information.

1 The individual has consented to the processing. Think about when you enter a competition – you often sign to agree that the information can be retained by the organiser of the competition.

2 Processing the information is necessary for the performance of a contract with the individual.

3 Processing is needed under a legal obligation, for example, in the case of teachers, child minders or people who come into contact with children, where you have to disclose any criminal records.

4 Processing is needed to protect the interests of the individual, for example, medical records

5 Processing is needed to carry out public functions, for example, in court.

6 Processing is needed to pursue the legitimate interests of the data controller or third parties (unless it could unjustifiably prejudice the interests of the individual).

There is also provision in the Acts to allow for processing sensitive personal information which might not normally be recorded. This would include information on ethnic origin, political opinions, religion, trade union membership, physical and mental health, sexual orientation, criminal proceedings or convictions. If an organisation intends to record any of this data they would have to meet at least one of a series of extra conditions. Here are examples of extra conditions.

- They have the explicit consent of the individual.

- The information is required by law for employment purposes – the example of those working with children, given above, would fit in here.

- They can prove that they need to process the information to protect the vital interests of the individual or another person.

- They are dealing with the judicial process or law administration.

The rights of the individual are clearly defined by the Data Protection Acts.

Subject access: you can find out what is held about you on computer.

Prevent processing: you can ask for a data controller not to process information which causes unwarranted damage.

Direct marketing: you can ask that your data is not used for direct marketing purposes.

Automatic decision making: you can object to decisions being made on your behalf on account of the data held.

Compensation: you can claim compensation from the data controller for damage or distress if they breach the act.

Rectify, block, erase and destruct: you can apply to court to order a data controller to change, block or destroy personal details if they are not accurate or have opinions based on inaccurate information.

Role of commissioner: you can ask the Commissioner to assess whether the Acts have been contravened.

These Acts have been amended by the introduction of the Freedom of Information (FOI) Act which applies to public authorities. The FOI Act gives a statutory right to information and provides for the release of exempt information in the public interest. Public authorities have to establish a publication scheme which means they commit to publishing information, classifying what information they will publish and indicate if there will be a charge for publishing the information. This will ultimately mean that information previously regarded as 'secret' will be available to all.

You can access a presentation on the Freedom of Information Act (2000) on the website www.informationcommissioner.gov.uk/eventual

You can access a useful factsheet on the Data Protection Act on the website www.informationcommissioner.gov.uk/eventual

Privacy and Electronic Communications (EC Directive) Regulations 2003

This covers unsolicited electronic marketing communications and supercedes the Telecommunications (Data Protection and Privacy) Regulations 1999. It covers telecommunication network and service providers and individuals and how publicly available electronic communications services are used for direct marketing purposes. It also covers unsolicited direct marketing activity by telephone, fax and electronic mail and automated calling systems. With e-mails, there are essentially two new rules:

1   The sender must not conceal their identity and must provide a valid address to allow opt-out requests.

2   Senders cannot send unsolicited marketing messages by e-mail to individual subscribers unless they have the subscriber's prior consent to do so.

This strict opt-in rule is relaxed only under the following circumstances:

- If the recipient's e-mail address was collected in the course of a sale or negotiations for a sale.

- If the sender only sends promotional messages relating to their similar products and services.

- If, when the address was collected, the recipient was given the chance to opt out which they didn't take. There must be an opt-out opportunity given with every subsequent message.

You can register with a central stoplist such as the Telephone Preference Service, Corporate Telephone Preference Service or Fax Preference Service to stop unsolicited telephone calls or faxes. You can also register with individual organisations who are sending the communication.

The Computer Misuse Act 1990

The main purpose of this Act is to specify offences against computer systems or data. It provides protection for systems and data. Within the Act there are three specific offences:

1 *Unauthorised access to computer material*
It is an offence to perform any function with the intention of securing unauthorised access to any program or data held in any computer. This is commonly referred to as 'hacking' or 'cracking'. An offence is committed if access results in data being altered, erased, used, ouput or copied or saved to any other storage medium. The offence carries a prison sentence.

2 *Unauthorised access with the intention of committing further offences*
This is the follow-on offence from offence 1. In offence 1 the offender gets into the system, in offence 2 they commit a further crime such as tampering with bank account details held on computer.

3 *Unauthorised modification of computer material*
This makes it a crime to modify the contents of anything accessed if there is an intention to modify – any program or data held is altered or erased or added to – and a knowledge that the person making the modification has not been authorised to do so. This offence covers the introduction of worms and viruses to a system

There is a Council of Europe Cybercrime Convention whose purpose it is to investigate and prosecute computer and computer-related crimes and facilitate international co-operation on this type of crime. They have drawn up a series of articles which act as guidelines to legislation. There is also a European Union Framework Decision which attempts to align member states' legislation to ensure that attacks against information systems would be dealt with in criminal law in the same way.

Although the Computer Misuse Act was written before many of the current developments in technology were envisaged, it is still deemed fit for purpose in view of the number of prosecutions which take place under the Act.

Check your Progress

Consider the following. Make a note of the legislation concerned and what you would do.

1 Janice works in the HR department. Janice notices that her boss has left her computer on and she is logged in. Janice is desperate to know how much the new admin assistant is being paid. She can access this information through her boss's machine. She phones you and asks you if you think she should look up the information.

2 Your mother is really fed up getting phone calls every night at dinner time from people trying to sell double glazing, home extensions and holidays. What advice would you give her?

3 You are convinced that there is a problem with the information your local college have about you. Every time you apply for a course there you are told the course is full. How could you find out what information they hold about you?

Internal Assessment

Here are some examples of the kind of questions you might be asked as part of your internal assessment.

1 Outline the benefits of e-commerce to an organisation. (2)

2 Describe two purposes of having a law to protect copyright. (2)

3 Using the Internet has helped everyone access information but there are some disadvantages in using the Internet to source business information. What are they? (2)

4 If you worked in an organisation with three branches why might your organisation consider installing video conferencing facilities? (2)

1 Outline two problems poor data management might cause in an organisation. (2)

2 Outline two ways in which good data management will benefit an organisation. (2)

3 What are the main principles behind the Data Protection Act (1998)? (2)

4 Describe four ways in which good ICT systems will help improve work flow. (4)

5 Outline three ways in which an organisation might try to ensure its data is kept securely. (3)

External Assessment

Here are some examples of the kind of questions you might be asked as part of your external assessment. An estimate of the marks assigned to each question is indicated and it would be anticipated that each question would form part of a larger question.

1 What is meant by back-up procedures? Why are they important? (3)

2 Outline the main purpose of legislation on Computer Misuse. (4)

3 Explain what is meant by video conferencing and using examples explain when it might be used. (4)

1 Describe three ways in which an organisation can inform employees of their role in ensuring security and confidentiality of electronically held information. (6)

2 Improvements in ICT have resulted in better workflow. Explain this statement using three examples. (6)

3 Using examples explain why electronic file management is important to organisations. (6)

CHAPTER 10

Word Processing

Intermediate 2 Level Outcomes:

This chapter contains explanations and exercise material for Intermediate 2 Information Technology for Administrators Outcome 3.

 Use a word processing document to present the solution to a business problem:

☆ **creating and completing letters and business reports**

☆ **using various features of word processing software**

☆ **integrating data from spreadsheets and databases including mailmerge**

☆ **printing documents and documents with merge fields.**

It also includes explanations and exercise material for Intermediate 2 Presenting and Communicating Information Outcome 2.

 Use ICT to present and communicate information:

☆ **creating and completing memos, forms and tables**

☆ **using various features of word processing software**

☆ **tables.**

Note: Layout and content of itineraries is included in Chapters 7 and 11.

Higher Level Outcomes:

 It also contains Higher Information Technology for Management Outcome 3.

Use ICT to solve business problems and communicate and present solutions:

☆ **letters, notice of meeting and agenda, minutes, reports and newsletters**

☆ **tables**

☆ **forms**

☆ **using various features of word processing software**

☆ **integrating data from spreadsheets or databases including mailmerge**

☆ **printing.**

The materials in this chapter will take a different format from previous chapters. The aim is not to provide you with instructions on how to use the software on your system but to give a general explanation of the features available and provide exercise materials in the form of in-tray exercises for practice.

House Style

Most organisations will have house styles for documents which are produced regularly. House styles will vary between organisations and will usually be a preferred method of layout, spacing, tone and content.

Task 1

Identify the preferred housestyle for your school or college for the following documents:

Letters
Memos
Reports
Notice of meeting and Agenda
Minutes

Task 2

Create headed paper for the following organisation.

John Nicholls
47 Great Emperor Street
GLASGOW
GF1 7JN

Telephone 0141 568 8000
E-mail customers@JNstores.co.uk

Word processing enables you produce and edit documents and use a series of features. The main advantage of using any kind of software application is that data can be transferred from one software package to another and time is not wasted inputting the same information into a different format. It is important that, as a user of software, you ensure that the data you key in or scan in, is accurate, up to date and in a format which can be used by others.

House styles have already been mentioned, but many organisations will also have a preferred font and size of font for general use. Large organisations may employ editors or publication experts whose job it is to check all documents which go into general circulation. You could expect to find this type of service in a bank or an insurance company, for example. All of these functions are there to try to ensure consistency of documentation.

You should now look carefully at the house style information you have on letters and memos and ensure you understand the spacing and layout.

Before keying in this section of correspondence you should know:

- acceptable layout for letters
- acceptable layout for memos
- how to display text
- how to embolden, underscore, use italics
- how to change a font and change the size of the font
- how to align text
- how to insert bullet points
- how to deal with the 24 hour clock
- how to change font and font size
- how to print a document
- simple printers' corrections.

You should discuss how you are going to file these documents and what traceable referencing system you are going to use. You will be asked to recall some of these documents at a later stage so they should all be saved, although you may not wish to save letters with the headed paper.

Here are some of the common printers' corrections you will meet:

Correction Signs

	Handwritten sign	Meaning
New paragraph	// or [or NP	Start a new paragraph
Insert	*h* eg *and h* ⊙*h*	Insert what is written beside this line exactly where indicated. If punctuation marks are to be inserted they are often circled.
Transpose horizontally	trs four ⌐or⌐ one psyh⌐cic	Move words or letters as indicated. More than 2 is usually shown using numbers
Transpose vertically	(circular arrows)	Change lines or sections or figures from one place to the other
Close up	(close up sign)	Remove any extra spaces
Leave a space	/ or #	Insert a space where the sign is located.
Stet	~~now~~ ~~then~~ ------	You should key in the words which have a dotted line underneath them. Stet meaning let it stand.
Delete	~~delete~~ ~~this~~	Delete any words or letters with a line through them
UC or Caps	u/c or caps _voluntary_ _corp_	Key in the letters or words underlined in capital letters
LC or lc	_Managers_ lc	Key in the letters or words underlined in lower case.
Run on	here⌐ ⌐once again	Do not start a new paragraph/section

In-tray documents Set 1 Day 1

You are working in the general office of the department store John Nicholls. The office supervisor will often ask you to help out with word processing requests, particularly when the office is busy. You are keen to develop your skills in this area. However, it is important that you make sure that what you produce is up to the high standards required.

These documents have been written by Margaret Ward, Sales Administrator.

In-tray Set 1 Day 1 – document 1

> Memo
>
> To Keith Walters
>
> From Margaret Ward
>
> Subject Easy-rest Suite Order number 298/450
>
> Please key this as a letter according to our house style.
>
> I have phoned this customer John Gillespie several times and the phone keeps ringing out. I can only assume he is on holiday as our records say he is not moving until the end of the month. I have written to the address we have for him to tell him his suite is now in stock. Please refer him to the General Office if any enquiries come through to you. We are anxious to deliver this suite as soon as possible. There is a balance of £1700 to pay on delivery.

In-tray Set 1 Day 1 – document 2

> MW/
>
> Today's date
>
> Mr John Gillespie
> 56 Halpin Street
> EDINBURGH
> EH42 5JK
>
> Dear Mr Gillespie – heading – Easy-rest Suite
>
> I am writing to tell you that your suite has now arrived at our warehouse and we are ready to deliver it to your new house in Leith. We have tried to contact you by phone on several occasions but have been unable to make contact. Could you please phone us on 0131 674 7888 to arrange delivery. There is a balance of £1700 to pay on delivery of the suite.
>
> NP [I look forward to hearing from you.
>
> Yours sincerely, Margaret Ward, Sales Administrator
> You should ensure that the phone number is emboldened

INFORMATION TECHNOLOGY

In-tray Set 1 Day 1 – document 3

Could you please prepare an A4 Notice for the Furniture department
For One day only

25% off all Trusleep beds

All beds fully guaranteed

In-tray Set 1 Day 1 – document 4

Key in the following passage in double line spacing, with the heading Updated Staff Safety Information as a centred emboldened heading in a larger font.

Following the installation of new escalators to the <u>f</u>urniture <u>d</u>epartment, please bear in mind that escalators will be switched off automatically when the Fire Alarm sounds. Each Floor Manager has been given specific instructions about evacuating customers and staff from their areas of responsibility.   *u/c*

All staff will be issued with additional pages for their <u>p</u>ersonal <u>s</u>afety <u>m</u>anual which was issued at the time of their employment with John Nicholls. Please ensure that you read this information and keep it in a safe place.   *u/c*

These instructions are displayed on <u>s</u>taff <u>n</u>oticeboards situated to the left of the entrance of all Staff Only areas.   *u/c*

In-tray documents Set 1 Day 2

This set of correspondence has to be keyed in for Lorna Green, HR Director.

In-tray Set 1 Day 2 – document 1

Please send the following Memo to all staff. The subject heading is Flexible Working Hours.

Over the last 3 months we have been negotiating with Staff Association representatives to reach agreement on introducing a system of flexible working hours which is workable for staff and flexible enough to meet our business needs. We have now decided on a flexitime system which will enable staff to 'bank' time which they work in addition to their core hours but which are not within designated overtime rates. Full details of the scheme will depend on your contract of employment as well as your length of service and the grade of post you hold.

In order to fully explain the system to you, there will be Staff Information Sessions which will be held between 9 and 10 every morning next week. Please book your place on this programme by speaking to your Manager and agreeing a date. Your Manager will then book your place with Human Resources.

continued ➤

It may help you understand the system if you are clear about your Contract of Employment i.e.

- are you permanent or temporary
- are you full-time, part-time or job-share
- how long have you worked for John Nicholls
- what grade of post do you currently hold.

Staff from Human Resources will be available to deal with all your questions.
If you wish you can make a further appointment to discuss your situation privately.

In-tray Set 1 Day 2 – document 2

Please prepare the following notice for all Staff Noticeboards A4 size

Flexible hours – Information sessions

Remember to look at your Contract of Employment for your

    permanent/temporary status

    full-time, part-time or job share

    length of service

    grade of post

Please bring this information with you

A healthy eating breakfast will be available at the meeting.

In-tray Set 1 Day 2 – document 3

Send the following letter to Ms M Harper, Littlejohn and Hope, Catering and Events Organisation, 67 Hanover Road, LIVINGSTON, LM32 7HT

Dear Margaret, Following our discussions about catering arrangements for the Information Sessions to be held between 9 and 10 every morning during the first week in October (please insert the dates), will you please arrange to provide

NP breakfasts for 50 Monday – Saturday.[As agreed we will ensure there are sufficient tables available to lay out the buffet and the room will be available to you from 8 each

NP day and access will be available through the staff entrance.[We confirm our booking is for the Californian Buffet at a price of £5.00 per person.

Yours sincerely, Lorna Green, HR Director

In-tray Set 1 Day 2 – document 4

> Memo to All Managers From LG Subject Flexible Working Sessions
>
> During the first week in October we will be holding Information Sessions to explain the new Flexible Working arrangements which have been agreed with the Staff
>
> NP Association. [I have asked all staff to speak to their Managers about which day they attend one of these Information Sessions. When you receive a request please phone or e-mail Joyce O'Malley (Ext 2455) to book a place. Places are limited to 50 per session and you should ensure before booking places that you still have sufficient
>
> NP staff available to serve our customers. [A Californian style breakfast will be served each morning.

In-tray documents Set 1 Day 3

In-tray Set 1 Day 3 – document 1

The following set of documents has been prepared by Barry Ward, Personnel Assistant.

Set up the following as a letter, without a date or inside address for using as a mail merge.

> Thank you for coming to interview last week. We are delighted to be able to offer you a temporary position as Sales Assistant at our Glasgow store. The hours of work will be 0900 – 1730 hours, working 10 out of 14 days. One night per week you will be expected to work until 1900 hours. You will be allowed a one hour lunch break. Your contract will start on 1 November and will terminate on 3 January 20... The rate of pay will be £6.50 per hour.
>
> If you wish to take up this offer please complete the attached acceptance and return it to us in the stamped addressed envelope before the 30th of the month.
>
> You should report for work on 1 November and ensure that you have your National Insurance Number and any relevant Tax documents with you on that day.
>
> I look forward to hearing from you. Yrs sinc Barry Ward, Personnel Assistant

On a separate sheet in double line spacing:

I _____ accept the offer of employment as a Temporary Sales Assistant in John Nicholls. I agree to the hours specified in your letter of _____ and the terms and conditions outlined.

I am/am not prepared to consider extending my hours of work, if required for an additional rate of pay of £8.00 per hour,

Signed _____

Date _____

Return to Barry Ward, Personnel Assistant, John Nicholls, 47 Great Emperor Street, Glasgow, GF1 7JN.

In-tray Set 1 Day 3 – document 2

Please lay out the following notice for Staff Noticeboards:

Induction of temporary staff 1 November

Temporary Christmas Staff will start their Induction on 1 November

Volunteers to act as Mentors are required to help with training staff on stock control and working with tills

Please volunteer to help new starts by contacting

Kyle in Personnel

Extension 478

In-tray Set 1 Day 3 – document 3

Set up the following as a letter, without a date or inside address for using as a mail merge.

Thank you for coming to interview last week. On this occasion we are unable to offer you a position as a temporary Sales Assistant at our Glasgow store. We had an exceptionally large number of applicants for these posts, however we will keep your name on record should more temporary staff be required. Applications will be retained for a maximum of 3 months.

I wish you every success in your job search.

Yrs sinc Barry Ward, Personnel Assistant

In-tray documents Set 1 Day 4

This batch of work is from Margaret O'Hare.

In-tray Set 1 Day 4 – document 1

Key in the following notice:

> IMPORTANT RECALL NOTICE
>
> The following product has been found to be faulty
>
> Baby Rabbit – pink, blue or lemon
>
> Maker –Cuddlytoys
>
> Price – £5.99
>
> It has been notified to John Nicholls that some of these toys sold in our <u>baby</u>   u/c
> u/c <u>department</u> between May and September of this year have faulty eye fixings.
>
> (stet) Please return ~~any of these~~ products to John Nicholls for a full refund

In-tray Set 1 Day 4 – document 2

> Memo To All Toy Department Managers Subject Recall of Baby Rabbit Soft Toys by Cuddlytoys
>
> The following toy has been recalled as a result of information received from the Health and Safety Executive.
>
> Baby Rabbit by Cuddlytoys
>
> Serial numbers 305, 306, 307
>
> Colours pink, blue, lemon
>
> The fault is in the eye fixing of the toys. Anyone returning a toy to the store should be offered a full refund and given a complimentary tea/coffee voucher. An alternative toy should be offered. We have recently taken stock of a batch of similar toys from America called Touchytoys. These should be in all stores by next week.
>
> It is important that you stress to customers that there have been no accidents with these toys, the withdrawal from stock is merely a precaution.[Thank you for your co-   NP
> operation

In-tray Set 1 Day 4 – document 3

Health and Safety Executive

54 Dryburgh Lane, London, WC4 5DG

Dear Sirs, Thank you for the information about Cuddlytoys Baby Rabbits. We have checked our records and we imported a total of 600 of these toys through Chiltern Importers. We have advised all of our stores to advertise the recall in their Toy Departments and we will be advertising the recall in the national and local press this weekend. We have already had 47 of these toys returned to us and a check of our stock shows that we still have 32 toys in stores throughout the country. These have, of course, all been withdrawn from sale.

I will write to you again in 4 weeks to let you know the situation. Meantime thank you for informing us of the problem so promptly.

Yrs ffy, Margaret O'Hare, Marketing Manager

In-tray Set 1 Day 4 – document 4

Memo To All Stock Depot Managers Subject Recall of faulty soft toys

The following toy has been recalled as a result of information received from the Health and Safety Executive.

Baby Rabbit by Cuddlytoys

Serial numbers 305, 306, 307

Colours pink, blue, lemon

Please ensure that any remaining stock of these toys is securely packaged and sent to Head Office as quickly as possible

In-tray documents Set 2

Tables from this section can be used by Intermediate 2 students. Meeting documents are part of the Higher syllabus, as are more complex letters. However these could readily be used by Intermediate 2 students too. Before tackling production of these in-tray documents you should be able to:

- lay out business letters with a tear off portion
- produce letters with more than one page
- lay out a table
- prepare a notice of meeting and an agenda
- prepare a chairperson's agenda.

The two page letters and tables are suitable documents for those studying Intermediate 2, as is the chairperson's agenda as an illustration of the use of tables. When you are dealing with letters which go on to a second page or letters with a tear off portion, you should always use the print preview to ensure that where you are splitting the letter for page 2 or where you want to insert the tear off section is appropriate.

In addition to the functions you used for In-tray Documents Set 1, within these documents you should know how to deal with the following instructions:

- align text
- use italics
- convert text to table
- use manuscript corrections
- use footnotes
- merge cells in a table.

Think about when you would align text to the right, for example, for a letter heading or when you might centre text, for example, for a notice. Although you can also justify text, i.e. ensuring the left and the right hand margin are even, this is less used in business than you might think. This is because it sometimes leads to distortion of text and spacing.

Use of italics and emboldening are simple ways of highlighting text to draw attention to particular words or headings. Text can also be enhanced by changing fonts, using block capitals or changing the size of text.

Following one of the main principles of using IT applications – that data should not need to be keyed in more than once – converting already keyed in text into a table and then adding one or more columns as required, is a good way of changing the format of text and saves it being keyed in for a second time.

Footnotes are used when additional relevant information is needed as an explanation but placing this information in the middle of a passage of text or table would detract from the overall impression of the data. The additional information appears at the foot of the page where the original reference appears. An end note is similar but an end note appears at the end of the entire document rather than at the foot of the page.

In-tray documents Set 2 Day 1

This group of documents was written by Margaret O'Hare, Marketing Manager.

In-tray documents Set 2 Day 1 – document 1

Letter to Mrs L Price, 34 Hillside Walk, Leith, LE3 4RT. Send the same letter to Mr A Halford, 22 Trent Road, Glasgow, G45 7NQ. His order number was 2449. The letter should fit on to one page. If it does not fit on to one page try to ensure that you are keying in the tear off portion in a sensible place.

Dear Mrs Price

Order Number 3569 – Brown leather settee

I was sorry to hear that there has been a problem with the settee you ordered from us in January. While it is our aim to please all our customers, I am sure you appreciate that we try to do this by dealing with reputable suppliers who can guarantee the quality of the goods they supply. In your case something has obviously gone wrong with the quality control system at Highrise Upholstery and we are currently taking up this matter with them. We will keep you informed of the outcome.

John Nicholls are obviously keen to resolve this matter as quickly as possible and we suggest that we pick up the settee and the 2 accompanying chairs from your house as soon as possible so that they can be returned to the manufacturer. We will leave you with a substitute suite until the matter is resolved.

Can you please complete and return the attached slip to me as soon as possible and I will make arrangements to uplift the suite at your convenience.

Yours sincerely Margaret O'Hare Marketing Manager

....

Mrs L Price, 34 Hillside Walk, Leith, LE3 4RT

Telephone ....

Could you please arrange to pick up a settee and 2 armchairs from the above address at the following time and date

Day .... Date ....

Time .... am/pm

In-tray documents Set 2 Day 1 – document 2

Letter to Jonathan Rico, Manager, Highrise Upholstery, Lindesfarne Industrial Estate, Grantham, GA56 7HG

Dear Mr Rico **Siena Suites – brown hide**

We have now received 3 different complaints from customers who have purchased hide suites from us over the last 3 months. All of these customers bought brown leather suites in ~~January/February~~ last year. The problem seems to be that the hides used are ageing. While we appreciate a certain amount of colour variation is inevitable in the hides used in a leather suite, in these 3 cases the colour variation is too obvious to be acceptable.

(stet)

From the point of view of customer care, we are very keen to resolve these complaints as quickly as possible. In all 3 cases the customers concerned are account holders with this company.

So far we have picked up all 3 suites from the customers and are holding them in our Glasgow warehouse ~~and~~ would be available for you to uplift *The suites* and/or inspect ~~them~~ at any time Monday-Friday by prior arrangement. We have provided each of the customers with an alternative suite at the moment but obviously this is only a temporary measure ~~and~~ has cost us *which* money as these suites cannot now be sold in the usual way. A copy of the text of the letter sent to our customers is shown below. (Insert a copy of the body of the letter you keyed in to Mrs Price and Mr Halford in italics.)

Could you please let me have your comments as quickly as possible so that we can move this issue forward. As you know our company sells a large number of your suites and we would be sorry to have to change suppliers because of a problem such as this.

I look forward to hearing from you.

Yours sincerely Margaret O'Hare, Marketing Manager

In-tray documents Set 2 Day 1 – document 3

Key in the footnote where indicated.

Summary of Sales for last year (20..)

Glasgow Branch		
Department	**Manager**	**Sales £000s**
Furniture	Kamal Ahmed	458
Cosmetics	Rena Carter	215
Bathrooms	Susan Shields	124
Cosmetics – JN only	Loraine Duval	230
Ladies Clothing	Naiem Reda	121
Children's clothing	Anne Wilson[1]	179
Gents Clothing	Alistair McKay	112
Electrical	Jeff Quigley	146
Household	Ellen Divers	213
China	Ruby Dalziel	215
Glassware	Gordon Stratford	122
Soft furnishings	Gary Davidson	413
Accessories	Sandra Melbourne	108
Gifts	Sonia Ben Arefi	104
Toys	Gail Shields	207
Sports	Orla Coyle	115

bold and italics in column headings

[1]Temporary Acting Manager

In-tray documents Set 2 Day 1 – document 4

Prepare the Notice of Meeting and Agenda for a meeting of the department managers. It should be held in the Board Room at 1000 hours, a week on Friday. Apart from the usual items please add to the agenda 'Sales figures', 'Comparison with previous year's trading' and 'Current outlook'. Insert an indication that this is a DRAFT document. You are the secretary of this committee.

In-tray documents Set 2 Day 1 – document 5

Using the Agenda that you set up earlier, convert the agenda items into a table so that the Chairman can write his notes prior to the meeting. Indicate that this item is a draft.

In-tray documents Set 2 Day 2

This group of documents were written by Jim Winters, IT Director.

In-tray documents Set 2 Day 2 – document 1

Prepare the Notice and Agenda for the next meeting of the IT Committee. Use headed paper. The meeting will be held in the Board Room on Monday 22 May 20.. at 1300 hours. Include in the agenda: minutes of previous meeting, matters arising, stock control software, staff development, etc. Put your name in as the Secretary and indicate that this document is a first draft.

In-tray documents Set 2 Day 2 – document 2

Using the Agenda that you set up earlier, convert the agenda items into a table so that the chairperson can write their notes prior to the meeting. Indicate that this item is a first draft.

In-tray documents Set 2 Day 2 – document 3

Prepare the following letter which will be given to customers who buy a computer in the store. There will not be an inside address and you should indicate that this is a draft letter. Print a copy on headed paper.

> Dear Customer
>
> **Peace of Mind Insurance**
>
> Insurance costs generally have risen substantially over the last few years but our premiums have remained substantially lower than the average charged to cover breakdown and repair of your new computer.
>
> How do we do this? We do it through:
>
> - buying only from first class suppliers who have a reputation for excellent quality products
> - providing good customer advice prior to purchasing
> - ensuring that the equipment you buy suits your needs
> - advising customers when they should be upgrading their equipment.
>
> What does our insurance include? In the first year we will guarantee to:
>
> - repair or replace any equipment failures (Put in a footnote here and put in the footnote Subject to certain restrictions detailed on page 4 of our Service Plan)
> - give advice to every customer on how to set up your home office to meet with the requirements of health and safety legislation
> - agree to trade in used equipment if, after following our advice, it does not meet your needs
> - carry out a suitability check, if requested, after 12 months has elapsed since purchase.
>
> *continued* ➤

Compare our prices. You have 30 days from the date on your receipt to take up our insurance option. For further details complete the slip below or e-mail insurance@jn.com.

Yours faithfully Jim Winters, IT Manager

....

Please send full details of your Peace of Mind Insurance to me at the following address

Name ....

Address ....

....

Postcode ....

E-mail ....

I have purchased ....

....

In-tray documents Set 2 Day 2 – document 4

Put in an appropriate reference and date. This letter is to go to John McCafferty, Southwood Logistics, 37 Woodside Walk, Burnside, GH6 7JK. It should be marked Confidential.

Dear Mr McCafferty

Keira McGill, 209/2B Highgrove Road, Maryhill, GLASGOW, G7 9LG

Thank you for your letter about Keira's application for the post of IT Manager at your Glasgow office. Keira has worked with this organisation since August 1994. At first she worked in the IT support and maintenance section which deals with all the IT systems used in our department store in Glasgow. During this time Keira proved herself able to deal well with people and she showed particular aptitude for dealing with those who had little or no experience with IT systems.

After 2 years Keira was promoted to Supervisor of this section, taking on additional duties and dealing with a huge increase in the volume of work, as well as the kinds of software and terminals used throughout the organisation. Part of her duties during this time was the training of new starts, temporary agency help and secondees in the IT department. All of these duties she carried out diligently and with good humour. After her maternity leave in 2001 Keira opted to continue her post on a job-share basis and has concentrated on the training and development side of the job since that time.

Keira has undertaken a number of courses at John Nicholls, in particular Oracle, networking and software editing courses and she has contributed greatly to the development of company-wide software developments, earning herself a reputation as one of the most competent IT specialists in the organisation. [Having had a close look NP at the Job specification and the Person specification you enclosed I would have no doubt about Keira's ability to carry out the role outlined. Keira has always been a popular and sociable member of staff. She gets on well with her colleagues, is

continued ➤

adaptable and flexible. Although I would be sorry to lose Keira as a member of staff, I would have no hesitation in recommending her to you.

I would be pleased to answer any further questions you may have.

Yours sincerely Jim Winters, IT Director

In-tray documents Set 2 Day 2 – document 5

Key in and enhance.

IT support staff

First Name	Surname	Branch	Department
Keira	McGill	Hightown	IT
John	Cavanagh	Edinburgh	IT
Rashid	Ahmel	Edinburgh	IT
Lynn	Forsyth	Hightown	Admin
Caroline	Harper	Hightown	Admin
Paul	Ganguly	Edinburgh	IT
Claire	Lee	Edinburgh	Electrical

In-tray documents Set 2 Day 3

This set of documents was prepared by Kamal Ahmed, Manager of the Furniture Department in Glasgow.

In-tray documents Set 2 Day 3 – document 1

Prepare the following letter for sending to Richard MacPherson, 9/11 Braeview Road, EAST KILBRIDE, EH4 5NH. Make sure this letter either fits on to one page or continues to a second page and leaves the tear-off portion in an appropriate place.

Dear Mr MacPherson

ORDER NO GH7865/11 – FITTED BEDROOM UNITS

Thank you for your order for Highline Oak Veneer bedroom furniture. As outlined to you when you placed your order and paid a deposit of £100, this furniture is made to suit your individual requirements and the exact price will be determined after our representative has visited your home and taken the required measurements. Following this initial survey, we will prepare a detailed estimate for you and make a further appointment with you to discuss any variations on the proposed layout and internal fitments. If you decide to proceed with the order, you will be required to pay a deposit of 25% of the price of the furniture when the order is placed. If you do not wish to proceed with the order your £100 will be refunded. [You can expect 6 weeks between NP the placing of the order and delivery. Once we have received delivery at our warehouse we will telephone you and agree when our fitter can call, confirm the work to be carried out including any wiring, and arrange a date for fitting. [To start this NP process, can I ask you to complete the attached slip or telephone me at the Glasgow store Ext 419 so that I can arrange for our representative to call.

I look forward to hearing from you.

Yours sinc etc

Insert a tear off portion with name, address, phone number and space for day and time of visit.

In-tray documents Set 2 Day 3 – document 2

Stock-taking – Tables and Chairs

Model	Tables	No of Chairs	Seat coverings	
			Fabric	Leather
Elsanta	4	20	14	6
Edinburgh	6	42	22	20
Highland	3	20	10	10
Shaker	4	32	12	20
Classic	2	27	11	16
Earnock	6	32	16	16

INFORMATION TECHNOLOGY

In-tray documents Set 2 Day 3 – document 3

Prepare a Notice of Meeting and Agenda for the team meeting. This is an informal meeting but Kamal usually sends out an agenda and notice. The meeting will be held in the department at 0845 hours on the 24th of this month. The agenda should have the following items: apologies, matters arising from the last meeting, household sales, stock-taking, any other business, date of next meeting.

In-tray documents Set 2 Day 3 – document 4

Convert the Agenda into a Chairperson's Agenda for Kamal so that he can prepare for the meeting and insert notes against the agenda items.

In-tray documents Set 2 Day 3 – document 5

This letter is to be included with a copy of our catalogue.

Letter to Mrs K Li, 490/2B North Erskine Road, ARRAN, AA3 8VB.

Dear Mrs Li

MAIL ORDER FURNITURE

Thank you for your letter of (insert yesterday's date). I enclose a copy of John Nicholls' 'Your Home' catalogue. This catalogue contains more than one thousand pages and brings thousands of branded products direct to your home.

You will see from the information enclosed there are a number of ways to order goods from this catalogue.

On-line ordering

You can order on-line by sending your order to yourhome@jn.com and paying by using your credit card or your debit card.

If you are an account holder with John Nicholls you can order on-line and charge the items ordered to your John Nicholls account.

Completing an order form

Order forms are to be found at the back of the catalogue and, once completed, you should send your order along with a cheque or credit card/debit card details to the address given, in one of the stamped addressed envelopes supplied. Better still, charge the order to your John Nicholls account.

In store ordering

You can also order any items in the catalogue from the Customer Service Department of any of our stores. Full details of store locations are in the back of the 'Your Home' catalogue.

If for any reason you are not delighted with the goods ordered we will, of course, arrange an immediate and full refund.

This is an easy way of shopping for stylish and fashionable items for your home. Most items in the catalogue will be delivered to you within one week of receiving your order. Some larger items may take longer but this will be clearly stated in the catalogue.

continued ➤

While delivery on the mainland is free of charge, we reserve the right to charge for delivery to offshore locations such as Arran. If you order on-line you can check the cost of delivery prior to sending your order. The charge for delivery will vary depending on the items ordered.

Should you require any further information please do not hesitate to get in touch.

Yours etc

In-tray documents Set 2 Day 4

This set of documents was prepared by Orla Coyle, Manager of the Sports Department in Glasgow.

In-tray documents Set 2 Day 4 – document 1

Prepare a Notice of Meeting and Agenda for a meeting of the staff in the Sports Department and representatives of the Marketing Department. The meeting will be held at 0800 hours in the Board Room on the last Friday in the month. The agenda will have only the following items: Nike promotion, Teenage Week, Children's Keep Fit Event and discounts available.

In-tray documents Set 2 Day 4 – document 2

Prepare a Chairperson's Agenda by converting the agenda items into a table and adding in the following against the relevant items.

Nike Promotion

Possible dates – 21–28 Feb or same week in March or April. Scottish Gold medallist attend for launch? Special Nike discount of 20% negotiated. Special stock items.

Teenage Week

Suggest first week in May or June, preferably May. Keep fit DVDs, street wear, rap and street dancing. Clothing needs to be ordered 3 weeks before.

Children's Keep Fit Event

Date – Easter hols – check with schools. Suggested trials trampoline, bowling, swingball, badminton, table tennis, in-line skates, running tests.

Discounts Available

Will JN offer additional discount? Nike will discount. Health Clubs will discount membership where there are teenagers or children in the family. Sports equipment companies will offer extra 10% off.

In-tray documents Set 2 Day 4 – document 3

Prepare this letter. Insert format for date and relevant reference but do not insert any inside address. Indicate that this document is a draft. You may use this for a mail merge later. Make sure the letter fits on to one page or leave the tear off section in a logical place on the second page.

Dear

TEENAGE WEEK

We have some very special promotions planned for the next few months. These will be of special interest to you and your youth groups and we can offer you all kinds of special deals during our promotions. The first promotion which may be of interest to you is the Teenage Week.

This week is aimed at the younger teenager. Press and television programmes are full of advice to encourage us all to get more active. This is our chance to inspire young people to keep active. This week will be activity based and will allow those pre-booked to take part in lots of events, some in the store and some in their own clubs and premises. Here are some of the activities planned.

- The chance to watch and dance with professional dancers and personalities who feature in keep fit DVDs. You can arrange for this activity to take place in your own club. (Insert a footnote here to say that certain minimum numbers and restrictions may apply.)

- Rap and street dancing competitions to be held in the Royal Concert Hall.

- 'How fit are you?' Using electronic exercise equipment in the store, experts will be on hand to test heart rates, lung capacity, flexibility and metabolic rate.

- Fashion shows which will take place in the store. These will concentrate on street wear and will use professional as well as local models chosen from volunteers.

- Special free one day visits to local health clubs available. (Insert a footnote to indicate that minimum purchase may apply.)

- Bowling with style. Themed events and discounted entry to several bowling alleys throughout the country.

Later on in the year we intend to hold a special Children's Keep Fit Event and various well known sportswear suppliers such as Nike will also be holding special promotions in our store.

I do hope you will join us at our first special event of the year.

Yours etc

Add on a tear off portion with contact name and address, name of organisation, contact phone number, list of events.

INFORMATION TECHNOLOGY

In-tray documents Set 2 Day 4 – document 4

Key in the following table and enhance to show information more clearly.

Sports Department

Supplier	Sales £s	
	July–December	January–June
Nike	22800	27900
Addidas	21200	32800
SweatyBetty	10200	14300
Sloggi	10078	12080
USA PRO	12764	13820
Videos/DVDs	**Sales (units)**	
	July–December	January–June
Latino Dance	180	240
Dancemix workout	120	300
Funky Fit	130	260
Total Body Plan	250	210
Housework Workout	220	270
NY Body Plan	290	420
Personal Trainer	130	220
Ultimate Challenge	135	330

In-tray documents Set 3

This set of documents is based on the keying in of tables. Day 1 and Day 2 in-tray exercises in this section are suitable for Intermediate 2. Day 3 is aimed at Higher only.

Before beginning this section, you should know how to:

- set up a table

- input data into a table

- add and remove borders round tables

- print a table

- save a table

- merge cells in a table.

Tables are a useful way of ensuring that text appears in columns. Remember you do not have to print a table showing the gridlines, you can print it without lines. This means that tables are often used for keying in documents which appear in columns, for example, some minutes might be keyed in like this. (Look back at the Action Minutes shown in Chapter 5.)

You can draw attention to particular parts of tables by using heavier borders or by shading some cells.

In-tray documents Set 3 Day 1 Tables

In-tray documents Set 3 Day 1 – Tables Task 1

Task 1

Input the following table:

Department	Name	Training	Date
Human Resources	Joyce O'Malley	Freedom of Information Act	13 November
Marketing	Parvinder Kaan	Freedom of Information Act	13 November
Furniture	Robert Bechal	Customer Care	4 November
Floorcoverings	Msim Paval	Stock control	30 November
Bathrooms	Kathy McAdam	Customer Care	4 November
Cosmetics	Lynn Fraser	Stock control	30 November

Save as Training Table Nov and print a copy.

In-tray documents Set 3 Day 1 – Tables Task 2

Task 2

New Starts for Christmas Period

Start Date	First Name	Surname	Mentor
15/11/..	Lynn	Marshall	PK
15/11/..	Pierre	Boucheron	MP
18/11/..	John	MacKay	MP
01/11/..	Dorian	Rohmer	PK
15/11/..	Kim	Lee	MP
01/11/..	Mark	Kedzierska	MP
03/11/..	Fiona	Galbraith	PK
15/11/..	Abdul	Bastani	PK

Save as New Starts Christmas, check and print a copy.

In-tray documents Set 3 Day 1 – Tables Task 3

Task 3

Key in the following document and display appropriately. Save and print a copy of the file. (If you have already keyed in In-tray documents Set 2 Day 1, copy and paste the information you need from document 3.)

Summary of Sales for last month.

Department	Manager	Sales £
Furniture	Kamal Ahmed	36500
Cosmetics	Rena Carter	18700
Bathrooms	Susan Shields	10045
Cosmetics – JN only	Loraine Duval	21008
Ladies Clothing	Naiem Reda	10021
Children's clothing	Anne Wilson	17359
Gents Clothing	Alistair McKay	10120
Electrical	Jeff Quigley	14560
Household	Ellen Divers	20141
China	Ruby Dalziel	12015
Glassware	Gordon Stratford	10922
Soft furnishings	Gary Davidson	23467
Accessories	Sandra Melbourne	10508
Gifts	Sonia Ben Arefi	10904
Toys	Gail Shields	10207
Sports	Orla Coyle	11215

INFORMATION TECHNOLOGY

In-tray documents Set 3 Day 1 – Tables Task 4

Task 4

Key in the following document and display appropriately. Save and print a copy of the file. (If you have already keyed in In-tray documents Set 2 Day 2, copy and paste the information you need from document 5.)

First Name	Surname	Branch	Department
Keira	McGill	Hightown	IT
John	Cavanagh	Edinburgh	IT
Rashid	Ahmel	Edinburgh	IT
Lynn	Forsyth	Hightown	Admin
Caroline	Harper	Hightown	Admin
Paul	Ganguly	Edinburgh	IT
Claire	Lee	Edinburgh	Electrical

In-tray documents Set 3 Day 2 Tables

Before altering these tables you should be able to:

- add a column to a table
- shade columns, rows and cells
- sort rows and columns
- add a row to a table
- edit the content of cells
- merge cells
- insert formula to total a series of cells
- insert formula to average a series of cells
- change the orientation of the table.

You will see in some cases we are treating this table as if it was a spreadsheet and entering formula to total or average a range of cells. This is usually only done in a table when there are a limited number of calculations. If you were using a table and noticed that lots of calculations were needed, you would be quicker copying the table into a spreadsheet file, performing the calculations and copying it back to the word processed document.

In-tray documents Set 3 Day 2 – Tables Task 1

Task 1

Recall the table you saved as Training Table Nov and make the following amendments:

- Add a column at the end of the table. The heading is Cost. Enter the following data in this column.

- Right align the data in the column.

Name	Cost
Joyce O'Malley	£250.00
Parvinder Kaan	£250.00
Robert Bechal	£45.00
Msim Paval	£130.00
Kathy McAdam	£45.00
Lynn Fraser	£130.00

- Shade the column Cost.

- Sort the table on Department.

- Add a row above the column heading row and insert the title Training Courses in November. Merge the cells in this row.

- Change the column title Training to Course.

- Add a row at the end of the table, merge the first 4 columns and enter the word Total and embolden it.

- Using the formula function, enter the total of the Costs in the last column. Embolden this total.

- Add a row above the Total row. Merge the first 4 columns and enter the word Average and embolden it.

- Using the formula function, enter the formula for average in the last column. Embolden this figure.

- Shade the cells where the Total and the Average figures appear, in a different colour from the rest of the column.

- Print a copy of the table in landscape format.

- Save the table in a way which shows this is your most recent version of the table.

In-tray documents Set 3 Day 2 – Tables Task 2

Task 2

Recall the file you called New Starts Christmas and make the following amendments:

- Delete the row with Mark Kedzierska's details, he will not now be starting.

- Add a column after the Mentor column with No of Hours as follows:

First Name	Surname	No of Hrs
Lynn	Marshall	20
Pierre	Boucheron	16
John	MacKay	16
Dorian	Rohmer	16
Kim	Lee	18
Fiona	Galbraith	20
Abdul	Bastani	20

- Add a row at the end of the table. Merge the first four columns and insert the word Total in block capitals and bold.

- Using the formula function, enter a total for the No of Hrs column in the last row. Embolden this total.

- Add a row above the Total row. Merge the first 4 columns and enter the word Average and embolden it.

- Using the formula function, enter the formula for average in the last column. Embolden this figure.

- Shade the cells where the Total and the Average figures appear, in a different colour from the rest of the column.

- Print a copy of the table in landscape format.

- Save the table in a way which shows this is your most recent version of the table.

In-tray documents Set 3 Day 2 – Tables Task 3

Task 3

Recall the file where you recorded the Sales figures for the month and make the following changes.

- Right align data in the last column. Shade the column for Sales.

- Sort the table on Department.

- Add a row at the end of the table. Merge the first 2 columns and enter the word Total and embolden and italicise it.

- Using the formula function, enter the total of the sales for the month in the last column.

- Embolden this total.

- Add a row above the Total row. Merge the first 2 columns and enter the word Average and embolden it.

- Using the formula function, enter the formula for average in the last column. Embolden this figure.

- Change the heading on the Sales £ to This month's Sales £

- Add a column after the Sales column with the following sales figures for last month. Right align the data in this column.

Department	This month's Sales £	Last month's Sales £
Furniture	36500	23450
Cosmetics	18700	23009
Bathrooms	10045	11257
Cosmetics – JN only	21008	20324
Ladies Clothing	10021	11467
Children's clothing	17359	16879
Gents Clothing	10120	11987
Electrical	14560	23789
Household	20141	28244
China	12015	15436
Glassware	10922	11231
Soft furnishings	23467	26750
Accessories	10508	6782
Gifts	10904	2431
Toys	10207	2251
Sports	11215	7689

- Save using a different name and print a copy of the amended table.

In-tray documents Set 3 Day 2 – Tables Task 4

Task 4

Recall the table you keyed in about IT staff and amend as follows:

- Shade the column with the heading Department.

- Sort the table on Department.

- Move the Department column to the start of the table.

- Add a column at the end of the table with the heading No of hours worked for other depts. It should contain the following data on the number of hours each person worked.

First Name	Surname	No of hours worked for other depts
Keira	McGill	10
John	Cavanagh	18
Rashid	Ahmel	10
Lynn	Forsyth	12
Caroline	Harper	10
Paul	Ganguly	11
Claire	Lee	12

- Add a further column at the end with the heading Charged per hour to cost centre and insert £13.50 for each person from the IT department, £11.50 for each person from Admin and £10.50 for each person from Electrical.

- Right align the figures in these last 2 columns.

- Add a row at the end of the table and insert the total of the hours worked for other departments.

- Enhance the table by emboldening and shading all columns which contain figures.

- Print a copy of the table in landscape format

- Save the table in a way which shows this is your most recent version of the table.

In-tray documents Set 3 Day 3 Tables

Before undertaking this you should be able to:

- sort using different levels

- insert formula for adding, subtracting, multiplying and dividing. Remember calculations in tables in Word is meant for occasional use. If you have a large number of calculations to do, you might be better copying and pasting the table to a spreadsheet file, performing the calculations and pasting it back to a Word file.

In-tray documents Set 3 Day 3 – Tables Task 1

Task 1

- Recall your latest version of Training Table Nov.

- Remove the first row and insert the text in this row as a heading to the table.

- Add a column at the end of the table with the heading Length of Course (days) with the following data in it:

Course	Length of Course (days)
Customer Care	.5
Stock control	1
Stock control	1
Customer Care	.5
Freedom of Information Act	2
Freedom of Information Act	2

- Add a further column at the end with the heading Daily rate and insert an appropriate formula to find the daily rate of each course.

- Msim Paval has now moved to the Furniture Department.

- Sort the table on Departments and within departments on the Date of the Training Course.

- Save and print a copy of the amended table.

In-tray documents Set 3 Day 3 – Tables Task 2

Task 2

Recall the table showing the New Starts for the Christmas Period.

- Add a column between Mentor and No of Hours showing the department where each new member of staff will work.

- Add a column at the end of the table with the heading No of weeks.

First Name	Surname	Department	No of Weeks
Lynn	Marshall	Gifts	6
Pierre	Boucheron	Toys	7
John	MacKay	Toys	8
Dorian	Rohmer	Gifts	5
Kim	Lee	Toys	7
Fiona	Galbraith	Cosmetics	4
Abdul	Bastani	Gifts	5

- Add a final column with the heading Total Hours of Contract.

- Using the formula function, calculate the number of hours each person will work.

- Enhance the table using shading and emboldening and remove any unnecessary cells.

- Sort the table on Department and within departments on Start Date and then the Surname of the new starts.

In-tray documents Set 3 Day 3 – Tables Task 3

Task 3

Recall the table showing the Sales figures of each department for last month and this month.

- Add another column with Increase/Decrease as the heading.

- Using the formula function enter the difference between the last 2 columns of Sales figures.

- Shade this column to enhance.

- Add a final column with the heading Estimated Annual Sales. Work out the estimated annual sales based on this month's sales figures.

- Insert the totals of the last 2 columns.

- Remove the empty cells in the Average row.

- Print a copy of the table and save the table indicating that this is your latest version of the data.

In-tray documents Set 3 Day 3 – Tables Task 4

 Task 4

Recall the table showing the amount of IT staff time charged to other cost centres last month.

- Add a final column with the heading Total amount charged to other departments.

- Using the formula function, calculate the total charged to other cost centres, against each person.

- In the total row at the end of the table, total the amount charged this month to other departments.

- Sort the data on Branch, then Department and then Surname.

- Save the table and print a copy in landscape format.

In-tray documents Set 3 Day 4

Tables are not only used for numerical data but are also used where columns of text are required. You should try to use tables wherever data or text is used in columns.

In-tray documents Set 3 Day 4 – Tables Task 1

 Task 1

Recall the Notice you keyed in for In-tray documents Set 1 Day 1 document 3 and add the following information at the end of the Notice.

Special offers on Trusleep beds		
Size	**Finish**	**Discount**
Single bed	Tapestry	25%
Double bed	Silver sheen	30%
King size	Hi-style	40%
Super King size	Tapestry	40%

In-tray documents Set 3 Day 4 – Tables Task 2

Task 2

Key in the following information for Kamal Ahmed.

Itinerary *h*   for Aberdeen visit *h*

25 March 20..

0900 hrs	Flight from Glasgow Airport to Aberdeen. Flight number BA34AB. Check in must be before 0800 hours
0945 hrs	Arrive in Aberdeen
1100 hrs	Meeting with Lorna Stewart, Furniture Department Manager from Edinburgh at Lorne Hotel, Union Street, Aberdeen.
1300 hrs	Lunch booked at Lorne Hotel with Robert Wise of Hammondcraft Furniture.
1430 hrs	Visit to Hammondcraft Furniture Showrooms. RW will arrange transport to showroom and back to airport.
1700 hrs	Flight from Aberdeen Airport to Glasgow. Check in must be before 1600 hours.
1745 hrs	Arrive Glasgow Airport

In-tray documents Set 3 Day 4 – Tables Task 3

Task 3

Recall the Memo you keyed in for Set 1 Day 4 Document 2 about faulty Baby Rabbits. Set up the middle part of the memo as a table.

In-tray documents Set 3 Day 4 – Tables Task 4

Task 4

Key in the following notice.

The following special offers are available in the Furniture Department as a result of surplus stock.

Carillon 7 piece dining room suite	This suite is available in light or dark oak. The table sits 6 people comfortably and the set comes complete with 4 standard chairs and 2 carving chairs, at a discounted price of £560 representing a saving of 30% against the list price. <u>Note</u> There may be a limited number of seat cover fabrics available with this offer.

continued ➤

Masterclass bookcase wall units	Fully fitted bookcase units giving a wall coverage of 3 metres by 2 metres are available at the special price of £499. This represents a saving of 25% on the manufacturer's list price. An unrepeatable offer. These units are available in Ash, Black or Light Oak.
Fanfare fitted bedrooms	Fully fitted bedroom furniture which can be tailored to meet your requirements, is available in store <u>NOW</u>. You buy the basic kit at £799 and our bedroom fitters will help tailor it to suit your needs. The basic kit is designed to fit out a double bedroom 3 metres by 4 metres. Any additional units required will be discounted by 30%. Available in Rosewood, Pine, Elm or Light Oak.

In-tray documents Set 4

Before keying in these documents you should be able to:

- lay out minutes of a meeting in a given housestyle
- insert comments
- insert footnotes
- insert endnotes
- create an automatic form – work with drop-down list fields, checkbox fields, text fields
- lay out a newsletter
- insert a watermark.

This set of documents is suited to those studying the Higher Administration course.

The style of layout of minutes will vary between boards and committees but generally most organisations will have a house style which applies to the records of all meetings within that organisation. You should look back to the chapter on Meetings (Chapter 3) for further examples of Minutes you could use to key in as practice.

Inserting comments in a document is a useful way of adding your thoughts on the content without actually changing the document – usually a document which was not written by you. When you look at a document created by another person, you can also opt to track changes which will show any changes you have made, such as deletions or insertions. This can be a useful tool when amending a document – particularly if you get a lot of interruptions. If you are inserting comments in a document you have keyed in, you will usually have to save it first and then re-save with the comments.

Footnotes and endnotes enable you to insert a brief explanation about the main text without interrupting the flow of the text. The software package will place a footnote in the footer at the end of the page where the reference appears or in the case of an endnote at the end of the document.

Automatic forms allow you to create a professional looking document quickly using a variety of pre-set tools. This includes drop down lists which limit what can be inserted as an answer, check boxes which allow you to tick or not and text fields which allow you to key in an answer.

Using a watermark is a useful way of indicating that a document is not in its final form. You would usually chose to use a semi-transparent version of a watermark so that it was apparent on all pages and clear to all readers of the document. The watermark can be removed once the document is no longer in draft format.

In-tray documents Set 4 Day 1

This set of documents has been prepared by Margaret O'Hare Marketing Manager.

In-tray documents Set 4 Day 1 – document 1

Prepare the following set of Minutes and indicate they are draft by using a watermark. Insert a comment after Board Room and ask if the Chairman wants you to put in the address of the Board Room.

John Nicholls

Minutes of Meeting of the Marketing Department held in the Board Room at 1000 hours on Friday (insert date).

Present: Margaret O'Hare in the Chair, Parvinder Kaan, Rosemary Forbes, Joe Mullen

Apologies: Apologies were received from Lou Grant

Minutes of Previous Meeting: The minutes of the previous meeting were read, approved and signed by the Chairperson.

Matters Arising from Minutes: The budget for marketing has now been decided and has increased by 8% on last year's figures. As agreed this money will be directed towards account holders to offer special promotions in the slower months of the year.

Sales figures: The team considered the comparative figures for this month and last month for each department and agreed that last month's Household promotion was reflected in the sales figures. This month's Furniture promotion was also clearly indicated in the figures. (Insert the table you keyed in earlier showing the Sales figures for the month – In-tray documents Day 1 Tables Task 3. Only the names of the departments and the sales figures are required). Insert a footnote at the end of the heading and in the footnote key in 'These figures were confirmed by John Leamington, Accountant and date 21 of the month'.

Comparison with previous year's trading: Based on the figures given above there appeared to be an overall increase of 4% on like for like sales. Confirmation of this figure is expected from the Finance Director within the next few days. (Insert a comment here asking if MO'H wants the figures to be inserted once they are available)

Current outlook: The Retail Consortium of Glasgow (insert an end note here and indicate in the end note that the Retail Consortium is a section of the Chamber of Commerce) have already indicated that the sector is buoyant and this is borne out by our current figures.

Any Other Business: The next in-store promotions will be in the Sports Department and the Cosmetic Department.

continued ➤

It was agreed that a Good News Sheet should be sent to all Department Managers. This should have headline information from our meetings

Date of next meeting The Board room at 1000 hours on the last Friday of the month (look up the date).

In-tray documents Set 4 Day 1 – document 2

Prepare a Good News Sheet for staff with the main items from the minutes. You should lay it out as attractively as possible. It will be printed in black and white. You should use graphics where appropriate to make it more attractive. It should have information under the following headings:

Title – Good News Sheet Edition 1

Heading – National Outlook – The info from current outlook

Heading – Sales are up – The info from comparison with previous year's trading

Heading – Promotions work – Last month's Household promotion was reflected in the sales figures. This month's Furniture promotion was also clearly indicated in the figures. Here are the figures. Look how well your department has done.

Heading – Coming Soon – The next in-store promotions will be in the Sports Department and the Cosmetic Department. Watch this space....

In-tray documents Set 4 Day 1 – document 3

Set up a form using the automatic form function with form fields which staff can use to extend our customer base. Indicate that it is a draft form and protect the form.

Tell us how we are doing

Are you a regular customer in this shop?
Set this up as a yes/no with drop down

How often do you shop in this shop?
Set this up as more than once a week, once a week, once a month, occasionally, with a drop down menu.

What do you like best about this shop? Make this a text box.

What do you like least about this shop? Make this a text box.

Do you come for particular promotions? Make this a drop down yes/no

Tick the box if you would like information on promotions. Make this a tick box.

Name, Address, Postcode, Phone number, Mobile phone number, E-mail should all be text boxes.

Completed on (insert date). Make this a text box.

In-tray documents Set 4 Day 2

This set of documents has been prepared by Jim Winters, IT Director.

In-tray documents Set 4 Day 2 – document 1

Prepare the Minutes of the IT committee from the following notes and indicate it is in draft form by using a watermark.

> Meeting held on May 20 at 1300 hours in the Board Room.
>
> Present – Jim Winters, in the Chair, Rashid Ahmel, John Cavanagh, Paul Ganguly, Claire Lee
>
> No apologies
>
> Minutes OK
>
> Matters Arising – JW welcomed CL to the meeting. Although CL works in the Electrical Department, she provides IT support for colleagues on the electrical floor.
>
> Helpline calls have continued to decrease this month reflecting better staff training and better support. The switch to chip and pin tills has been straightforward and has created no problems.
>
> Stock control software – New software will be introduced in September. The programme is based on Qstock (Insert a footnote here to indicate that Qstock is a registered trademark) software which has been tailored to suit our needs.
>
> Staff development – Staff development workshop with the software providers on June 3 for all committee members. This will be an in-house all day training session. IT staff will then roll out training on the stock control system to all staff in ½ hour sessions in the training time on Wednesday mornings. These training sessions will be organised by the HR department.
>
> Any Other Business – Increase in problems connected with changing till rolls. Staff training needed. Speak to department managers to deliver on Wednesday mornings. (Insert a comment here and ask who is to speak to the Managers).
>
> It was agreed that a brief questionnaire should be sent to Department Managers to identify any further staff development required and the extent of development needed.
>
> DONM 24 June at 1300 hours in the Board Room
>
> Space for signing and date

In-tray documents Set 4 Day 2 – document 2

Prepare an IT newsletter for Edinburgh with the following information. Use graphics and enhancements to make this an attractive document. It should be designed to be read on-line as it will go on the company intranet.

Qstock is coming. This is the name of our new integrated stock control software. What can it do for you? It will update immediately any sales made from stock and can let you know exactly how many goods we have in stock *and* accurately at any time. It will automatically re-order stock of standard items for you. What do you have to do? You decide on your standard stock items and set them up with a minimum and maximum level. Every time an item is sold *of stock* your stock control system is updated and supplies are re-ordered weekly. You can ask for Alarms to be set and every morning when you log on you can see the items which should be causing you alarm – eg the items which are not moving, those which are in limited supply or are causing problems, allowing you the freedom to discount or ~~up~~ your *raise the level of* minimum stock.

You will be trained by our own staff in this simple system. Meantime if you want to know more about it access the intranet and check it out.

with IT!

Help

Want help? Try the Helpline X999. No question is too silly but sometimes what you need is someone to show you what to do, not just talk you through the steps. Remember we have an IT expert on each floor to provide help with tills and computers. You should never be stuck. Here are the people to ask:

Claire Lee
Rashid Ahmel
John Cavanagh
Paul Ganguly
Jim Winters

Want to learn more?

John Nicholls has linked up with Edinburgh College, Glasgow College and Hightown College to allow you to learn more about IT. You can study IT Passport (Insert an endnote at the end of this paragraph. The end note should read 'Any course you undertake when in the employment of John Nicholls should be added to your Personal Development Plan and may be used as part of your Performance Management Review evidence') These courses will not cost you anything – John Nicholls will pay the cost of the course and pay any travelling expenses incurred. This can even be arranged on a distance learning basis so that you can ~~do it~~ *study* in your own home. Speak to Joyce O'Malley in Human Resources for further information.

What help do you need?

Department Managers are currently being asked to comment on staff development requirements. Please pass any comments to your Department Manager.

INFORMATION TECHNOLOGY

In-tray Set 4 Day 2 – document 3

Set up a form using the automatic form function with form fields to gauge the level of IT support needed. Indicate that it is a draft form and protect the form.

IT Staff Development requirements

Name (Insert text box)

Department (Insert text box)

How many full time staff do you have in your department? (Insert text box)

How many part-time staff do you have in your department? (Insert text box)

How many of your staff have received training in operating the new tills? (Insert drop down list with none, 1-5, 5-10, 10-15, more than 15)

Can all your staff access the intranet? (Insert yes/no box)

How many staff require training in its use? (Insert text box)

Do all staff check e-mail regularly? (Insert yes/no box)

How many staff require training in its use? (Insert text box)

Do you send work rotas to staff electronically? (Insert yes/no box)

How many staff will require training in the new Qstock stock control system? (Insert text box)

In-tray documents Set 4 Day 3

This set of documents was prepared by Orla Coyle, Manager of the Sports Department in Glasgow.

In-tray documents Set 4 Day 3 – document 1

Prepare the Minutes of Meeting of the Sports Department for the meeting held on (insert the date of the last Friday in last month) at 0800 hours in the Board Room in Glasgow. Indicate they are in draft form by using a watermark.

Present – Orla Coyle (Chair), Margaret O'Hare (Marketing department) Greg Hannah, Jon McIntyre, Max Xum, Ted Johnstone (Marketing)

Items discussed – Nike Promotion, Teenage Week, Children's Keep Fit Event and Discounts Available.

Nike Promotion – It was decided to hold the promotion on week beginning 22 March. The promotion will last for 7 days. Marketing agreed to try and get a Scottish sports celebrity to attend on Day 1 and agreed to prepare a press release for all local and national papers once arrangements were finalised. Nike had agreed to discount all Nike products ordered in the preceding 6 weeks by 20%. Special stock items, in particular children's trainers and track suits, would be discounted by at least a third during this week. (Put in a footnote here 'This discount will continue to run from 22 March to the end of the Children's Keep Fit Event'.)

NP

continued ➤

NP Teenage Week – It was agreed that this promotion would start on the first Saturday in May (insert the date). All DVDs which feature pop stars and pop groups would be highlighted and discounted. Marketing agreed to do price checks on those identified for the promotion. OC agreed to order appropriate clothing for promotion in May. Sporty Health Clubs will discount their membership fee by 25% and will discount subscriptions by 10% per month for 3 months, where there are teenagers or children in the family. Marketing will NP investigate hiring someone from the entertainment world for a personal

NP appearance to start the promotion. Children's Keep Fit Event – Will take place the first 2 weeks in April. GH and MX agreed to measure the space available for a trampoline, swingball and table tennis. The cost of hiring an in-line skating rink was £300 per day and it was agreed that the in-line skating trial would not take place. Running tests could be organised on fitness machinery in the store. All NP purchases would entitle the purchaser to one $^1/_2$ hour session in Gobowl or one $^1/_2$ hour session on the Skate-in rink at Braeside shopping centre. Sporty Health Clubs have donated a one year family membership as a prize. JMcI agreed to design an application form which could be completed for customers, on line at the point of sale.

Discounts Available – JN will offer 20% discount on all sports equipment – 10% will trs be recoverable form the sports equipment suppliers. Nike discounts will apply (see NP Teenage Week above). Sporty Health Clubs will discount membership where there are teenagers or children in the family (see Teenage Week above).

Date of Next Meeting – it was agreed to meet again in 4 weeks (insert date) to discuss promotion of the events and guest appearances.

In-tray documents Set 4 Day 3 – document 2

Prepare a newsletter for Glasgow customers with an outline of the above information. Use graphics and enhancements to make this an attractive document. It should be designed to be a single page and should be on headed paper.

In-tray Set 4 Day 3 – document 3

Set up a form using the automatic form function with form fields to record the information for the Prize Draw for Family Membership of the Sporty Health Club. Indicate that it is a draft form and protect the form.

On Headed paper

How would you and your family like to be members of one of Glasgow's top Health Clubs?

Sporty Health Clubs are offering you the chance for you and your family to join in the fun at Sporty Health Clubs for a whole year free of charge. (Insert a footnote 'No cash alternative will be available') All you have to do is complete the following form and answer the simple questions at the end. (Insert footnote which should read Terms and conditions of Sporty Health Clubs must be accepted at the time of accepting the prize).

Name (Insert text box)

Address (Insert text box)

continued ➤

Telephone number (Insert text box)

e-mail address (Insert text box)

Which of the following sports does not use a ball? (Insert a drop down menu and enter Tennis, Squash, Badminton, Lacrosse)

Which member of the Royal Family was part of an Olympic team? (Insert a drop down menu and enter Prince Charles, Princess Anne, Prince Andrew, Prince Edward)

What is the most popular sport in the UK? (Insert a drop down menu and enter Swimming, Fishing, Running, Badminton)

I would be happy to be involved in any publicity should I win the prize draw (Insert Yes/No box)

In-tray documents Set 4 Day 4

This set of documents was prepared by Lorna Green, HR Director based in Glasgow.

In-tray documents Set 4 Day 4 – document 1

Indicate that this is a draft document.

Meeting of Department Managers held Wednesday 14 November, at 1100 hours in Room 104, Glasgow.

Present – Lorna Green, Chairperson, Sandra Melbourne, Susan Shields, Anne Wilson, Ruby Dalziel, Rena Carter, Loraine Duval, Jeff Quigley, Kamal Ahmed, Alistair McKay. Apologies – Sonia Ben Arefi, Gordon Stratford

Minutes – okayed by group and signed. Matters arising – Several temporary members of staff had been appointed for the Christmas period. Discussion – re where they should be placed. Decided gifts, toys and cosmetics. Most start in November.

Extended hours – discussion re Christmas opening times. Decided will be 8pm Thurs, Fri and Sat in December. Allows restock and ordering and redisplaying activities. Unions have agreed.

Sales figures – (Insert the figures from the table you keyed in with each department's sales figures – your answer for Set 3 Day 2 Tables Task 3. Insert an endnote at the end of the table to indicate that these are provisional figures. Reference this endnote to the Heading.) Figures discussed. Agreed that promotions have had an important impact on figures. Questions raised about budget for promotions.

Christmas decorations – simulation of Christmas decorations was shown – thematic approach – all silver and blue. Ice cavern for Santa in Toy Department.

Any Other Business – What are opening hours after Christmas? Closed Boxing Day, open day after from 0800. Revert to usual hours after that.

continued ➤

Date of next meeting – January 7 at 1100 hours. (Insert a comment box here and ask if Lorna wants you to book a room).

Signature

Date

In-tray documents Set 4 Day 4 – document 2

Set up a one page Christmas Newsletter for staff with a paragraph on each of the above topics. Include graphics to draw attention to each section. Insert the table with departmental sales figures. (Indicate with a footnote that these are draft figures.)

In-tray documents Set 4 Day 4 – document 3

Set up a form using the automatic form function with appropriate form fields to record staff opinions of the newsletter. Use headed paper and the appropriate tools available when using form function.

Do you read the staff Newsletter regularly – yes/no

Where do you read it – the canteen, at home, in your department, on the notice board, somewhere else?

Do you find the layout – eye-catching, interesting, boring, don't know

Do you think the content is – essential, important, boring, irrelevant

Would you like the opportunity to contribute to the Newsletter – yes/no

Would you like your own copy – use a check box here

Do you have a department newsletter – yes/no

Please insert any suggestions for improvement – insert textbox here.

In-tray documents Set 5 Day 1

Integration of data

Before tackling this set of documents you should be able to:

- Set up a database table.
- Query a database table.
- Merge information in a database table to a form letter.
- Print data in label format.
- Copy and paste data from a spreadsheet to a word processed document.
- Copy and paste chart from a spreadsheet to a word processed document.

It is often useful to copy data from one application package to another so that you can retain it or organise it in a particular way. You have already used tables in word processing to calculate some simple figures but if you were going to do a large number of calculations, you would be

better to do the calculations in a spreadsheet and import the answer into the word processing file. Charts are often used to illustrate information and these can also be set up in a spreadsheet and imported into a word processing file.

Information from databases in the form of tables or queries can also be imported into word processing files. Information from a database is most frequently used to merge data with word processed data so that mail merge letters and documents can be produced. It is good practice when doing a mail merge to print a copy of the letter showing the merge fields for your hard copy file along with the database query showing where the letters went rather than save copies of each letter either electronically or in hard copy.

In-tray documents Set 5 Day 1 – document 1

This is a list of staff who applied for temporary Christmas jobs. You may recognise some of the names from a table you prepared earlier. Set this up as a database table. Make reference number the primary key. Query the table and find all of those who were successful at interview. Using the letter you prepared in In-tray Set 1 Day 3 document 1, prepare a mail merge to all those who were successful. Print a copy of the form letter with merge fields and print labels for the envelopes.

First Name	Surname	Address	Town	Postcode	Phone number	Reference number	Successful?
Lynn	Marshall	35 Miller Street	GLASGOW	G45 7LK	0141 9987880	57	yes
Pierre	Boucheron	907 Great Western Road	GLASGOW	G67 0PL	0798 576880	58	yes
John	MacKay	52 Hill Street	MOTHERWELL	ML5 8JN	01698 767577	59	yes
Dorian	Rohmer	89 Little Road	MILNGAVIE	MG56 9HJ	0141 9528888	61	yes
Kim	Lee	9 Grange Road	STIRLING	SS5 7BV	01798 678655	62	yes
Mark	Kedzierska	18 Thomson Drive	GLASGOW	G76 8QT	0141 8447570	64	yes
Fiona	Galbraith	35 Green Road	GLASGOW	G14 9BH	0141 4532222	66	yes
Abdul	Bastani	70 Greatbridge Street	FALKIRK	FK6 8HJ	07785 756442	68	yes
Jim	Kerr	20 Primrose Hill	GREENOCK	GR5 9HN	01987 578677	70	no
Anthea	Feguson	25 Waterside Drive	BISHOPTON	BR5 9GF	07709 698444	71	no
Paul	Gillespie	31 Dalzell Road	WISHAW	ML5 8HY	07798 200745	73	no

INFORMATION TECHNOLOGY

In-tray documents Set 5 Day 1 – document 2

Query the database table for those who were not successful at interview and merge the result of this query to the letter you set up in In-tray Set 1 Day 3 – document 3. Print address labels and a copy of the form letter with merge fields.

In-tray documents Set 5 Day 1 – document 3

Set up the following information in a database file. You are going to start a database table with information on departmental managers.

Manager info			
Department	**First Name**	**Surname**	**Extension number**
Furniture	Kamal	Ahmed	261
Cosmetics	Rena	Carter	263
Bathrooms	Susan	Shields	262
Cosmetics – JN only	Loraine	Duval	264
Ladies Clothing	Naiem	Reda	265
Children's clothing	Anne	Wilson	266
Gents clothing	Alistair	McKay	267
Electrical	Jeff	Quigley	268
Household	Ellen	Divers	269
China	Ruby	Dalziel	270
Glassware	Gordon	Stratford	271
Soft Furnishings	Gary	Davidson	272
Accessories	Sandra	Melbourne	273
Gifts	Sonia	Ben Arefi	274
Toys	Gail	Shields	275
Sports	Orla	Coyle	276

Recall the table you keyed in for In-tray documents Set 3 Day 2 Tables Task 3. It should look like this.

Summary of Sales for last month.

Department	Manager	This month's Sales £	Last month's Sales £
Accessories	Sandra Melbourne	10508	6782
Bathrooms	Susan Shields	10045	11257
Children's clothing	Anne Wilson	17359	16879
China	Ruby Dalziel	12015	15436
Cosmetics	Rena Carter	18700	23009
Cosmetics – JN only	Loraine Duval	21008	20324
Electrical	Jeff Quigley	14560	23789
Furniture	Kamal Ahmed	36500	23450
Gents Clothing	Alistair McKay	10120	11987
Gifts	Sonia Ben Arefi	10904	2431
Glassware	Gordon Stratford	10922	11231
Household	Ellen Divers	20141	28244
Ladies Clothing	Naiem Reda	10021	11467
Soft furnishings	Gary Davidson	23467	26750
Sports	Orla Coyle	11215	7689
Toys	Gail Shields	10207	2251
Average		**15480.75**	
Total		**247692**	

Copy this information into a spreadsheet file and, using an appropriate chart, show each department's figures for the last 2 months in one chart.

Key in the following memo for this month's departmental managers' meeting which will be sent to Name of the Manager and Department (use your database table to do a merge here), from Margaret O'Hare, Subject – Current Sales figures. Print a copy of the memo with merge fields and one copy of the memo with the merge printed.

I attach a copy of the sales figures for the last 2 months which show clearly how much difference promotions can make to departmental results.

(Insert the chart here)

Please join us for a short informal meeting at 1800 hours on Thursday when you can learn about the promotions we have in store for you over the coming months. A light buffet will be served.

INFORMATION TECHNOLOGY

In-tray documents Set 5 Day 1 – document 4

Set up the following database table which you will use to contact staff who work in the IT support area. You already have some of this information in a table prepared for Set 3 Day 1 Tables Task 4 (IT Support Staff).

IT Staff				
First Name	**Surname**	**Branch**	**Dept**	**Staff No**
Keira	McGill	Hightown	IT	4256
John	Cavanagh	Edinburgh	IT	7821
Rashid	Ahmel	Edinburgh	IT	2009
Lynn	Forsyth	Hightown	Admin	8645
Caroline	Harper	Hightown	Admin	2331
Paul	Ganguly	Edinbuirgh	IT	3117
Claire	Lee	Edinburgh	Electrical	4007

Send a memo to all these staff from Jim Winters, IT Director.

To (Name from database)

Subject IT support in (Branch from database)

I have recently been doing an analysis of the time you spend supporting and training other members of staff in addition to your usual job. Firstly can I thank you for all the extra help you have been giving your colleagues and secondly can I ask you to let me know of any particular problem areas you are encountering where staff might benefit from extra training. As you know we have a different system in our Glasgow branch where we have dedicated IT support staff.

I have already had a number of requests for additional training to be given in the area of searching for product codes which have been inaccurately given or searching on our buyers database for new products requested but in the (*insert the name of the branch here*) branch this may be causing difficulties.

I intend to provide all managers with a clear indication of the proportion of your time which is spent supporting staff and I am confident that this will lead to a review of salary grades within the IT section. Once again thank you for the support you are giving to your colleagues.

In-tray documents Set 5 Day 1 – document 5

Recall the table you keyed in for In-tray documents Set 3 Day 2 Tables Task 4. It looks like this:

IT support staff

Department	First Name	Surname	Branch	No of hours worked for other depts	Charged per hour to cost centre	Total amount charged to other depts
Electrical	Claire	Lee	Edinburgh	12	£10.50	£126.00
IT	Rashid	Ahmel	Edinburgh	10	£13.50	£135.00
IT	John	Cavanagh	Edinburgh	18	£13.50	£243.00
IT	Paul	Ganguly	Edinburgh	11	£13.50	£148.50
Admin	Lynn	Forsyth	Hightown	12	£11.50	£138.00
Admin	Caroline	Harper	Hightown	10	£11.50	£115.00
IT	Keira	McGill	Hightown	10	£13.50	£135.00
Total				83		£1040.50

Copy this table into a spreadsheet and add another column with Total hours spent on support as the heading.

- Subtotal the hours for Edinburgh and for Hightown.

- Add in a row to indicate that Glasgow has the equivalent of 70 hours a week available for supporting staff in other departments.

- Prepare a chart which shows these hours and the branches.

Send this memo from Jim Winters to all department managers using the database already prepared in in-tray documents Set 5 Day 1 – document 3 to do it as a mail merge, from Jim Winters. Subject – IT Support.

As you know we have recently been looking at the work done in the IT area in supporting staff throughout the organisation to deal with our new systems. This has been particularly important in the Hightown and the Edinburgh branches where there are no dedicated IT support staff. We analysed the time spent by staff in a typical week with a view to getting a clear picture of what time is being spent supporting staff. The purpose of this review was to provide information for a possible review of IT staff salaries.

The following table shows how much this support is costing us at the moment.

(insert the table here)

A further analysis in terms of hours spent in each branch can be clearly seen in the diagram below.

(insert the diagram here)

continued ➤

INFORMATION TECHNOLOGY

As an organisation we now need to decide how to pay for this support either by dedicated staff or by using departments as cost centres for the amount of staff time they use. Either way you will note that the IT staff time is being provided at a very low rate compared to that which would normally be paid to IT support staff.

This Memo will form the basis of discussion at our next managers' meeting.

In-tray documents Set 5 Day 2

In Higher you are also required to be able to:

- dynamically link a chart or a graph from a spreadsheet
- import the result of a database query to a word file.

There are some cases where you would dynamically link data and some cases where you would not. In many organisations, the preference is to keep the data in the document correct as it was on the date on which the document was issued but in some cases it is more important to have up-to-date information available. When data is linked like this the information would often be available on an intranet rather than in hard copy as the whole purpose is to ensure that up-to-date information, rather than historical information, is available. This approach is often used in regular reports, for example, one part of a minute of meeting which has a standard format and gathers information from the same standard documents each month, or in financial reports.

In-tray documents Set 5 Day 2 – document 1

Go back to the database table you keyed in for in-tray documents Set 5 Day 1 – document 3. This was a database with information on departmental managers. You are going to add to the design of this table by adding a field for starting date. The dates are as follows.

First Name	Surname	Start Date
Kamal	Ahmed	23/03/2001
Rena	Carter	12/02/1997
Susan	Shields	21/03/1984
Loraine	Duval	06/04/1998
Naiem	Reda	14/07/2001
Anne	Wilson	16/07/2002
Alistair	McKay	22/11/2000
Jeff	Quigley	24/02/1998
Ellen	Divers	17/05/1992
Ruby	Dalziel	03/08/1991
Gordon	Stratford	30/11/2001
Gary	Davidson	27/10/1996
Sandra	Melbourne	22/04/1994
Sonia	Ben Arefi	05/05/1995
Gail	Shields	18/02/1987
Orla	Coyle	22/03/1990

Query this database and arrange the result in alphabetical order. You want to know who started before 1 January 1995. Save this query. Do a second query for those before 1990 and a third one for before 1985.

Key in the following memo from Joyce O'Malley, HR Administrator to Lorna Green, HR Director. Subject: Long Service – Managers

I have looked at the information we have on our Managers in the Glasgow store and their length of service. Those who started before 1995, 1990 and 1985 are shown below.

(Insert the result of your queries here)

Would you like me to draft a letter to these Managers about their Long Service Awards?

In-tray documents Set 5 Day 2 – document 2

Prepare this letter to all managers who are due to receive a Long Service Award – that is, those who started before 1 January 1995. Use the Glasgow store address as the letters will be handed out.

> Dear…
>
> On looking at your records I noted that as you started with the company on (insert the date), you are eligible to receive one of JN's first Long Service Awards. This is a new recognition scheme which we are introducing this year. Your loyal service to JN is being recognised with a £200 gift token.
>
> From 2005 you will receive a further £100 for every further 5 years service. Your first gift voucher will be presented to you on (put in next Friday's date) at 1300 hours in the Board Room in Glasgow. I look forward to seeing you there. Yours sinc Lorna Green HR Director.

In-tray documents Set 5 Day 2 –document 3

Go back to the spreadsheet file you prepared for in-tray document Set 5 Day 1 – document 3 (Summary of Sales) and dynamically link the chart you created to the following document.

> Memo to go to (Insert Manager's name and Department from your Manager's database) from Margaret O'Hare Marketing Manager. Subject – Sales figures.
>
> At the end of every month this Memo will be sent to all Department Managers. It is being sent in hard copy as I know many of you like to look at your paperwork when you are on the shop floor. This information will be updated automatically as the figures submitted by you at the end of each month are amended once returns, omissions, or special orders are taken into account. It is also available to view on the intranet.
>
> (Insert the diagram in a way in which it will be updated as soon as the figures are changed in the spreadsheet file)
>
> I hope you find this information useful.

In-tray documents Set 5 Day 2 – document 4

Go back to the document you keyed in for in-tray document Set 5 Day 1 – document 5. Change the way you linked the chart and the table to a dynamic link. Then change the figures in the spreadsheet for Glasgow to 60 hours (one of the Glasgow staff has cut their hours of work).

In-tray documents Set 6 Reports

Before keying in these reports you should be able to:

- lay out a report in house style
- insert footers with name, date, time and filename

- insert page breaks
- customise bullets
- set up a database table
- integrate data from a database
- set up a spreadsheet file
- create a chart in a spreadsheet
- integrate data and a chart from a spreadsheet
- change line spacing
- insert header
- change font and size of font
- use spellcheck.

In-tray documents Set 6 Day 1 Reports

In-tray documents Set 6 Day 1 – report 1

The following document was given to you by Jean Brass, Human Resources Department. You are asked to lay out this report in John Nicholls' house style with each section of the report numbered as indicated. Jean likes to use Arial font throughout. You should indicate in the header that the report is in draft format and take account of the printer's corrections indicated. Insert a footer with name, date, time and filename in a small size font.

Report of the arrangements made by the committee for the Charity Day in aid of Comic Relief.

1 Date The date for Red Nose Day is now confirmed as 5 March 20.

2 Fundraisers A number of possible ways of raising funds were discussed and the following were chosen to receive John Nicholls' sponsorship.[Fancy Dress NP
– John Nicholls will sponsor all employees with a £5 donation per person for all those who dress up for the occasion.[Prize Draw – All customers will receive NP
a free prize draw ticket for every £5 spent in store the week beginning 1 March. The Prize draw will take place on the Saturday afternoon at 1700 hours. One prize will be donated by each participating department (except the Toy Department) and should be of approximately £100 in value. The star prize will
NP be £1000 to spend in store.[Funniest Picture – There will be a sponsored drawing competition for children and young people under the age of 12. This will be divided into 3 categories. Under 5s, Over 5 but under 9, Over 9 but under 12. The competition will be judged at 1400 hours on Saturday. The main prize will be £100 John Nicholls vouchers plus a Young Artist's set. There will be 2nd and 3rd prizes of Artists sets provided by Reeves Artistic Materials.[Cosmetic treats will NP
be provided at a number of counters. For a voluntary donation, customers can have their make-up done free of charge. These treatments cannot be pre-booked but will be available at Clarins, Estee Lauder, Benefit and John Nicholls'

continued ➤

NP own counters.[All tips received in the Beauty Spa Rooms will be donated by staff. A notice to this effect will be prominently displayed. Normal charges will apply
NP for these pre-booked treatments.[All tips received in the Hairdressing salon will be donated by staff. A notice to this effect will be prominently displayed. Normal charges will apply for these pre-booked treatments.[Collection buckets. These NP will be placed beside all tills for voluntary donations from customers.

3 Publicity Publicity is being sought for this event. Press coverage will be encouraged. The Marketing Department has already contacted a number of
NP local papers.[The Marketing Department have also informed over 70 primary schools in the Glasgow area of the event and included entry forms for the painting competition with the information.[A flyer has gone to all account NP
NP holders with their February account.[Four volunteers have agreed to go to BBC Scotland in the evening with a giant cheque and will hopefully appear on television.

4 The total sum raised last year was £26,857.15. (Insert an asterisk here and on a separate page put the details shown below into a spreadsheet, create a chart and import it into the last page of this report). It is hoped to raise even more this year. Our target is £30,000.

Information for spreadsheet and chart

Breakdown of Last Year's figures		
Department	Competition	Donations
Sports	Prize Draw	£5,334.00
Cosmetics	Donations	£3,589.00
Toy	Various	£11,860.00
Hairdressing and Beauty Spa Rooms	Donations	£2,876.50
Restaurant	Donations	£3,197.65
Total		**£26,857.15**

In-tray documents Set 6 Day 1 – report 2

You are asked to lay out this report in John Nicholls' house style with each section of the report numbered. You have been asked to use Arial font throughout. You should indicate in the header that the report is in draft format and take account of the printer's corrections indicated. Use double line spacing throughout. Your footer should contain the date, time, your name and the file name. Key in all abbreviations in full.

John Nicholls Best Value Initiative.

NP **1** Terms of Reference[Following the report on the financial health of John Nicholls, issued by our auditors Smith, Smart and Wooley, the John Nicholls Board has decided to annotate and make public, expense items as part of the recommended BVI. (Insert an asterisk and at the end of the report on a separate page key in this *NOTE: This will include expenses paid to individual employees over a certain amount and also Directors' expenses. An example is shown below. Then key in the information spreadsheet I have attached at the end, show it in an appropriate chart and import it into the last page of the report.) This report is the first in a series of reports which will show where best value is achievable.

NP **2** Procedure[All expense items which fall into the publishable category will be identified. Existing procedures will be logged and amended to ensure compliance with auditor recommendations.

NP **3** Findings[A sophisticated and fully auditable system of logging all claimed expenses already exists, gathered by various members of the administrative
NP support staff.[The methods and format used to track and log this data
NP currently vary between depts.[The Board agreed to appoint a Project Manager to lead the BVI and has appointed Miriam Goldberg from the Finance Dept (Edin). Her appointment commenced on April 8 (year).[MG is currently   NP working on a project plan which will identify the key milestones involved in the introduction of formal standardised systems of recording all relevant expenses. This project plan will be presented to the Board at their June meeting. A note of those currently eligible to claim expenses which would be analysed in this way is shown in Appendix 1.[All participants are encouraged   NP to feed back comments on the information provided in particular in terms of
NP level of detail or presentation of data.[Any feedback should be given to Dept Managers by 15 May (year).

NP **4** Conclusions[Once the project plan is written and accepted by the Brd (anticipated date the end of July (year)) the BVI will be launched.[Publicity will NP be extensive to all employees and will include (bullet these with square or arrow type of bullets) payslip info, posters, team meeting items, specific launches, dept process manual, staff dev for admin staff.

NP **5** Recommendations[The project should be viewed as project of prime importance; one which should enhance JN's ability as an org to meet mkt needs by controlling costs as well as meeting the requs of our stakeholders
NP under the Data Protection Act.[The Project Plan produced will detail the order in which each set of summaries will be reviewed.[Each department should   NP show its commitment to the project by allowing a cross-dept approach to be taken to logging travel expenses as a pilot project. (Expense information to be put into a spreadsheet and an appropriate chart compiled showing the maximum allowed compared with the average amount spent in each category. Import this to a new page at the end of the report with the heading Appendix 1).

continued ➤

Allowable expenses for Authorised Managers					
	Organised by JL	Maximum amount before review	Preferred suppliers	Existing procedure	Average amount spent last year
Mileage	No	£2,000	BP	yes	£1,800
Air fares	Yes	£3,000	BM, Easyjet, BA	yes	£2,800
Subsistence	No	£1,500	N/A	yes	£2,500
Petty cash	No	£500	N/A	yes	£590
Uniform dry cleaning	Yes	£800	Scotclean	yes	£400
Trade journals	Yes	£500	E-map	yes	£830
Conferences	Yes	£1,000	N/A	yes	£1,900
Trade fairs	Yes	£1,000	N/A	yes	£2,780
Sundries	No	£500	N/A	yes	£690

Staff authorised to claim expenses.

Import the information from In-tray documents Set 5 Day 1 Document 3 – a database table with departmental managers' information. You need full name and department. Import it here and add on the additional Directors' names to the table. For department put Directors under Board. This should also go into Appendix 1

Jonathan Wiley
Lawrence Haverford
Jennifer Scott
Marie-Louise Leclerc

In-tray documents Set 6 Day 1 – report 3

You are asked to lay out this report in John Nicholls' house style with each section of the report numbered as indicated. Use Arial throughout. You should indicate in the header that the report is in draft format. Use double line spacing throughout. Number the pages leaving page 1 blank. Include your name and the file name, as well as the date in the footer in a small sized print. All the abbreviations should be shown in full.

Report of HR dept on the impact of days lost due to sickness in JN

1 Terms of Reference

As a result of the substantial rise in days lost to JN through sickness over the past few years, the Brd requested statistical information from the HR Director.

2 Procedure

A full analysis of sickness absence information will be used to identify any trends and provide information which can be used to inform policy decisions.

All absences should be reported to the HR dept in the first instance.

Any phone calls received by individual departments should be logged and the information passed on to the HR dept within one hour of receipt.

Once an absence has been reported HR staff will log the absence on the sickness report.

When employees return to work after a short absence, they should report in person to the appropriate HR staff and complete the relevant self certification documents.

In cases of prolonged absence, staff should send in all sick lines for the attention of the HR department.

All information on absences should be recorded on a daily basis by HR staff.

This information will be entered initially on to a spreadsheet by the appropriate HR staff.

The information held on spreadsheet will subsequently be transferred to Sickness Manager software. This will be done on a weekly basis by HR staff. This software automatically generates pro-forma correspondence and ensures all days lost to sickness are logged for each member of staff.

3 Findings

On close examination of the data held by HR dept there has been little systematic analysis of absences within or between departments. As a result the Joint Negotiating Committee has agreed that these figures should be analysed and compared as long as individual members of staff and their sickness records are not made public.

4 Conclusions

From this month, figures will be available to the Brd which will highlight absences and show comparable figures between departments.

5 Recommendations

It is recommended that the Joint Negotiating Committee is empowered to examine these figures in detail and review the internal processes currently used.

It is recommended that the Joint Negotiating Committee is empowered to discuss ways of addressing any problems identified within departments where high absentee rates are apparent and ensure that a consistent approach is taken throughout the organisation.

continued ➤

An example of the kind of information which will be available to the Joint Negotiating Committee is shown below in both graphical and tabular format. The figures inserted are for illustration only.

Staff Absent Due To Ill Health in XXX Department				
	Jan	**Feb**	**Mar**	**Totals**
Days lost to ill health	7	8	5	
Days lost for other reasons	3	2	4	
Permitted absences	2	1	2	
Total working days in department	110	100	112	
% of time lost to ill health				

(Insert missing figures in the above table)

(Insert a graph showing % of time lost to sickness each month for the department)

It is recommended that the JN Staff Association and all JN Unions, as well as individual JN employees, have the opportunity to respond to any proposals decided by the Joint Negotiating Committee.

It is recommended that Dept Managers are also invited to comment on any proposals, either collectively or individually.

It is recommended that the Joint Negotiating Committee publish its proposals in June of this year.

In-tray documents Set 6 Day 2 Reports

Before keying in these reports you should be able to:

- Insert an endnote.
- Insert numbered paragraphs as sub-sections.
- Dynamically link data from spreadsheets.
- Dynamically link charts or graphs from spreadsheets.
- Change line spacing.
- Use styles for headings and be able to alter these styles.

In-tray documents Set 6 Day 2 – report 1

Recall the first report you keyed in for Jean Brass and make the following amendments:

1 Change the asterisk to a footnote.

2 Dynamically link the data you set up as a spreadsheet and chart.

3 Set up all headings as styles – Report should be Heading 1, bold, 16 point; numbered sections should be Heading 3, bold, 13 point.

4 Number all pages except the first page.

5 Remove your name and the time from the footer. Change to your initials, date and file name.

6 Number all subsidiary paragraphs as appropriate, for example, 2.1, 2.2, 2.3, etc. within each numbered section.

In-tray documents Set 6 Day 2 – report 2

Recall the report you keyed in about BVI and make the following amendments:

1 Set up all headings as styles – the title of the report should be Heading 1 which should be bold, 16 point; numbered sections should be Heading 3, bold, 13 point.

2 Remove your name and the time from the footer. Change to your initials, date and file name.

3 Change to single line spacing.

4 Number all subsidiary paragraphs 2.1, 2.2, 2.3, etc. within numbered sections.

5 Number all pages except the first page.

6 Dynamically link the data you set up as a spreadsheet and chart.

In-tray documents Set 6 Day 2 – report 3

Recall the report you keyed for the HR Department about Absence and make the following amendments:

1 Dynamically link the data you set up as a spreadsheet and chart.

2 Set up all headings as styles – Report should be Heading 1, 16 point; numbered sections should be Heading 3, 13 point.

3 Remove your name and the time from the footer. Change to your initials, date and file name.

4 Number all subsidiary paragraphs 2.1, 2.2, 2.3, etc. within numbered sections.

5 Change to single line spacing.

In-tray documents Set 6 Day 3 Reports

Before undertaking this section you should be able to:

- Format the front page differently.
- Number sections within a booklet.
- Insert a table of contents.
- Shade text.
- Box text.
- Change the style of headings.

1 Put all reports into one document and treat each report as a separate section.

2 Number the pages within each section so that the report reads as one document.

3 Ensure all reports are in the one typeface – Arial, and that all have the same styles of headings which should be Heading 1, 14 point, bold, and Heading 3, 12 point, bold.

4 These reports have to be gathered together as Current Reports for the Chief Executive who has been on holiday for the last few months. Create a front sheet with John Nicholls boxed and shaded and the words Current Reports. Centre this information on the front page.

5 Remove any references to draft.

6 Insert a table of contents on the second page.

CHAPTER 11

E-diary, E-mail and the Internet

Intermediate 2 Level Outcomes:

I2 This chapter includes explanations and exercise material for Intermediate 2 Presenting and Communicating Information Outcome 1.

Using the Internet to search for and extract information for a given purpose:
- ☆ **integrate information from the Internet into a word processing document**
- ☆ **inserting a hyperlink to URL in a word processing document**
- ☆ **using various techniques and tools to aid your search.**

I2 From the same Unit, it also includes content from Outcome 2.

Use ICT to present and communicate information:
- ☆ **itineraries**
- ☆ **e-diary functions**
- ☆ **e-mail functions.**

Higher Level Outcomes:

H From Higher Information Technology for Management this chapter includes from Outcome 3.

Use ICT to solve business problems and communicate and present solutions practice in using:
- ☆ **e-mail features**
- ☆ **e-diary features**
- ☆ **internet features.**

E-mail

You will already have used e-mail throughout your course and you should now be familiar with some of the advantages of using this system of communication. If you have forgotten them, look back at Chapter 9 for a reminder.

Just as you do in an address book, you should now have built up a number of e-mail addresses – addresses of people you contact regularly – and these should be filed in your e-mail address book. You were asked in Chapter 9 Task 1 to set up a group of names so you should also have at least one group in your address book. Remember using a group in this way saves time,

particularly if it is a regular group you contact, such as members of a committee. You only need to identify the group and anything you send will automatically go to all of them.

Task 1

Look at your incoming e-mails. If you have a long list of e-mails there, you should now set up folders within your e-mail system and file them. You should really only have the mail pending in your in-tray just as you would only have the items to be dealt with in your desk in-tray if you were dealing with letters and memos. Try to name your files logically just as you would a hard copy file.

Task 2

You should now set up automatic out of office messages for all the school/college holidays for the year and indicate that you will not be available. Use the facility that allows you to write your own message. Anyone sending you an e-mail will get an out of office message from your system.

There are various ways of tracing an e-mail. You should be able to trace it by date, name or subject. Check that you know how to do this. This is why it is always easier if you have filed e-mails properly in folders – part of a search will already have been done as your work will be organised in a logical way.

Task 3

You should also ensure that you know how to set up an automated response. Try this facility with the next e-mail you receive. Remember, however, it is always better to acknowledge an e-mail, no matter how briefly, with a few words.

An important part of dealing with e-mails is using correct e-mail etiquette. Information on correct e-mail etiquette was included in Chapter 9.

Occasionally you will be asked to print e-mails, for example, your boss may want to compose a lengthy response to an e-mail received. Generally speaking e-mails should not be printed. In some systems the e-mail box is kept deliberately small so that individuals do not keep e-mails stretching back over years. You will know if you have a system which limits the size of your e-mail box as you will keep getting mail warning signs telling you your in-box or e-mail files are too big. If you have a system like this you may need to sort out the e-mails you want to keep and delete the rest. You would transfer those you wanted to keep to your network drive.

Check your Progress   11.1

1   When would you use cc and bcc in e-mail?

2   Why would you use urgent sparingly?

3   Explain how you would attach a file.

E-Diary

E-diary software is essentially internal to an organisation. The e-diary is a useful way of keeping track of what people are doing and where they are. Most e-diary systems have a facility to allow preferences to be stated. This means that you can set up your diary to:

1 allow selected people to read only

2 allow selected people, such as your manager or admin assistant, to set up appointments for you in your absence

3 keep your diary private.

To get the most out of a diary system organisations usually choose option 1 so that if you are trying to set up a date for a meeting with another person, you can see when they are free and send them an invitation to a meeting.

Most diary systems let you set up a meeting, stating the time, date and place of the meeting and identify who you want to invite to that meeting. The invitations will then be sent out to the participants' e-mail addresses and they will be asked to accept or decline the invitation. This means that you can usually find a date and time for a meeting which suits everyone.

Diaries can be viewed in different ways: usually two days to a screen, a week to a screen, a month to a screen. Although a diary can be printed out, this should only be used sparingly. The danger with an electronic diary is that you forget to enter appointments and what is on your system may not be entirely accurate. As a result, if you are keeping both an electronic diary and a traditional diary, you should ensure that you update and align them both regularly.

Task 4

Throughout the course you should mark up any events in your e-dairy, for example, any internal assessments, appointments with your teacher/lecturer, any deadline dates for submission of work.

Task 5

Some diaries also have the facility to incorporate to do lists. You should look at the facilities available with your diary and see what other facilities it has available.

Task 6

Set up your diary so that you do your e-mail filing on the 2nd of each month.

Task 7

What would you do if you were trying to set a date for a meeting and no dates were available when everyone was present?

Internet

We have already looked at the advantages and disadvantages of using the Internet in Chapter 9. You probably use the Internet for leisure interests but using it for business can be different. Here are some definitions which might be useful to you. You will use these but may not know their proper name.

Task 8

Using the site http://webopedia.com find the following terms

Browser
Cookie
Search engine
Save this site as one of your favourites.

Task 9

You should now follow some of the hyperlinks which are shown in one of the documents above.

Check your Progress   11.2

1   What is the history feature? Give an example of when you might use it.

2   When would you mark a website as a favourite? Give an example.

ICT In-tray documents Set 1

Before doing this set of documents you should know how to:

- use the Internet for travel information

- set up favourites

- lay out an itinerary (see Chapter 7 for a sample layout)

- indicate that this is a draft, for example, by using a watermark or other indicator

- use a footnote

- insert a hyperlink

- e-mail a note with attachments of documents 1, 2, 3 and 4 to your teacher/lecturer.

ICT in-tray documents Set 1 – document 1

You are working in the Marketing section of John Nicholls and have been asked to make travel arrangements for the following people to attend a conference in the Hilton Hotel, Green Park in London.

Margaret O'Hare, the Marketing Manager, who will be travelling from Edinburgh.

Margaret Ward, Sales Administrator, who will be travelling from Aberdeen.

Naiem Reda, the Ladies Clothing Manager, who will be travelling from Glasgow.

Alistair McKay, the Gents Clothing Manager, who will be travelling from Glasgow.

Using the British Midland, Easyjet and British Airways websites you should research flights for them to be at the conference which starts at 1100 hours on the last Monday of next month.

Look up the Hilton website and see the availability of rooms for the Monday night. Indicate on the itinerary with a footnote that you have not booked these rooms, only checked availability. If the rooms are not available find another suitable Hilton (John Nicholls has an account with this company).

The conference finishes at 1500 hours on the Tuesday and all staff have indicated they want to come home that night.

Prepare a simple itinerary for staff using your house style. Naiem Reda and Alistair McKay should go on the same flight. The itinerary should include a hyperlink to the Hilton website so that staff can see if they want to be at that hotel.

Print one page of information about the hotel.

Indicate that the itinerary is a draft.

ICT in-tray documents Set 1 – document 2

Margaret O'Hare had indicated that although she will be travelling down from Edinburgh she wants to go back into Glasgow airport as she is expected in the Glasgow store on Wednesday. She will need a hotel in Glasgow on the Tuesday night and the Wednesday night. Can you please alter her itinerary.

ICT in-tray documents Set 1 – document 3

Margaret O'Hare has asked you to find out train times from Glasgow to Aberdeen on Thursday of the same week and to find a suitable central hotel in Aberdeen for that night. Also find her a suitable train time back to Edinburgh on the Friday afternoon. Prepare in itinerary format.

ICT in-tray documents Set 1 – document 4

Create a table with the title Conference Costs and include the following column headings:

Name, Cost of Air fare, Overnight accommodation, Conference Cost (each delegate costs £150) and Total cost (excluding taxis and incidentals). Input the date from the flights and hotels chosen and total the columns.

ICT in-tray documents Set 2

You should know how to:

- search for relevant data on the Internet
- insert hyperlinks to your own documents
- insert hyperlinks to websites
- lay out forms
- use your e-diary and print weekly information
- e-mail data to your teacher/lecturer – documents 1, 2, and 3 should be e-mailed to them.

ICT in-tray documents Set 2 – document 1

Using the information you found out in Task 8, complete the following document and display appropriately.

Updating your vocabulary

From time to time you may come across computing terms with which you are not familiar. When this happens you should always try to find out what these terms really mean so that you can use them properly.

A good site for your new vocabulary and one which is updated regularly is http://webopedia.com and here you will find an easy route into finding a clear definition. You simply key in the word you want to know and press go. The definition which appears will often have hyperlinks to other parts of the site which will give you a fuller explanation of the terms used.

Here are some new terms which have been added to the John Nicholls handbooks recently. (Insert the 3 terms you looked up and copy in the website definitions of these terms.)

We intend to add to your knowledge regularly in the Newsletter which appears on the intranet so if you come across any interesting new computer terms let us know.

ICT in-tray documents Set 2 – document 2

Key in this article for the John Nicholls Newsletter which will go on the intranet.

Travelling for John Nicholls

When you are away on business for the organisation you may need to make travel arrangements. This should always be done by completing the appropriate forms and submitting them to your named administrative assistant. This is a copy of the updated form.

(Insert a hyperlink to the Travel Request Form (TR1) detailed in Chapter 7. You should key in the form and/or save it as Travel Request Form to your network file and insert a hyperlink.)

continued ➤

If you are using your own transport, you require to get prior permission from your departmental manager and then claim back the mileage at the following rate:

30 pence per mile

You may find the following Internet sites of use to you when calculating distance travelled and working out the most appropriate routes (insert a minimum of two websites which can be used for this purpose in the format that they can be accessed). These sites will give you an estimate of the time taken for the journey as well as distance and route.

You would also require to complete form CL1 for each journey. The full form is available in the Forms Section of the intranet and should be completed and e-mailed to your line manager as soon as possible after the journey has been completed. (You should insert a hyperlink to the Expenses Claim Form CL1 detailed in Chapter 7. You should key in the form and/or save it to your network file and insert a hyperlink here.)

All accommodation arrangements must be made through John Nicholls. When accommodation arrangements are confirmed you will also receive a note of the rates of subsistence currently being permitted. All accommodation arrangements must be requested on Accommodation Request Form ACR1.

ICT in-tray documents Set 2 – document 3

John Nicholls has a number of overseas visitors coming to Edinburgh for the Fashion Festival planned for the last week in April of next year. You have been asked to give them some information on the kind of accommodation available for single rooms in a city centre location.

Draw up a table with the following column headings:

> Name of hotel; No of single rooms; Price per night, Inc Breakfast; Location; Telephone number; Notes (this column is for any additional information, for example, prices are only valid until…)

Complete the table with a minimum of six hotels, with 3, 4 or 5 stars which are located near Princes Street. Your boss intends to include this information in the welcome pack for overseas visitors.

ICT in-tray documents Set 2 – document 4

Set up the following events in your e-diary.

- You are going to the Salary Committee meeting on Tuesday of next week at 1300 hours until 1600 hours.

- You are on a staff development course all day next Thursday in the Milton Hotel.

- You have an appointment with Personnel at 1500 hours on Friday.

- Reserve the time between 0900 hours and 1000 hours on the next four Fridays for personal development planning.

Take a print out of your diary for next week.

CHAPTER 12

Spreadsheets

I2 This chapter contains explanations and exercise material for Intermediate 2 Information Technology for Administrators Outcome 1.

Use spreadsheets to solve business problems:

- ☆ **work with multiple spreadsheets**
- ☆ **link data within worksheets using named cells**
- ☆ **use formulae and functions – maximum, minimum, count, the IF function, combine formulae, absolute cell references**
- ☆ **create charts – bar charts, column charts, formatting of information on axes**
- ☆ **printing – worksheets, parts of worksheets, embedded charts and separate charts.**

Note: Integrating data from a worksheet, including a chart, has already been covered in Chapter 10 Word Processing.

Higher Level Outcomes: ⫸

H It also includes explanations and exercise material for Higher Information Technology for Management Outcome 3.

Use ICT to solve business problems and communicate and present solutions:

- ☆ **working with cells and cell data – formatting, working with comments**
- ☆ **managing work book – linking worksheets, inserting page breaks**
- ☆ **working with named cells and ranges of cells**
- ☆ **data consolidation – summary worksheets, pivot tables and charts**
- ☆ **functions –countif, round mathematical function, V and H lookups**
- ☆ **sorting – filtering on two criteria, grouping and outlining**
- ☆ **charts – customising data series in rows and columns**
- ☆ **importing data from a database table**
- ☆ **printing – worksheets, parts of worksheets, value and formulae view, separate and embedded charts.**

Note: Importing data from a word processed document and exporting dynamically linked data have already been covered in Chapter 10 Word Processing.

In addition to the In-tray exercises included in this chapter, simple spreadsheets (many with charts) are included as part of chapter 10 Word Processing in In-tray Set 6. Those undertaking Intermediate 2 are advised to complete these simple spreadsheets first. The spreadsheets in this chapter have been written to extend problem solving skills.

Spreadsheet programs enable you to produce complex statistical and arithmetic data in a standardised format which you can alter to suit your needs. One of the main advantages of using software of this type for calculations is that anything you create in spreadsheet format can be transferred to other software packages and time is not wasted inputting the same information into a different format. It is important that you try to ensure any data keyed in is accurate and up to date.

You have already looked at housestyles for word processed documents. Many organisations also have housestyles for spreadsheets; indeed in some organisations, spreadsheets are set up by the 'owning' section for use by other sections, so the layout is pre-determined. When this happens it is usually set up as a pro-forma document with all formulae and formats already set up. All that those completing the spreadsheet have to do is fill in the blanks. An example of this kind of approach would be an overtime spreadsheet set up by the section responsible for paying wages but completed by the administrator in the section where the work is actually carried out.

When you are keying data into a spreadsheet you should always be aware of the formatting used and any formula already set up. You should look over the entire spreadsheet first before keying in any data and you may find it helpful to take a printout of the formulae used. For example, you should generally not key in the £ sign but should use the format facility for currency and the £ sign will show automatically. The format facility should also be used to determine how many decimal places you want in your answer, the format for date, etc.

While spreadsheets were designed for use primarily for statistical and numerical data, many organisations use them as mini-databases as data can be sorted and filtered and subsequently printed. Many people find spreadsheet software simpler to use than database software and it has a big advantage in enabling different versions of the same spreadsheet to be retained by using the Save As facility. It is also useful to know that if you have a large table to lay out, your word processing software may have insufficient space for the information you need – using a spreadsheet might be more appropriate.

The MAXIMUM function can be used to help you find the highest number in the range identified. The MINIMUM function is used to find the smallest number in the range identified. The COUNT function will give you the total number of numerical or date entries in the range identified but note it will not count alphabetical entries – for this you would need to use the COUNTA function.

Every cell in a spreadsheet has a different cell reference and spreadsheets are based on the principle that cell references are relative, that is, that both the row number and the column letter of each cell address changes when you copy the cell. You can change this default by overwriting and making the address an absolute cell address so that neither the row nor the column changes. When you copy a formula an absolute cell address will remain the same.

Many people find it easier to work with numbers when they name cells, for instance, you might name the cell with the VAT rate as VAT. When you want to include this cell as part of a formula you can use the name VAT rather than identify the cell address. A range of data can also be named.

You can use a number of different types of chart when you want to show your data graphically. Using a chart to illustrate your figures makes it easy to spot trends and easier to remember relationships. You can place your chart on a separate page or embed your chart within a spreadsheet. It is often a good idea to show data in two or three different chart styles before

INFORMATION TECHNOLOGY

deciding which is the best way of illustrating your information. Once you have decided on the type of chart to use, you may need to change the size of the fonts used on chart titles and headings so that all information can be seen. It is important to do this as your chart may be reduced in size at a later stage or it may be transferred to another software application. You often have to ensure that all labels are still legible and it is important that you check this before finally saving your chart.

Remember you can navigate your way about a spreadsheet in different ways – using your mouse to click on the cell you want to go to or using the arrow keys or using specific commands to take you to the start or to the end of a large spreadsheet or to the start or the end of a row or a column.

In-tray Spreadsheets Set 1

Before starting this set of spreadsheets you should be able to:

* copy a table from Word into a spreadsheet
* navigate a spreadsheet table
* insert data
* insert formulae for adding, subtracting, multiplying, dividing
* format cells
* merge cells
* shade cells
* insert borders in cells
* name sheets in a spreadsheet file.

In-tray spreadsheets Set 1 Day 1 – spreadsheet 1

Find the table you created in Chapter 10 Word Processing for In-tray Set 3 Day 1 Tables Task 3. It should look like this. It was a summary of the sales made in John Nicholls last month.

Summary of Sales for last month.

Department	Manager	Sales £
Furniture	Kamal Ahmed	36500
Cosmetics	Rena Carter	18700
Bathrooms	Susan Shields	10045
Cosmetics – JN only	Loraine Duval	21008
Ladies Clothing	Naiem Reda	10021
Children's clothing	Anne Wilson	17359
Gents Clothing	Alistair McKay	10120
Electrical	Jeff Quigley	14560
Household	Ellen Divers	20141
China	Ruby Dalziel	12015
Glassware	Gordon Stratford	10922

continued ➤

Department	Manager	Sales £
Soft furnishings	Gary Davidson	23467
Accessories	Sandra Melbourne	10508
Gifts	Sonia Ben Arefi	10904
Toys	Gail Shields	10207
Sports	Orla Coyle	11215

- If you have already keyed it in and saved it as a Word file, copy the file into a spreadsheet file. If you have not keyed it in you should key it into a spreadsheet file.

- Call the file Sales Summaries.

- Format the Sales figures column as £s with no decimal places.

- Insert the following data into a fourth column as shown below.

Department	Manager	Sales £	Sales this year so far
Furniture	Kamal Ahmed	36500	126800
Cosmetics	Rena Carter	18700	62458
Bathrooms	Susan Shields	10045	36918
Cosmetics – JN only	Loraine Duval	21008	55897
Ladies Clothing	Naiem Reda	10021	37826
Children's clothing	Anne Wilson	17359	60119
Gents Clothing	Alistair McKay	10120	34527
Electrical	Jeff Quigley	14560	52765
Household	Ellen Divers	20141	52281
China	Ruby Dalziel	12015	28624
Glassware	Gordon Stratford	10922	27514
Soft furnishings	Gary Davidson	23467	51781
Accessories	Sandra Melbourne	10508	27819
Gifts	Sonia Ben Arefi	10904	18242
Toys	Gail Shields	10207	22716
Sports	Orla Coyle	11215	29178

- Change the heading of column 3 to Sales for March and the heading of column 4 to Sales for year to date.

- Add in a column at the end with the heading Total Sales to add the two sales figures together. Copy this formula down the table.

- Add in a row at the foot of the table with the label Total.

- Merge the first two columns in this row and insert a formula to total each of column C, column D and column E.

INFORMATION TECHNOLOGY

- Put a border round each of the cells in this totals row and shade this row. Make sure these totals are formatted in currency.

- Name this worksheet March.

- Print a copy of the spreadsheet in landscape format.

In-tray spreadsheets Set 1 Day 1 – spreadsheet 2

This trial spreadsheet was set up for illustration purposes in Chapter 10 when Set 6 Day 1 Report 3 was keyed in. If you have already keyed it in as a spreadsheet file, recall it and edit it. If you have not yet keyed it in as a spreadsheet, do so now.

Staff Absent Due To Ill Health in XXX Department				
	Jan	Feb	Mar	Totals
Days lost to ill health				
Days lost for other reasons				
Permitted absences				
Total working days in department				

You will require this spreadsheet for the IT Department.

- Call the file Absence Summary.

- Name the sheet IT Dept and change the heading appropriately.

- Format all of the numerical data to one decimal place.

- Insert the following data as three columns to the left of January with the headings Coding, First name and Second name and add in the following information:

	First Name	Second Name	Coding	Jan	Feb	Mar	Totals
Days lost to ill health							
	Claire	Lee					
	Rashid	Ahmel					
	John	Cavanagh					
	Paul	Ganguly					
	Lynn	Forsyth					
	Caroline	Harper					
	Keira	McGill					
Days lost for other reasons							
	Insert same names here as above in the next 7 rows						
Permitted absences							
	Insert same names here as above in the next 7 rows						
Total working days in department							

- Enter the following data:
  - Claire Lee had 4 days off each month due to ill health
  - John Cavanagh had 3 days off in January due to ill health and 7 days permitted absence in February
  - Caroline Harper had 2 days off in February which come under the Days lost for other reasons and so did Keira McGill and Rashid Ahmel
  - Paul Ganguly had 3 days off in March due to ill health
  - Enter zeros where no other entry is indicated.
- Insert a row above Total working days called Total days off work.
- The Total working days in the department are January – 125, February – 115, March – 124.
- Enter the appropriate formulae to make all calculations, copying formulae where necessary.
- Print a copy of the spreadsheet in landscape format.

In-tray spreadsheets Set 1 Day 1 – spreadsheet 3

Set up a spreadsheet called Stock Control with information on the minimum and maximum stock levels, movement of stock in and out, and balance at the start and end for the month of March.

Item	Min	Max	In	Out	Balance at start	Balance at end
Hotpoint Model 483	6	15	5	0	6	
Model 355	5	10	4	2	5	
Model 528	5	10	6	4	6	
Indesit Model 08X	5	10	7	6	7	
Model 90X	5	10	8	3	8	
Model 06X	5	10	6	7	7	
Phillips Whirlpool B22	6	12	8	8	8	
Whirlpool B24	5	10	6	8	7	
Whirlpool B26	6	12	9	10	5	
Miele Advanced	5	10	6	8	7	
Superadvanced	5	10	5	7	5	
Sonic	5	10	6	8	9	

- Alter the spreadsheet to show the make of each type of washing machine in a separate row with an enhancement. Do not merge the cells in these rows.
- Work out the balance of stock at the end of the month by inserting a formula and copying it down.

- Insert a row at the end of the spreadsheet to show the totals of each column. (Do not total the minimum or maximum columns.)

- Name the sheet as Washing machines.

- Save the spreadsheet file as Stock control.

- Print a copy of the worksheet in landscape format so that it fits on to one page.

In-tray spreadsheets Set 1 Day 2

Before undertaking these spreadsheets you should ensure that you know how to:

- create charts and embed them in worksheets

- create charts where data is separated

- change the size of font used in labels on worksheets

- express one figure as a percentage of another

- use the functions maximum and minimum

- print worksheets to fit to a page.

In-tray spreadsheets Set 1 Day 2 – spreadsheet 1

Recall the spreadsheet file Sales Summaries.

- Create a chart which shows the March sales figures for all departments. Place the chart on the same page as your spreadsheet. Ensure that you can read all the labels easily.

- Create a final column in the spreadsheet which shows the March sales as a percentage of total sales. Show this to one decimal place.

- Add a row to the end of the spreadsheet to show the biggest contribution (in percentage terms) any of the departments made to total sales. Merge the other cells in this row so that only two cells are outlined.

- Add a row to the end of the spreadsheet to show the smallest contribution (in percentage terms) any of the departments made to total sales. Merge the other cells in this row so that only two cells are outlined.

- Print your worksheet so that it fits on to one page.

In-tray spreadsheets Set 1 Day 2 – spreadsheet 2

Recall the Spreadsheet file Absence Summary. You will be working on the IT worksheet.

- Add in rows in appropriate places to subtotal the days off for each month for each category of absence.

- Amend the formula you have used to show total absences for each month.

- Add a final row which shows the absences due to ill health as a percentage of total working days in the department. Show this to one decimal place.

- Add a row to the end of the spreadsheet to show the greatest number of absences in one month due to ill health.

- Add a row to the end of the spreadsheet to show the smallest number of absences each month.

- Merge cells in each of the last four rows so that the first three columns are merged in each row.

- Create a pie chart which shows the absence due to ill health subtotalled figures for January, February and March – showing the figures as a percentage of the total. Place the chart on the same page as your spreadsheet.

- Print your worksheet so that it fits on to one page – landscape.

In-tray spreadsheets Set 1 Day 2 – spreadsheet 3

Recall the spreadsheet file Stock Control. You will be working on the worksheet Washing machines.

- Add in rows in appropriate places to subtotal the In, Out and Balance columns for each make of machine.

- Insert formulae to insert these subtotals.

- Add in a column at the end to show the highest number of washing machines in stock in any brand/model.

- Add in a column to show the lowest number of washing machines in stock in any brand/model.

- Create a chart to show the stock in hand of each type of washing machine and change the size of the fonts in the labels to ensure that it can all be read. Embed the chart in the spreadsheet sheet.

- Print your worksheets so that it fits on one page.

In-tray spreadsheets Set 1 Day 3

Before undertaking these spreadsheets you should ensure that you know how to:

- Duplicate/copy a worksheet within a spreadsheet file.

- Use the COUNT function or the COUNTA function.

- Use the IF function.

- Delete a chart.

- Use text orientation techniques in charts and cells.

- Name a cell.

- Link spreadsheets through named cells.

There are lots of ways of copying spreadsheets. The simplest is to copy and paste but there are other ways which you should explore which allow you to copy the formats you have already set up as well as the data. Often copying is used to save time and ensure consistency of layout. You should always name your new worksheet.

The IF function allows you to use spreadsheets to help in decision-making. It is sometimes called the logical function and its purpose is to ask:

INFORMATION TECHNOLOGY

> IF(logical test, the value if the logical test is true, the value if the logical test is false)

For example, if you were trying to get the spreadsheet to show that all of the students who received more than 50 marks in a test would get a pass but those who did not would fail, your logical test or IF statement would look like this:

> IF(the cell with the mark in it was equal to = or more than > 50, Pass, Fail)

The result would be shown in the cell as either Pass or Fail.

In-tray spreadsheets Set 1 Day 3 – spreadsheet 1

Recall the file Sales Summaries. You will start off using the worksheet for March but you should read carefully which worksheet you will use throughout the exercise.

- Duplicate your existing worksheet and call the new worksheet Forecasts.

- Working on the Forecasts spreadsheet:

  - Delete the chart.

  - Insert a row at the end of the worksheet with the label Number of Departments and using the COUNT or the COUNTA function, find out how many departments' sales are in this spreadsheet.

  - Using the IF function insert a final column to identify which departments might get a bonus if we paid bonuses to those where March sales made up 25% or more of the total sales. Make the heading of this column Bonus?

  - Change the orientation of the heading in the last column Bonus? to be vertical left aligned.

- Working on the March spreadsheet:

  - Set up a named cell with the name Commission with the content 2.5%.

  - Using this named cell in your formula, calculate how much commission John Nicholls would have to pay each department for their March sales.

  - Total the amount of commission and name this cell Totalcommission.

- Working on the Forecast spreadsheet insert the label Total of commission to be paid in the last row of the spreadsheet.

  - Using the named cell Totalcommission link the spreadsheets with this named cell.

  - Set up a cell with the name Expected Percentage. John Nicholls would expect the March sales to amount to 23% of total sales. Using this as an absolute cell address, add a last column to this spreadsheet showing any increase/decrease from the expected percentage.

- Working on the March spreadsheet amend the figure for the Gift Department's March sales to £14200.

- Print a copy of both of the worksheets in the spreadsheet file.

In-tray spreadsheets Set 1 Day 3 – spreadsheet 2

Recall the file Absence Summary.

- Duplicate your IT worksheet to another sheet and call the new worksheet Forecasts. You will now work on the Forecasts Sheet.

    - Delete the chart on the Forecasts worksheet.

    - Insert a row at the end of the worksheet with the label Number of Staff and using the COUNT or COUNTA function, find out how many staff returns are included in this spreadsheet.

    - Using the IF function insert a final column to identify which members of staff should be referred for absence counselling. This is available to those with 10 or more days absence due to ill health over 3 months. The heading for this column should be Counselling?

    - Copy this formula down the column only to the end of the section.

    - Align the heading in the last column Counselling? vertically.

    - Add a last column to calculate how many days in total each person has lost for all reasons. Show this column heading vertically.

    - Set up a named cell called Bonus with £25 as its content

    - If an employee has no time off he/she will get a bonus of £25. Using an appropriate formula which includes the named cell Bonus, show this on your spreadsheet.

- In the last row of the IT spreadsheet insert the label Possible Bonus if no days are lost and insert the named cell Bonus.

- Print a copy of both worksheets in the spreadsheet.

In-tray spreadsheets Set 1 Day 3 – spreadsheet 3

- Duplicate your existing stock control worksheet to another sheet and call it April Stock Sheet.

- Delete the chart on the April Stock Sheet.

- Change the heading of In to In in March, Out to Out in March, Balance at start to Balance at start of March and Balance at end to Balance at start of April.

- Change the heading to Stock Control Washing Machines – April.

- Insert a row at the end of the spreadsheet and insert a formula to find out how many models we hold in stock.

- Using the IF function insert a final column to identify the models of which we have more than the maximum stock. Insert a warning. The heading for this column should be Stock Alert.

- Copy this down the column and remember to delete the result beside any subtotals or heading rows.

- Align the heading in the last column Stock Alert to go diagonally.

- Print a copy of the worksheet April Stock Sheet on one page.

In-tray spreadsheets Set 1 Day 4

Before being able to do this, you should be able to sort and filter information.

Data can be sorted in different ways in a spreadsheet. At its simplest, sorting can be done by choosing to re-arrange data based on a column, such as alphabetical order or date order. Using language you are familiar with from databases, you can sort using a primary, secondary and tertiary sort key.

Alternatively you can sort data so that you are only looking at specific types of information, for example, all those who work in the Electrical Department. This type of sorting is usually done using autofilter.

In-tray spreadsheets Set 1 Day 4 – spreadsheet 1

- In your Sales Summaries spreadsheet sort the departments in alphabetical order.

In-tray spreadsheets Set 1 Day 4 – spreadsheet 2

- In your Absence Summary spreadsheet filter the data to find all entries for Claire Lee.

In-tray spreadsheets Set 1 Day 4 – spreadsheet 3

- In your Stock Control spreadsheet filter data to find all washing machines where we hold 13 washing machines in stock.

In-tray spreadsheets Set 1 Day 5

Before starting this set of exercises you should be able to:

- Set up and look up a vertical and a horizontal lookup table.
- Insert comments.
- Use the ROUND functions.
- Name a range of data.

Inserting comments allows you to add in some narrative which will not be seen by those accessing hard copy of the spreadsheet. It is usually only visible to those looking at the data on screen. It is useful to identify figures which seem out of place – too big or too small – or are only provisional. Comments can be added, altered or deleted. They should be treated like electronic sticky notes and while the whole message is usually only visible when your pointer is above the cell in which they are written, they are identifiable usually by a marker – in Microsoft Excel this is a red triangle.

Rounding figures can be done by choosing to show only whole numbers or a certain number of decimal places or it can be done by using the functions ROUND, ROUNDUP, ROUNDDOWN.

To save you keying in data again you can use already keyed in data or communal data, look it up and reference it to your spreadsheet. This is called automatic table lookups or VLOOKUP (vertical lookup) or HLOOKUP (horizontal lookup).

Rather than you having to find the correct value in a big table, you simply identify where the matching information is held and the programme finds the correct value. Your lookup table has to have certain attributes. The values you want looked up must be in the first column of a vertical lookup table or the first row in a horizontal lookup data table.

The values in the lookup table should be sorted in ascending order by rows in a VLOOKUP or in columns by the HLOOKUP. The values in the first column or row must be unique – a bit like a primary key in a database.

In-tray spreadsheets Set 1 Day 5 – spreadsheet 1

Using your March spreadsheet:

- Round up the Total commission paid to whole pounds.

- Add a comment beside the Gift department to check these figures – they seem very high.

In-tray spreadsheets Set 1 Day 5 – spreadsheet 2

Using the IT spreadsheet:

- Add in a comment beside Claire Lee's name in the Absence Due to Sickness section saying that this requires immediate referral to a Counsellor.

- Round down the total number of working days lost to ill health to a whole number.

In-tray spreadsheets Set 1 Day 5 – spreadsheet 3

Using the April Stock Sheet:

- Put in a comment beside the model of Whirlpool which went below the minimum stock level and ask why.

- Add the following codings into your main spreadsheet. Miele and Phillips are Code D, Indesit machines are code B and Hotpoint are Code A.

- Set up a Lookup table. Name the range Maintenance with the following information about Maintenance Costs. You will use this table again in this spreadsheet.

Coding	Annual cost of Maintenance
A	£55
B	£60
C	£85
D	£105
E	£120
F	£80
G	£95

- Use the Lookup table to link the two tables so that the cost of maintenance shows in your main spreadsheet.

- Set up a horizontal lookup table with delivery information, based on the same coding. Name the range Delivery.

Coding	A	B	C	D
Delivery cost	£25	£30	£30	£25

- Use the Lookup table to link the two tables so that the cost of delivery shows in your main spreadsheet.

In-tray spreadsheets Set 2 Day 1

In this set of exercises you will have to:

- Set conditional formatting.

- Insert data simultaneously in different worksheets.

- Prepare summary spreadsheets using data consolidation techniques, named cell techniques or linking sheets through individual cells – you should make sure you know how to use all of these techniques.

- Change colours in a chart.

- Delete comments.

When the layout of a spreadsheet is going to be standardised throughout a department or organisation it is a good idea to set up the parts which are needed in each worksheet in a standardised way with enhancements and headings and calculated figures in the same part of the spreadsheet. This makes it easier for everyone to find the relevant information that they need. You can enter common information like column headings and row headings, headers, footers, etc. in different worksheets at the same time but you can also enter formulae and enhancements like this too. If you enter data in this way you can then transfer data from individual worksheets very easily to a summary worksheet.

Any changes you make to the individual sheets are then automatically updated in the summary sheets – this does not happen if you simply copy and paste the data from individual cells. In this Set you will be using summary sheets. While you are free to set the summary sheets up any way you wish, you should use these exercises to ensure you know how to use the consolidation facilities of your software, how to link individual cells and how to use named cells to transfer the information you need to a summary sheet. In the next Set we will look at using some of the automatic ways of setting up summaries and consolidating data.

Conditional formatting is a way to apply a formatting consistently throughout a range of data or cells, for example, if a minus sign is showing you might want to show figures in RED or if minimum stock level is reached you might want to show figures in GREEN.

In-tray spreadsheets Set 2 Day 1 – spreadsheet 1

You are going to set up a spreadsheet for the Ladies Department – Petite. This will have four suppliers on it: Precis, Minuet, Principles and JN own brand. The layout of each spreadsheet will be the same and the worksheets should be set up at the same time.

Item	Colour	Ref	8	10	12	14	16	Cost price	Mail Order Code
Jacket			3	4	6	6	4		A
			3	4	6	6	4		
			3	4	6	6	4		
			3	4	6	6	4		
Skirts									B
			3	4	6	6	4		
			3	4	6	6	4		
			3	4	6	6	4		
			3	4	6	6	4		
Trousers									B
			3	4	6	6	4		
			3	4	6	6	4		
			3	4	6	6	4		
			3	4	6	6	4		
Dresses									A
			3	4	6	6	4		
			3	4	6	6	4		
			3	4	6	6	4		
			3	4	6	6	4		
Blouses									B
			3	4	6	6	4		
			3	4	6	6	4		
			3	4	6	6	4		
			3	4	6	6	4		

continued ➤

Item	Colour	Ref	8	10	12	14	16	Cost price	Mail Order Code
Knitwear									C
			3	4	6	6	4		
			3	4	6	6	4		
			3	4	6	6	4		
			3	4	6	6	4		

- You should calculate subtotals for each size and calculate the value of stock for each item throughout all of these sheets.

- Set up a lookup table for Mail Order with the following information:

Code	Cost
A	£4.50
B	£2.50
C	£3.50

- Once you have set up each of the worksheets enter the following information about the Autumn stock received. John Nicholls always orders the same number of items in each size from each supplier. The colours, reference numbers and costs will vary but the mail order code will remain the same for each category of clothing.

Precis

Item	Colour	Ref	Cost price	Mail Order Code
Jacket	Red	P001R	£85.00	A
	Black	P001B	£85.00	
	Pink	P001P	£85.00	
	Grey	P001G	£85.00	
Skirts				B
	Red	S001R	£35.00	
	Black	S001B	£35.00	
	Pink	S001P	£35.00	
	Grey	S001G	£35.00	

continued ➤

Item	Colour	Ref	Cost price	Mail Order Code
Trousers				B
	Red	T001R	£40.00	
	Black	T001B	£40.00	
	Pink	T001P	£40.00	
	Grey	T001G	£40.00	
Dresses				A
	Red	D001R	£70.00	
	Black	D001B	£70.00	
	Pink	D001P	£70.00	
	Grey	D001G	£70.00	
Blouses				B
	Red	B001R	£30.00	
	White	B001W	£30.00	
	Pink	B001P	£30.00	
	Grey	B001G	£30.00	
Knitwear				C
	Red	K001R	£30.00	
	White	K001W	£30.00	
	Pink	K001P	£30.00	
	Grey	K001G	£30.00	

Minuet

Item	Colour	Ref	Cost price
Jacket	Navy	MJN01	£87.00
	Brown	MJB01	£87.00
	Green	MJG01	£87.00
	Purple	MJP01	£87.00

continued ➢

Item	Colour	Ref	Cost price
Skirts			
	Navy	MSN01	£32.00
	Brown	MSB01	£32.00
	Green	MSG01	£32.00
	Purple	MSP01	£32.00
Trousers			
	Navy	MTN01	£29.00
	Brown	MTB01	£29.00
	Green	MTG01	£29.00
	Purple	MTP01	£29.00
Dresses			
	Navy	MDN01	£48.00
	Brown	MDB01	£48.00
	Green	MDG01	£48.00
	Purple	MDP01	£48.00
Blouses			
	Navy	MBN01	£26.00
	Brown	MBB01	£26.00
	Green	MBG01	£26.00
	Purple	MBP01	£26.00
Knitwear			
	Navy	MKN01	£27.00
	Brown	MKB01	£27.00
	Green	MKG01	£27.00
	Purple	MKP01	£27.00

Principles

Item	Colour	Ref	Cost price
Jacket	White	PrJW1	£75.00
	Orange	PrJ02	£75.00
	Black	PrJB3	£75.00
	Red	PrJR4	£75.00
Skirts			
	White	PrSW1	£29.00
	Orange	PrS02	£29.00
	Black	PrSB3	£29.00
	Red	PrSR4	£29.00
Trousers			
	White	PrTW1	£27.00
	Orange	PrT02	£27.00
	Black	PrTB3	£27.00
	Red	PrTR4	£27.00
Dresses			
	White	PrDW1	£48.00
	Orange	PrD02	£48.00
	Black	PrDB3	£48.00
	Red	PrDR4	£48.00
Blouses			
	White	PrBW1	£19.00
	Orange	PrB02	£19.00
	Black	PrBB3	£19.00
	Red	PrBR4	£19.00

continued ➤

Item	Colour	Ref	Cost price
Knitwear			
	White	PrKW1	£22.00
	Orange	PrK02	£22.00
	Black	PrKB3	£22.00
	Red	PrKR4	£22.00

John Nicholls Own Brand

Item	Colour	Ref	Cost price
Jacket			
	Black	0BB1J	£50.00
	Blue	0BB2J	£50.00
	Red	0BR3J	£50.00
	Brown	0BB4J	£50.00
Skirts			
	Black	0BB1S	£22.00
	Blue	0BB2S	£22.00
	Red	0BR3S	£22.00
	Brown	0BB4S	£22.00
Trousers			
	Black	0BB1T	£21.00
	Blue	0BB2T	£21.00
	Red	0BR3T	£21.00
	Brown	0BB4T	£21.00
Dresses			
	Black	0BB1D	£39.00
	Blue	0BB2D	£39.00
	Red	0BR3D	£39.00
	Brown	0BB4D	£39.00

continued ➤

Item	Colour	Ref	Cost price
Blouses			
	Black	0BB1B	£17.00
	Blue	0BB2B	£17.00
	Red	0BR3B	£17.00
	Brown	0BB4B	£17.00
Knitwear			
	Black	0BB1K	£16.00
	Blue	0BB2K	£16.00
	Red	0BR3K	£16.00
	Brown	0BB4K	£16.00

- Set up a summary sheet showing the total value of stock for each category of clothing for each supplier and the overall value.

- Conditionally format the Total Value cell to show in RED any type of clothing where we have more than £15,000 of goods in stock.

- Insert an appropriate comment that figures showing RED are considered to much stock.

- Save and close this spreadsheet.

In-tray spreadsheets Set 2 Day 1 – spreadsheet 2

John Nicholls want to extend the use of the style of spreadsheet you set up for the Ladies Clothing to the Gents Clothing. You have been asked to set up a similar style of spreadsheet for the Prestige brands.

- Each worksheet should have the same information – Timberland, Burberry, Gant.

- Row headings should be:

  Jackets, Knitwear, Shirts, Trousers, Accessories.

  Sizes 36, 38, 40, 42, 44 for Jackets, and Knitwear.

  Shirt sizes 15, 15$\frac{1}{2}$, 16, 16$\frac{1}{2}$, 17, 17$\frac{1}{2}$.

  Sizes 28, 30, 32, 34, 36, 38, 40, 42 for trousers.

  No sizes for Accessories.

- Like ladies fashions in the previous exercise, the same number of items of stock are ordered of each brand. The same lookup information for postage and packing should be used here as used in the ladies fashion. Jackets and Knitwear will be A, Trousers and Shirts will be B and Accessories C. The sizes are shown below and should be entered simultaneously on the appropriate worksheets.

INFORMATION TECHNOLOGY

INFORMATION TECHNOLOGY

Item	Size 36	Size 38	Size 40	Size 42	Size 44			
Jackets	2	2	3	3	1			
	2	2	3	3	1			
	2	2	3	3	1			
	2	2	3	3	1			
Knitwear	2	2	3	3	1			
	2	2	3	3	1			
	2	2	3	3	1			
	2	2	3	3	1			
	Size 15	Size 15½	Size 16	Size 16½	Size 17	Size 17½		
Shirts	5	6	7	7	4	3		
	5	6	7	7	4	3		
	5	6	7	7	4	3		
	5	6	7	7	4	3		
	Size 28	Size 30	Size 32	Size 34	Size 36	Size 38	Size 40	Size 42
Trousers	2	2	3	4	4	4	4	3
	2	2	3	4	4	4	4	3
	2	2	3	4	4	4	4	3
	2	2	3	4	4	4	4	3
Accessories	No							
	5	Wallet						
	12	Scarf						
	15	Tie						
	10	Toilet bag						

● Add in the following data about Autumn stock received. The cost of each item for each brand is shown below and needs to be entered on each individual sheet as follows:

  – Burberry jacket, trousers and knitwear colours brown, navy, black, and oatmeal.

  – Shirt colours cream, blue, camel, check.

  – Costs are jacket £110, knitwear £55, shirts £35, trousers £45, wallet £45, scarf £55, tie £30 and toilet bag £40.

- Gant jacket, trousers and knitwear colours camel, grey, black, cream.

- Shirt colours blue, pink, grey, green.

- Costs are jacket £90, knitwear £50, shirts £30, trousers £40, wallet £12, scarf £18, tie £15, toilet bag £18.

- Timberland jacket, trousers, and knitwear colours black, charcoal, buff, tweed.

- Shirt colours blue, pink, white and grey.

- Costs are jacket £98, knitwear £70, shirts £35, trousers £45, wallet £15, scarf £28, tie £22, toilet bag £24.

- Subtotal the amount of stock in each size and in each colour.

- Using the price as an absolute address, calculate the value of stock held for each category of goods and the overall value of stock held in each brand.

- Prepare a summary sheet to show clearly each category of clothing and the value of stock held from each supplier as well as the overall value of stock.

- Conditionally format the value of any stock where we have more than £12,000 in stock to show in RED.

- Add a comment to any RED figures to indicate 'Action required'.

- Save and close this spreadsheet.

In-tray Spreadsheets Set 2 Day 1 – spreadsheet 3

Set up a spreadsheet to record mileage with the column headings shown below plus each day of the week and relevant totals.

First Name	Second Name	Department	Car Type

- The departmental managers are Susan Shields – Bathrooms – who has a Mazda MX5, Jeff Quigley – Electrical – who has a VW Golf GT, Gary Davidson – Soft furnishings – who has a Vauxhall Vectra 1.9 and Ellen Divers – Household – who has a Toyota Yaris 1.8.

- You should enter common data simultaneously and name each worksheet, as Week 1, Week 2 etc.

- The mileage done in Week 1, 2 and 3 is shown below.

	Mon	Tues	Wed	Thurs	Fri
Susan Shields	34	0	0	87	15
Jeff Quigley	22	0	0	0	32
Gary Davidson	44	76	45	0	0
Ellen Divers	27	43	0	0	0

(side margin) INFORMATION TECHNOLOGY

	Mon	Tues	Wed	Thurs	Fri
Susan Shields	14	0	0	37	15
Jeff Quigley	27	0	8	0	12
Gary Davidson	40	79	34	0	80
Ellen Divers	29	4	0	18	0

	Mon	Tues	Wed	Thurs	Fri
Susan Shields	36	9	7	87	25
Jeff Quigley	21	0	0	3	12
Gary Davidson	56	6	15	0	0
Ellen Divers	20	14	0	65	9

- The current mileage rate is 42 pence per mile. You should set this up in an absolute address. Name the cell Mileage Rate.

- Using the mileage rate as an absolute reference you should set up appropriate formulae to calculate how much each department manager will be claiming for mileage on all spreadsheets.

- Set up a summary sheet to show the total amount claimed over 3 weeks by each department manager as well as the overall total.

- Conditionally format the totals so that any claim over £100 is shown in Red.

- Add the Comment to any cell showing in red High Mileage Claimed.

- Save the workbook as Mileage Information.

In-tray spreadsheets Set 2 Day 2 – spreadsheet 1

Recall the spreadsheet based on Ladies Fashions:

- delete the comments in the Summary Sheet

- prepare an appropriate chart to show the relative value of each type of stock held, enhancing the title of the chart and changing the colours used from the default to shades of red/blue.

- save the file.

In-tray spreadsheets Set 2 Day 2 – spreadsheet 2

Recall the spreadsheet based on Gents Fashions:

- delete the comments in the Summary Sheet

- prepare an appropriate chart to show the relative value of each type of stock held, enhancing the title of the chart and changing the colours used from the default to shades of blue and/or green.

- save the file.

In-tray spreadsheets Set 2 Day 2 – spreadsheet 3

Open the workbook you saved as Mileage Information.

- Delete the comments on the Summary Sheet

- Set up a chart on the Summary Sheet to show the amount claimed by each manager over the three weeks, showing only the manager's first name and amount claimed. Show the title Mileage Claimed in Arial bold italics and change the scale so that it shows only whole numbers. Show the information for each department manager in the colours red, white, green and blue in that order.

- Save the file.

In-tray spreadsheets Set 3 Day 1

Before undertaking this group of exercises you should be able to:

- import information from a database
- use the countif function
- set up and use pivot tables
- set up and use pivot charts
- print formulae view worksheets
- group and subtotal automatically
- copy worksheets
- sort on more than one field
- filter.

You have already looked at some ways of summarising data but there are lots of ways of consolidating and summarising data when using spreadsheets. Pivot tables allow you to consolidate data and show it in a summary form. This technique is most suited to summarising data which is entered on a day-to-day basis into a spreadsheet. You can highlight the information you want to summarise and where you want totals to be displayed. A pivot table report is interactive and allows you change the way data is shown. You can also show this information in chart format known as a pivot chart.

You can also summarise data by grouping or outlining and subtotalling using the software features. These techniques are best used when data is entered on an incremental basis yet you still wish to know running totals. Other techniques used to help find or view data more easily are sorting on one or more criteria and filtering so that you only view the data you want to see.

In-tray spreadsheets Set 3 Day 1 – spreadsheet 1

Go back to the data you entered in a database file in Chapter 10 Set 5 Day 1 – document 3. Here you started a database with Departmental Managers' Information (you later added to the database in Set 5 Day 2 – document 1 in Chapter 10). Using this database import the fields with Department, First name and Surname into a spreadsheet file – it should look like this:

Department	First Name	Surname
Furniture	Kamal	Ahmed
Cosmetics	Rena	Carter
Bathrooms	Susan	Shields
Cosmetics – JN only	Loraine	Duval
Ladies Clothing	Naiem	Reda
Children's clothing	Anne	Wilson
Gents clothing	Alistair	McKay
Electrical	Jeff	Quigley
Household	Ellen	Divers
China	Ruby	Dalziel
Glassware	Gordon	Stratford
Soft Furnishings	Gary	Davidson
Accessories	Sandra	Melbourne
Gifts	Sonia	Ben Arefi
Toys	Gail	Shields
Sports	Orla	Coyle

- Add a column to enter the sales information for week ending 7/5/.. as follows:

Department	Sales to 7/5/..
Furniture	£78800
Cosmetics	£16300
Bathrooms	£12400
Cosmetics – JN only	£3500
Ladies Clothing	£32800
Children's clothing	£24500
Gents clothing	£26700
Electrical	£25600
Household	£12400
China	£5400
Glassware	£3100
Soft Furnishings	£10600
Accessories	£9200
Gifts	£2300
Toys	£1900
Sports	£7800

- Insert an appropriate formula to calculate commission due at $2^{1}/_{2}\%$.

- Add in the following data:

Department	Sales to 14/5/..	Sales to 21/5/..
Furniture	£65700	£42500
Cosmetics	£16700	£13400
Bathrooms	£13300	£14200
Cosmetics – JN only	£1690	£1600
Ladies Clothing	£44200	£35600
Children's clothing	£26700	£25700
Gents clothing	£25600	£27000
Electrical	£25800	£27200
Household	£13000	£12700
China	£7800	£9800
Glassware	£4200	£5200
Soft Furnishings	£10700	£11200
Accessories	£10200	£11700
Gifts	£3500	£3700
Toys	£2900	£3100
Sports	£9200	£8700

- Calculate commission earned at the same rate as before for each week.

- Set up a pivot table to show the total sales for each week and the total commission paid.

- Set up a separate pivot table to show commission paid each week for each department and throughout the shop.

- Create a pivot chart to show this data.

- Using the Countif function work out how many departments will gain more than £600 commission in a week.

- Save your file ensuring you name each worksheet you have used with an appropriate name.

In-tray spreadsheets Set 3 Day 1 – spreadsheet 2

You are asked to set up a spreadsheet to record the hours worked by temporary Christmas staff. You will find their names in the database table you used for word processing Set 5 Day 1 – document 1 in Chapter 10. The database table is shown below. If you have not already keyed it in you should do so now.

First Name	Surname	Address	Town	Postcode	Phone number	Reference number	Successful?
Lynn	Marshall	35 Miller Street	GLASGOW	G45 7LK	0141 9987880	57	yes
Pierre	Boucheron	907 Great Western Road	GLASGOW	G67 0PL	0798 576880	58	yes
John	MacKay	52 Hill Street	MOTHERWELL	ML5 8JN	01698 767577	59	yes
Dorian	Rohmer	89 Little Road	MILNGAVIE	MG56 9HJ	0141 9528888	61	yes
Kim	Lee	9 Grange Road	STIRLING	SS5 7BV	01798 678655	62	yes
Mark	Kedzierska	18 Thomson Drive	GLASGOW	G76 8QT	0141 8447570	64	yes
Fiona	Galbraith	35 Green Road	GLASGOW	G14 9BH	0141 4532222	66	yes
Abdul	Bastani	70 Greatbridge Street	FALKIRK	FK6 8HJ	07785 756442	68	yes
Jim	Kerr	20 Primrose Hill	GREENOCK	GR5 9HN	01987 578677	70	no
Anthea	Feguson	25 Waterside Drive	BISHOPTON	BR5 9GF	07709 698444	71	no
Paul	Gillespie	31 Dalzell Road	WISHAW	ML5 8HY	07798 200745	73	no

- Query the database to find only those who were successful in gaining employment and show their first names, surnames and reference numbers.

- Transfer this information into spreadsheet format and call the spreadsheet Temporary Christmas Staff.

- Add columns for logging the sales made at the end of each day. Each temporary employee will log their total sales at the end of each day before clocking off.

- Sort your spreadsheet on surname before inputting the data.

Sales are as follows for week 1:

First Name	Mon	Tue	Wed	Thu	Fri	Sat	Sun
Abdul	£334.00	£534.00		£348.00	£870.00	£1,098.00	£1,145.00
Pierre	£526.00		£889.00	£768.00	£890.00	£1,050.00	£1,698.00
Fiona	£1,087.00	£987.00	£899.00		£2,085.00	£2,340.00	£3,278.00
Mark		£5,247.00	£5,340.00	£667.00	£5,268.00	£5,266.00	£5,678.00
Kim	£3,200.00	£3,100.00		£2,890.00	£4,189.00	£5,561.00	£5,760.00
John		£1,024.00	£1,090.00	£1,478.00	£1,780.00	£2,561.00	£2,341.00
Lynn	£2,300.00	£1,400.00		£1,478.00	£1,456.00	£1,899.00	£1,600.00
Dorian	£567.00		£635.00	£644.00	£698.00	£780.00	£886.00

- Add another section to the spreadsheet to enter the sales for Week 2 as follows:

First Name	Mon	Tue	Wed	Thu	Fri	Sat	Sun
Abdul	£343.00	£554.00		£368.00	£815.00	£1,156.00	£1,070.00
Pierre	£516.00		£832.00	£715.00	£800.00	£1,156.00	£1,078.00
Fiona	£1,009.00	£902.00	£890.00		£1345.00	£1,896.00	£2,341.00
Mark		£4565.00	£2432.00	£612.00	£2341.00	£2,231.00	£4,325.00
Kim	£2300.00	£2560.00		£2089.00	£4,090.00	£5,111.00	£5,001.00
John		£1,870.00	£1568.00	£1,332.00	£1,556.00	£2,232.00	£2,928.00
Lynn	£1340.00	£1446.00		£1,351.00	£1,998.00	£1,775.00	£1,998.00
Dorian	£789.00		£789.00	£988.00	£798.00	£980.00	£1,886.00

- Insert a subtotal for each person's weekly sales.

- Using these figures group and outline using the automatic feature of your software so that you can see the day-by-day figures or the weekly figures.

- Using the Countif function work out how many people have sold more than £10,000 each week.

- Save your spreadsheet.

In-tray spreadsheets Set 3 Day 1 – spreadsheet 3

Recall the database you set up in Chapter 10 for Set 5 Day 1 – document 4. Query the database to transfer the following information into a spreadsheet file – First name, Surname, Branch, Dept and Staff number.

IT Staff				
First Name	**Surname**	**Branch**	**Dept**	**Staff No**
Keira	McGill	Hightown	IT	4256
John	Cavanagh	Edinburgh	IT	7821
Rashid	Ahmel	Edinburgh	IT	2009
Lynn	Forsyth	Hightown	Admin	8645
Caroline	Harper	Hightown	Admin	2331
Paul	Ganguly	Edinburgh	IT	3117
Claire	Lee	Edinburgh	Electrical	4007

- You should add on some of the information from a spreadsheet file you used in Set 5 Day 1 – document 5 (Chapter 10) which showed the hours worked for other departments.

First Name	**No of hours worked for other depts**	**Charged per hour to cost centre**	**Total amount charged to other depts**
Claire	12	£10.50	£126.00
Rashid	10	£13.50	£135.00
John	18	£13.50	£243.00
Paul	11	£13.50	£148.50
Lynn	12	£11.50	£138.00
Caroline	10	£11.50	£115.00
Keira	10	£13.50	£135.00

- You are now going to add in the information from the Glasgow branch as follows: (All are charged out at £13.50 per hour.)

First Name	**Surname**	**Dept**	**Staff No**	**Hrs for other depts**
Ann	Little	Admin	6984	9
Margaret	Reilly	IT	1076	22
Jim	McCoist	IT	6193	18
Gianni	Matonti	IT	4186	23
Lena	McCoist	IT	4003	12

- Complete the totals to match with the previous data.
- Sort on branch, surname and then first name.
- Set up a pivot table to show the total number of hours and the amount charged to other departments.

- Using the Countif function work out how many people have had over £150 charged out.

- Apply conditional formatting to this column and show any amounts over £150 in red.

- Save your file ensuring you name each worksheet you have used with an appropriate name, such as IT Hours.

In-tray spreadsheets Set 3 Day 2 – spreadsheet 1

Open the main spreadsheet with Departmental Sales and Commission information.

- Duplicate your original worksheet on to a second sheet. Name the new worksheet Auto Subtotal.

- You have been asked to alter the main spreadsheet and change the layout so that you show the sales vertically, week 1 above week 2 above week 3.

- Remove the Countif row.

- You are asked to outline each week's sales with a border and change the column headings to Sales.

- Sort or group the data on Department.

- Using the facilities of your software subtotal the sales and commission giving a subtotal for each department and for the whole shop.

- Copy the spreadsheet to another sheet, call this worksheet Formula.

- Change the view to formula view.

- Print the information only about the China Department showing the formula used.

- Save your spreadsheet.

In-tray spreadsheets Set 3 Day 2 – spreadsheet 2

Open the spreadsheet for Temporary Christmas Staff.

- Duplicate your Day 1 worksheet and call it Temporary Christmas Staff Day 2.

- Create a pivot table to show the sum of each person's sales for the two weeks given.

- Create a pivot chart to show this data and make sure that you show only whole pounds.

- Save this worksheet with an appropriate name.

- Copy Temporary Christmas Staff Day 2 and call the new worksheet Subtotals.

- Sort the worksheet on surname.

- Using the facilities of your software, subtotal the sales for each person and for all the temporary Christmas staff.

- Change the worksheet so that all the formulae show.

- Filter to show only Abdul Bastani's information.

- Print a copy of this information in formula format.

- Save the whole file.

In-tray spreadsheets Set 3 Day 2 – spreadsheet 3

Open the file which recorded the IT hours charged to departments.

- Duplicate your main Day 1 worksheet and call it Autosubtotal.

- Sort on department, surname and first name.

- Using the automatic features of your spreadsheet programme subtotal the number of hours worked and the total amount charged to other departments.

- Copy this spreadsheet and rename Autosubtotal and use this worksheet to show all formulae.

- Print the IT Department information only showing formulae used.

- Save the whole file.

CHAPTER 13

Databases

Intermediate 2 Level Outcomes:

This chapter contains explanations and exercise material for Intermediate 2 Information Technology for Administrators Outcome 3.

Use a flat database to solve business problems:

- ☆ **selecting field types as required**
- ☆ **altering properties**
- ☆ **adding/deleting fields and records**
- ☆ **sorting records**
- ☆ **using queries**
- ☆ **filtering data**
- ☆ **creating a database form**
- ☆ **producing reports**
- ☆ **datasheet formatting**
- ☆ **printing tables, forms, queries, reports, selected records/fields.**

Note: Integrating data from a database into a word processing document is covered in Chapter 10.

Higher Level Outcomes:

It also covers Higher Information Technology for Management Outcome 3.

Use ICT to solve business problems and communicate and present solutions:

- ☆ **working with relational databases**
- ☆ **working with queries, forms and reports**

Databases

A database is an organised collection of information relating to a particular subject. A telephone book, the Yellow Pages and a filing cabinet are examples of databases. The advantage of a computerised database lies in its ability to manipulate data very quickly and in many different ways. For example, queries will enable you to ask questions and allow you to sort your data in a particular order. Reports will allow you to display your data in a format that is well designed and easy to understand and forms are very good for inputting data.

In this section you will be using a flat database. This is a database which contains a single table. When designing your database it is important to ensure that you think very carefully about the purpose of your database and the end user requirements, including any forms and reports you will need. You will need to identify fields for each table, assign a primary key to make sure no two records are the same, and determine how the tables are going to be related (you will do this at Higher level). You can then go on to create the tables and enter the data.

Set 1 In-tray exercises in this section are suitable for Intermediate 2. Set 2 exersies are aimed at Higher only.

Before beginning this section, you should know how to:

- create a database file
- design a table with appropriate field names and data types
- add a primary key
- save a table
- change field properties
- open a database and enter, edit and delete data
- create and use queries (use a range of expressions when querying and use a query to perform a multi-column sort)
- sort records in a table based on one or two fields
- hide and unhide a column in a table
- format column width
- create a report from selected fields from a table and query
- add a footer to a report
- print a table and report.

Instructions to Teachers/Lecturers

Your teacher/lecturer will provide you with the following file. Alternatively, you should key in the following table yourself.

EMPLOYEE DETAILS.MDB. This is a flat database and consists of a single table called **Staff**.

INFORMATION TECHNOLOGY

Staff ID	Sname	Fname	Department	Add1	Add2	Pcode	Tel No	Date of birth	Start Date	Scale Point
219	Adams	Derek	Administration	62 Brittannia Way	Clydebank	G61 6XY	0141 951 2362	26/12/49	17/08/1989	3
220	Marshall	Lynn	Human Resources	21 Bell Street	Kilsyth	G65 3CK	01236 777994	11/07/63	21/02/1989	1
224	Lee	Kim	Sales and Marketing	30 Hillhead Street	Glasgow	G25 7BN	0141 570 9321	21/05/85	05/07/2001	2
225	Kedzierska	Mark	Sales and Marketing	30 Deans Ave	Dalmuir	G81 6YB	01389 873455	25/08/85	12/03/2004	1
228	Singh	Gurbhaj	Administration	19 Second Ave	Bothwell	G71 4WA	01698 435517	17/10/79	26/11/1998	4
230	Ramsay	Shiela	Administration	7 Oak Drive	Bishopbriggs	G64 9LA	0141 772 2300	12/12/83	17/4/2004	2
231	Murphy	Delan	Administration	27 Iona Court	Kilmarnock	KA3 1AP	01563 980006	16/07/81	16/07/2002	1
232	Wallace	Mason	Administration	9 Shore Road	Ayr	KA6 5RT	01292 087913	26/09/76	13/10/1997	5
235	Kaur	Pavinder	IT	15 Loch View	Bearsden	G61 9LG	0141 942 3908	07/06/84	11/02/2004	2
236	Chow	Mylee	Sales and Marketing	97 Reservoir Avenue	Milngavie	G62 3DK	0141 956 7869	11/02/62	16/07/1979	5
237	Chung	Kwok	Administration	1 Elizabeth Road	Kirkintilloch	G66 3TY	0141 776 3421	07/11/63	10/11/1981	5
238	Ellsweiller	Hans	IT	31 Stirling Drive	Motherwell	ML1 7RS	01698 874367	11/01/64	16/09/1984	5
239	Rodriguez	Roberto	IT	8 Main Street	Lennoxtown	G66 1AS	01360 136247	18/11/75	08/09/1995	3
240	Lynch	Susan	Sales and Marketing	43 Croy Road	Kilsyth	G65 1FG	01236 357865	12/06/72	23/12/1995	3
241	McDonald	Colin	Human Resources	97 Gourock View	Greenock	PA16 4FD	01475 498256	30/09/73	12/12/2001	4
242	Ross	Alison	Sales and Marketing	69 Old Course Road	Hamilton	ML3 4TD	01698 564239	27/10/76	05/06/2001	2

You will be asked to create the following files.

CHILDREN'S BOOKS.MDB. This is a flat database and consists of a single table called **Books**.

TRAINING.MDB. This is a flat database and consists of a single table called **Training Events**.

CUSTOMERS.MDB. This is a flat database and consists of a single table called **Products**.

GYM.MDB. This is a flat database. It consists of a single table called **Customer Details**.

In-tray documents Set 1 Day 1 – database 1

 This is a list of children's books held in stock in the Toy Department of John Nicholls. Set the information up as a database called Children's Books. Design a table called Books and format fields appropriately. Make the ISBN (International Standard Book Number) the primary key. Change the field sizes of Title, Author and Publisher fields to 35.

Title	Author	Publisher	Price	Age	ISBN
Dotty the Dog	Jane Bradshaw	Prentice Press	£7.99	2	221
Best Friends	Ellis Troy	Prentice Press	£4.99	5	222
The Big Fight	Edward Dupont	Pondlife	£5.99	5	223
Am I An Alien?	Louise Penderleith	Collins	£6.99	4	224
Is That for Me?	Jackie Sheldon	Collins	£4.99	5	225
The Crocodile who Went on Strike	Mary Flood	Michael Lewis	£6.99	4	226
Are We There Yet?	Susan Troy	Goodlife	£7.99	6	227
Whatever!	Marc Snowdown	Prentice Press	£5.99	7	228

- Sort the table in descending order of ISBN and print a copy of the table on one page. Make sure all data is fully visible.

- Add the field Publication Date as the last field to the database. Set the format to short date format. Complete using the information given below:

  (You only want to use the Title and Publication Date Fields. Hide all the other columns.)

Title	Publication Date
Dotty the Dog	03/09/2004
Best Friends	04/10/2003
The Big Fight	04/04/2002
Am I An Alien?	23/09/2003
Is That for Me?	17/02/2003
The Crocodile who Went on Strike	23/06/2002
Are We There Yet?	18/03/2002
Whatever!	29/05/2002

- Print the records showing only the columns Title and Publication Date. Unhide the columns.

- Search the database for all books which are published by Prentice Press or Collins.

- Sort the result of this query in ascending order of Publisher and descending order of Price.

- Save this query as Prentice and Collins.

- Print this query showing all fields.

- Create a report from this query to include the fields ISBN, Title, Author, Publisher and Price in this order. Insert your name as a footer in this report.

- Save the report and print a copy.

In-tray documents Set 1 Day 1 – database 2

Create a new database called Training for staff training events which will take place in John Nicholls in November and December (for staff at Hightown branch). Format fields appropriately. Use the YES/NO format for the Inhouse field. Change the field properties so that start time and finish time have numbers to two decimal places (short time) and save the table as Training Events but do not set a primary key.

21 November 2005 – IT Training Word/Excel 9.00am–4.00pm	**First Name**	**Last Name**	**Staff ID**	**Training**	**Stime**	**Ftime**	**Inhouse**	**Date**
	Norma	Smith	450	IT Training (Word)	9.00	4.00	YES	21/11/05
	Edward	Morton	451	Freedom of Information Act	1.00	4.00	YES	03/12/05
28 November 2005 – Manual Handling Course 9.15am–4.00pm	Katie	Singh	453	Manual Handling	9.15	4.00	NO	28/11/05
	Katie	Singh	453	IT Training (Excel)	9.00	4.00	YES	21/11/05
	Niela	Hussain	454	IT Training (Excel)	9.00	4.00	YES	21/11/05
3 December 2005 – FIA 1.00pm–4.00pm	Patrick	O'Brien	455	Manual Handling	9.15	4.00	NO	28/11/05
	Susan	Docherty	456	Manual Handling	9.15	4.00	NO	28/11/05
	Matthew	Adams	457	Freedom of Information Act	1.00	4.00	YES	03/12/05
	Grant	Smith	458	IT Training (Word)	9.00	4.00	YES	21/11/05

- Add the following records:

Yvette Fazzoli, Staff ID 480 – she will be attending the training courses on Word and Manual Handling

Gavin Lafferty, Staff ID 487 – he will be attending the Manual Handling course

Pierre Cousin, Staff ID 421 – he will be attending the FIA course.

- Delete the record for Grant Smith.

- Sort in decending order of Training and then print a copy of the table in landscape orientation on one page. Make sure all data is fully visible.

- Search the database for all inhouse courses running in November. Sort the results of this query in alphabetical order of surname. Save the query as Inhouse Courses Running in November and print showing all fields.

- Create a report from this query to include the fields Staff ID, Name and Training. Give the report the heading Inhouse Training in November. Insert your name as a footer on this report.

- Print this report.

In-tray documents Set 1 Day 1 – database 3

Create a new database file called Customers for the Lighting Department in the John Nicholls store. Add a table called Products to the database file and complete using the information given below. Format the fields appropriately. Use the YES/NO format for the Discontinued field. The products must be given a unique code number so assign the field type for the Product ID as Autonumber and define this field as the primary key.

Product ID	Product	Unit Price	Units in Stock	Re-order Level	Discontinued
1	Dark Wood Lamp	£26.99	5	10	YES
2	Hudson Table Lamb	£39.99	9	20	NO
3	Shinto Wooden Floor Lamp	£49.99	9	10	YES
4	Mini Wooden Lamp	£14.99	30	15	NO
5	Chocolate Ceramic Lamp	£39.99	14	10	NO
6	Curtain Droplights	£16.99	22	15	YES
7	Rubber Star Lights	£16.99	14	20	YES
8	Sparkle Candle Vase	£12.99	9	5	NO

- Print a copy of the table on one page. Make sure all data is fully visible.

- Make changes to the following records:

  The cost of the Sparkle Candle Vase is £14.99

  There are only 3 Dark Wooden Lamps in stock.

- Add the following new range of products which have just come in from the supplier:

  20 Lilly Lights at £14.99 each. Re-order level is 5.

  20 Mesh Flower Lights at £19.99 each. Re-order level is 5.

- Search the database for all products which have less than 10 units in stock and which will be discontinued. Save the query with the name Under 10 Units in Stock.

- Print the query showing the fields Product, Unit Price, Units in Stock, Discontinued.

- Search the database for all products which have 30 or less units in stock and which will not be discontinued. Sort the results of this query in ascending order of unit price and ascending order of product.

- Save the query with an appropriate name.

- Print the query showing all the fields.

- Create a report from this query to include all fields except the discontinued field. Insert an appropriate title and insert your name as a footer.

- Print a copy of the report.

Forms will allow you to add, update and view records in a table one at a time. They allow you to view data on screen in a more organised and attractive way. Forms are based upon the order of a table or a query.

In addition to the features you used for the above in-tray documents, before beginning this section you should know how to:

- create a database form

- enter, edit and delete data

- insert footer details

- produce a report from a form

- print a form.

In-tray documents Set 1 Day 2 – database 1

Open the database called Children's Books.

- Sort the records in ascending order of book price.

- Create a columnar form.

- Use this form to add new records which were published on 24 August 2003:

  Up, Up and Away by Mark Reid. Publisher is Collins & Sons, price $4.99. The book is suitable for 4 year olds. (ISBN 229)

  Lost and Found by Anna Greg. Publisher is Collins & Sons, price $8.99. The book is suitable for 2 year olds. (ISBN 230)

- Save the form as Children's books.

- Print the forms for the two new records.

- Close the form and the database file.

In-tray documents Set 1 Day 2 – database 2

Create a new database called Gym to record those staff who have joined a local gym which offered Edinburgh staff a concession rate. Design a table called Customer Details and complete using the information given below. Format fields appropriately. Assign the Customer ID field as AutoNumber and set the primary key on this field.

INFORMATION TECHNOLOGY

Customer ID	Surname	First Name	Add1	Add2	Pcode Date	DOB	Mobile No	Status	Join Date	Female
1	Smith	Hannah	4 Dalserf Court	Edinburgh	EH7 3DG	07/11/63	07811338756	1	31/12/04	Yes
2	Connelly	Margaret	16 Forth View	Dalgety Bay	KY11 6PT	08/10/80	07810684491	1	18/12/04	Yes
3	Bjornsson	Mary	22 Margueriete Ave	Edinburgh	EH6 5MR	07/12/84	07854199569	1	31/12/04	Yes
4	Tai	Sarah	22 Brodie Gdns	Bathgate	EH48 9TR	08/07/63	07969225632	3	18/11/04	Yes
5	Grassieq	Anna	12 Craigside Court	Mid Calder	EH53 7RT	05/06/82	07771942178	2	17/10/04	Yes
6	Majid	Abdul	22 Lloyd Street	Livingston	EH54 3WT	08/08/70	07947198326	1	13/03/05	No
7	Granger	Arthur	2 Bromfield Road	Dalgety Bay	KY11 9TY	06/11/80	07990347712	2	13/03/05	No
8	Sinclair	Jack	36 Earls Court	Dalgety Bay	KY11 9UY	08/09/80	07969327834	3	04/12/03	No
9	Maloney	Marie	22 Ronay Street	Livingston	EH54 5PB	07/10/60	07810275667	1	04/08/05	Yes
10	Friel	Henry	25 Sandyhill Terrace	Dalgety Bay	KY11 6NR	18/11/66	07932745662	3	04/08/05	No

- Sort the above database in ascending order of Surname.

- Create a columnar form to enter the following additional membership details – this will allow you enter and view them one at a time.

  Marie Maloney, 22 Ronay Street, Livingston EH54 5PB. DOB 10/07/60. Her mobile no is 07810275667 and join date 04/08/05. Membership status is 1

  Henry Friel, 25 Sandyhill Terrace, Dalgety Bay, KY11 6NR DOB 18/11/66. His mobile no is 07932745662. Same join date and membership status is 3.

- Margaret Connolly has changed address. Recall her form and change the address to 44 Madison Ave, Dalgety Bay KY11 4AY.

- Add the following data to the form footer: John Nicolls – Edinburgh.

- Print a copy of the form displaying Margaret Connolly's details.

- Create a report based on the Customer Details. Do not include the fields for DOB, Mobile No and Female in the report. Give the report an appropriate title and make sure all headings are fully visible.

- Add your name as a footer.

- Save this report and print a copy.

In-tray documents Set 1 Day 2 – database 3

Open the database file Employee Details and sort in ascending order of Surname.

- Create a form of your design to add details for the following temporary staff who joined Sales and Marketing (Scale Point 2) on 12/10/2005:

  Maria Shorlin, 26 Rona Avenue, Glasgow G31 7PR. Tel 0141 551 6234. DOB 27/12/82.

  John McGuire, 36 Lockend Road, Glasgow G33 2RU. Tel 0141 771 1295. DOB 11/02/86.

- Use the form to make the following changes:

  Lynne Marshall has changed her telephone number. Her new telephone number is 01236 884786.

  Derek Adams has now left the company. Delete his record.

- Add the following data to the form footer: John Nicholls – Glasgow. Print the record for Lynne Marshall.

- Close the form.

- Create a report based on the employee details. Sort in alphabetical order of Department and then numerical order of Staff ID. Print the report on one page.

- Close the database.

You have already practised querying and sorting to view and manipulate records in the database. You can also use filters to select records in a database. Filters are used in conjunction with tables, reports and forms. In this section you will use filter by selection which will allow you to use a filter to select records using one field. Filter by form will allow you to use a filter to select records using more than one field. Filtering will allow you to limit the records you want to view. What is the difference between a sort and a filter? – sorts simply rearrange the order of your data whereas filtering restricts the records you want to view and hides the other records from view.

You can modify the appearance of the datasheet to make the data easier to work with and view. You can change the font, row height, column width and the attributes of the datasheet (such as background colour and gridline colour).

In addition to the features you used for the above In-tray exercises you should know how to:

- Filter by form.
- Filter by selection.
- Print results of a filter.
- Modify the appearance of the datasheet:
  - Change the font, row height and column width.
  - Changing background colour, gridline colour and datasheet border.

In-tray documents Set 1 Day 3 – database 1

Open the Database Children's Books.

- Use a filter to find those books published by Prentice Press.
- Modify the appearance of the datasheet:
  - Change the font to Comic Sans (or similar font) and increase size to 14 pt.
  - Increase the row height.
  - Change the cell effect.
- Print the records making sure that all data is fully visible and fits on to one page.
- Remove the filter and do not save changes.
- Use a filter to find those books suitable for children 5 years old and over and which cost more than £5.00.
- Print the records on one page.
- Remove the filter before you close the database file.

In-tray documents Set 1 Day 3 – database 2

Open the database file Employee Details.

- Use a filter to find details of staff who stay in the Glasgow area.
- Modify the appearance of your datasheet, for example, change the cell effect.
- Print a copy of these records.
- Remove the filter.
- Use a filter to find staff who work in Sales and Marketing and live in the Glasgow area.
- Print a copy of these records.
- Remove the filter and close the database.

In-tray documents Set 2

At Higher level you will use a relational database. A relational database uses relationships to establish connections between tables. You need at least two tables to establish a relationship. Remember:

- You need a common field in both tables.

- Common fields must have the same data type (number fields must have same field size).

- Both fields usually have the same name.

- The linking field in the primary table is usually the primary key and the linking field in the other table (or the related table) is called the foreign key.

For example, Customer Ref is the primary key in the customers table but the foreign key in the orders table. The relationship between the customers table and the orders table is one-to-many. The orders table can contain lots of orders from the same customer. This is the most common type of relationship.

Enforcing referential integrity will ensure that any changes you might make will not impair the relationships established in your tables. Select Cascade Update to ensure changes in a Primary Table automatically update the Foreign Key field. Cascade Delete Related Records ensures that when records are deleted in a primary table corresponding records in a related table will also be deleted.

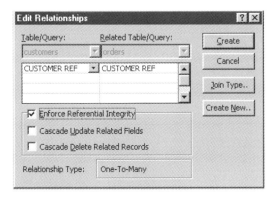

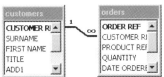

Before beginning this section, you should know how to:

- use primary and foreign keys

- create one-to-many relationships

- enforce referential integrity

- cascade updates and deletes

- edit and delete relationships

- print database relationships

Working with queries, you should know how to:

- query on a minimum of two fields from multiple tables (involve use of wildcards)
- use AND, OR or NOT to join query criteria together to create more complex conditions
- use aggregate functions in queries
- use a calculated field
- sort on a minimum of two fields from multiple tables within a query
- create a graph from query
- export data to a word processing document.

Working with forms – adjusting the appearance to make them look more attractive – you should know how to:

- design fields and establish order of data entry
- establish order of data entry
- set style and alignment and apply decorative enhancement
- insert graphic and header and footer
- modify properties
- move, align, delete and edit components of form
- print forms.

Working with reports, you should know how to:

- create a report from a table or query
- use calculations within a report
- modify the layout of reports to ensure data is visible
- insert report header, page header or footer
- print reports.

Intructions to Teachers/Lecturers

The following tables should be made available for the students. Alternatively, the students may key in the following tables.

GYM.MDB. This is a relational Database with 2 tables: Customer Details and Membership Status.

CUSTOMERS.MDB. This is relational Database with 3 tables: Customers, Orders and Products.

EMPLOYEE DETAILS.MDB. This is a relational Database with 4 tables: Staff, Payroll Details, Scale Point, Holiday Details.

GYM.MDB

TABLE: CUSTOMER DETAILS

Customer ID	Surname	First Name	Add1	Add2	Pcode	DOB	Mobile No	Status	Join Date	Female
1	Smith	Hannah	4 Dalserf Court	Edinburgh	EH7 3DG	07/11/63	07811338756	1	31/12/04	Yes
2	Connelly	Margaret	44 Madison Ave	Dalgety Bay	KY11 4AY	08/10/80	07810684491	1	18/12/04	Yes
3	Bjornsson	Mary	22 Margueriete Ave	Edinburgh	EH6 5MR	07/12/84	07854199569	1	31/12/04	Yes
4	Tai	Sarah	22 Brodie Gdns	Bathgate	EH48 9TR	08/07/63	07969225632	3	18/11/04	Yes
5	Grassieq	Anna	12 Craigside Court	Haddington	EH53 7RT	05/06/82	07771942178	2	17/10/04	Yes
6	Majid	Abdul	22 Lloyd Street	Livingston	EH54 3WT	08/08/70	07947198326	1	13/03/05	No
7	Granger	Arthur	2 Bromfield Road	Dalgety Bay	KY11 9TY	06/11/80	07990347712	2	13/03/05	No
8	Sinclair	Jack	36 Earls Court	Dalgety Bay	KY11 9UY	08/09/80	07969327834	3	4/12/03	No
9	McLaren	Agnes	5 Waverley Crescent	Bathgate	EH48 5GD	19/07/59	07810179879	3	17/11/04	Yes
10	Walthew	Kerry	10 Highfield Road	Mid Calder	EH53 1ET	21/10/86	07771243544	1	21/03/03	Yes
11	Johnston	Hannah	2 Lammermoor Crescent	Edinburgh	EH4 3ST	01/12/73	07947112113	3	19/10/04	Yes
12	Bell	Grant	13 Muirside Avenue	Selkirk	TD7 6GK	16/09/69	07811921327	2	2/11/05	No
13	McPhee	William	6 Victoria Road	Grangemouth	FK3 9YS	12/07/86	07947459879	2	11/07/03	No
14	Evans	Meghan	26 Castle Court	Dunfermline	KY12 5AD	17/12/79	07795070908	1	25/10/04	Yes
15	Sharif	Rosina	16 Cadzow Street	Linlithgow	EH49 7EV	04/05/66	07968579897	1	08/08/03	Yes

continued ➤

Customer ID	Surname	First Name	Add1	Add2	Pcode	DOB	Mobile No	Status	Join Date	Female
16	Mohammed	Niela	9 Pitt Road	Whitburn	EH47 8BN	21/03/55	07810089078	3	04/02/04	Yes
17	Collina	Gianni	52 Bothwell Road	Haddington	EH41 2QM	29/10/71	07811097768	2	15/03/05	No
18	Eriksson	Magnus	16 Nelson Avenue	North Berwick	EH39 6XC	01/06/86	07854210913	3	7/11/04	No
19	Baxter	Colin	91 O'Connell Street	Edinburgh	EH2 1HM	13/09/72	07969546712	3	01/10/05	No
20	Harris	Walter	4 Alexandra Street	Dalgety Bay	KY11 9SH	09/11/63	07771217097	1	29/05/05	No
21	Watson	Beverley	1 Oxford Street	Edinburgh	EH9 1PS	23/05/86	07947909547	2	09/09/03	Yes
22	Wilson	Rachel	19 Park Road	Livingston	E54 5GF	08/09/54	07990201326	3	12/08/04	Yes
23	McIntyre	Johnny	21 Merkland Park	Dunfermline	KY12 7SK	19/02/66	07810579895	2	27/01/05	No
24	Maloney	Marie	22 Ronay Street	Livingston	EH54 5PB	07/10/60	07810275667	1	04/08/05	Yes
25	Friel	Henry	25 Sandyhill Terrace	Dalgety Bay	KY11 6NR	18/11/66	07932745662	3	04/08/05	No

GYM.MDB

TABLE – MEMBERSHIP STATUS

Status	Membership Type
1	Pay as you go
2	Direct Debit
3	Subsidised

CUSTOMERS.MDB

TABLE: CUSTOMERS

Customer Ref	First Name	Surname	Title	Add1	Add2	Pcode	Phone No
1	Abdul	Abahari	Mr	1 High Street	Glasgow	G1 2TA	0141 552 3987
2	Annette	Differ	Mrs	109 Westland Way	Glasgow	G14 2DG	0141 429 3255
3	Jason	Corlett	Mr	10 Southesk Drive	Bishopbriggs	G64 7LT	0141 772 4598
4	Peter	Murphy	Mr	40 Sandbank Ave	Glasgow	G12 5TR	0141 332 3876
5	Alison	Wilkie	Miss	33 Eastmains Ave	Glasgow	G33 3PG	0141 779 2765
6	Jon	Singh	Mr	100 Dumbarton Road	Glasgow	G14 2TA	0141 517 9879
7	Jessica	Siochowicz	Mrs	21 Burmola Street	Lennoxtown	G66 2MN	01360 236789
8	Mary	Horrocks	Mrs	22 South Street	Cumbernauld	G67 6GH	01236 546765

continued ➤

Customer Ref	First Name	Surname	Title	Add1	Add2	Pcode	Phone No
9	Alison	Benjamin	Mrs	6 Woodcroft Ave	Ayr	KA6 9KL	01292 709812
10	Andrew	Neil	Mr	19 Keal Crescent	Kilmarnock	KA3 1QT	01563 409890
11	Nasser	Hussain	Mr	29 Waverley Gardens	Bishopbriggs	G64 4DG	0141 772 3934
12	Shiela	Winters	Ms	26 Stirling Drive	Cumbernauld	G67 8UM	01236 547657
13	Sara	Li	Miss	14 Jura Grove	Kilmarnock	KA3 8YN	01563 430975
14	Ashok	Dahwan	Mr	57 Friars Way	Cumbernauld	G67 9YH	01236 439087
15	Talal	Karkouri	Mr	33 Ashgrove Park	Cumbernauld	G67 3WS	01236 002235
16	Vanisha	Patel	Mrs	39 Victoria Road	Bishopbriggs	G64 1DK	0141 772 9806
17	Leonard	Jacob	Mr	3 Greenside Avenue	Kilmarnock	KA3 5BC	01563 320907
18	John	Stratham	Mr	76 Cumbria Drive	Kirkintilloch	G66 2FT	0141 776 2309
19	Robert	Elliot	Mr	36 Highbury Lane	Kilmarnock	KA3 7TY	01563 127651
20	Pamela	Mills	Ms	40 The Leas	Milngavie	G62 4WQ	0141 956 3879
21	Jaqueline	Allan	Miss	24 Stretford Road	Ayr	KA6 9OP	01292 786548
22	Fiona	Clark	Mrs	16 Windsor Drive	Kilmarnock	KA3 2TH	01563 237890
23	Neil	Thomas	Mr	73 Charlton Road	Glasgow	G33 9AZ	0141 779 3345
24	Alan	Stewart	Mr	7 Trossachs View	Bishopbriggs	G64 8EW	0141 772 4908
25	Lesley	Manning	Mrs	19 Gordon Avenue	Ayr	KA6 2VM	01292 100908

CUSTOMERS.MDB

TABLE: ORDERS

Order Ref	Customer Ref	Product Ref	Quantity	Date Ordered	Delivery Date	Supplier Ref
1	1	2	1	21/01/05	23/02/05	1041
2	7	4	1	26/02/05	14//02/05	1042
3	7	1	2	03/01/05	13/03/05	1043
4	9	8	2	12/12/04	14/01/05	1032
5	6	3	10	13/01/05	17/03/05	1471
6	8	2	2	15/01/05	18/02/05	1888
7	9	2	1	18/01/05	21/01/05	1760
8	2	3	1	18/01/05	24/02/05	1340
9	22	9	1	19/01/05	24/02/05	1223
10	22	10	2	19/01/05	24/02/05	1475

CUSTOMERS.MDB

TABLE: PRODUCTS

Product Ref	Product	Unit Price	Units in Stock	Re-order Level	Discontinued
1	Dark Wood Lamp	£26.99	3	10	Yes
2	Hudson Table Lamp	£39.99	9	5	No
3	Shinto Wooden Floor Lamp	£49.99	9	10	Yes
4	Mini Wooden Lamp	£14.99	30	15	No
5	Chocolate Ceramic Lamp	£39.99	14	10	No
6	Curtain Droplights	£16.99	22	15	Yes
7	Rubber Star Lights	£16.99	14	20	Yes
8	Sparkle Candle Vase	£14.99	9	5	No
9	Mesh Flower Lights	£19.99	20	5	No
10	Lilly Lights	£19.99	20	5	No

EMPLOYEE DETAILS.MDB

TABLE: STAFF

Staff ID	Fname	Sname	Department	Add1	Add2	Pcode	Tel No	Date of birth	Start Date
220	Lynn	Marshall	Human Resources	21 Bell Street	Kilsyth	G65 3CK	01236 777994	11/07/63	21/02/1989
221	Pierre	Boucheron	Human Resources	33 Corr Street	Cambuslang	G72 7PL	0141 641 8777	12/08/82	08/08/2000
222	John	MacKay	Human Resources	14 Hollyhill Grove	Cumbernauld	G67 5TD	01236 599998	21/02/80	15/10/2001
223	Dorian	Rohmer	Human Resources	2 Lugie Road	Coatbridge	ML5 2WS	01236 420396	21/08/84	01/09/2000
224	Kim	Lee	Sales and Marketing	30 Hillhead Street	Glasgow	G25 7BN	0141 570 9321	21/05/85	05/07/2001
225	Mark	Kedzierska	Sales and Marketing	30 Deans Ave	Dalmuir	G81 6YB	01389 873455	25/08/85	12/03/2004
226	Fiona	Galbraith	Sales and Marketing	22 St Germains Ave	Glasgow	G33 4DF	0141 959 2314	27/05/80	21/06/2002
227	Abdul	Bastani	Sales and Marketing	2 Peel Place	Glasgow	G20 8VB	0141 946 3000	28/09/84	30/07/2000
228	Gurbhaj	Singh	Administration	19 Second Ave	Bothwell	G71 4WA	01698 435517	17/10/79	26/11/1998
229	Ross	McDonald	Administration	6 Gallowhill Road	Glasgow	G33 2DP	0141 779 2357	25/11/81	01/03/1999
230	Shiela	Ramsay	Administration	7 Oak Drive	Bishopbriggs	G64 9LA	0141 772 2300	12/12/83	17/04/2004

continued ➤

Staff ID	Fname	Sname	Department	Add1	Add2	Pcode	Tel No	Date of birth	Start Date
231	Declan	Murphy	Administration	27 Iona Court	Kilmarnock	KA3 1AP	01563 980006	16/07/81	16/07/2002
232	Mason	Wallace	Administration	9 Shore Road	Ayr	KA6 5RT	01292 087913	26/09/76	13/10/1997
233	Audrey	Robertson	IT	22 Fossil Grove	Hamilton	ML3 2DG	01698 278643	03/04/84	21/04/2001
234	Pamela	Brown	IT	3 Wodhead Court	Bishopbriggs	G64 9LA	0141 772 6598	09/07/78	01/02/1999
235	Pavinder	Kaur	IT	15 Loch View	Bearsden	G61 9LG	0141 942 3908	07/06/84	11/02/2004
236	Mylee	Chow	Sales and Marketing	97 Reservoir Avenue	Milngavie	G62 3DK	0141 956 7869	11/02/62	16/07/1979
237	Kwok	Chung	Administration	1 Elizabeth Road	Kirkintilloch	G66 3TY	0141 776 3421	07/11/63	10/11/1981
238	Hans	Ellsweiller	IT	31 Stirling Drive	Motherwell	ML1 7RS	01698 874367	11/01/64	16/09/1984
239	Roberto	Rodriguez	IT	8 Main Street	Lennoxtown	G66 1AS	01360 136247	18/11/75	08/09/1995
240	Susan	Lynch	Sales and Marketing	43 Croy Road	Kilsyth	G65 1FG	01236 357865	12/06/72	23/12/1995
241	Colin	McDonald	Human Resources	97 Gourock View	Greenock	PA16 4FD	01475 498256	30/09/73	12/12/2001
242	Alison	Ross	Sales and Marketing	69 Old Course Road	Hamilton	ML3 4TD	01698 564239	27/10/76	05/06/2001
243	Wilma	Miller	Administration	53 Clyde Street	Motherwell	ML1 2MB	01698 864367	14/02/69	13/02/1992
244	Peter	Smythe	Sales and Marketing	17 Viking Way	Largs	KA30 8YG	01474 786342	13/05/77	22/06/1995

EMPLOYEE DETAILS.MDB

TABLE: SCALE POINT

Scale Point	Salary
1	£15,000.00
2	£18,000.00
3	£20,000.00
4	£25,000.00
5	£30,000.00
6	£35,000.00

EMPLOYEE DETAILS.MDB

TABLE: PAYROLL DETAILS

Staff ID	Overtime	Travel	Subsistence
220	£150.00	£19.80	£7.16
221	£125.00	£45.70	£12.80
222	£130.00	£32.80	£10.15
223	£162.00	£47.50	£15.45
224	£75.00	£0.00	£0.00
225	£92.00	£0.00	£0.00
226	£127.00	£37.65	£12.50
227	£135.00	£43.70	£17.75
228	£95.00	£25.00	£7.50
229	£100.00	£31.00	£9.50
230	£75.00	£0.00	£0.00
231	£55.00	£7.45	£3.75
232	£125.00	£32.72	£15.10
233	£97.00	£52.75	£26.40
234	£115.00	£37.80	£17.95
235	£175.00	£58.00	£29.85
236	£85.00	£18.75	£9.20
237	£128.00	£42.20	£15.75
238	£105.00	£38.00	£12.80
239	£165.00	£52.00	£33.80
240	£85.00	£0.00	£0.00
241	£85.00	£0.00	£0.00
242	£97.00	£0.00	£0.00
243	£125.00	£0.00	£0.00
244	£95.00	£8.48	£0.00

continued ➤

EMPLOYEE DETAILS.MDB

TABLE: HOLIDAY DETAILS

Staff ID	Holiday Entitlement	No of days taken
220	30	12
221	30	10
222	30	12
223	32	9
224	28	8
225	30	13
226	35	7
227	38	6
228	30	11
229	35	14
230	30	8
231	30	10
232	28	9
233	32	7
234	32	15
235	30	9
236	35	10
237	30	7
238	30	6
239	30	12
240	32	14
241	35	9
242	30	11
243	30	8
244	30	10

In-tray documents Set 2 Day 1 – database 1

Open the Gym database and update:

- Set an appropriate primary key for Membership Status table.

- Create an appropriate relationship to link the two tables and apply referential integrity with no cascade options.

- Print a copy of the relationship.

In-tray documents Set 2 Day 1 – database 2

Open the Customers Database and update:

- Make sure appropriate primary keys have been set for the three tables.

- Create appropriate relationships to link the tables.

- Apply referential integrity and check the boxes for Cascade Update Related Fields and Cascade Delete Related Records.

- Print a copy of the relationships.

In-tray documents Set 2 Day 1 – database 3

- Open the Employee Details Database and update.

- Make sure appropriate primary keys have been set for the four tables.

- Create an appropriate relationship to link the tables.

- Apply referential integrity with no cascade options.

- Print a copy of the relationships.

In-tray documents Set 2 Day 2 – database 1

Use the Membership Status and Customer Details tables.

- Open the Membership Status table. Add a new Membership Type for Senior Citizen.

- Add the following details for a senior citizen (use the expand indicator on the table window):

  James Carter (Customer ID 26), 11 Hill View, Dalgety Bay, KY11 6TR Mobile No 07878889997. DOB 7/11/45. James joined on 5 October 2005.

- Provide a list of all customers who are senior citizens or who benefit from a subsidised membership. Sort in order of membership type and then town. Print the result of this query showing first name, surname, add 2 (town) and membership type.

- Find those customers who live in the Dalgety Bay or Edinburgh area who have opted for a Pay As You Go membership. Sort the results of this query in alphabetical order of town then join date.

- Save the query and print on one page.

- We need information on those customers with postcodes beginning with KY or EH who joined after 1 January 2003.

- Create a report based on the above query showing all fields except Customer ID, Mobile No, Female and Status. Group on membership type and then Add2. Arrange customers in

alphabetical order of surname within these groupings. Give the report an appropriate heading and reformat the font type and size. Also, change the font colour to red.

- Amend the Add1 label to read Street and Add2 label to read Town.

- Modify the report to ensure all data is fully visible.

- Print the report.

In-tray documents Set 2 Day 2 – database 2

Use the Customers, Orders and Products tables.

- Find the order details for all those customers who have a postcode starting with G1 who were promised a delivery date of February 2005. Save this query with an appropriate name and print showing the fields Order Ref, Product, Product Ref, Delivery Date, First Name, Surname, Add1, Add2 and Postcode.

- Search for all products which were ordered between 7 January and 21 January 2005. Sort the results of this search in descending order of date ordered and ascending order of surname.

- Save the query and print showing First Name, Surname, Add1, Add2, Postcode, Product, Product Ref, Date, and Quantity Ordered.

- Find the lowest, highest and average price of products available in the Lighting Department at John Nicholls.

- We need to establish the total cost of products ordered by Mrs Fiona Clark from Kilmarnock. Design a suitable query to show customer details and product details. Save the query with a suitable name and print.

- The manager of the Lighting Department needs to know the total value of products ordered by our customers. Design a suitable query to show product, unit price, and total order value. Save the query as Product Sales and print.

In-tray documents Set 2 Day 2 – database 3

Use the Scale Point, Payroll Details, Staff and Holiday Details tables.

- We need names, addresses, telephone numbers and date of birth of staff except for those who work in the IT Department. Sort the results of this query in alphabetical order of department and alphabetical order of surname. Save the query with an appropriate name and print.

- We need information on staff who are on scale point 3 and above and who work in the Human Resources Department or Sales and Marketing Department. Design a suitable query to show staff names, department, scale point and salary. Arrange in descending order of scale point and numerical order of surname. Save this query with an appropriate name and print.

- We need to establish those members of staff who live in the Glasgow area who were born after 1 January 1980. Design a suitable query to show staff names and address details and date of birth. Arrange in alphabetical order of department and alphabetical order of date of birth.

  Save this query with an appropriate name and print.

- Due to an expected upturn in customers over the coming months, the Human Resource Manager requires an audit of all annual leave taken so far in order to ensure suitable staff coverage. Design a suitable query to ascertain all holiday entitlement and the number of days taken so far for all staff in every department. Arrange in ascending order of department and descending order of holiday entitlement.

Save the query with an appropriate name and print.

What is the average number of days taken on holiday to date?

- We need to ascertain total overtime and expenses for each member of staff. Design a suitable query to show staff names and department. Arrange in alphabetical order of surname.

  Save the query with an appropriate name and print.

- We also need to ascertain our total overtime and expenses by department. Design a suitable query to show the department and total cost fields. Arrange in alphabetical order of department. Save the query as Total Overtime and Expenses by Department and print.

In-tray documents Set 2 Day 3 – database 2

- Create a report based on the query Product Sales. Group by product. Use the summary options to include a sum of the total order value for each product.

- Give the report an appropriate title and reformat the font type and size. Also, change the colour of the font.

- Save the report as Product Sales and print.

- Build a column chart on this query to show the total income from each product. Save as Product Sales Chart and print a copy.

- The manager of the Lighting Department wishes to make a presentation on product sales at the next staff meeting. Write a memo to John Harris, the Manager of the Lighting Department, enclosing a copy of the report Product Sales which you have already created.

  (Copy the report across to Word and insert below memo.)

In-tray documents Set 2 Day 3 – database 3

- Create a report on the query Total Overtime and Expenses by Department. Group by department. Use the summary options to include a sum of the total overtime and expenses by department.

  Give the report an appropriate title and reformat the font type and size. Also, change the colour of the font.

  Save the report as Total Overtime and Expenses by Department and print.

- Build a pie chart on the query Total Overtime and Expenses to show the total cost by department. Save as Total Overtime and Expenses By Department Chart and print.

- The manager of the Human Resources Department wishes to discuss overtime and other expenses at the next budget control meeting.

  Write a memo to Brian Edmonds, the Manager of the Human Resources Department, enclosing a copy of the report Total Overtime and Expenses by Department.

  (Copy the report across to Word and insert below memo.)

In-tray documents Set 2 Day 4 – database 1

You have been asked to improve the appearance of the Health and Fitness form to make it easier for new staff to enter customer details. The Health and Fitness form is based on the Gym database.

- Select the form Health and Fitness. Add the title Health and Fitness. Make it 24pt, colour red and apply a shadow effect.

- Change the label First Name to read Name.

- Move Surname text box and drag up and to the right of First name.

- Remove the label Surname.

- Change label Add1 to read Street.

- Change label Add2 to read Town.

- Right align all text labels, change font size to 10 pt and embolden.

- Insert the graphic gym.jpeg (or a suitable graphic image) somewhere in the form. Resize, if necessary.

- Print out records 1 to 3 in form format.

- Save the form as Health and Fitness New Format.

- Close the form.

The form should now look something like this:

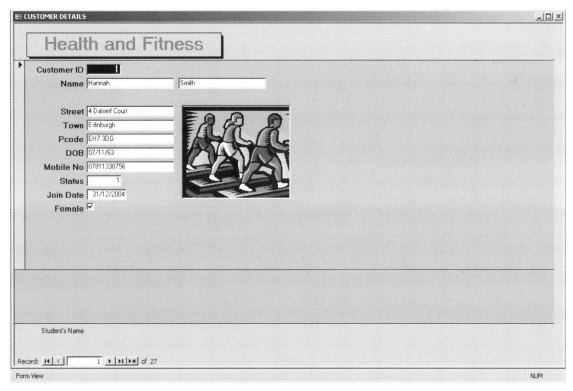

In-tray documents Set 2 Day 4 – database 2

You have been asked to improve the appearance of the Customer Details form to make it easier for new staff to enter customer details. The Customer Details form is based on the Customers database.

- Select the form Customer Details. Add the title Customer Details in the form. Reformat the font type and size. Add a background fill colour to the label.

- Change the label First Name to read Name.

- Move Surname text box and drag up and to the right of First name.

- Remove the label Surname.

- Change label Add1 to read Street.

- Change label Add2 to read Town.

- Format the text labels to italic.

- Change the background colour of the form.

- Save the form as Customer Details New Format.

- Print out one record in form format.

The form should now look something like this:

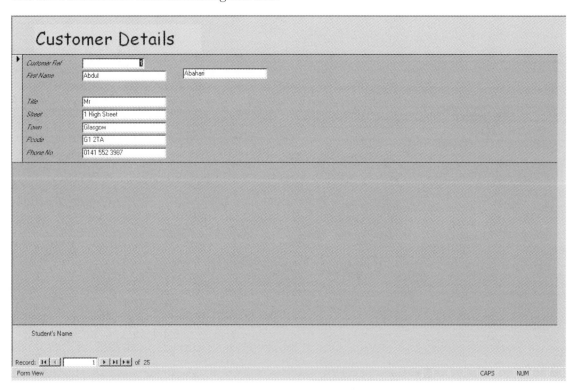

In-tray documents Set 2 Day 4 – database 3

You have been asked to improve the appearance of the Employee Details form to make it easier for new staff to enter staff details. The Employee Details form is based on the Employee Details database.

- Add the title John Nicholls – Employee Details. Format the font, size. Add background colour to the label to make it stand out.

- Experiment with setting special effects, colours and borders. For example:

  - Set all the field labels as raised.

  - Set the form header as sunken.

  - Change border widths.

  - Apply some colours to different parts of the screen to make it look more attractive.

It may be a good idea to rename and reposition text labels as in previous form exercises.

- Save the form as Employee Details New Format.

- Print out one record in form format.

In-tray documents Set 2 Day 5 – database 1

- Open the Gym database.

- Delete the relationship that exists between the customer details table and the membership status table.

- Print a copy of the relationship.

CHAPTER 14

Presentations

Intermediate 2 Level Outcomes:

I2 This chapter contains explanations and exercise material for Intermediate 2 Presenting and Communicating Information Outcome 3.

Use presentation software to present and communicate information including:

☆ **modifying and enhancing a presentation as required**

☆ **creating additional slides**

☆ **printing slides in a required view**

☆ **e-mailing the presentation.**

Higher Level Outcomes:

H It also includes explanations and exercises for Higher Information Technology for Management Outcome 3.

Use ICT to solve business problems and communicate and present solutions:

☆ **advancing slides automatically timed to accommodate speaker notes**

☆ **promoting and demoting slides and text within slides**

☆ **importing data from the Internet**

☆ **setting up a hyperlink to URL**

☆ **creating and printing notes.**

Presentation software allows you to create, organise and display presentations in the form of overhead projector slides, computer presentations and handouts.

To make a presentation look consistent you can apply a template to all your slides – and then add your own text and some graphics. You can then customise the text, colour and graphics in your slides to give the presentation the look you want.

Many organisations will use their own house style template to which they have added their own logo, with perhaps specific information in the header/footer and their own choice of font and colour scheme. House styles will vary between organisations. The advantage of using a house style template is that it ensures consistency of layout and saves time in the preparation of the presentation.

Task 1

Find out if your school/college has their own house style template which they use for presentations. What do you think are the main advantages of using a house style layout for presentations?

You will use the Slide Master and/or Title Master facility to give your presentation a consistent look. This will incorporate such features as background colour, colour of text, font and font size to control the look of all the slides in your presentation. Masters have placeholders for title text, paragraph text or bullet points, date and time, footer details and slide numbers. Title Master will control the look of the Title Slide which is usually the first slide of your presentation. You will have to alter the Master slides when you want to add or delete any of the above features.

Sometimes you may want a particular slide to stand out from all the others, perhaps because of a change of topic. In this case you can reformat the background and colour of one or some of your slides.

Higher level students may complete the In-tray presentations in Set 1 before attempting those in Set 2.

In-tray Presentations Set 1 Day 1

Before tackling the following in-tray exercises you should know how to:

- Create a new presentation.
- Use and customise bullets.
- Add text to a slide.
- Save slide presentation.
- Use a Slide Master or Title Master to apply and change background and colour scheme of your presentation.
- Apply a design template.
- Define and redefine fonts and styles.
- Insert footer objects.
- Be familiar with language used in presentation software – levels of text, font size, master slide.
- Print presentation in slide format.

In-tray presentations Set 1 Day 1 – presentation 1

You have been asked to create a short presentation of three slides on Absence Management.

- Create a Slide Master as follows:

  Change the background colour of all slides to white.

  Master title style – apply a showdown effect, embolden and change font size to 40.

  Insert text box with header Absence Management above Master Title Text. Centre the text box and header.

  First level text style – change font size to 28. Change to a style of bullet of your own choice.

  Second level text style – change font size to 24. Apply a different style of bullet from the one used in the first level text style.

- Using the Title Master select a different font and change font size to 44.

  Use header/footer to insert www.shaw.uk.com in the lower left corner of slide. Add your name to the centre and insert slide number in the right hand corner. Use a different font for footer details. Make sure these details are entered on all slides.

Slide 1

- Select a bulleted list layout and add the title Staff Responsibilities
- Add the following:

  Contact Line Manager at earliest opportunity – lst level

  Contact should be made personally – lst level

  Absence of 4 days or more – 1st level

  Employee to indicate likely extent of absence – 2nd level

Slide 2

- Add the following text:

  Absences of less than 7 days – lst level

  Employee complete a self certificate statement – 2nd level

  Absences of 7 days or more – 1st level

  Submission of a Doctor's Line – 1st level

Slide 3

- Add the title Supervisor's Responsibilities.

- Key in the following text – all 1st level

  Record reports of absence timeously in appropriate document.

  Ensure absences do not impact on your department's efficiency levels.

  Treat ALL cases of ill health amongst your staff with sympathy.

  Maintain regular contact.

  Identify any abuses of system.

- Save presentation as Absence Management.

- Print a copy of the presentation in slide format.

You can create a table in a slide to allow you to add information into rows and columns. Different types of charts can also be inserted and formatted, i.e. bar chart, pie chart, etc. You can also create an organisation chart to show people's position within a company.

Before you begin presentation 2 you must be able to:

- Create a chart, table and organisation chart within presentation software.

- Print presentation in handout format.

In-tray presentations Set 1 Day 1 – presentation 2

Create a short presentation of four slides for the Customer Services Manager on Mystery Shopping.

Using the Slide Master:

- Apply a design template of your choice.

- Above the master title text insert a text box with the text Mystery Shopping. Centre this text box. Make the font size 18 and embolden.

- Insert an appropriate graphic to appear at the top right hand side of all slides.

Using title master:

- Change the font and increase the size of master title text. Make sure the text is centred.

Using header/footer:

- Insert your name and slide number at the bottom of all slides except the first.

Slide 1

- Select title slide and key in the main title Mystery Shopper.

- Add subtitle John.Nicholls@glasgow.co.uk

Slide 2

- Insert the heading Measuring Customer Service.

- Add the following with styles as indicated:

  Objectives include – 1st level

  Adhering to legal requirements – 2nd level

  Maintaining organisational standards – 2nd level

  Identification of training needs – 2nd level

  Ensuring honesty of staff – 2nd level

  Continuous improvement – 2nd level

Slide 3

- Create a clustered 3D column chart from the following information

	2000	2001	2002	2003	2004
No of Complaints	252	208	139	97	51

- Add the title Complaints Over Last 5 Years

Slide 4

- Using the Organisation Chart layout, enter the organisation chart for the Customer Services Department as shown:

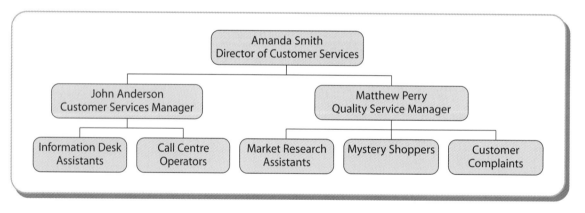

- Add the title Meet the Customer Services Team.

- Save presentation as Mystery Shopper.

- Print a copy of the presentation in handout format.

Many different slide layouts come with presentation software. You may wish to scroll through the layout options to view the different slide layouts, for example, Title Slide. You can also change line spacing, font size and bullets in your presentation.

Before beginning presentation 3 you should know how to:

- Change slide content layout.
- Change line spacing and font size.
- Customise bullets.

In-tray presentations Set 1 Day 1 – presentation 3

Create a short presentation of three slides on the Health at Work Week:

- Apply an appropriate template, such as Edge from the task pane (or something with a white background).
- Number the slides and add your name as a footer (excluding title slide).

Slide 1

- Select the title slide layout and add the title Health at Work Week! Insert a suitable piece of clip art. Resize and centre to ensure that it looks effective.

Slide 2

- Change slide layout to placeholder for text and clip art.
- Add the title Benefits.
- Type the following in the text column:

  Improve health and well-being

  Improve morale

  Reduce stress.

- Double click placeholder to insert a suitable image
- Increase line spacing within the bulleted list
- Format the bullets as ticks

Slide 3

- Change the slide layout to title and table layout.
- Add the heading *Events Include*:
- Double click the table icon, select two columns and three rows. Add the following text to your table:

Edinburgh Branch	Big Breakfast Bike Rides Health Clinics
Glasgow Branch	Big Breakfast Race for Life Health Clinics
Hightown Branch	Big Breakfast Stress Management Health Clinics

INFORMATION TECHNOLOGY

- Save the presentation as Health at Work Week.
- Print the presentation in handout format.

In-tray presentations Set 1 Day 2

You can add special effects to make your slides look more interesting for example, allow transition between slides and animation of objects or slides.

Before you begin this section, you must be able to:

- Add a slide.
- Import data from a word processed document.
- Change slide order.
- Apply slide transitions.
- Use bold, italics and centring
- Animate text/objects.
- Find and replace text.

In-tray presentations Set 1 Day 2 – presentation 1

Recall the presentation Absence Management.

- Add a new slide (make this slide 4). Select title slide and insert the word processing file Mission Statement. Your teacher/lecturer will supply this file or you should key it in yourself using the following text.

> John Nicholls is committed to the continued development of personnel policies on occupational health and welfare in association with staff associations and government initiatives which promote health in the workplace.

- Enter the title Mission Statement – centre this heading.
- Recall slide 3.
  - Delete second bulleted item
  - Embolden word ALL in the second bulleted item
  - Embolden the word must and make italic in third bulleted item
  - Add final bulleted item:
    Refer staff to Occupational Health Unit where appropriate (1st level)
- Change the slide order so that slide 4 becomes slide 1.
- Increase the line spacing within the bulleted lists in slides 2 and 3.
- Save and close the presentation.
- Print a copy of the presentation in handout format.

In-tray presentations Set 1 Day 2 – presentation 2

Recall the presentation Mystery Shopper and make the following amendments:

Slide 2

- Underline the words Objectives include:
- Move the bulleted item Ensuring honesty of staff to be the second bullet item
- Choose a different font for 2nd level bullet list
- Apply an animation effect on the title.

Slide 3

- Insert the following text below the chart. Embolden (or change the colour to yellow) and change text to italics:

  80% reduction in complaints over past 5 years
- Apply a transition effect to all slides.
- Apply a different animation effect to the title of every slide.
- Save this presentation.
- Print a copy of this presentation in handout format.
- E-mail the completed presentation to your teacher/lecturer.

In-tray presentations Set 1 Day 2 – presentation 3

Recall the presentation Health at Work Week and make the following amendments:

- In slide 2 apply an animation effect to the bulleted list.
- Go back to slide 1. Apply an animation effect to the title.
- Change the background colour of slide 3 only to pale yellow.
- Amend the data in the table as follows:
  - Embolden heading
  - Delete the word branch from each row in the first column
  - Find Health Clinics and replace with Health and Fitness Clinics
  - Reduce font size of text within table.
- Apply a transition effect to all slides.
- Save the presentation.
- Print the presentation in handout format.
- E-mail the completed presentation to your teacher/lecturer.

In-tray presentations Set 1 Day 3

Before beginning this section, you should know how to:

- Align, distribute and group objects.

- Insert action button to hyperlink to first slide.

In-tray presentations Set 1 Day 3 – presentation 1

Your manager wishes you to add a Supervisor's Checklist to keep them on track.

- Recall the presentation Absence Management.

- Create a new slide (make this slide 5).

- Enter the heading Supervisor's Checklist.

- Using autoshapes, draw six circles. Resize the circles until the slide is similar to the picture below.

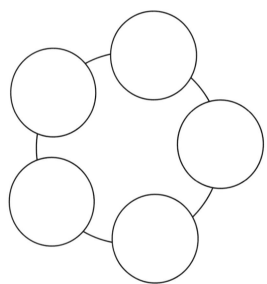

- Enter the following text – centre text within individual circles.

  Main circle: ABSENT STAFF – embolden this heading.

  Other circles: Treat with sympathy

  Offer O H Services

  Identify any abuses

  Keep regular contact

  Make staff feel valued

- Group the drawing and align centre (remember you will have to select Relative to Slide otherwise the drawing objects will be aligned within the object group).

- Ensure all text is fully visible.

Using Slide Master:

- Insert an action button at bottom to hyperlink to the first slide.
- Select the action button: Home.
- In the lower-right corner of the slide, drag to create a Home Action Button.
- Hyperlink to first slide.
- Save the presentation.
- Print a copy of the completed presentation in handout format on a maximum of two pages.
- E-mail this presentation to your teacher/lecturer.

In-tray presentations Set 1 Day 3 – presentation 2

You are working in the Human Resources Department and have been asked to make some amendments to a short presentation of four slides (filename Working with VDUs) which will be presented to the new word processing operators during their induction sessions. You will need the John Nicholls Logo (word processing file) and the spreadsheet file Sickness Record.

- Open the file Working with VDUs. Your teacher/lecturer will supply this four slide presentation file or you should create it yourself. It should contain the following information:

1
Working with VDUs

Health and Safety (DSE) Regulations

2
Common Illness

3
Who is covered?

Any employee at John Nicholls who **regularly** requires the use of DSE for a significant part of each working day.

4
Protect yourself!

- Adopt comfortable posture and postural change
- Adjust furniture and equipment to suit your needs
- Give consideration to the layout and positioning of workstation equipment

---

- Save this file as Induction.
- Edit the Master Slide as follows:
  - Master title style – embolden, centre and change font size to 40.
  - Insert a text box with the header Working with VDUs above Master title text. Centre the header information.

- First level text style – change to italic and change font size to 28. Change to a style of bullet of your own choice.

- Second level text style – no emphasis required and change font size to 24. Apply a different style of bullet from above.

- Place a John Nicholls logo at the top right corner of slide. Make sure the logo does not overlap the text frame.

- Using the Title Master

  Change the main title font to Algerian (or other appropriate font) and change font size to 40.

  - Insert footer details to appear on all slides. Add your name in a very small font at left hand side of the footer area. Insert the slide number on the right hand side of the footer area. Insert two action buttons side by side in the centre of the footer area. Link one back to the previous slide and link the other to the next slide.

- The initials DSE should be replaced with the words Display Screen Equipment throughout the presentation.

Slide 1

- Add the date 1992 after Display Screen Equipment Regulations

- Apply an animation effect to the title Health and Safety (Display Screen Equipment) Regulations 1992

- Add the following information to the bottom of the slide:

  The company intranet is the principal source of Health and Safety Information on the above.

Slide 2

- Change layout of slide to one that includes a placeholder for a bulleted list and image.

- In the first column, create a bulleted list of the following problems:

  Muleskeletal problems

  Visual discomfort

  Mental stress

- Change the line spacing within the bulleted list.

- Add an appropriate image, picture or photograph and apply an animation effect to the picture.

Slide 3

- Remove the words at John Nicholls from the first line of the bulleted item.

- Change the slide order so that slide 3 is slide 2.

Slide 4

- In the second column, create a bulleted list with the following three points:

  Ensure screen is cleaned regularly

  Ensure you take regular breaks

  Report problems promptly following company procedures

- Change font size to 24pt within this slide and ensure consistency of line spacing.

Slide 5

- Create a new slide and select appropriate slide layout

- Insert the chart from the file Sickness Record. Your teacher/lecturer will supply this file or you should create the chart yourself. It should look like this:

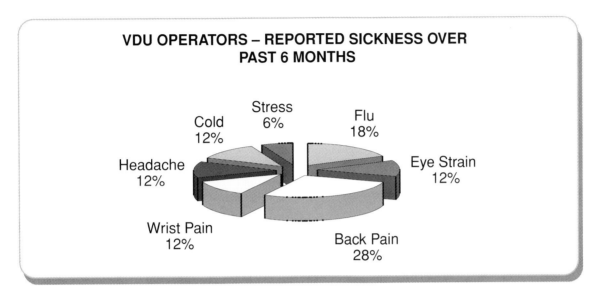

- Apply a transition effect to all slides.

- Change the background colour of slide 4 only – make sure all text is visible.

- Save the presentation.

- Print a copy of the completed presentation in handout format on two pages.

- E-mail this presentation to your teacher/lecturer.

In-tray presentations Set 2 Day 1

You will be required to make use of presentation software with a greater degree of confidence at Higher level. You will be required to use the Internet to obtain necessary information. Presentation software will allow you to connect to a web page by inserting a hyperlink directly into the presentation or by placing an action button which connects to the web page when selected in your slide.

In order to hold the audience's attention you will need information that is relevant, but it must be also interesting and timely. Presentation software also makes it easy for promotion and demotion of text within slides which allows for the audience to focus on certain parts. When making a presentation you can also advance slides automatically to show the next slide after a set number of seconds. This can be useful if you are delivering the presentation to a live audience and are using speaker notes to help you.

Before beginning this section, you should know how to:

- Advance slides automatically timed to accommodate speaker notes.
- Promote and demote slides and text within slides.
- Import data from the Internet.
- Hyperlink to URL.
- Create and print notes.
- Access incoming message with attachment.
- Send e-mail with attachment.
- Send e-mail with attachment and mark URGENT.

In-tray presentations Set 2 Day 1 – presentation 1

To carry out this in-tray exercise your teacher/lecturer may email the following to you:

Subject: *Absence Management*

Message: *I attach a short presentation which will be used during the Sickness and Absence Monitoring Training sessions. Please make amendments as necessary and forward to me for my consideration.*

Signature: *Human Resources Assistant*

Attachment: *Absence Management.ppt*

Alternatively, you should create the initial presentation yourself. It should contain five slides as follows:

1
Mission Statement

John Nicholls is committed to the continued development of personnel policies on occupational health and welfare in association with staff associations and government initiatives which promote health in the workplace.

2
Staff Responsibilities

- Contact Line Manager at earliest opportunity
- Contact should be made personally
- Absence of 4 days or more
  - Employee to indicate likely extent of absence

3

- Absence of less than 7 days
  - Employee complete a self certificate statement
- Absence of 7 days or more
  - Submissions of a Doctor's Line

continued ➤

4
Supervisor's Responsibilities

- Record reports of absence timeously in appropriate document
- Treat ALL cases of ill health amongst your staff with sympathy
- Regular contact **must** be maintained
- Identify any abuses of system
- Refer staff to Occupational Health Unit where appropriate

5
Supervisor's Checklist

You are required to make some amendments to the file Absence Management which has been e-mailed to you by your teacher/lecturer as follows:

- Open Absence Management.
- Change background colour and texture on all slides.
- Using the Title Master, insert a hyperlink to www.shaw.uk.com at bottom of the slide.
- Apply a transition effect to all slides.
- Set up the presentation to advance all transitions automatically after one minute. Also leave the On Mouse Click option on and set the speed to medium.
- In Slide 1, remove the animation effect from the title.
- In slide 2, demote the last bulleted item Employee to indicate likely extent of absence.
- Create a Notes page for the last slide and type the following:

  Diagram to be added to Employee Handbook

- Add your name and slide number as a footer on all pages.
- Save the presentation.
- Print a copy of the presentation showing all slides on one page and in handout format. Also print a copy of the Notes page.
- E-mail the copy of the completed presentation to your supervisor. Mark this email URGENT.

In-tray presentations Set 2 Day 1 – presentation 2

To carry out this In-tray exercise your teacher/lecturer may email the following to you:

Subject: *Induction Session – Working with VDUs*

Message: *I attach a short presentation which will be used during the induction session for our new word processing operators. Please make amendments as necessary and forward to me for my consideration.*

Signature: *Human Resources Assistant*

Attachment: *Induction.ppt*

Alernatively, you should create the initial presentation yourself. It should contain five slides as follows:

1

Working with VDUs

Health and Safety (Display Screen Equipment) Regulations 1992

The company intranet is the principle source of Health and Safety Information on the above

2
Who is covered?

Any employee who regularly requires the use of Display Screen Equipment for a significant part of their working day

3
Common Illness

4
Protect yourself!

- Adopt a comfortable posture and postural change

- Adjust furniture and equipment to suit your needs

- Give consideration to the layout and positioning of workstation eqiupment

- Ensure screen is cleaned regularly

- Ensure you take regular breaks

- Report problems promptly following company procedures

5

You are required to make some amendments to the file Induction which has been e-mailed to you by your teacher/lecturer as follows:

- Open Induction.

- Insert a hyperlink to www.hse.gov.uk at bottom of this slide 1.

- Reorder slides so that slide 3 becomes slide 2.

- In slide 2 promote Visual Discomfort and Mental Stress to the same level as Muleskeletal Problems.

- Apply the same slide transition to all slides.

- Set up the presentation to advance the slides automatically at one minute intervals.

- Change the background colour of all slides.

- Create a Notes page for the last slide and type the following:

    - Mention that we will be giving training on use of company intranet in 2 weeks time. **It is essential that all employees attend**. Give out list of selected dates and times and ask staff to let you know by end of week which slot will suit.

- Insert your name and slide number as a footer on all slides.

- Save the file as Induction 2.

- Print a copy of the presentation showing all slides on one page and in handout format. Also print a copy of the Notes page.

- E-mail the copy of the completed presentation to your supervisor. Mark this email URGENT.

In-tray presentations Set 2 Day 1 – presentation 3

As part of John Nicholls community initiatives you have been asked to create a presentation about a Club/Café for 15–17 olds in the area to go and meet friends in the evenings and weekends to keep them off the streets. You should use five slides and include the following:

Slide 1 Design a club name and logo (include an example of Clipart).

Slide 2 Aims of club. Create a bulleted list, for example:

- to provide a safe environment for teenagers to meet and socialise at weekends

- to give teenagers experience in running a small business

You can demote and promote bullet points here if you want to expand with examples

Slide 3 Include an organisation chart showing the management structure for the club with Paid Youth Leader followed by three elected members, specialist staff and members.

Slide 4 An example of a handout designed to advertise the club (include two examples of Clipart here).

Slide 5 Import a suitable example from the Internet of a club where a similar venture was successful, for example, access the Rhyl Youth Café website on www.youth-cafe.co.uk. Copy and paste a couple of relevant sentences.

- Apply a suitable colour scheme to your presentation.

- Apply transitions between slides and timings so that slides appear automatically.

- Apply some custom animations.

- Create a Notes page for one of the slides and add appropriate information to this (for example, Slide 5 – copy and paste further examples).

- Save your presentation as Drop in Club.

- Print the slides in the form of a single-page handout.

- Also print out the Notes page only.

- E-mail this presentation to your teacher/lecturer.

Index

Answers

Chapter 1 Working Effectively

Task 1

Junior administrative job in supermarket office	
Duties	**Personal qualities**
Perform routine office work including dealing with mail, filing, photocopying.	Good communication skills.
	Enthusiastic.
Be able to use word processing and spreadsheet software.	Energetic.
Provide support for buyers.	
Experienced administrative assistant/receptionist	
Duties	**Personal qualities**
Reception duties to deal with customers and staff.	Cheerful.
Word processing skills.	Friendly manner.
	Quick.
	Accurate.
	Pay attention to detail.
	Able to work on your own.
	Good level of education.
	Two years experience.
	Willing to learn.
Personal assistant	
Duties	**Personal qualities**
Expert in Word.	Able to communicate well with clients.
Expert in Excel.	Good telephone manner.
Expert in Powerpoint.	Able to work under pressure.
Supervise clerical staff.	Flexible.

Task 2

Students should be encouraged to look on the Internet for job vacancies. If this is not possible, the teacher/leacturer may wish to provide some local job advertisements to use for this task. There is no 'right' answer to this question, completion will depend on the jobs chosen. Answers can be keyed into Admin1task2 (on CD ROM).

Check your Progress (1.1)

1   This will require the student to look back at the person specification for the job and try to identify how they could provide evidence. They should copy the qualities on to a table and add a second column to key in what evidence they could provide. Some examples are shown below.

Person specification	Personal experience
Have experience of working in an administrative capacity in an office environment and/or be qualified to Standard Grade General Level, SVQ Level II or equivalent.	Any work experience. Any Standard Grades.
Have the ability to prepare standard written communication and be able to communicate information clearly, including by telephone, using standard grammatical form with a variety of internal and external customers.	Any Communications/English qualifications. Any portfolios of work produced at school/college. Any work experience which had telephone skills.
Be able to work with others and as part of a team.	Hobbies, sports, class work which involved working with others.
Be able to organise own work for given priorities, tasks and objectives; be able to identify, and propose solutions for routine problems.	Evidence of working with a big project, such as in Standard Grade, compiling portfolios of work, hobbies.
Be able to understand and carry out basic numerical calculations.	Qualifications, jobs, hobbies which use number work.
Be customer focused.	Dealing with customers, such as visitors on open days at school/college, work experience, part-time job.
Be confident and competent in dealing with telephone enquiries.	Examples of where they deal with the phone, including part-time work, work experience, training.
Preferably have experience with standard word processing and spreadsheet packages.	Qualifications, examples of work, training undertaken/being undertaken.

2   Good communication skills including the ability to deal with front office duties. Dealing with switchboard. Other qualities (Pupils/students should be expected to look at other job descriptions to get suitably worded personal qualities which suit the reception job.) Pleasant manner, approachable, customer focused, good telephone manner, cheerful, friendly, etc.

3   Job 6. The level of responsibility, for example, advice on procedures, planning visits, implies a level of responsibility which is not there in Job 4 or 5.

4   Administrative duties, IT skills and communication skills.

Task 3

Students/pupils should complete the table in accordance with their current skills. They should be encouraged to complete these accurately and the teacher/lecturer should discuss their responses with them. Each student/pupil is likely to have different 'answers'. This document is available as Admin1task3 on the CD ROM.

Task 4

General target	SMART target
Learn to drive	Pass my driving test by (insert date) can then be split into getting a provisional licence, booking driving lessons, doing theory test and booking tests.
Save some money	Save £X per week or per month in xxx bank by (insert date)

Task 5 and 6

The student should complete the table and use it as the focus of discussions with teacher/lecturer. Teacher/lecturer may like to ask the questions posed to help completion of the table in class, so that the PDPs are completed at the same time. Completing electronically can encourage integration of skills (sending the form to teacher/lecturer by e-mail), as can allowing a certain time each week for discussion of PDPs and getting pupils/students to set up a meeting with teacher/lecturer during these times using their electronic diaries. The information completed will vary between individuals. The form is available as Admin1task5 on the CD ROM. Time needs to be allowed for each person completing this task.

Check your Progress 1.2

1 Development of the individual as a person, not just an employee, makes you feel more valued and may bring out other qualities that your organisation did not know you had.

2 Achievement can be measured if targets are SMART. Did you achieve it? Yes/no. If not why not? What did not happen can be traced and amended so that the target can be achieved.

3 Highflyers will often overtake targets quicker than the dates set. They need to refocus by having targets reviewed more regularly and have something new to aim for. This enables them to judge their own progress.

Task 7 and 8

Individual answers will differ. Student/pupil should identify their own time wasters and solutions to dealing with them. Teacher/lecturer should comment on, rather than correct, these tasks, focussing on how the student might avoid wasting time.

Task 9

The table shown is Admin1task9 (on CD ROM). Some suggestions are shown.

Time stealer	How can you stop this stealing your time?
Interruptions by telephone	Limit time spent on phone calls. Divert calls when busy. Use voice mail. Deal with calls only at specific times of the day, accessing voice mail and making outgoing calls, (first thing in the morning).
Looking for lost papers	Limit time spent. File as you go so things do not get lost. Minimise paperwork by keeping things electronically and doing electronic searches.
Communicating problems	Use more than one method where people are difficult, (e-mail and phone). Try to do face-to-face communication and have someone else present if the situation is difficult.
Meetings going on longer than expected	Set an end time for meetings. Start on time regardless if all are present.
You re-do one part of the job again and again	Complete all of the task, leave and then re-visit rather than focussing on one bit.

Task 10 and 11

There are no set answers to these tasks. Students should be encouraged to evaluate their own actions.

Check your Progress 1.3

1 Answer should include details like the following:

Try to keep a note of what you are being asked to do. Demonstrate electronic methods and written methods you use to store helpful lists/data. (To do list, carry forward lists). Demonstrate how you use your diary, how you would write in regular tasks into your diary when you need to do them, rather than when they are needed, tell them whose work gets priority.

2 Columns with date, priority, task, complete and notes, for example, for carrying forward, (P for priority)

Date	P	Task	Complete	Notes

3 See above. You may wish to indicate only urgent or prioritise on 1-5 basis, 1 being high priority. Teacher/lecturer may wish to introduce any templates on the diary system being used to help with time management.

Task 12

For example, job interview, customer complaints, bad news to staff, (redundancy, an issue which has caused bad feeling in the past). In face-to-face you can see the body language and gauge reaction better. You can therefore re-word or re-arrange what you were going to say.

Task 13

When there are lots of applicants, it allows you to pre-screen them without having to give up lots of time to interview them. Allows the organisation to form an impression of the applicant and then compile a shortlist. Allows a judgement to be made on their oral communication skills and telephone skills.

Task 14

Group discussion should bring out the following points:

1   Tell your boss at a better time/confirm what you told them by e-mail/let them know as far in advance as possible.

2   Explain organisational policy. Ask her to send information to the office address and mark it personal if she wishes and assure her you will pass it on unopened.

3   Phone the organisation and tell them that your application is in the post or deliver it by hand.

4   Remind them tactfully that this is not appropriate. If the situation does not improve tell your boss.

Task 15

- The main principle of the new system is to ensure that all time is logged effectively and the Principal intends to check data to ensure its accuracy. The principle purpose of carrying out this check is to ensure that everyone records data in accordance with the principles laid down in the staff handbook.

- Formally – structured, officially, properly

  Formerly – previously, before, in the past.

- There are too many people wanting to undertake this course so we are going to have to divide them into two groups. If your name is in group one you will require to report to the Board Room at two o'clock on Friday to start the course.

- There were so many volunteers wanting to do that course that they were asked to put their names down on a waiting list. They're going to be informed as soon as there is another course available.

Internal Assessment Intermediate 2 Questions

1   Answer should include the following:

Used to check the skills someone already has; Helps identify the training they need; Must be answered honestly; Skills are usually connected with a particular job role.

2   Answer should include three from:

Organised; Helpful; Able to use initiative; Good telephone manner; Good communication skills; Flexible; Able to work as part of a team.

3   Answer should include three from:

1) Information which has been missed out and not passed on.
2) Information which has been overlooked.
3) Information which has been distorted as people put on their own bias.
4) Conflicting information received from different sources.
5) Communication difficulties due to language, age, personalities involved.
6) Difficulties in understanding or retaining what was said.

Internal Assessment Higher Questions

1   Answer should include two from:

Able to work unsupervised; Able to organise and supervise the work of others; Able to communicate well with those at a higher level in the organisation; Able to lead a team; Able to provide training and support to other members of a team; Able to work on their own initiative.

2 Answer should include three from:

Time spent at work is wasted; Staff become demoralised; Work does not progress quickly and keeps other sections back; Targets are not achieved and plans become meaningless; New projects are not started and the business does not move forward; No spare time to progress ideas.

3 Answer should include two from:

Allows major projects to be tracked; Allows the organisation to identify where targets are not being met and to take corrective action; Allows other sections to rework their plans; Allows extra resources to be allocated if needed; Lets managers be in control of their area of work.

4 Benefits to the organisation should include two from:

Staff turnover falls; Absenteeism reduces; Accidents decrease; Complaints decrease; Errors in work fall; Productivity increases; Good team provides good induction.

Benefits to the individual should include two from:

Support from other members of the team; Few underlying conflicts – good teams sort their own problems; Ready supply of mentors to learn new skills; Good teams tend to be happy at their work.

External Assessment Higher Questions

1

Person specification	Job description
Used to detail personal qualities and attributes.	Lists what people are required to do in the job.
Used by employer to help identify qualities needed.	Used by applicants to judge if they can do the job.
Lists core skills like communications.	Outlines responsibilities.
Details qualifications.	Details where the job fits into overall organisation.
Should be available for all jobs but particularly useful when recruiting as can form the basis of interview.	Should be available for all jobs and should help grade pay rate.

2 Answer should include points like the following, linked with phrases such as 'compared with', 'as opposed to', 'in comparison to' etc.

Administrative assistant	Senior administrator
Works under supervision	Supervises others
Little decision making involved in job	Makes decisions and decides priorities
Has their priorities decided for them	Prioritises their own work and other people's work
Is not able to delegate to others	Can delegate to others
May order resources but does not make decisions about resources	Manages resources and makes decisions about resources
	Takes an overview
Works to a short timescale	Takes on longer term tasks

3 Answer should include points such as:
All members of the team are supported which helps learning on the job, mentoring, covering for absence, training for different job roles, developing for promotion. All of these factors lead to fewer customer complaints and better productivity. People are happier working in teams and this results in lower absenteeism, lower staff turnover, better quality work, few accidents and a better working environment.

4 Answer should include points such as:
looks at progress made; alters targets/timelines in accordance with reality; ensures development is in line with the goals of the organisation; checks that any identified staff development has taken place; gives the opportunity to discuss, analyse and record performance; gives the opportunity for the individual to speak privately to the reviewer.

Chapter 2 The Work Environment

Check your Progress 2.1

1 People's lives are much busier today and, as a result, they are demanding high quality services outside traditional hours – hence the increase in 24 hour banking/insurance call centres and 24-hour mail order catalogue services. Retailers, under strong competitive pressures, have had to extend opening hours following both a demand for longer weekday openings and the Sunday Trading Act 1994, which allows 6 hours trading on Sundays. Flexible working arrangements include part-time, job-share, flexi-time and home-working. Use of Flexible working arrangements allows employer to investigate better ways to recruit and retain valued staff to meet changing customer requirements.

2 It describes the many different facets of work, workers and the workplace. The range of practices may include **flexibility of work** – employers may offer a variety of flexible working arrangements including part-time, job share and flexi-time; **Flexibility of workers** – use of contingency staff on temporary part-time or fixed term contracts to cover holiday and busy periods; **Flexibility of the workplace** – in order to save space hot-desking may be introduced.

3 Answer should include:

Allows John Nicholls to use staff to cover busy periods and cover absence; Workers may be more committed because they hope to gain a permanent position within the organisation; John Nicholls does not have to renew contract.

4 The subcontracting/contracting out of certain activities particularly non-core activities. The organisation engages a supplier to perform a non-core activity for example, cleaning, catering or payroll instead of employing more staff.

5 Benefits could include:

Organisation can agree short term contracts with the subcontractor to ensure performance and low costs are maintained; Organisation able to cancel contracts without the associated obligation of providing for staff should the service provided not meet suitable standards; Savings in recruitment and training.

Problems could include:

Lack of control over the subcontracted staff and the services they provide. The only way an organisation can show dissatisfaction is by not outsourcing for a second time

Check your Progress 2.2

1 Benefits could include:

Reduces or eliminates punctuality problems and the need to discipline staff for being late. People who are always late can make up their time later in the day or take a shorter lunch; Reduces absence rates – staff can organise personal appointments like dental appointments in flexi-time; Flexi-time can create a greater sense of responsibility and commitment from employees; Allows extension of opening hours i.e. branches of banks which are now open between 8am and 6pm.

Disadvantages could include:

Extra costs including the purchase of recording equipment and its maintenance; the cost of administering the scheme; Increased heat, lighting and security costs due to longer opening hours; Heavier burden placed on managers as they have to organise the level of staff cover needed at any particular time; Making decisions on when people can take a 'flexi day' – ensuring enough staff cover and supervisory staff available to cover this; Communication difficulties – it is important to always be clear when staff are in the office outside core times.

2 A positive answer could include:

Gives greater freedom for people to organise their working lives and suit personal needs; Travelling can be easier and cheaper if outside peak times; Gives staff responsibility for their work and they are not disciplined for not being in at the start of the day. This can create an improved working environment; If people stay late to finish a task they can take the time off later in the accounting period.

3 Answer could include:

If you want to keep up to date in your professional and skilled work without a full-time commitment; If you were looking to ease back in to work after not working full-time for some time, such as after long-term sick leave or maternity leave; If you needed to balance care of children and/or elderly relatives with working.

Check your Progress 2.3

1 Answer could include:

Increase in home-working/tele-working, for example, Purchasing team at John Nicholls spend a lot of their time at various suppliers locations and time is split between home and office. Networked computers with electronic mail would allow them to keep them in touch with suppliers and stores within the organisation.

Increase in hot-desking.

2 Tele-working benefits to employee could include:

Better work/life balance; Ability to access different types of work without changing location; Reduces (or eliminates) travel time – also reduces stress;

Employee can choose their own work schedule.

Tele-working disadvantages to employee could include:

Self discipline is required. The employee needs to set their own goals; Employees may feel isolated with little or no social contact. A compromise of this arrangement is best i.e. the ability to work some of the time in office and some of the time at home; Employees may not have the space at home for the office.

Tele-working benefits to employer could include:

Employers may retain staff because they can balance work with looking after children/elderly parents; Freeing up office space and associated savings offsets equipment costs for tele-workers; Higher productivity because of improved concentration and fewer interruptions at home; Increased motivation and commitment because no travel involved.

Tele-working disadvantages to employer could include:

Not suitable for all jobs i.e. some jobs involve extensive face-to-face contact with customers; Not suitable for all employees. Employees must be able to work on own and be quite self disciplined; Costs of equipment; Managing tele-workers – different style of management is required for managing remote workers.

Career breaks advantages to employee could include:

Opportunity to combine family and other commitments with work.

Career breaks disadvantages to employee could include:

Can become isolated from the workplace; Can affect their continuity of employment.

Career breaks benefits to employer could include:

Allows organisations to keep valuable staff who might otherwise leave.

Career breaks disadvantages to employer could include:

Costs involved in maintaining contact with the employees.

3 Organisation:

- Provision of flexible working arrangements means that employers can recruit and retain valued staff and meet changing customer requirements more easily.

- Can cut costs by using peripheral workers, for example, fixed term contracts to cover busy periods and boost productivity.

- Improve in the quality of work if employees are able to choose a working arrangement which allows them to balance work with commitments at home. It usually results in increased productivity and improved morale (workers are more energetic).

- Reduces stress and time off work.

- Introduction of hot-desking means that savings in office space can be made or office space can be used for other purposes.

Individual:

- Individuals can access work and training when they otherwise may not have been able to, such as when they have to look after young children/sick relatives.

- Can balance work with other commitments.
- Reduces stress levels, increases energy, motivation and commitment.

Check your Progress 2.4

1 Answer should include six from:

Name and address of Employer; Name and address of Employee; Job title and grade; Date of Commencement of continuous employment (for those workers on a fixed term contract a clause will be included which specifies the date at which the contract terminates); Duties attached to the job; Hours of work (i.e. full-time, part-time, job-share); Location (home address will need to be given here for home-workers/tele-workers); Working times and breaks; Pay details; Holiday entitlement; Sickness and absenteeism; Pension inclusion/exclusion; Disciplinary rules and procedures; Grievances procedures; Notice requirements.

2 permanent contract – of no fixed duration

fixed term – a contract of employment which is of a fixed duration.

Check your Progress 2.5

1 A suitable answer would be:

The study of the relationship between man and his working environment. Movement should be natural, rhythmical and symmetrical – work tools and equipment should be within easy reach; should work sitting down, where possible, in an adjustable, supportive chair, and with convenient desk heights etc.

2 Answer could include:

The employee: boost the morale and well being; encourage staff to stay.

The employer: increase productivity; improve efficiency.

Check your Progress 2.6

1 Employer advantages could include:

- Easier supervision of staff – everybody is working in an open area which can be seen by one supervisor.
- Economy in floor space, lighting and heating – no space is lost to internal walls and doors.
- Flexibility of layout – any expansion or change of work or procedures and consequent increase of staff and equipment can be accommodated.
- Minimises movement of staff and documents. Delays in the flow of work caused by moving papers and people from room to room are eliminated.
- Communication between staff is easier. You can see if a member of staff is at their desk by simply looking around.
- Morale of staff is enhanced by the pleasant, spacious appearance of the office.
- A more sociable atmosphere is created because artificial barriers between people working at different levels in the organisation are removed.

Employer disadvantages could include:

- More noise. One person's phone call or meeting may disturb everyone.
- Encourages chit-chat amongst staff so staff can be more easily distracted.
- Lack of privacy can be a problem, especially if disciplinary or personal issues are involved.
- Staff may have difficulty reaching agreement about appropriate levels of lighting, heating and ventilation.
- Managers can be distracted by routine matters.
- More chance of infections spreading throughout the office.

Employee advantages could include:

- Communication between staff is easier.
- Resources can be shared.

Employee disadvantages could include:

- More noise.
- Lack of privacy.
- Staff may have difficulty reaching agreement about appropriate levels of lighting, heating and ventilation.

2 Answer could include:

- creation of meeting rooms to allow privacy and ensure confidentiality.
- use of acoustic screens and barriers to minimise noise problems.
- ensure all legal aspects such as adequate heating, lighting and method of air conditioning have been satisfied to minimise the risk of infections.

3 Answer should include an explanation of how ensuring workers and equipment are grouped together will assist communication and work flow.

Task 1

Student to name six regulations and outline their main features. Six possible regulations are outlined as follows:

Management of Health and Safety at Work Regulations 1992

This regulation requires the employer to undertake risk assessment of their work activities. Employer is required to:

- Carry out suitable and sufficient risk assessments of their working activities – this includes everyone affected by working activities, including employees and visitors to the organisation.
- Record in writing the significant findings of the assessment and any group of workers identified as being significantly at risk.
- Review any assessment when there is reason to suspect it is no longer valid or where there has been a significant change.

Workplace (Health, Safety and Welfare) Regulations

This deals with workplace safety for everyone in the workplace. Employer is required to assess and monitor specific areas and is required to:

- provide suitable and effective ventilation
- provide suitable and sufficient lighting
- ensure temperature is reasonable
- ensure workplace is clean
- provide sufficient space for employees
- provide suitable seating
- ensure floors and traffic routes are sufficient
- provide suitable and sufficient washing facilities and drinking water
- provide sufficient toilets
- provide suitable and sufficient accommodation for clothing (and changing facilities if required).

Health and Safety (Display Screen Equipment) Regulations 1992

This refers to visual display screen/computers in the place of work and aims to reduce muscular and other physical problems.

All employers must:

- Carry out ongoing assessment of workstations to assess and reduce risks.
- Ensure workstations and related furniture comply with minimum requirements.
- Ensure employees plan their work to include breaks.
- Provide employees with information and training.
- Offer eye tests on request.

Minimum requirements for workstations include:

- VDUs – clearly formed and clearly defined characters; stable image on the screen; adjust brightness/contrast control; swivel and tilt easily; free from reflective glare
- Software – appropriate for task
- Keyboards – detachable or moveable; has a matt surround; sufficient space in front of the screen; easy to use
- Desks – sufficient size for equipment to allow employees to feel comfortable; stable with matt finish
- Chairs – adjustable in height; adjustable back rest
  (Candidates may discuss factors relating to the environment such as space requirements, lighting, heating and ventilation).

Provision and Use of Work Equipment (PUWER) Regulations 1992

This deals with the safe use and maintenance of equipment in the workplace. In brief employers have to ensure that:

- All equipment is suitable for the purpose it is required for and is well maintained and has been 'risk assessed'.
- All users of the equipment are adequately trained in the use of the equipment.
- Safety literature for all equipment is readily available and, where appropriate, on display.
- The equipment itself has all the necessary safety features (such as visors/shields) fitted, has been installed correctly by authorised personal and all waste products are suitably disposed off without causing a hazard to employees.
- All supervisors are adequately trained in the use and safety instruction for the equipment.

The definition of equipment is any item used to assist the employee complete their task, such as a screwdriver, a milling machine or a word processor.

Manual Handling Regulations 1992

This deals with the practices used by employers to ensure the health and safety of employees in relation to the lifting, moving and transporting of goods/items. Employers must take all reasonable steps to ensure no injury comes to employees and all necessary lifting and moving aids are in place, used and maintained. All staff should be suitably training in correct moving and handling procedures to ensure that risk from injury is reduced.

Personal Protective Equipment (PPE) Regulations 1992

This deals with the requirements of employers to provide personal protective equipment to employees. Personal Protective Equipment must conform to all British and European standards and be in good condition and well looked after. It must fit the wearer well and be fit for the intended purpose. Suitable storage for the equipment should be provided.

Task 2

Employer could be liable for breaching: Health and Safety at Work Act 1974; Management of Health & Safety at Work Regulations 1992; Workplace (Health, Safety & Welfare Regulations) 1992.

Task 3

1   Health and Safety Executive (HSE) Inspectors and local authorities share responsibility for enforcement of health and safety legislation.

2 The powers of the enforcement officers include: entering and inspecting premises at any reasonable time (even unannounced); taking photographs, samples of water, measurements etc.; interviewing and asking people questions if they think this is essential; issuing improvement notices; issuing prohibition notices; prosecuting people and organisations.

3 There are penalties for failing to comply with health and safety legislation. If health and safety issues are identified Inspectors and local authorities will try to negotiate an improvement by serving an improvement notice but may need to close premises, issue fines or even prosecute, which may result in imprisonment.

4 Failure to comply with these requirements can lead to disciplinary action and even prosecution.

Task 4

Security of information:

- Ensuring that only authorised users can get into the computer system – i.e. through passwords. Passwords will have to be changed on a regular basis. Passwords should not be given to anyone else and should not be written down.
- Logging into the system allows the system administrator to check who is doing what. What you have accessed can be traced.
- Use screen savers so that information can be hidden from passers by or when employees are not at their desk.

Security of visitors:

- Visitors should report to reception, which should be manned at all times.
- Reception should be informed of expected visitors.
- Visitors should be asked to sign in and out and issued with an identification pass.

Security of staff:

- Installation of security cameras and CCTV.
- Ensure visitors are monitored.
- Installation of toughened glass screens and panic buttons where staff are in contact with members of public.

Security of equipment:

- Tag or security mark all computers and valuable pieces of equipment.
- Make sure equipment is stored in a safe place.
- Lock away small items of equipment when not in use.

Internal Assessment Intermediate 2 Questions

1a Any five for one mark each from:

Name and address of Employer; Name and address of Employee; Job title and grade; Date of Commencement of continuous employment (for those workers on a fixed-term contract a clause will be included which specifies the date at which the contract terminates); Duties attached to the job; Hours of work (i.e. full-time, part-time, job-share); Location (home address will need to be given here for home-workers/tele-workers); Working times and breaks; Pay details; Holiday entitlement; Sickness and absenteeism; Pension inclusion/exclusion; Disciplinary rules and procedures; Grievances procedures; Notice requirements.

1b Advantages for employee (any one for one mark):

They may suit workers who do not want to be tied down for long periods of time; Workers may enjoy a higher rate of pay to compensate for lack of permanency.

Disadvantages for employee (any one for one mark):

Many workers report a lack of feeling of belonging to the organisation because of the fixed-duration of the working arrangement; Less job security.

Advantages for employer (any one for one mark):

They allow the employer to use staff to cover busy periods and absences; Workers may be more committed because they hope to gain a permanent position within the organisation; Employer does not have to renew contract; Allows the employer to 'try out' employees.

Disadvantage for employer (any one for one mark):

More administration involved when contracts are to be renewed; Employees may not be as motivated as permanent staff.

2a Any two for one mark each from:

Workers do not have their own desks; workers are allocated work space according to their needs; workers may keep their personal belongings in lockers when not in the office; hot-desks may be depersonalised so that they can be used by anyone – this means no photos or personal belongings in your workspace; in some organisations workspaces/hot-desks may be allocated on a first come first served basis (such as call centres) but in others workspaces can be booked in advance.

2b Benefits to the employer (any one for one mark):

Lower corporate office costs; Allows staff to be in control of where they work; Enables staff to work in a wide range of locations; Can prevent cliques forming.

Disadvantages to the employee (any one for one mark):

Can lead to poor morale if staff are continually working with strangers; Reduced productivity if staff are continually working with strangers.

3 Any four for one mark each from:

Where sensitive information is being stored, many organisations will employ security guards and may use Closed Circuit TV (CCTV) to monitor visitors; Minimise the number of entrances and exits; Issue identification passes to staff; User identification such as electronic keypad or card reader required to gain access to rooms where confidential information is stored; Only issue keys to nominated personnel; Check all rooms at end of each day to ensure windows and doors are locked; Use security guards to prevent unauthorised access which could lead to theft and vandalism.

4 One mark for each valid point regarding legislation (maximum six marks):

Health and Safety at Work Act 1974 requires employers to provide and maintain a working environment for employees that is without risk to health and ensure that all equipment and systems of work are safe and without risks to health.

Health and Safety (Display Screen Equipment) Regulations 1992 requires employers to:

Carry out ongoing assessment of workstations to assess and reduce risks; Ensure workstations and related furniture comply with minimum requirements; Ensure VDUs are free from glare and adjustable; Ensure desks are large enough to accommodate equipment and employee requirements; Ensure employees plan their work to include breaks; Provide employees with information and training; Offer eye tests on request.

External Assessment Higher Questions

1 Any four for one mark each:

- Provision of flexible working arrangements means that employers can recruit and retain valued staff and meet changing customer requirements more easily.

- Costs can be cut by using peripheral workers, for example, fixed term contracts to cover busy periods and boost productivity.

- Improvements in the quality of work if employees are able to choose a working arrangement which allows them to balance work with commitments at home. It usually results in increased productivity and improved morale (workers are more energetic).

- Reduced stress and time off work.

- Introduction of hot-desking means that savings in office space can be made or office space can be used for other purposes.

2 One mark for each appropriate point made.

- Cellular office or traditional design is the name given to the concept of separate rooms of varying sizes for individual workers, or group of workers.

- Open plan office design is based on the concept of large areas of floor space with no dividing walls.

- Cellular ensures the privacy of the group or individual i.e. can hold confidential discussions.

- Cellular – noise level is kept to a minimum.

- Cellular – security of information is easier – doors can be simply closed/locked.

- Cellular – easier to control levels of heating and lighting.

- Open plan – easier supervision of staff – everybody is working in an open area which can be seen by one supervisor.

- Open plan – economy in floor space, lighting and heating – no space is lost to internal walls and doors.

- Open plan – flexibility of layout – any expansion or change of work or procedures and consequent increase of staff and equipment can be accommodated.

- Open plan – minimises movement of staff and documents. Delays in the flow of work caused by moving papers and people from room to room are eliminated.

- Open plan – communication between staff is easier. You can see if a member of staff is at their desk by looking around.

3 One mark each for any four points:

- Intranet. Many organisations create a health and safety folder which has the Health and Safety Policy Document and procedures and other related information such as workplace checklists, accident report forms.

- Notice boards. These can be used to provide general information. Information must be updated regularly and notice board should be kept tidy by removing out of date information.

- E-mail, memo or newsletter. Changes to procedures can be communicated in this way. Bottom of document should be dated to allow for identification of the most up to date version. Each member of staff receives their own copy of the document.

- Training Sessions. Used to keep staff informed and to disseminate information, such as on Risk Assessment when staff move to different jobs.

- Posters. A good way to communicate prohibitions such as 'you must not do'. They are usually a red circle on a white background with a diagonal bar across. Examples include no smoking, no entry. Posters are also designed to give warnings to people – i.e. alert staff to a hazard. This type of poster will have a yellow background with a triangular border and a symbol and/or lettering in black. Examples include warning of a slippery surface or uneven floor. Posters are also used to inform people of what they must do, such as keep fire door shut or wear hearing protection. Posters can also be used to communicate safe conditions. They will have white lettering and/or symbols, for example, fire exit and drinking water. Many organisation display a Health and Safety poster informing staff of health and safety provision in the workplace (in accordance with the Health and Safety Information for Employees Regulations 1989).

- Videos and role plays exemplify and encourage good practice, such as working at the VDU, lifting heavy objects. Fire drills are used on a regular basis to familiarise staff with procedures.

- Safety Meetings. Employees can be kept up to date with any changes and new regulations, codes of practice or guidelines. Most large organisations have Health and Safety Committees which include both union and management members to ensure all staff have a channel of communication about health and safety issues.

4 One mark each for any three.

All employers must:

Carry out ongoing assessment of workstations to assess and reduce risks; Ensure workstations and related furniture comply with minimum requirements; Ensure employees plan their work to include breaks; Provide employees with information and training; Offer eye tests on request.

Chapter 3 Meetings

Where notices, agendas, minutes and action minutes are used, they should be combined with word processing activities to ensure students are laying out the documents in the preferred housestyle. The styles used here are suggestions only.

Task 1

Part 1

John Nicholls

NOTICE OF MEETING

A meeting of the Social Committee will be held in the Boardroom at 1400 hours on Friday (insert date).

AGENDA

1 Apologies for absence

2 Minute of previous meeting

3 Matters arising from minutes

4 Children's Christmas Party

5 Staff Christmas Party

6 Charity Fun Run

7 Any other business

8 Date of next meeting

Student's name
Secretary

Today's date

Part 2

John Nicholls

NOTICE OF MEETING

Social Committee Meeting – (insert date).

CHAIRPERSON'S AGENDA

AGENDA ITEM	NOTES
1 Apologies for absence	Jim Martin will not be there
2 Minute of previous meeting	
3 Matters arising from minutes	
4 Children's Christmas Party	
5 Staff Christmas Party	
6 Charity Fun Run	
7 Any other business	
8 Date of next meeting	

Task 2

Part 1

John Nicholls

NOTICE OF MEETING

A meeting of the Pay and Salaries Negotiating Committee will be held in the Boardroom at 1430 hours on 12 January 20..

AGENDA

1 Apologies for absence

2 Minute of previous meeting

3 Matters arising from minutes

4 Review of Pension Provision – Report of Sub-committee

5 Any other business

6 Date of next meeting

Student's name
Secretary

Today's date

Part 2

John Nicholls

NOTICE OF MEETING

Pay and Salary Negotiating Committee on 12 January 20..

CHAIRPERSON'S AGENDA

AGENDA ITEM	NOTES
1 Apologies for absence	
2 Minute of previous meeting	
3 Matters arising from minutes	
4 Review of Pension Provision	Report of Sub-committee
5 Any other business	
6 Date of next meeting	

Check your Progress 3.1

1 Answer should contain the following points:

List of items that will be discussed, listed in order of discussion. Headings should convey the content of the discussion. Chairman's agenda should be more detailed – additional notes if known and space available at right hand side for any comments or notes of the meeting. Not always used but useful as an aide memoire.

2 Answer should contain the following points:

Informal – not usually set procedures, notes not always taken, not usually held at regular intervals, no requirement for notice in advance of meeting. Usually called on an informal basis, such as by phone, e-mail. Formal – for a specific purpose, special rules apply, often regularly held, documents record the calling and progress of the meeting, named person is responsible for the paperwork, calling the meeting and recording decisions.

3 To testify to the accuracy of the record, to indicate that the record has been passed by those who attended as accurate. File both electronically and in hard copy so that previous paperwork can be accessed at a meeting if required. If electronically held, facilities to ensure access to previous decisions, such as laptop with network/wireless connection, should, be available.

Task 3

If you were using a meeting to communicate, keeping staff informed, tracking progress, looking for ideas, bonding teams together, telling a group bad news you would choose to keep it informal. Why? – people are more likely to speak up, no set prior notice needs to be given, no formal record is kept, can be called quickly.

Task 4

Standing orders will hold the 'rules'. This will contain information on the purpose of the committee, how much notice has to be given before a meeting can be held, how many members the committee has, how long members serve on the committee, how members are elected to the committee, how the office bearers are elected (usually the chairperson, secretary and treasurer) and what their duties are, and how many members form a quorum.

Check your progress 3.2

The following would be recorded in the minutes:

- The minutes of the previous meeting were taken as read, agreed and signed by the Chairperson.

- The Motion 'the presentation will take place in the Royal Scot Hotel on 27 January' was proposed by John Smith and seconded by Wendy O'Hara and unanimously carried. An amendment that all members of the marketing department past and present be invited, was not carried.

- The meeting was adjourned due to a severe snow storm. The date of the next meeting will be agreed at a later date.

2 Wasted time for participants, lack of preparation may influence decisions, (frustration and annoyance) and an inability to get through the agenda items.

Check rooms are comfortable and laid out as requested, resources are in working order, signage is in place, reception knows of visitors, stationery requirements and extra copies of documents are available, attendance list is prepared and available, minutes of last meeting are available for chairperson to sign, switch phone through to voicemail or a colleague and arrive early to welcome visitors.

3 The motion – a proposal put before the meeting.

The proposer – the person who proposes a motion and speaks on behalf of it.

The seconder – the person who seconds the motion showing that they back the proposal.

An amendment was proposed and seconded – a suggested change to the original motion, proposed and seconded by two members of the committee.

Following discussions, the proposer used the right to reply – the original proposer may wish to have the final few words and correct any errors or misjudgements on the original motion.

A vote was taken and passed – the members decided that they agreed with the motion and voted for it.

The resolution – once passed a motion becomes a resolution.

A rider – the original motion now has an added clause which does not change the meaning but adds to it.

4 Casting vote – A vote which is tied, i.e. the same number of people vote for as against, can use the chairman's casting vote to break the deadlock. Whichever way the chair votes will decide.

Action minutes – A summary minute which identifies who will do what by when. Will be only a summary of what actions result from the meeting not a summary of the whole proceedings.

Verbatim – A word for word record of what happened.

Quorum – The number of people needed for a meeting to take place.

Abstain – Eligible to vote but chose not to vote – to abstain.

Internal Assessment

1 *Chairman's agenda* – An agenda with space for the chairperson's notes. Usually for formal meetings. Good for inexperienced chairperson. Help chairperson keep a summary of their notes before the meeting as well as what happened at the meeting. Layout could be shown.

Attendance register – Records all of those present at the meeting. Useful for the secretary when drawing up Minutes of the meeting. Allows a cross check if expenses are being claimed. Often used to check that only authorised people are present, for example at an AGM.

Action minutes – Record what actions have to be taken as a result of the meeting. Usually have an identified person to carry out the action and usually the date when the action has to be done is also identified. Not usually a summary of the process of the meeting, merely the actions arising from the meeting.

2 Annual General Meeting takes place once a year, set date, advance notice to all those eligible to attend. Purpose is to elect office holders and directors, discuss the organisation's performance including financial performance and to look at future plans. Gives all the stakeholders the opportunity to speak about the organisation's plans.

On the other hand an Extraordinary General Meeting will only be held under exceptional circumstances. It will be open to all those eligible to attend an AGM but is usually called to discuss a particular issue which cannot wait until the next AGM. Will still require advance notice and may need the agreement of a number of shareholders.

3 Answer two from:

a Seconder – the person who follows the proposer in backing a proposal or motion. The seconder does not usually have to talk about the motion.

b Adjournment – This is where a meeting is stopped or discontinued until a date in the future. This is rare but may be done due to bad weather, ill health or an emergency situation.

c Abstain – Someone who is eligible to vote has decided not to vote. This often happens because they disagree with the motion but do not want to disagree with the people they usually align with on the committee.

d Quorum – The number of people who have to be present before the meeting can begin. This number is set in the 'rules' governing the meeting – standing orders or articles of association or constitution.

4 a e-mail – Papers can be sent electronically and stored electronically which saves space and is quicker. The sender can check they have been received and opened. Documents can be read on screen at meetings. Amendments can be made and redistributed easily.

b e-diary – Diaries within an organisation can usually be scanned to find a date when all participants are free. Invitations to meetings can be sent and responses are returned to sender. Changes to venue and times are easy and quick to send. You can check that all messages have been opened/received. Key dates can be flagged up for distributing information and preparing materials.

c video-conference – Saves travelling time and costs involved. Allows those who would not be able to participate in a meeting to take part (those who are located at a distance). Allows more face to face communication to take place. Pace of the meeting may need to be slower than usual. Often requires technical support and some training for those involved.

External Assessment

1   Answer should be split into before the meeting, at the meeting and after the meeting.

Before the meeting: check room for layout and comfort, check resources are there and working, signage in place, reception is aware of visitors, paperwork and spare copies as well as stationery are available. Ensure minute of previous meeting is available for chair's signature and an attendance list is also available.

At the meeting: read minutes if required, inform meeting of any apologies, provide any papers requested, take notes with particular attention to actions which have to be done, ensure attendance list is signed by all and distribute expense forms if needed.

After the meeting: clear and tidy the room and remove signs, let anyone covering another job know the meeting has finished. Ideally key in the minutes as quickly as possible after the meeting and check accuracy with the chairperson, follow up your own actions and prepare a list of actions for the chairperson. Write the date of the next meeting in your diary and send an electronic invitation to members of the committee. Also note when papers have to be sent out in your diary. Return any files or papers to the correct file.

*Ineffective organis*ation *prior to a meeting* may mean the meeting has to be cancelled or postponed, it may over-run if you have not organised the Agenda correctly or people may not have had time to read the papers resulting in poor discussion. Mismanagement may damage the reputation of you and your organisation as you mess people about. Not following proper procedures may invalidate any decisions you have made.

2   Students should identify the differences laid out below and link them together to compare and contrast with appropriate phrases such as 'on the other hand', 'conversely', 'in comparison', etc.

E-mail	E-groups
Allows you to send papers.	Allows papers to be posted on an e-group so they are available to all in the e-group.
Does not allow discussion.	Allows discussion.
Controlled by the sender.	Not usually controlled but an open forum.
Allows only accurate information to be sent to all.	Additional information which is inaccurate could be added as there is often no policing.
You can trace who has received and opened e-mails.	You cannot trace who has read only who has contributed to the discussion.
Allows documents to be sent confidentially to others.	Those logged in as group members can access discussion. May not be appropriate when people leave.
Allows members to file documents in their e-mail or electronically.	E-group members have to trace back arguments and discussions.

3

Costs *Traditional meeting*	Costs *Video conference*
Cost of transport and accommodation, cost of time away from home base	Hire of venue.
Face-to-face communication.	May not be relaxed with the technology to allow benefit of face-to-face communication.
No technical support needed.	Technical support costs may be high.
If you miss the meeting you only have the minute.	If you miss the meeting you can also have it recorded.
Chairman has to develop only chairing skills.	Chair may not have the skills to get the best out of the technology, will need to allow for delays ensure all are included, use of camera to focus on who is speaking.
More flexible in taking turns to speak.	Often have to allow for a delay in speech reaching everyone. Summaries are needed regularly.
Must address the chair.	People must wait for their turn to speak otherwise they will not be heard/seen by all.
Benefits *Traditional meeting*	**Benefits** *Video conference*
No interruptions as all are out of their own workspace.	Same.
Allows people to get to know each other.	Can be more stilted than traditional face-to-face.
May be hidden networking benefits for people working together.	Inclusive.

4 Secretary would check there is a quorum, inform the chairperson who would call the meeting to order. Chairperson would usually welcome everyone to the meeting and either the chairperson or the secretary would inform the meeting of any apologies received. The secretary would read the minutes or the meeting would agree that the minutes can be taken as read, any amendments would be made or they would be agreed and signed by the chairperson. Any matters which were arising from the last minutes, such as follow up actions, would be reported on. Then the specific business of the meeting would begin.

5 Students should identify the differences and they should then use appropriate words such as 'compared with', 'as opposed to', 'in comparison with', 'on the other hand' to link the two sets of features.

Traditional minutes	Action minutes
Full account of meeting.	Only the actions required are recorded.
Names of proposers and seconders and full motions recorded.	Names of proposers and seconders not recorded unless an action ensues.
Have to be signed by the chairperson.	Do not have to be signed by the chairperson.
Formal language.	Formal language.
Resolutions worded exactly.	Resolutions not recorded unless an action follows.
Copies sent to all who attended and usually to all eligible to attend.	Copies usually sent to all who attended but always to those with actions to perform.

Chapter 4 Recruitment and Selection

Task 1

A Job Description clearly defines the duties and responsibilities associated with the job. It may include any constraints, such as working at a different location. It determines what tasks have to be done in the job. After determining what tasks have to be carried out, a Person Specification will be drawn up which states the personal qualities and attributes needed to do the job. This is a summary of the most important knowledge, skills and characteristics required in order to be able to do the job to the required standard.

Task 2

Examples of suitable answers are shown. The candidate may have formatted their answers differently but they should have included the following information.

JOB DESCRIPTION

Job Title: Human Resources Assistant

Grade: 2

Location: Edinburgh

Responsible to: Human Resources Manager

OVERALL PURPOSE:

To provide an efficient secretarial and administrative service to the HR team.

STAFF RESPONSIBILITIES: n/a

SPECIFIC RESPONSIBILITIES:

- To provide a shorthand service to the HR team.

- To receive and assist visitors.

- To carry out any word processing duties.

- To carry out any reprographic duties.

- To undertake any telephone duties when necessary.

- To maintain the manual and computerised filing system.

- To assist with the organisation of interview rooms/events.

JOB SPECIFICATION

Job Title: Human Resources Assistant

Grade: 2

Location: Edinburgh

Responsible to: Human Resources Manager

	Essential	Desirable
Qualifications	SVQ Level 2 in appropriate discipline or equivalent	
Work Experience	At least 2 years' experience in an office environment	
Skills	• Excellent oral/written communication • Keyboard • IT • Organisational • Word processing • Telephone • Other administrative skills including manual/computerised filing, photocopying	• Shorthand
Special Attributes	• Able to priorities own workload • Able to work under pressure • Able to work as part of a team • Self confident • Able to listen • Able to communicate sensitively	
Specific Training	None	None
Other Requirements	None	None

Check your Progress 4.1

1   Any five from:

- Local newspapers can be used to advertise unskilled and semi-skilled jobs.

- National newspapers can be used to advertise professional and managerial positions.

- Technical/professional journals can be used to advertise professional and managerial positions.

- Jobcentres are usually used to advertise unskilled and semi-skilled jobs and temporary jobs.

- Agencies are usually used to advertise temporary positions such as administrators, secretaries, bank staff, IT staff, nurses and some specialist staff such as software engineers.

- The Internet is now used to advertise a wide range of occupations including graduates. E-recruitment now plays an important role in the recruitment and selection processes. The use of e-mail and the Internet is fast becoming an integral part of recruitment and selection strategy.

2 Positions can be advertised internally using the corporate intranet, on notice boards and in weekly newsletters.

3 Advantages include:

It is less expensive to advertise internally than externally; It is less expensive to interview and select internal candidates because expenses do not need to be paid; The induction and training processes will be less expensive if the person already works in the organisation. The recruitment process may be quicker because of this and because less notice needs to be given; Existing employees will have the opportunity to enhance their career; Further job opportunities may be created as a result of recruiting internally; The organisation can make use of its large pool of existing workers; Candidates are known to the organisation so there is less chance of selecting the wrong person; The motivation of the existing workforce may be enhanced due to a good internal promotion policy.

Disadvantages include:

There is a smaller pool of workers to choose from; The organisation will need to advertise another job (quite often lower-end jobs) if the new job is filled by an internal candidate; There is less opportunity to bring new skills, ideas and experience into organisation; There can be a lack of stability in work teams due to team members regularly moving to other positions; There can be a lack of ownership of tasks due to employee expectations of moving on to another job.

Check your Progress 4.2

1 The interviewer should:

Book an appropriate interview room; Match the Person Specification against the application form to decide on areas to investigate at the interview; Read all other relevant documentary evidence – CV, references etc.; Decide on suitable questions to ask the candidate to ensure that they obtain the information they want from the candidate; Confer with colleagues who may also be present at the interview to ensure they are both taking the same approach, who will ask what questions and identify areas for further discussion; Decide whether or not there is a need to carry out any testing, such as a word processing test.

2 Main qualities include:

Listening and observing skills; questioning skills; ability to build and maintain rapport with the candidate; ability to summarise and make relevant notes about the candidate; ability to control the interview.

Staff conducting interviews must also be aware that all interviews must be conducted within the Law – all candidates must be treated fairly and equally.

Check your Progress 4.3

1 Training is the learning of an activity to gain specific knowledge and skills in order to carry out a job.

Development is concerned with future needs rather than current ones. It focuses more on career growth than immediate performance.

2 A staff appraisal process is one way to help identify and evaluate the training and development needs of staff and thus improve work performance. This is done by appraising current strengths and weaknesses of staff and assessing their career development potential.

3 The process usually starts with the completion of an appraisal form. Then an appraisal interview is conducted by the relevant Line Manager. This usually happens once a year. The appraisal process should be viewed as an opportunity for honest and open self assessment. Any training and development requests from members of staff usually relate to the job role. Goals set at the appraisal meeting will reviewed at the next appraisal meeting.

Often performance is graded, such as 1-5; in this case 5 would be the highest (highly effective) and the gradings would drop down through 4 (effective), 3 (satisfactory), 2 (ineffective) and 1 (very ineffective). Staff who receive higher grades may be considered for promotion or pay increases.

4 Problems could include:

- The appraiser may not possess the necessary interview skills.

- The appraiser may rely on their own perceptions, own likes/dislikes about some of their subordinates to reflect any assessment made about the candidate.

- Where pay is linked to appraisal, employees/appraisees may try to hide any difficulties in the job in order to obtain a pay increase.

- There can be loss of morale where staff expectations regarding promotion are not met.

Check your Progress 4.4

1 Continuing Professional Development – often shortened to CPD – implies both the commitment of the individual and the commitment of the organisation. In order to implement a CPD system, the member of staff must make a commitment to develop and move on in some way and that commitment should be endorsed and actively supported by the organisation.

2 There are obvious advantages to the organisation of committing to CPD, including improved performance of the organisation, more satisfied customers and greater motivation amongst employees.

Advantages to the individual of undertaking CPD include:

- Improved employee performance because they are equipped with new skills and experience.

- Job security. Employees who are multi-skilled and versatile can adjust to changes in the work environment more easily.

- Reduced stress. Employees can cope with changes more easily.

- Increased motivation and job satisfaction.

- Access to further promotion due to the development of skills and experience.

- May lead to increase in salary.

3 In-house training

This may be on-the-job, i.e. done in the course of employees carrying out their normal work, perhaps through job rotation or work shadowing, or it may be off-the-job, where people are removed from their own work environment, for example, to a computer suite for IT training.

External Training

Many organisations employ their own full-time training staff and seek assistance from specialists when required. External training may take place at a college, university or private training centre and may also involve a secondment opportunity. For example, administrative staff at John Nicholls could be sent to a local college to learn shorthand because the Training and Development team do not possess this skill. Staff may go to college or university to gain a formal qualification.

Check your Progress 4.5

1 Disciplinary procedures will be instigated by management where an employee does not meet these or other standards set for their job.

Grievances are raised by employees to management when employees feel they are genuinely aggrieved.

2 The disciplinary procedure will involve several stages:

- verbal warning

- written warning

- final written warning

- suspension (with/without pay)

- dismissal.

The grievance procedure will involve several stages:

- Employee raises grievance with immediate supervisor.
- If the matter is not settled the employee has right to see next level of management. Employee can take a representative.
- Employee has right to meet with senior management and can take a representative.
- If employee is still not satisfied they have the right to appeal to the Managing Director.

Check your Progress 4.6

1   It is important for the HR Department to monitor all cases of sickness and absence because every occurrence of staff absence/illness is money lost.

Problems associated with staff absence and illness include disruption to the flow of work, dissatisfaction amongst other workers, increased workload for staff that are at work.

2   Support strategies could include a modified workload for an agreed period, phased return to work, temporarily reduced hours.

3   Flexible work patterns and leave arrangements:

Organisations have found that staff are less likely to be absent where flexible work patterns are available which fit in with family responsibilities and other commitments. Staff are usually invited to apply for changes to their working arrangements and consideration will be given to the individual and the needs of organisation.

Some organisations provide leave arrangements over and above those normally expected (annual leave, maternity leave, parental, paternity leave, adoption leave). The additional leave may include:

- Carer's leave – an entitlement to take time off to deal with certain unexpected or sudden emergencies involving a dependent.
- Special discretionary leave – requests from members of staff for short periods of paid and/or unpaid leave in circumstances not covered by other policy provisions.
- Childcare – many organisations are now providing nursery facilities and Kids Clubs which run during school holidays. These facilities may be in partnership with local authorities.
- Career development opportunities – many organisations offer a range of development opportunities in conjunction with the organisation's training and development policy such as secondments and sabbaticals.

Other services may include provision of free hairdressing, subsidised canteen and free car parking. Social and recreational events and activities may be promoted, such as an annual outing or Christmas party or sporting competitions.

Internal Assessment Higher Questions

1   Internal recruitment (any three points for one mark each):

- The post is advertised internally before going outside the organisation.
- The post would be advertised internally via the corporate intranet, on notice boards and in weekly newsletters.
- It is less expensive to advertise internally than externally.
- It is less expensive to interview and select internal candidates because expenses do not need to be paid.
- The training and induction processes will be less expensive.
- The recruitment process may be quicker because of this and because less notice needs to be given.
- Existing employees will have the opportunity to enhance their career.
- Further job opportunities may be created as a result of recruiting internally.
- The organisation can make use of its large pool of existing workers.

External Recruitment (any three points for one mark each):

- Vacancies are advertised externally through newspapers, magazines, professional journals, job centres, schools, colleges, agencies and the Internet.

- The organisation attracts a wider pool of workers from home and abroad, for example, European job seekers often use the Internet to search for jobs in other EU countries.

- There is more chance of recruiting a 'good-fit' because the organisation is recruiting from a wider pool.

- New workers can bring new skills and innovation to the organisation.

2   One mark for each point; maximum of two marks for each test.

Skills tests:

- Skills tests are used to ascertain existing skills level.

- Skills tests are used to find out if the candidate has the ability to do the job, such as typing and shorthand skills, communication skills, numerical ability.

Psychometric assessment tests:

- Psychometric assessment tests are used to obtain a profile of the candidate covering both personality and intellectual ability. The tests have been developed by psychologists.

- Psychometric tests include personality tests. This test is used to explore a candidate's personality traits.

- A personality test can also help identify strengths and weaknesses and ascertain whether or not the candidate is a team player, a risk taker, cautious, aggressive etc.

3   Advantages to the organisation (one mark for each point for maximum of three):

- improved performance of the organisation

- satisfied customers

- motivated employees

Advantages to the individual (one mark for each point for maximum of three):

- Improved employee performance because they are equipped with new skills and experience.

- Job security. Employees who are multi-skilled and versatile can adjust to changes in the work environment more easily.

- Reduced stress. Employees can cope with changes more easily.

- Increased motivation and job satisfaction.

- Access to further promotion due to development of skills and experience.

- May lead to increase in salary.

4   One mark each for maximum of two:

- improved sickness and absenteeism

- earlier resolution of grievance problems

- increased output

- increased motivation

- happier staff.

External Assessment Higher Questions

1   Answer should include two of the following for one mark each:

- Job Description clearly defines the duties and responsibilities associated with the job.

- It may include any constraints, such as working at a different location.

- It determines what tasks have to be done in the job.

Answer should also include two of the following for one mark each:

- After determining what tasks have to be carried out, a Person Specification will need to be drawn up which states the personal qualities and attributes needed to do the job.

- A Person Specification is a summary of the most important knowledge, skills and characteristics required in order to be able to do the job to the required standard.

- A Person Specification is a useful tool to help ensure every candidate is treated equally and fairly in the interview process (measured against the same criteria).

- Usually the Person Specification and Job Description are used together to determine full details of what has to be done in the job and the qualities needed to do the job well.

2 Employer advantages (any one for one mark):

- The interview gives the employer the opportunity to assess whether or not the candidate will be able to perform well in the job.

- It also gives the employer the opportunity to assess the candidate's motivation for the job.

Employer disadvantages (any one for one mark):

- Some candidates are known to exaggerate their skills, experience and ability.

- Other candidates may possess excellent interview techniques which allow them to perform well at the interview. These candidates may not necessarily perform as well in the job.

Candidate advantages (any one for one mark):

- The candidate has the chance to build upon what they have written in the Application Form and to learn more about the job and the organisation.

- It gives the candidate the opportunity to ask questions and decide if they want to take up any job offer given.

Candidate disadvantages (for one mark):

- May be nervous and not perform well at interviews.

3 In-house training (one mark for each valid point; maximum of three):

- Training at the workplace may be on-the-job – done in the course of the employees carrying out their normal work, for example through job rotation or work shadowing.

- Employees may feel more comfortable in familiar surroundings.

- May be more cost-effective than external training.

- Can be more easily tailored to meet the individual's and organisation's needs, such as induction training.

- Can be arranged as and when necessary.

External training (one mark for each valid point; maximum of three):

- May take place at a college or university in order for the employee to gain a formal qualification.

- Employees are not as easily distracted by interruptions in a different environment.

- Employees have the opportunity to widen their perspective, the ability to network with others, exchange views and ideas which can enhance motivation and encourage new ideas.

- The organisation has little control over the length and content of training course and it may not address all needs of individual and the organisation.

Chapter 5 Customer Service

Task 1

Marks and Spencer's Mission statement, 'Our vision', is to be the standard against which all others are measured. Obtainable from their website.

Local college – Some examples are:

Central College of Commerce Glasgow – We provide quality lifetime learning for a changing world.

Edinburgh's Telford College – Bringing learning to life.

Perth College – Our mission is to meet the needs of our customers by providing high quality education, training and related services.

Task 2

There are no set answers to this task but each group should give the best instance of good service and the best instance of bad service and identify why they were good and bad.

Task 3

Answers are on the websites in full. Students should use search engines to find websites.

Task 4

Answers will vary between schools but all colleges should have a student charter and this can normally be accessed on their websites.

Check your Progress 5.1

1   The most suitable survey would be a focus group so that feedback can be quick and you can choose to speak not just to people who use the service but people who choose not to use the service.

2   Service level agreements document the quality and standard of the service so both provider and buyer know what they will receive. If things go wrong there will be a documented route to solving difficulties.

Task 5

Most websites of retailers now document their customer care policies and complaints procedures. They will usually document the first place to complain when something goes wrong and suggest contacting head office if no satisfaction is received from branch level. Students should know where to complain first and what to do if they do not receive a satisfactory response.

Task 6

Answers will vary depending on the information accessed.

Internal Assessment Intermediate 2 Questions

1   Answer should include at least two of the following: guarantee of standard of service, guarantee of consistency, information of a reliable standard, knowing what to do if something goes wrong, dealing with a reputable organisation instils confidence.

2   Answer should include at least two of the following: good publicity, regular repeat business from loyal customers, extra loyalty results in bigger turnover, good reputation means better recruitment and more customers, good internal relations within the organisation.

3   Answer should include a description of a mission statement such as: a mission statement is a short statement of the main intentions of the organisation, a cross between a slogan and a summary of their aims. It is important as it conveys the ideals of the organisation to potential customers.

Internal Assessment Higher Questions

1   Answer should include two from the following: bad publicity resulting in loss of business, falling market share, lost customers, legal action, increased resources needed to sort out problems.

2   Answer should include two from the following: good publicity, repeat orders, increased customer loyalty, enhanced reputation, bigger market share, better internal relations and high morale among staff.

3 Answer should include a definition such as: a SLA sets and clarifies expectations between the customer and the provider in terms of quality of standard of service to be provided. It should include at least three of the following: documents responsibilities and has a service part detailing the services, conditions, standards and responsibilities of both parties and any penalties; outlines how disagreements and complaints will be handled; outlines how effectiveness will be measured; outlines how and when the agreements will be revised.

Benefits should include two from the following list: clarifies expectations by setting boundaries and expectations for both parties, sets key performance indicators so both parties know what to expect and will know when standards have not been met, outlines compensation, outlines complaints procedures.

4 A focus group brings together groups of customers for the purpose of feeding back information on products or services. Used when you want a pre-determined number of customer responses, when you want instant answers, when you want customers to feel valued, when you have difficult questions to ask and you want face-to-face responses.

External Assessment Intermediate 2 Questions

1 Answer should include at least three of the following: bad publicity, poor reputation, falling market share, dissatisfied customers, legal action, increased resources being spent on dealing with complaints.

2 Answer should include a definition of a mission statement, for example, a short summary of the organisation's intentions. Organisations choose to have a mission statement to convey their core values and direction to the public. It sets the standard for their image.

External Assessment Higher Questions

1 Students should use two from: written, telephone, focus groups, face-to-face interviews, mystery shopper, membership group, and compare and contrast under the following headings:

	Written	Telephone	Focus group	Face-to-face	Mystery shopper	Membership group
Speed	Slow	Quick	Quick	Quick	Quick	Slow
Unbiased	Yes	Yes	Influenced by others in group	Yes	Limited selection of experience	Biased
Expensive	Yes	No	Variable	Variable	No	No
Level of response	Low	Variable	Good	Good	Good	Good
Depth of response	Low	OK	Good	Good	Good	Good
Feel opinion is valued	No	No	Yes	Yes	No	Yes

2 Customer Service Policy – lets the standards, procedures and policy of the organisation be known to all its customers. Seen as an open approach, encourages trade and trust. If there is a problem you know how to complain and how to get the issue resolved.

Chapter 6 Functional Departments

Check your Progress 6.1

1 Selling furniture is likely to take place in a showroom, as well as by representatives who will sell the furniture throughout the country or even overseas. The sales department will deal with customers, enquiries, orders and distribution. It may have to arrange to store the furniture – until it can be shipped – unless there is a warehousing section – and it will have to deal with guarantees and after-sales service. It will keep a check on the volume of goods in stock and sold and will ensure that any necessary follow up market research is carried out to make sure the products manufactured are what customers want. (This may be done in a specialist marketing department in large organisations.)

2 A specialist purchasing department allows an overview to be taken of stocks held of raw materials as well as finished goods. It will contribute to ensuring that supplies are delivered where and when they are needed and that they are of the right quality. A separate purchasing department will enable savings to be made by bulk buying for the organisation. It will have close links to warehousing and storing facilities. A Purchasing Department will ensure market market prices are paid, that quality is consistent, that good credit terms are agreed and that goods are delivered on time.

Check your Progress 6.2

1 You should check that the goods received are those ordered and that you are not paying for something you did not order or where the quality is not right. You should check the calculations and ensure that any discount promised has been deducted.

2 You would not pay an invoice if:

you had a regular order with the organisation and paid when you received a statement; if goods had been returned; if goods were not satisfactory and were going to be returned; if goods had not been received; if the wrong goods had been delivered.

Internal Assessment Intermediate 2 Questions

1 Manpower planning, dealing with recruitment, pay negotiations, training and development, appraisal and performance review, grievance procedures, employment legislation, keeping up-to-date personnel records, advising staff on employment and personal issues, welfare, dealing with pay (although the actual payment is likely to be made by the finance department).

2 A delivery note is sent with the goods from the seller to the buyer. It has the same details as the invoice, i.e. quantity, reference number and description of goods and order number. Goods are usually signed for when they are received so there will be a space for signing and a space for the date. A delivery note does not usually contain any information on price.

3 A job description is a list of the duties and tasks which are attached to a particular job. It is useful for both employee and employer as it is a reference point for the job, it confirms that the job is graded correctly and it can be referred to in any disputes. It will usually have information such as grade, hours of work and place of employment.

External Assessment

1 Answer should include two from the following list: You might need to deal with letters of enquiry which are sent to you by potential purchasers asking about prices, delivery, discounts and availability of the goods you sell. Catalogues/price lists/quotations which you send to a potential buyer detailing the goods you have available, delivery arrangements and prices.

Order: Sent from potential purchasers to you detailing the quantity, description, reference number and price of the goods they wish to buy.

Delivery Note: Sent by the sales department to the purchaser along with the goods, detailing the quantity, description, reference number of the goods being delivered.

Invoice: Sent by the seller to the buyer with the same information as the delivery note but including prices, discounts and VAT.

Credit Note: Issued by the seller to the purchaser if goods are returned. Shows the quantity, description, reference number and prices which will be deducted from the amount owing.

2 The main functions of finance department are to provide financial accounting services – managing the capital and cash of the organisation.

Management accounting services – giving managers accurate financial information to help them in their decision-making. Information like predictions, forecasts and analyses.

Financial reporting services – systematically collecting all the figures needed to work out asset values and profits, such as sales to date, amounts owing, etc.

3 Restricting who can sign purchase orders allows controls to be put in place which stop theft and fraud. Allows purchasing to be centralised and enables a check to be kept on the amount spent. The larger the number of people allowed to sign purchase orders, the greater likelihood of irregularity and fraud.

Chapter 7 Travel

Check your Progress 7.1

1   Air advantages include: savings in time, secure car parking facilities, good in-flight facilities .

Air disadvantages include: higher cost, have to travel to and from airports, luggage restrictions, delays, long check in time is often required, travel time can be increased if departure is delayed, jet lag due to time differences on long flights, fear of flying.

Rail advantages include: comfortable method of travel – you can undertake work while at your seat, less tiring than flying, quite fast, seat reservations can be made in advance of travel, good on-board facilities – most trains include an on-board catering service (some first class services have telephone, television, photocopier and fax machines installed).

Channel Tunnel advantages include: fast – Eurotunnel offers the fastest route to France crossing from Folkstone to Calais in under 35 minutes and Eurostar takes you right from the heart of London to heart of Paris, can take your car, loading and unloading is quick and easy, frequent shuttle service, efficient customs arrangements in place which means time is not wasted, relatively cheap, little chance of getting seasick.

Rail disadvantages include: travel time can be increased if the train is delayed, seat is not guaranteed if you do not reserve in advance.

Channel Tunnel disadvantages include: operating difficulties can cause delays and even cancellations, travelling to France in this way is the least exciting of cross channel options.

Road – Private car/car hire advantages include: able to suit yourself – not tied to flight/rail times, able to choose route – use quickest and best roads, relatively cheap.

Road – Private car/car hire disadvantages include: can get lost if unfamiliar with roads – traveller will need necessary maps and other related documentation, can be tiring if long journey, can break down –traveller will need relevant documentation in case of accident/breakdown, additional cost of toll roads – traveller will require change.

Road – Travel by taxi advantages include: convenient, traveller does not have to worry about parking, can be quick, do not have to be familiar with the area.

Road – Travel by taxi disadvantages include: can be expensive especially for long journeys, sometimes difficult to book or call taxis, such as at peak times, delays if roads are busy.

Travel by sea advantages include: can take your car on most services, relatively fast, secure quayside parking, excellent on-board facilities – cafes, bars restaurants, cinemas, gym and sauna. On some ferry services the traveller can pay a supplement to access meeting areas with access to a desk, telephones and fax facilities.

Travel by sea disadvantages include: not as fast as air travel, delays and cancellations due to bad weather, travel sickness if seas are rough, ferry ports may not be near city centres.

2   Factors to be considered include: distance to be travelled, organisational policy and procedures, purpose of trip, time available, preferences of traveller, budget available.

3   The main areas include: hotels/airlines/hire car firms that can be used, class of travel, mileage allowance, subsistence allowance, distance to be travelled before overnight accommodation can be allowed, health and safety guidelines such as insurance, arrangements for vaccinations/inoculations, length of trips and driving times.

4   • Travel Agent

Many can provide a complete business travel service to help organisations manage travel and provide more choices to the traveller. Travel agents usually provide the following services and information – air, rail, road and sea travel (the travel agent can book tickets for you), information on hotels (the travel agent can also book your hotel accommodation), currency, passport and visa requirements, insurance requirements and general information on places of interest to visit, cultural information, national holiday dates etc.

- Internet

    Websites can provide information on flight, ferry, bus and train times (bookings can also be made) and hotels (bookings can also be made). Can also access street maps, health advice and advice on passports/visa etc.

- Travel Organisation

    As above

Check your Progress 7.2

1 Administrator should consider:

departure/return dates; that cost is within the agreed price limit of the organisation. Also a good idea to check that the cost includes the price of breakfast; preferences of the traveller, for example smoking/non-smoking, type of hotel, facilities required, special requirements; location of the hotel (so that time is not wasted getting to and from appointments), check-in and check-out times, car parking facilities (where appropriate), method of payment.

2 Any eight from: restaurant on site, 24-hour room service, connection for laptop, air conditioning, satellite television, direct dial phone, mini bar, hairdryer, trouser press, automatic wake-up call, money exchange, valet parking, valet/laundry, multi-lingual staff, fitness centre, sauna, beauty parlour, business centre, city transportation.

3 Jet lag causes the traveller to feel fatigue, discomfort and disorientation due to crossing different time zones. The traveller may need a day of rest before their first appointment.

4 Advice to combat jet lag could include: drink plenty of fluids to avoid dehydration, avoid alcohol, undertake gentle exercises to reduce discomfort and swelling of the feet.

5 Information to be included on an itinerary could include:

- name of traveller, date and purpose of the trip

- precise times of travel

- exact travel details, including method of travel, check-in times, name of airport and departure times, flight numbers. Travel by ferry should include details on seat reservations and sleeping berths

- accommodation details – hotel name, address and telephone number

- details of business meetings including location and times and information on clients

- other documentation might include: documents which are necessary for a meeting, passport – all UK nationals traveling outwith the UK will need a passport, visa – needed for entry to certain countries, insurance – personal and vehicle cover, tickets for trip, letters and faxes of confirmation of hotel booking and car hire, emergency numbers for credit card insurance cover, vaccination certificates, information on culture, laws and customs of a particular country.

6 Additional documentation could include: medical documentation, information on culture, laws and customs of Japan.

Check your Progress 7.3

1 Advantages include:

accepted world wide as payment for goods and services; can obtain instant cash from ATMs and banks no matter where you are in the world without having to carry large amounts of cash or travellers' cheques.

2 The expenses claim form allows the traveller to claim back any out-of-pocket expenses and travel/accommodation costs.

Travellers will be asked to include receipts to make sure that no errors have been made and the amount is correct and also to ensure the expenses claimed are within the budget available.

Internal Assessment Intermediate 2 Questions

1 Any four for one mark each: name of the traveller, purpose of the trip, destination, date of departure, date of return, any individual preferences for travel/accommodation, special requirements, budget of the trip, if applicable.

2a The main document required is an itinerary. (One mark)

2b The itinerary provides a summary of all the travel arrangements, accommodation and events. (One mark)

2c The itinerary should include (any four for one mark each):

- Heading with the name of traveller, date and purpose of the trip.

- Precise times of travel, exact travel details including method of travel. Also check-in times/name of airport/departure times/flight numbers/seat reservations/sleeping berths.

- Accommodation details – hotel name, address and telephone number.

- Details of business meetings including location and times and information on clients.

- Other documentation might include: documents which are necessary for a meeting, passport – All UK nationals traveling outwith the UK will need a passport, visa – needed for entry to certain countries, insurance – personal and vehicle cover, medical documentation, tickets for trip, letters and faxes of confirmation of hotel booking and car hire, emergency numbers for credit card insurance cover, vaccination certificates, information on culture, laws and customs of a particular country.

External Assessment Intermediate 2 Questions

1 Eurostar

Advantages include (any two for one mark each): fast, frequent services, relatively cheap, no crowded airport check-in required, no lengthy transfers, can be less tiring than flying.

Disadvantages include (any two for one mark each): operating difficulties can cause delays and even cancellations, travel time can be increased if train is delayed.

Air

Advantages include (any two for one mark each): relatively quick, can be cheap if you are able to benefit from low-cost air tickets, secure car parking facilities, good in-flight facilities – some airlines have installed payphones, laptop computers and faxes, improved airport facilities including restaurants, shops, meeting rooms, executive lounges.

Disadvantages include (any two for one mark each): higher cost, travel to and from airports, restrictions on luggage you can take, delays due to bad weather/technical problems, long check in times are often required, travel time can be increased if departure is delayed.

2 Factors to consider include:

Travel (any three for one mark each): purpose of trip, preference of traveler, time available, destination, budget .

Accommodation (any three for one mark each): cost is within the agreed price limit of the organisation; preferences of the traveller, for example smoking/non-smoking, type of hotel; facilities required ie gym and meeting room, special requirements, including preferred location, disabled access, car parking facilities.

3a Credit card advantages include (one for one mark): used and accepted worldwide as payment for goods and services, ability to obtain instant cash from ATMs and banks no matter where you are in the world, no need to carry large amounts of cash or travellers' cheques.

Credit card disadvantages include (one for one mark): if the traveller loses a card the ability to replace it is hampered due to the lack of a permanent address and the timescale involved in banks providing replacements, banks can add extra charges onto customers for using their cards for payment or obtaining cash whilst abroad.

Travellers' cheques advantages include (one for one mark): accepted world-wide, traveller does not have to carry large amounts of cash, can be refunded if lost or stolen.

Travellers' cheques disadvantages include (one for one mark): in some countries the traveller may need to cash them in at a bank or hotel where a surcharge may be added and proof of identification required.

Currency advantages include (one for one mark): Can pay for routine expenses.

Currency disadvantages include (one for one mark): cannot be replaced if lost, cannot be replaced if stolen.

Chapter 8 Information and Decision Making

Task 1

a primary external

b secondary external

c primary internal

d primary internal or external (depends on where it was carried out)

Internal Assessment

1 Statistical information which can be measured. Examples could include individual department and organisation's total sales figures, departmental and organisational staffing costs, departmental and organisational absence rates.

2 Strategic Managers require a broad long term outlook which takes account of what is happening in the whole market. They should be aware of outside factors which affect their organisation and competitors. They should look at government policy and statistics, local government policy and information, information on competitors and any similar related industries.

3 Students should link similar characteristics pointing out the main differences with linking words such as 'in comparison with', 'as opposed to', etc.

Primary	Secondary
Gathered for your own purposes.	Gathered for another purpose.
Specific and focused on a particular purpose.	You don't always know why the information has been gathered.
Should be easy to analyse as you gather it the way you want it.	May need to be sifted to find relevant parts.
Difficult to source if external.	Can be bought in.
Expensive to gather if external.	Can be bought in and is therefore cheaper.
Can be gathered when you want it.	Unlikely to have a say when it is gathered.
Can be laid out how you want it.	No say over layout.

Examples would include:

Primary – internal sales figures, customer surveys

Secondary – retail sector figures, market research information of a general nature, government statistics.

External Assessment

1 Answer should include four features from the following list with a brief explanation of what this means and an example such as that indicated.

Timing – regular month reports of sales;

Relevant – no point in comparing entirely different organisations with your own;

Accurate – amount of sales – the greater accuracy is needed lower down the organisation at operational level;

Objective – given in a way that does away with bias, such as overestimating turnover to get more staff;

Available and Accessible – if available in the organisation all should know it exists and how to access it, such as use intranet to show information which will help staff morale;

Cost Effective – expensive primary information should only be paid for if the cost of investigation warrants it, perhaps focus groups;

Complete – should ensure that all the facts and not just censored information is available, for example, information on taxes or local authority plans for an area;

Traceable – the source of the information should be noted – this ensures it is real information and not made up.

2

Level of management	Information requirements
Strategic	Broad viewpoint Long term Externally sourced information Not in great detail Answers what ifs
Tactical	Wider than operational but not as wide as strategic Medium term Mix of external and internal information Quantitative information Mix of routine problems and ones which need initiative
Operational	Detailed narrow viewpoint Internal information Short term decisions Set procedures for dealing with routine problems Making it happen

3 Answer should compare features of focus group with those of market research, linking and contrasting features with suitable linking words such as 'in comparision with', 'by contrast', etc.

Market Research	Focus Group
External	Internal
Broad focus	Narrow focus
Usually secondary although it could also be primary	Primary
Slow	Quick
Less interactive	Interactive
Uses	
Strategic and tactical decision making	Operational and tactical decisions
New developments	Product/customer service improvements
Entirely new products	Variations in products
Sites of new stores	Siting of facilities

Chapter 9 ICT: Its Uses and Impact

Task 1

- This task requires the candidate to use their e-mail system and log in a minimum of four addresses and one group.

- The pupil/student has to set up a group with three or four class members and you. You should receive a note from them that they have set up the group and you will be asked to acknowledge receipt.

- The pupil/student is asked to set up a folder to retain e-mails for this group and to save the acknowledgements into this folder.

- In Chapter 10 students/pupils will be asked to do word processing tasks and they should set up a folder for each task they will undertake. When they reach this stage you should suggest that they e-mail their work to you, you correct with comments and return. You may like to identify which tasks would be suitable for this as you may not choose this way of looking at all student work.

- An out of office message should be set up for the next school/college holiday.

- Ensure students know how to print an e-mail.

Task 2

There is no correct answer for this. Students are asked to look at the website which gives advice and details on writing e-mails as well as an example of the kind of e-mail policy organisations are now adopting.

Task 3

Students/pupils are asked to access this website to find out how to set up groups, look at different kinds of groups and work out how to create their own groups.

Check your Progress 9.1

1   Allows you to send a set of documents quickly to a group of people without having to key in e-mail addresses individually. All you need to do is click on the group name, write the e-mail and attach the attachments. With a committee the same group of people would receive the same information at regular times.

2   This is a cheap way of fans airing their views and swapping news, communicating with other fans or simply reading what other people with the same interests think.

Task 4

Documents could be printed at a central point in the floor, data could be backed up centrally, less paper in the organisation, information saved centrally could be accessed more easily by all. E-mail, common folders for common documents (policy, procedures, forms, etc.), should lead to higher quality standards throughout the organisation.

Task 5

encryption – the translation of data into a secret code before it is stored or sent. To read the encrypted data you have to be aware of the code or have a password to read the data.

hacking – usually used to describe the act of accessing computer program language illegally with a view to altering what it does. A hacker is someone who accesses a computer program without authority, usually with a view to stealing information.

firewall – a system designed to stop unauthorised access to your computer system. Usually a software barrier which will protect your system from 'intrusion'.

virus – a program or piece of code which is loaded on to your computer without your knowledge and runs without your permission. Viruses often duplicate themselves and fill the memory on your computer, making your software unusable.

Task 6

While this will vary between schools, colleges and centres you should take the opportunity to let students know how this happens.

Task 7

There is no answer for this activity. Students are accessing information on the Freedom of Information Act.

Task 8

There is no answer for this activity. Students are accessing a Factsheet on the Data Protection Act.

Check your Progress 9.2

1   You should advise Janice not to access this information. She is breaking the law as she does not have authorised access to this information.

2   You should tell her to register with the Telephone Preference Service who will ensure that she receives no more calls of this type.

3   You should ask for a copy of the information they hold on you and check that it is accurate.

Internal Assessment Intermediate 2 Questions

1   Benefits should include a minimum of four from:

Open 24 hours a day 7 days a week; Low overheads of staff or rent; Brings your products directly to those who want to buy them; Your organisation can receive orders when no-one is there; Your market is world wide; Presentation, placement, display, selling and paying for goods is all done on screen; You can trace exactly what a customer bought and where their interests lie.

2   Answer two from the following with a brief description:

Allows exclusive ownership; Stops unauthorised copying; Covers anything which has been recorded, as soon as it has been recorded; Copying fees go back to the person who produced the materials.

3   Disadvantages should include a minimum of four from:

Accuracy may be doubtful; Some information may be old but has not been removed; Information is not always well organised; Finding information can take some time; Sometimes you get into a loop and keep going back to the same spot, other times sites may crash; You can waste a lot of time finding the right information; You can suffer from equipment or software problems.

4   Advantages should include:

Saves time and travelling costs; Allows for better communication between branches; Ensures that people from all branches can attend meetings; Helps stop the head office mentality where everyone is expected to go to one office.

Internal Assessment Higher Questions

1   Answer should include two from the following list with explanations and examples:

Difficulty in finding files unless all use the same standards and ways of filing – leads to slower working; Confusion will result from different conventions and practices being used; Old files which are out of date may not be deleted and some staff may be using older versions of files and documents; Backing up is essential in case mistakes are made and files accidentally erased; Customers could be lost and money lost when files are not kept well, as you may be unable to locate customer information; There may be litigation as a result of poor file management, due to information being wrongly recorded.

2   Answer should include two from the following with explanation:

Saving all information on to the network allows everyone to access it; Setting up folders in a logical way accepted by the organisation speeds up the retrieval; Checking filing regularly to ensure documents are not out of place keeps files tidy; Ensure filing is up to date means everyone uses the most up-to-date information.

3   Answer should include two from:

- The Act balances the rights of individuals and the rights of others for using their personal information.
- Data controllers have certain obligations.
- Data subjects have certain rights.
- Organisations have to register if processing personal information and agree to:

   fairly and lawfully process data, use it for limited purposes, hold data which is adequate, relevant and not excessive, keep data accurate and up to date, ensure data is not retained longer than needed, ensure data is processed according with the individual's rights, keep data secure, ensure data is not transferred to countries outside the EU unless there is protection for the individual.

4   Answer should include four from the following:

Information can be gathered from a wider area; Information only needs to be keyed in once; Gathering information is quicker; Sending information to different parts of the organisation is quicker; Enquiries can be dealt with speedily; Information can be accessed by several people at one time; Access to good information means better decisions are made; Information is likely to be more accurate; Less staff involved in routine tasks; More flexible working practices can be adopted; Information can be sent out quickly; People can access updated information from anywhere; Standardised formatting can help understanding.

5   Answer should include three from the following with explanations (at least one from each section).

Physical security should include points like:

alarms, security guards, restricted access to the public; ensuring adequate power supplies, encryption of sensitive data; special arrangements made for those who access computer data from home and when travelling.

Data security should include points like:

ensuring only authorised people get into the system, e.g. passwords; logging on and occasional checks of who is doing what by IT or supervisor; levels of access being set appropriate to level of seniority and job role; virus scanners, firewalls, filtering software, intrusion detection; e-mail and Internet policy which is known to all; staff awareness of virus problems and need to report any problems.

External Assessment Intermediate 2 Questions

1   Backs up procedures ensure that organisations can continue business even if a disaster strikes their business. A back up is a duplicate copy of the data held on your system.

- Back ups are usually taken every 24 hours.

- Stored away from the main office or in fireproof/bombproof stores.

- Taken by a designated person.

They are important to ensure that the organisation can recover from loss of data due to accident or sabotage or virus attack. Organisations try to ensure they can be up and running within 24 hours.

2   To specify offences against computer systems and identify three main offences:

1)   hacking – unauthorised access to computer material,

2)   committing a further crime after gaining unauthorised access to computer material

3)   modifying the contents of computer material, for example, using a worm or virus or altering something you do in 1 or 2.

3   Video conferencing joins people up by allowing them to see each other and talk using computers and web cams or specific video conferencing hardware and software.

Allows you to talk to people who are not geographically close on a one to one basis, for example, for a management performance review;

Hold meetings which might otherwise involve a lot of travelling and cost, such as a meeting of all store managers; Involve those who are distant in general meetings like an address by a chief executive.

External Assessment Higher Questions

1   Any three of these. Posters, screen notices, induction programmes, staff handbook, intranet and staff development events. The employee's role would be outlined and the danger to the organisation of breaches of security should be included in the content.

2   An explanation of input, processing and output followed by exemplification of how each has had changes due to ICT should include, access to information by all; speed; less routine tasks; better flow of information as opposed to paper; less need for everyone involved to be based in one office; more effective use of office space; and three examples such as call centre approach to dealing with customers and complaints; those involved in selling being able to access up to date information on availability of products due to remote access facilities; more use of flexible working arrangements allowing homeworking; better use of office facilities; more use of e-commerce to sell and buy goods, etc.

3   Answer should include points such as:

- access to other people's files means quicker, more cost effective working (i.e. insurance company)

- better information means better decision making; dynamically linked information will be up to date

- allows most use to be made of each person's work as work does not have to be done twice in different departments (all information keyed in only once)

- files must be kept up to date and housekeeping performed regularly or people will use out of date information

- staff training on data security becomes an issue as data must be kept safely for legal and competitive reasons. All staff should be aware of legal implications
- staff will have to be well trained about how things are filed so that information is up to date and accurate
- back ups and disaster recovery are very important.

Chapter 10 Answers

These answers are on the CD ROM. The house styles indicated are not meant to be prescriptive but are meant to provide students with examples. The teacher/lecturer may wish to edit solutions to suit their own house style and should indicate to students whether they are to supply answers in hard copy or send as email attachments.

Chapter 11 Answers

Task 1

This task is to ensure that candidates can set up folders for their e-mail files. You will need to check these by looking at the folders they have set up as each student/pupil will choose different folders.

Task 2

This task involves the student sending out of office messages during the school/college holidays. You should ask them to demonstrate how they do this and ensure that it has been activated by sending all an e-mail to all after 'close of business' one day.

Task 3

Ensure that you receive a minimum of one automated response from each pupil/student but discourage the use of this facility. Encouragement should be given to acknowledging receipt by replying more fully.

Check your Progress 11.1

1   You would use cc when you want the recipient of the e-mail to know where copies had been sent. You would use bcc when you did not want the recipient to know who else had received a copy of the correspondence, for example, you might send bcc to your boss when you are dealing with an awkward colleague so that your boss knows what is happening or how an issue is progressing.

2   If urgent is used all the time it would lose its high priority standing.

3   Most systems have a paperclip to indicate an attachment and you usually click on the paperclip and then scroll through your files to identify which file you wish to attach. Some systems will only attach files which are not already open.

Task 4

This asks students/pupils to mark up class events in their diaries (deadline dates, internal assessment dates, appointments with teacher/lecturer). The answers will vary from student to student.

Task 5

Students/pupils are asked to explore their software to see if to do lists or other facilities are incorporated. This will vary from system to system.

Task 6

Students/pupils are asked to set up a recurring date in their diaries for the 2nd of each month to do their e-mail filing.

Task 7

You would set a date when you know the majority of people will be available and when the information in the calendar of the people who already have appointments looks as if it might be flexible.

Task 8 and Task 9

Answers should be printed out from a website and should show definitions. Examples provided below.

Browser – a software application used to locate and display web pages, i.e. Microsoft Explorer.

Cookie – a way of identifying users and preparing customised web pages for them, usually reflecting their tastes and previous purchases.

Search engine – this allows you to use key words to search for information on a particular topic, i.e. Google.

Students should save the site http://webopedia.com as one of their favourites and should follow through one of the hyperlinks shown in one of the sites to aid understanding.

Check your Progress 11.2

1   When you want to find a recently visited website. For example, when you looked at a bargain holiday and want to find it again. When you had not finished reading the information you needed. When you can't remember where you found the information you can trace it through your web history.

2   When you use the website on a regular basis for example, business travel sites like airlines, train times, route finders; leisure sites for shopping, pop groups, music, films.

Solutions to In-tray exercises Day 1 documents 1, 2, 3 and 4, and Day 2 documents 1, 2, 3 and 4 can be found on the CD ROM. Teachers/lecturers should decide if students are to provide answers in hard copy or in electronic format.

Chapter 12, 13 and 14 Answers

All solutions can be found on the CD ROM.